First Edition

Organizational Communication

Foundations for Business & Management

Alan Jay Zaremba
Northeastern University

THOMSON
SOUTH-WESTERN

Australia · Canada · Mexico · Singapore · Spain · United Kingdom · United States

THOMSON

SOUTH-WESTERN ™

Organizational Communication: Foundations for Business & Management
Alan Jay Zaremba

Editor-in-Chief:
Jack Calhoun

Team Leader:
Melissa Acuña

Acquisitions Editor:
Jennifer Codner

Developmental Editor:
Taney Wilkins

Marketing Manager:
Larry Qualls

Production Editor:
Robert Dreas

Manufacturing Coordinator:
Diane Lohman

Compositor:
Carlisle Communications Ltd.

Printer:
Transcontinental Printing, Inc.
Louiseville, Quebec

Design Project Manager:
Rik Moore

Internal Designer:
Brenda Grannan
Grannan Art & Design

Cover Designer:
Rik Moore

**Cover Photographer/
Illustrator:**
Robin Jareaux
Artville, LLC

Photography Manager:
John Hill

Photo Researcher:
Darren Wright

COPYRIGHT © 2003
by South-Western, a division of
Thomson Learning. Thomson
Learning™ is a trademark used
herein under license.

Printed in Canada
1 2 3 4 5 05 04 03 02

For more information contact
South-Western, 5191 Natorp
Boulevard, Mason, Ohio 45040.
Or you can visit our Internet site
at: http:www.swcollege.com

ALL RIGHTS RESERVED.
No part of this work covered by
the copyright hereon may be
reproduced or used in any form
or by any means–graphic, electronic, or mechanical, including
photocopying, recording, taping,
Web distribution or information
storage and retrieval
systems–without the written permission of the publisher.

For permission to use material
from this text or product, contact
us by
Tel (800) 730-2214
Fax (800) 730-2215
http:www.thomsonrights.com

**Library of Congress
Cataloging-in-Publication Data**
Zaremba, Alan Jay.
    Organizational communica-
tion: Foundations for business &
management / Alan
    Zaremba.–1st ed.
        p. cm.
    ISBN 0-324-15865-3
    1. Communication in
organizations. 2. Communication
in management. I. Title.

HD30.3.Z3695 2003
651.7–dc21   2002190387

ISBN: 0-324-15865-3

To the memory of my grandfather, Joe Zaremba, an honest man and independent thinker who never failed to point out what he felt was "ridiculous."

When I began college, my grandfather, an immigrant, sent me a short letter. "You are building your skyscraper now," he wrote. I was grateful then, and have continued to value that message.

We are all, I suppose, "building our skyscrapers" daily. I feel fortunate to have had a grandfather who provided a foundation of integrity and support for the construction.

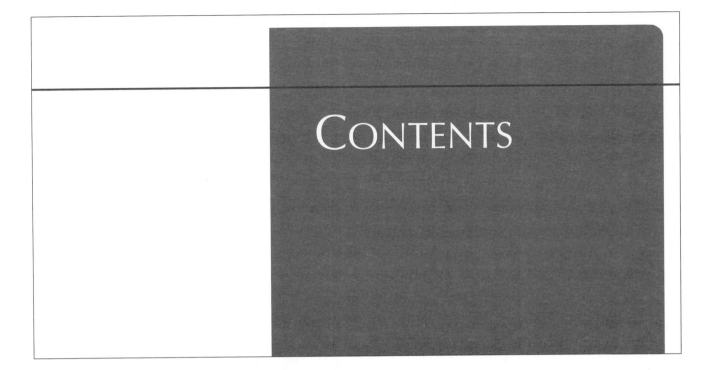

CONTENTS

6 Communications Networks 120

7 Communication Climate and Organizational Culture 146

PART 3 COMMUNICATION SKILL SETS 175

8 Communicating in Meetings 176

9 Making Presentations in Organizations 204

10 Improving Interpersonal Communication: Working with Difficult (and Not So Difficult) People 232

14 Assessing Organizational Communication Quality 326

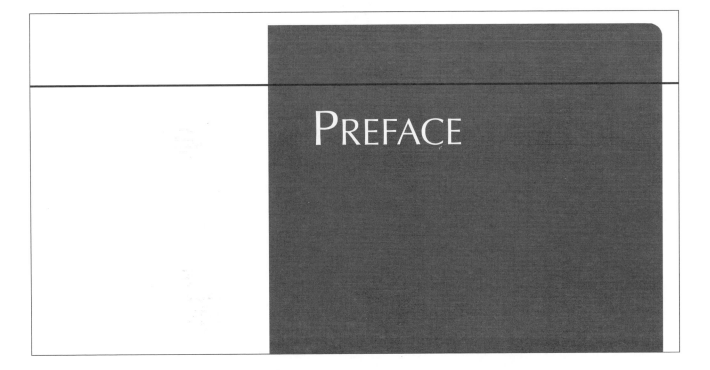

PREFACE

This book is based on the premise that communication is an integral and not peripheral dimension of organizational activity. I have set out to explain *why* communication is important for organizations and *how* individuals within organizations can become more effective organizational communicators.

As you will see, in each chapter I have included excerpts from interviews I've conducted with senior level managers in various organizations. The purpose of these interviews was to complement the academic material presented in the text with what I've referred to as "Practitioner's Perspectives." Academics have long argued that communication is vital for organizations. I thought it would be valuable to readers to present the perspectives of practitioners on the subject.

I expected to hear the interviewees comment that communication was an important part of their organizational activity. However, I was somewhat surprised to hear these individuals talk about communication so passionately and unconditionally as "critical," "essential," "crucial" and in one case, "the whole ball game." What each person had to say varied, of course; however, the theme was always the same: weak organizational communication can undermine an operation regardless of the technical qualities of the employees or the value of a particular product.

Whether the topic is *communicating during meetings, making presentations, intelligent use of e-mail, communicating during crises, communicating cross-culturally, the ethics of communication, establishing channels for interaction, clear writing, relaying job tasks, or communicating recognition,* the message from both academics and practitioners is consistent: communication is central to organizational activity. And it is this point that is central to this book. Those who go into the work world must recognize that effective internal communication is a fundamental plank in any thriving operation.

There are a number of people who were very helpful with this project, and I want to gratefully and sincerely acknowledge them.

Taney Wilkins, who served as developmental editor for the book, was as fine an editor as anyone could possibly desire. She is professional, punctual, sensitive, and intelligent. I am very fortunate that Taney was assigned to this project.

Donna Glick, my dear companion for 15 years, read the drafts of chapters and in some cases read them multiple times. She was patient with me when I became difficult, and I am very appreciative of her insights and support. My brother, Dr. Robert Zaremba, read several of the chapters and was consistently helpful with suggestions to improve the manuscript. He was willing to respond to the most arcane questions and sleuth them out with his various sources. My colleague, Dr. Kevin Howley, read the introductory chapter in the very early stages of the book's development. His comments were both encouraging and edifying. Kevin was involved with his own manuscript at the time, so I was particularly appreciative of the hours he spent with mine. I have always been impressed with Dr. Howley's energy and his willingness to help a colleague with meaningful suggestions and alternative perspectives. Larry Glick, Donna's brother, and as ethical of a person as there is, read the chapter on ethics and made substantive suggestions which I incorporated into the text. He spent hours with me analyzing the sections and commenting as diplomatically as one must during such times about ways to improve the chapter. I was very fortunate that the prepublication reviews of this book were quite good. The reviewers' comments about the chapter on ethics were extraordinarily supportive. I am very grateful to Larry for his help. Also, my mother, a former legal secretary, read two chapters for me with a keen eye for detail and syntax at a time when she most assuredly would have preferred to be doing something else. I am grateful for the hours she spent. Colleagues Elise Dallimore, David Marshall, Joanne Morreale, Ana Ilha, Michelle Lee, Karen Buzzard, Murray Forman, Alison Hearn, Jacqueline Sweeney, Sam Lotuff, and Lisa Thompson consistently asked me about the work and were encouraging in ways that one can only appreciate when one has been involved in such an undertaking. Leslie Donnell, librarian at the Kennedy school of government, was indefatigable in her sleuthing out transcripts for me, which I had just about given up on finding. Ron Peres, in our Department of Communication Studies, helped scan close to a hundred cases and interviews, which would have devoured many hours that I was able to spend writing. Naomi Dean in the department's central office was helpful with photocopying and providing dry humor when it was necessary. I am indebted to the 20 persons who gave up their time to be interviewed for the Practitioner's Perspective segments. Special mention here to Peter Jenkins, CEO of Boston Warehouse; Theresa Bullock now with Boston College; and J. P. Fingado, COO of Cerner DHT. My college buddy, Barry Kirschner, now an extraordinarily successful attorney, was helpful in connecting me to a number of interviewees and I'm grateful to him for his effort. John Aiken, of Day and Zimmermann, and Pat Faley, of the Direct Marketing Association were also very helpful in recommending appropriate interviewees for the Practitioner's Perspective components of the text.

It was Pamela Person from South-Western who signed me up for this book and I am grateful to her for seeing merit in the project and working with me as we discussed contractual arrangements. Jennifer Codner, acquisitions editor at South-Western, was very welcoming and encouraging. Bob Dreas at South-Western and Janet Kiefer at Carlisle Publishers Services were my connections as the book went into press and, like everyone else affiliated with South-Western, Bob and Janet were helpful and personable. Darren Wright was similarly professional as he worked with me on obtaining photos for the book.

There are likely many more whom I have forgotten with these acknowledgments and I apologize in advance for the omissions. To all of you who have helped me, I wish to communicate my thanks.

ALAN ZAREMBA
NORTHEASTERN UNIVERSITY

ABOUT THE AUTHOR

Alan Zaremba earned his doctorate from the University of Buffalo, and B.A. and M.S. from the University at Albany. He has been on the faculty at Northeastern University in Boston since 1981. From 1976–1981 he taught at the State University of New York College at Fredonia.

Dr. Zaremba is a recipient of both Northeastern University's Excellence in Teaching Award, and the State University of New York Chancellor's Award for Excellence in Teaching. He has written many articles on the interdependent subjects of management and communication. In June 2001, Zaremba was one of two alums to receive his undergraduate alma mater's *Excellence in Education* award.

Dr. Zaremba is the author of two other books:

Mass Communication and International Politics: A Case Study of Press Reactions to the 1973 Arab-Israeli War

and

Management in a New Key: Communication in the Modern Organization.

Part

1

FOUNDATIONS

© PHOTODISC

1

Organizational Communication: An Introduction

When I go into a company the first thing I notice is that communications are very poor. . . . You talk to several people and it's almost as if they're in different companies.

—Management Consultant Michael Lobiondo[1]

Organizational communication is the vital link in the chain of events that is the process of managing a business. It is the single factor that makes an organization viable, successful, effective, enduring.

—Roy Foltz in "Communication in Contemporary Organizations."[2]

The first executive function is to develop and maintain a system of communication.

—Chester Barnard in *The Functions of the Executive*[3]

© GETTY IMAGES/PHOTODISC

ABSTRACT

Organizational communication is a relatively new field. The first college textbook about the subject was published only 30 years ago. Many universities did not have a single foundational course in organizational communication until the 1980s or early 1990s. The growth in the last decade has been rapid. Now, scholars and business practitioners alike identify communcation as (a) central to organizational activity, (b) multi-dimensional, and (c) problematic.

Most of us know, first hand, that organizational communication can be difficult. We may

- attend poorly run meetings,
- hear long and rambling "briefings",
- be aware of co-workers who don't listen or are argumentative for what appears to be sport,
- or watch the company grapevine overwhelm formally communicated messages.

Organizational communication deals with all of these areas and many others. This chapter introduces organizational communication to the reader.

OBJECTIVES

When you have completed this chapter, you should be able to:

- ☐ **Define *organizational communication*.**
- ☐ **Discuss why scholars and practitioners consider communication central to organizational success.**
- ☐ **Identify several areas of organizational communication study.**
- ☐ **Debunk some myths about organizational communication.**
- ☐ **Describe the range of topics and scope of this book.**

COMMUNICATION: AN INTEGRAL COMPONENT OF ORGANIZATIONAL SUCCESS

Why Study Organizational Communication?

Over the last 20 years I have collected statements from persons who were asked to describe communication problems they have had in their organizations. You will see these cases throughout the book. Before we go any further in this introductory chapter, consider some case synopses that follow. For each one please address the following four questions:

- Do these cases seem common? Have you experienced the situation yourself or do you know of others who have had similar experiences?
- What are the roots of the problem? That is, why do you think these problems surfaced? Were people unskilled? Insensitive? Busy with other matters?
- What might be the long-term repercussions (if any) of the situation that is described.
- If you had been in the position of the person narrating the problem, how might you have attempted to address the issues?

1. Our meetings do not start on time and they are characterized by rambling orations. At no time does anyone in these meetings, including the department chair, attempt to end these irrelevant discussions by speaking out. A meeting that should last only 30–45 minutes lasts an hour and a half.

2. The problem I have is simply a matter of credibility and trust. I don't believe that my employers are being honest when they send me information. At the meetings the reps speak beautifully and do great power point. The memos are written impeccably. However, when I read that "we did this because of whatever" I tend to question the legitimacy of the claim.

3. Teleconferencing seems like a good idea on the surface but, ironically, it doesn't work all that well in times of globalization. We have teleconferences with our American offices and they want to set up a time which is very inconvenient to those of us in Europe, Asia, Australia, and Africa. In general, one region or culture doesn't seem to be very considerate of the needs of other regions and cultures.

4. When I attend briefing sessions from people in technical support I find myself lost. They use terminology that I do not understand. People ask questions that are beyond me, and I am frustrated because of the time wasted and also because I need this information. Yet no one appears willing to take the time to digest it for me.

5. The problem here is that the only messages I get are negative. It would be nice if every once in a while I heard something good about what I'm doing. But what happens is I get a sour face or a down e-mail, letting me know that such and such is in crisis or flawed. It's dispiriting and erodes my confidence.

6. I come to work in the morning and am flooded with electronic mail messages. Most of these have been broadcast and are irrelevant to me. It takes me quite a while to weed through them and, on occasion, I have missed some relevant communications because I've inadvertently deleted them.

7. I often get information too late for me to do anything about it. Last week I received a predated request for a lengthy report that was due the next day.

8. I'm a mid-level manager and need feedback on reports I send up the line. I need this feedback to make sure that the work I'm submitting is on target and what "they wanted." Despite repeated direct requests I get no direct response. My colleagues tell me that unless there's a problem I won't hear about it. Nevertheless, I'm not really comforted by the grapevine and need to know how I am doing.

What are the root causes of these problems? Can any of these problems affect the long-term health of an organziation?

Basic Principles

Communication is a vital and intrinsic part of management. Delegation, control, measurement, and motivation cannot exist without it.[4]

There are 14 chapters in this book. There are sections on presentations, meetings, interpersonal communication, new communication technology, crisis communication, intercultural organizational communication, and many other topics. It is my hope that you remember all that is here and find all subjects to be important and valuable. If, however, you retain only a few details from the entire book, please remember these three related points.

- Communication is a central and not peripheral component of organizational effectiveness. It is not a frill. It is vital. It is as integral to organizational success as your heart is to your health. You might be able to function with a weak heart, but the weakness will put stress on parts of your otherwise sound body. Eventually there will be a breakdown.

- Communication is a pervasive activity in organizations. It is not something that only some people in organizations must do or something that occurs infrequently. The responsibilities of managers and employees require regular effective communication.

- Organizational communication is multifaceted and deceptively complex. It may seem as if becoming an effective communicator in organizations is a relatively simple matter. It is not. The range of communication issues affecting organizations is large and, often, the cause of any one communication problem is more complicated than it appears to be.

There are several research studies that support these claims. A 1999 Watson Wyatt study found that "an organization's communication planning and programming are critical factors contributing to the success of an organization."[5] Reinsch Jr. and Shelby refer to "a growing body of literature [that] demonstrates a link between communication and business performance."[6] Allen, Gotcher, and Seibert examined a decade of organizational communication research and found "sixty seven articles that link communication to outcomes such as performance, productivity and commitment."[7] Several studies document the high percentage of time employees actually spend communicating and the difficulties these employees have when communicating.[8] It is not surprising that research also suggests that employers often identify communication and interpersonal skills as the number one attribute they look for when evaluating a potential associate.[9]

What Does It Mean to Say That Communication Is Central? Communication is necessary for nearly all forms of organizational activity and therefore necessary for organizational success. Communication shapes, limits, and defines perceptions of individuals and organizations alike.

W. Charles Redding is often called the "father of organizational communication." Redding was a Purdue University professor whose 1972 book *Communication Within the Organization* is the first textbook in the field.[10] A prolific author, Redding is referred to as an academic pioneer and as one who did a "great deal to launch the field of organizational communication."[11] One of the last things he wrote before his death in 1998 was the preface to a book on organizational communication consulting. In it he made some comments about the centrality of organizational communication that are unequivocal.

> In every instance of organizational malaise that comes to mind, at some time and in some way, human communication behavior has been significantly involved. Indeed there are scholars who have persuasively made the case that a communication failure is at least one of the basic sources underlying *every* organizational failure.[12]

Phillip Tompkins was one of Redding's Purdue University students who became a prolific author in his own right. In 1993 he wrote a book entitled

Inefficient organizational communication was a contributing factor in the disastrous explosion of the space shuttle Challenger on January 28, 1986.

©ROGER RESSMEYER/CORBIS

Organizational Communication Imperatives. In the book Tompkins describes his involvement as a communication consultant for the Marshall Space Flight Center (MSFC). He traces the history of the MSFC from its leadership under Dr. Wernher von Braun, through the disaster of the Space Shuttle Challenger explosion, and up to the renewal of the MSFC under the leadership of J. R. Thompson. It is Tompkins's contention—and he makes a very strong case—that the source of the Challenger disaster was inefficient organizational communication.[13]

Tompkins uses his experience and the case of the MSFC to argue that organizations indeed have communication "imperatives." The message is that if organizations do not meet their communication imperatives the result will be some type of disaster. The disaster may not be as grand or grave as what happened to the Challenger, but the results will be destructive nonetheless.

The centrality of organizational communication goes beyond the consequences of poor communication. Communication actually can be seen as an element of *the very fabric* that is the organization. Pace and Faules write,

> When the organization is conceived as people interacting and giving meaning to that interaction communication becomes an organizational making function rather than just an organization maintaining one. Communication does not just service the organization; it is the organization. . . . Communication, then, is central to organizational existence and does more than simply carry out organizational plans.[14]

Consultant Paul Strassmann made the following claim:

> My view is that the principal job of the CEO is to be the information and communication architect for the firm. In the information age all that matters is information and communication. Just remember this, organization means communication, communication means connectivity, connectivity means knowledge, that's the mantra.[15]

Mantra or otherwise communication is central.

Communication Is a Pervasive Activity.

Either through direct observation within a corporation or looking at a variety of studies which have been published, a good percentage of a manager's total behavior is some form of communication—most indicate 70–80%.[16]

At first glance, this may seem like an inflated statistic. Do managers in organizations really spend 70 percent of their time communicating?

If you consider the nature of organizational activity the statistic will not be surprising. Mintzberg identifies 10 managerial roles in his book, *The Nature of Managerial Work*. They are:

- Liaison
- Monitor
- Disseminator
- Spokesperson
- Negotiator

- Figurehead
- Leader
- Entrepreneur
- Disturbance handler
- Resource allocator[17]

Penley, Alexander, Jernigan, and Henwood argue that the first five of these listed roles are *explicitly* communication related. Even the second five require managers to be skillful communicators.[18]

Mintzberg's book related to managers, but all employees' behavior involves a high percentage of communication. How many of your organizational activities do *not* involve communication? Waiters need to interact with diners, bar staff, kitchen help, and managers. Office administrators need to communicate with suppliers, colleagues, superiors, and clients. Lawyers interact with judges, juries, and assistants who do legal research. The postal worker at the counter has to communicate with the mail carriers, mail handlers, those who deliver parcels, neighboring offices, and central administration.

Let's examine three (of the many) reasons why communication in organizations is such a pervasive activity and so essential for organizational success.

Organizations function by operating interdependently. In order for a company to make a product or offer a service, the various units within the organization must interact. Even organizations with highly specialized divisions of labor and levels of expertise are inherently interdependent. Therefore, the quality of communication between units, and between employees within departments, is likely to affect the corporate product. Product quality directly affects corporate profit or whatever else marks the income for a particular organization. Poor internal communication, therefore, can quickly damage the corporate "bottom line." Can your university be as efficient as it could be if the registrar is unaware of the policies of each academic department? How would students know which courses have prerequisites? How would the registrar know what students are eligible for classes? How would your college know if you've completed the requirements for graduation? How successful can a publishing company be if, for example, the sales representatives don't communicate with the people who edit and write the books? Can a professional theater survive if the set designers do not interact with the director and actors, or if marketing personnel is unaware of changes to the production schedule?

Organizations must relay information about job expectations and procedures; be prepared to receive responses to the messages they communicate; and respond intelligently to the feedback in a timely way. If managers can neither write nor speak effectively, how can employees be clear about responsibilities? Be aware of organizational policies? Gauge how well or how poorly management thinks the individual employees are doing? Similarly, if organizational men and women cannot make intelligent decisions about what types of communication channels to utilize (for example, e-mail or face-to-face communication) then other employees may get information that's not clear, or too late, or irrelevant to them. Communication is not a "one shot" linear act. Those who send messages have to assume (and should desire) that receivers will have questions, comments, and reactions to the messages that they have communicated. If those who send messages are unprepared to receive, react, and respond to feedback, then information will not flow as efficiently as it needs to.

Poor internal communication can result in bruised interpersonal relationships that directly or indirectly undermine the efficiency of an organization. We know intuitively, for example, that it is essential for engineers who have designed a building to communicate with construction personnel who are actually putting the building together. If key figures in each area are at odds because of what's perceived as condescending snubs from the past, then the messages sent between these persons and units may be abridged or poorly relayed. To avoid speaking with an estranged other, an engineer may send an e-mail when face-to-face communication is really what is necessary. A construction worker may retrieve the message too late to utilize the essential information.

In order to be effective, then, the people who work in organizations need to understand that communication is part of what they do, and an *important* part of what they do. These people—employees, managers, and executives—need to not only be aware of the *importance* of communication, but also must be *capable* of communicating effectively. Without this understanding and capability, otherwise knowledgeable, intelligent, and skilled personnel are likely to undermine the health of the organization.

To illustrate how all-encompassing organizational communication is in our daily lives, consider the following description of a "typical morning."

Several topics that are discussed in this book are alluded to in the narrative. You will see references to *nonverbal messages, written communication, the use and misuse of new communication technology; effects of unethical communication and difficult personalities; intercultural communication; the organizational grapevine; the communication climate; use and misuse of fliers and other printed messages;* and the *need to communicate effectively in meetings and presentations.*

To how many organizations do you belong? How often must you communicate to be effective as a member of these organizations? Is this a typical morning?

Focus on Applications

A typical morning

Usually before I leave for work I check my e-mail. Like many of you I have a home computer and can access the Internet and my e-mail without having to go to the office. It seems as if the number of daily electronic mail messages left for me has quadrupled in the last year. This morning I drink my morning coffee as I weed through the notices about a stranger's retirement party, computer downtimes, and opportunities to join the Credit Union. There are three messages that I need to respond to and I do so. I'm still in my bathrobe.

After I shower and dress I check my work voice mail. There are four calls. One is left by a friend who belongs to a club where I too am a member. She informs me of a meeting to be held next week in the evening. I jot down the appointment and listen to the three others. One amuses me. The caller claims to be sorry to have missed me because she'd like to chat. Our work voice mail, however, records the time a caller has left a message and she has called late at night, apparently *to avoid speaking to me as opposed to chatting.* She will have no idea of what message she's *really* left on the machine, that is, that she's trying to *avoid* a conversation. The third message is from a student who'd like me to speak to her club—the Lebanese student association—about communicating and the Middle East. The fourth is a broadcasted message to remind all faculty and staff to register for medical benefits. There's been a change this year. We are now to register by the end of the month on our intranet site. It's all being done on-line.

I'm about to leave when my wife informs me that the mayor's office called yesterday and left a message on our home answering machine. The neighbors in our community are in an uproar about a new car lot to be placed in a park near our homes. The park commissioner claimed to notify us all about the construction and seek our input. This was an unethical and deceptive claim. What had happened was that the commissioner had mailed fliers out about a meeting to discuss possible changes to the park. At what passed for a meeting, the commissioner had spoken ambiguously about several ideas. There was no talk of the car lot. Now, claiming that she had received input from the community, she plans to construct the lot. As a result of what we neighbors consider unethical and strategically ambiguous communication, I am now a member of the Neighborhood Order for Wondering About Youth. It sounds awkward, but we liked the acronym regarding the car lot: NOWAY. Our group will have a hearing with the mayor. My job is to meet with the others and devise a list of topics to be discussed at the meeting.

It's 8 A.M. I have not had solid food, nor have I had a face-to-face interaction with anyone other than my wife. I have two meetings to attend and a presentation to give. I have responded to four e-mails. I have been involved with five organizations: my university, NOWAY, the City of Waltham, the Lebanese Student Association, and the Mt. Auburn Health Club. I know a colleague wants me to think she desires to talk to me but only if I am in my office at 12:23 A.M. I know to use the intranet to register for medical benefits instead of meeting face to face with an HR representative.

On my drive to work I begin to count the number of drivers who are using cell phones. It seems as if two out of five are on the phone. Today, I decide to go through a toll booth with a human being. The line is just as short. I see my man Richard S. is taking the tolls. My man Richard S. has not smiled in 11 years if our brief interactions can be generalized. I've never heard him utter a sound. When I put the two quarters in his outstretched hand I am taken again by his calluses. I wonder if he has a second job in construction or if his hand has gotten that way from dealing with change.

When I arrive at work the woman who sells me a muffin is her usual happy self. "Hola," she says. "Como estas?" I respond. It is Esther's mission to have me speaking Spanish fluently before we both leave the university. I know some Spanish and had begun to converse with her about my purchases in Spanish a few years ago. Now she discourages any English from me. I protested. "If I only speak Spanish I'll get tuna instead of chicken salad."

"How do you think *we* feel?" she responded and then laughed while spewing Spanish at a dizzying rate to her colleagues who all got a chuckle. Today, as I leave the cafeteria and wave "adios" I hope I have a carrot and not a bran muffin.

(continued)

The woman who sits in the dean's office is the first person I see when I get into my building. She is the antidote to Richard S. She smiles, apparently genuinely, each time I walk into the building. It's nearly a joy to walk through the door and say "good morning" to her. There's nothing perfunctory about her greeting. We talk for a moment about her upcoming twenty-fifth wedding anniversary. She is positively energized by the prospects of the celebration. If she were to quit I wonder if the Dean would jump out of the window. She is as efficient as pleasant, and I am amazed at how she handles her meetings, diplomatically addresses abrasive faculty members, and communicates to college staff about upcoming events.

I get to the department office and go to my mailbox. Among other items therein I find a notice about the college council—a legislative committee that I sit on; the minutes from a sabbatical committee meeting I attended; a letter from the president about the September 11th tragedy; and a *printed* invitation to join the Credit Union. There's also a note from a student who would like to take an Independent Study. The note is particularly self-aggrandizing in an attempt, I assume, to convince me that I should take on the assignment. I wonder if the student is as good or as self-impressed as he appears to be. The message I received from his note might have been different if I could have heard his tone of voice or seen his facial expressions while he listed the accomplishments. The note is extraordinarily well-written and the list of achievements so long that I begin to think that he may be every bit as impressive as he claims to be. Perhaps I should be taking an Independent Study from him. There are some questions I have about his request, but he is not present, nor has he left any phone number, nor e-mail address. The note has, however, included a request for me to get back to him.

I leave the department center and head for my office. I deliberately avoid going past Robbie's office. If he catches me I will feel obliged to listen to him speak interminably about his complaint du jour. Robbie is a very abrasive personality whom we all seem to avoid. Detours around his office are such that I wonder if the carpet surrounding his office door will remain forever pristine. Unfortunately, he is a senior member of the department and we do need to interact with him regularly, but we routinely attempt to get information informally from alternative sources to avoid being waylaid. Today, I am successful navigating the route without an encounter.

On the bulletin board outside my door is a business card from a textbook salesperson. Also someone has taken the liberty of posting a notice advertising a meeting protesting the prohibition of contraceptive sales at the bookstore. This posting obscures my posting announcing my office hours, phone number, and e-mail address.

I've not yet opened my office door.

- ☐ How pervasive is organizational communication?
- ☐ How many interactions do you have before you *begin* your day?
- ☐ What is the impact on organizational success of an inability to understand the value of communication for organizational success?

Organizational Communication Is Multifaceted and Complex.

. . . Communication actually consists of a great deal more than what individual managers say or information that managements publish. Corporations frequently overlook *this obvious point* when they attempt to improve their communication systems.[19] (Emphasis added)

Organizational communication is multifaceted and complex.

©CORBIS

A problem with organizational communication is that there are varied interpretations of what the word communication means in organizational contexts. To some communication refers to speaking, listening, and writing skills. To others communication is perceived as something related to the technologies that are employed to facilitate communication. Improving communication to these persons means improving the electronic methods of disseminating information in an organization. Still others think of printed matter—newsletters, magazines, and internal memoranda—as what is meant by internal communication. Organizational communication issues include all of these areas and many more. For example, communication problems in organizations might involve

- The inappropriate use of print or electronic communication. An overabundance of memos, bulletins, e-mails, and internal letters.
- A hyperactive grapevine. An unusually active informal communication network that spreads inaccurate information.
- Informational briefings/presentations that are neither informational nor brief and are perceived as time wasters by subordinates.
- A credibility problem within the organization that makes employees wonder about the ethical foundation of the organization and the truth of the messages they do receive.
- Poor intercultural communication reflecting an ignorance of, or insensitivity to, diverse needs and cultural differences.
- A defensive communication climate, which discourages employees from utilizing their inherent communication skills.
- Poor updating of the organizational intranet resulting in outdated information that is accepted as current by intranet users.
- A heavy and inappropriate reliance on committees and meetings.
- An ineffective or unskilled method of interpersonally communicating to employees regarding how well or how poorly they are doing.
- A weak interoffice mail system that results in correspondence being received late.

Overlooking the *obvious point* that organizational communication is multidimensional can create communication problems. If one is under the assumption, for example, that "business presentation skill" is a phrase that's synonymous with "organizational communication effectiveness," then administrators and consultants may design speaking skill programs under the assumption that these skill interventions will improve communication effectiveness. These programs, at best, will deal with a component of organizational communication and, at worst, deal with a meaningless component. Creating a program that provides the illusion of dealing with the core and/or breadth of organizational communication, while leaving the overall problems intact, creates a double negative. The central employee communication problems are likely to not be addressed and yet the organization believes that they have been meaningfully addressed.

Breadth of Topics

The Association for Business Communication (ABC) is an academic organization that publishes the *Journal of Business Communication* and *Business Communication Quarterly*. Annually the organization meets to discuss various issues germane to the field. The diversity of topics discussed at the ABC meetings is indicated by the list below, which reflects the focus of papers presented at recent conventions.

- Assessing abrasive interpersonal communication styles
- Communicating sympathy to employees who've suffered personal losses
- Communicating with employees who are handicapped
- Creating feedback loops for employees to communicate with employers
- Crisis communication planning
- Cultural effects of communicating in international business
- Development of non-English-speaking cliques in predominately English-speaking organizations.
- Effects of corporate climate and culture on communication
- Effects of gender on communication in groups and dyads
- Effects of the organizational grapevine
- Ethical issues in business communication
- Interviewing techniques
- Intranet development and effective organizational communication
- Making quality presentations
- Nonverbal communication in organizations
- Same site electronic meetings
- Subordinate to superior communication issues
- Use and abuse of electronic mail
- Using communication to create a team atmosphere
- Using visual support for presentations
- Writing reports collaboratively after team problem solving

Sometimes people assume that academics are not in touch with the "real world." Yet the topics listed above are very much real-world issues. This is supported by looking at the varied subjects that were discussed at recent meetings of the IABC, the International Association of Business Communicators. The IABC, unlike the ABC mentioned above, is an association comprised predominantly of communication practitioners. The members are not those who study communication in the academy, but those who work in industry as communication professionals. Topics at these IABC practitioner meetings similarly reflect the diversity and breadth of organizational communication issues.[20]

Multifaceted Problems

In 1999 I completed a study of 140 persons who were managers or who aspired to be managers. All of these persons were part-time MBA students who worked during the day full time or who had very recently been employed full time (within 1 year of the time of the study). Each of the subjects was asked to describe a communication-related problem they had at work. They could describe any problem and were encouraged to select incidents that were particularly difficult and ones for which they would like to have, or have had, some solution. Subsequently, a content analysis of the descriptions was conducted.[21]

The results support the conception of organizational communication as multifaceted. Forty percent of all problems dealt in some way with the absence of communication channels that permitted communication. For example, one manager commented that she needed to get information from a specific source but had little to no access to that source. Without the contact and resulting exchange of information, the manager could not clearly nor accurately inform her own subordinates so that they could intelligently complete their tasks. Not only did this manager have little access to the source, she claimed to have few avenues available to communicate the need to have such access to anyone who might have prevailed upon the source to be accessible.

Thirty-two percent of the problems referred to issues with the quality of messages received in terms of timeliness, pertinence, credibility, and the manner used to disseminate the messages. For example, one manager claimed to be dunned with broadcasted voice mail that was irrelevant. Sometimes, she confessed, she would abort a message before listening to it in its entirety in order to get through her voice mail messages. On one occasion this habit created a big problem for her since a portion of the purged message was in fact pertinent, yet she was unaware of the relevance nor the content of the message since in her haste she had deleted it prematurely.

Fifteen percent of the messages dealt with communication "climate" issues that tended to discourage managers and employees from exercising their inherent communication skills. One respondent wrote that the tensions within his department were so high that persons were reluctant to share information fearing that any information shared might be somehow used against the person who had communicated it. In a particular instance information that had not been communicated created a crisis because incorrect assumptions regarding eventual product cost had been based on incomplete information.

Thirteen percent dealt with communication skill issues, for example, how to run a meeting or communicate during meetings; how to communicate sensitive personal information; how to communicate interculturally; how to persuade others; how to use vocal inflection appropriately; and how to listen effectively. For example, several respondents commented about counterproductive tendencies during meetings including hogging speaking time, unclear articulation of messages, contentious and gratuitous personal attacks, and time-wasting orations that were only tangentially related to the meeting topics.

Clearly, when employees think about communication and communication failure what they consider problematic transcends individual skill set issues. Organizational communication is far more encompassing than individual listening, speaking, reading, and writing skills. Communication does indeed consist "of a great deal more than what individual managers say or information that managements publish."

What is essential for organizational communication?

As we discussed earlier in the chapter, Phillip Tompkins has made the argument that organizations must meet their communication imperatives or suffer some type of organizational disaster. The "explosions" will not typically be as dramatic, visible, or even as disastrous as that which befell NASA and the Challenger in 1986, but they will similarly have corrosive consequences for the organization. Does this make sense to you? Can poor communication in organizations really cause "explosions"?

For each of the following statements, indicate how important the item is for successful organizational communication. Use the following labels. Indicate whether the item is

- ☐ Imperative
- ☐ Somewhat important
- ☐ Neither important nor unimportant
- ☐ Somewhat unimportant
- ☐ Not important at all

For those that you identify as imperative indicate what might be the repercussions of not meeting that imperative.

1. All organizational personnel (managers, executives, employees) must be able to orally express ideas.
2. All organizational personnel must be able to express ideas in writing.
3. All organizational personnel must be active and efficient listeners.
4. All organizational personnel must be able and willing to read distributed material.
5. All organizational personnel must be able to use so called *new technology* (for example, the intranet, electronic mail, the World Wide Web).
6. All organizational personnel must be able to lead a meeting with 3 to 15 members.
7. Information distributed throughout the organization must be perceived as credible.
8. Information distributed throughout the organization must be timely.
9. Information distributed must be accurate.
10. Information distributed must be sent to only those receivers to whom the information pertains.
11. The method for communicating the information must be appropriate. For example, one must know when to use e-mail, face-to-face communication, the phone, and meetings.
12. All personnel must be aware of organizational policies.
13. All personnel must be aware of their individual tasks.
14. All personnel must be aware of how well or how poorly they are doing in their job.
15. All personnel must feel as if other staff members are concerned about their personal needs. Therefore, it is essential for colleagues to ask, tactfully, about personal issues that may or may not be peripheral to work.
16. Networks must be established linking related departments.
17. Channels must be established allowing superiors to formally and regularly relay information to subordinates.
18. Channels must be established allowing subordinate staffers to communicate *problems* to superiors.

19. Channels must be established allowing subordinate staffers to communicate *ideas* to superiors.
20. Networks must be established allowing communication to external audiences (for example, media, prospective students).
21. The informal network (i.e., grapevine) needs to be harnessed.
22. All personnel must feel supported and get supportive messages when they deserve them.
23. All personnel must get constructively critical messages when they deserve them.
24. All personnel must feel as if they participate in decision making that affects their jobs.
25. Messages from and by all staff members should reflect a commitment to organizational excellence.
26. Information that can be shared should be shared.
27. A proactive crisis communication plan must be in place so that the organization will be able to expeditiously communicate in times of such crises to internal and external audiences.
28. All communications should be concerned with ethical issues. Specifically, information communicated must be honest.
29. Sensitivity to the needs and concerns of a multicultural population must be the rule when communicating.
30. The organization must self-assess communication quality periodically.

MYTHS REGARDING ORGANIZATIONAL COMMUNICATION

Before we proceed further it is a good idea to examine some myths or misunderstandings about what is meant by organizational communication. By debunking these myths it is likely that the focus for this area of study will become clearer.

Myth #1: *Organizational communication is relevant only to businesses and those who study business.* While organizational communication is certainly applicable to business and many of you may well be pursuing a degree in business, organizational communication is not a study just confined to businesses. We are all organizational men and women regardless of where we work. We belong to athletic clubs, churches and synagogues, civic associations, and assorted other organizations. The head of your sorority is a manager of sorts who must communicate information to the sisters in your organization and solicit communications from them. Your minister is in a similar position and must deliver homilies, use communication skills to counsel membership, and persuade the congregants that she or he is doing a good job. Your soccer teammates need to communicate with you while you're playing. The captain needs to relay the sentiments of your team to the coach. The coach has to convince the league coordinators to come up with the funds for new nets or uniforms. If you stop to think about it, you are probably now involved as a member or quasi-member of three or four organizations that are not businesses in the traditional sense of the word. Some have argued that the family unit itself can be considered an organization.[22]

Therefore, the notion that only those people who are going into business need be concerned about organizational communication is an inaccurate conception. It is true that in this book the focus is on organizational communication in business contexts, but organizational communication principles are applicable to any organization.

Myth #2: *It is easy to train someone to be an effective communicator in organizations.* It is not easy to train someone to be a good communicator. Even if we were to simply (and incorrectly) define organizational communication as a speaking skill phenomenon, it would be foolish to assume that it's easy to train someone to be an effective speaker. However, if we define communication correctly as a multifaceted phenomenon, the assumption that someone can be crash course trained to be competent is not just incorrect, it is absurd. It would be as short-sighted as assuming that someone could become good at math by taking a 1- or 2 day cram course. Imagine hiring an accountant who couldn't do arithmetic computations on the basis of the notion that she or he could do "everything else" and could be trained to add subsequently. Hiring someone who can do "everything else" but cannot communicate makes no sense given the central and multidimensional nature of communication in organizations. "You can't run [managers] through a charm school and have natural communicators."[23]

Myth #3: *Organizational communication is the role of Human Resources or Corporate Communication people. It does not pertain to the average employee or manager.* Human Resources (HR) and Corporate Communication departments certainly have communication-related responsibilities. However, this does not mean that the average employee does *not* have communication-related responsibilities. The average employee needs to be able to

- Articulate ideas to colleagues
- Listen effectively
- Communicate during meetings
- Use e-mail efficiently
- Write memos
- Persuade colleagues
- Communicate interpersonally during appraisal, selection, and informative interviews
- Use the intranet
- Communicate cross-culturally
- Make ethical decisions regarding how and what to communicate
- Know when, what, and how to communicate information

When these responsibilities surface employees don't and can't call HR representatives and have them complete the chore. Organizational communication is a responsibility of every employee.

Myth #4: *People know how to communicate. We can all speak. We can all hear. Most of us can use the Internet. Certainly intelligent people can communicate well.* Most of us can communicate to some extent. This does not mean we can communicate well. To assume that all people because of their *capabilities* have *abilities* is to make an incorrect assumption. In his autobiography, Lee Iacocca, the former Chrysler CEO made the following observation:

I've known a lot of engineers with terrific ideas who had trouble explaining them to other people. It's always a shame when a guy with great talent can't tell the board or committee what's in his head.[24]

Iacocca is not the only person to know people like the engineers to whom he refers. We all know bright people who are weak communicators either because they don't understand what it means to communicate or because they cannot express what they need to write or say.

We have heard the expression, "It doesn't take a rocket scientist to figure out. . . ." Tompkins carefully documents that NASA rocket scientists could not understand or could not implement effective organizational communication strategies at the Marshall Space Flight Center in the mid-1980s.[25] The brilliant physicist, Richard Feynman, who was a member of the Roger's Commission that investigated the causes of the Challenger disaster, was startled when he came to the conclusion that, apparently, some of the rocket scientists were *deliberately* making it difficult for communication to take place.[26] More about Feynman's theory of organizational communication appears in Chapter 6. However, it's clear that intelligence does not guarantee communication competence.

Myth #5: *Sharing a sophisticated vocabulary makes a group, and members of that group, effective organizational communicators.* A person is not necessarily an effective communicator because she or he knows a great many words. Being able to use words correctly for various audiences is an asset. Being able to understand a great many words is also an asset. However, extensive vocabularies do not, in and of themselves, guarantee effective communication.

Lawyers, doctors, technicians, even communication professionals have their own lexicon—a common language that they use among themselves and can understand. Having this shared language is helpful for those who are speaking to others within a similar group. However, knowledge of sophisticated pieces of information or language does not eliminate communication responsibilities. Lawyers may be able to speak "legalese" to their colleagues and may even be able to impress clients with jargon, but knowledge of terms doesn't preclude the need to inform associates about trial times, or to inform clients about what they need to do to prepare for court, or to select the best method for communicating any piece of information.

In short, language while important is not the lone criterion for organizational communication success.

DEFINING ORGANIZATIONAL COMMUNICATION

"All books end in definition" is the way one author began a monograph.[27] By this he meant that at the end of a book the reader ought to have a clearer, more defined understanding of the topic. In the same way as all *books* end in such definition, all good introductory chapters should also end in definition. We have been defining organizational communication throughout the chapter. At this point we know that organizational communication is pervasive, central to organizational success, multi-dimensional, and complex.

There are many definitions of organizational communication. Some, however accurate, are cumbersome and difficult to understand rendering them less than valuable to a person studying organizational communication for the first time. Perhaps it is easier at this point in the chapter to examine these definitions now that you are more familiar with organizational communication. Some of the definitions follow.

Organizational communication is

- The process whereby members gather pertinent information about their organization and the changes occurring within it.[28]

- The coordination (by communication) of a number of people who are interdependently related.[29]
- The process of creating and exchanging messages within an organization in order to help that organization cope with the uncertainties of a changing environment.[30]
- The process of creating, exchanging, interpreting (correctly or incorrectly), and storing messages within a system of human interrelationships.[31]
- The study of sending and receiving messages that create and maintain a system of consciously coordinated activities or forces of two or more people.[32]

These definitions all have valuable attributes. Organizational communication is a field of study. It does involve creating, sending, receiving, and interpreting information. Effective organizational communication does help organizations cope with uncertainty and does exist within a complex system of interrelationships. Let's try to digest these definitions and provide a simple one that can be used for this foundational course:

Organizational communication is the study of why and how organizations send and receive information in a complex systemic environment.

Systemic environment is likely the only confusing phrase in our definition. It will be explained more thoroughly in Chapter 2. However, for now consider the organization as a combination of persons and departments that have a common goal and are, therefore—directly or indirectly—interdependent. This interdependence creates a system. What happens to one part of the organization has a direct or indirect effect on other parts. Organizational women and men need to acknowledge the systemic nature of their environment when considering *why* they must communicate and *how* they must communicate. This systemic phenomenon is one of the factors that makes communication in organizations different from communications that you might have with your best friend or any other individual acquaintance.[33]

THE SCOPE OF THE TEXT

This book will explain the comprehensive nature of organizational communication. In Part 1 we put down the floorboards of the study by discussing

- Organizational theory
- Communication principles
- Ethical issues in organizational communication

In Part 2 we explain how organizational communication meets the needs of a systemic environment by examining

- Information management
- Communication networks
- Communication climate and culture

Part 3 discusses communication skill sets. In this section we examine principles and "how to" dimensions relating to

- Communicating in meetings
- Making oral presentations
- Interpersonal communication
- Written communication

In Part 4 we examine three topics that have become particularly relevant in these early years of the new millennium:

- Organizational communication in the global, intercultural village
- Crisis communication
- Communication auditing

Practitioner's Perspectives and Ethical Probes

As you have seen in this introductory chapter, case studies and explanatory exercises will be interspersed throughout the book. In addition, you will find two other regular features in the text.

The first is called *Practitioner's Perspective*. These sections will present segments of interviews conducted with executives who offer their insights on the importance of communication for organizational success. These inclusions will complement the research and perspectives of organizational communication scholars.

The second feature is called *Ethical Probe*. These segments (which are in addition to the chapter dedicated to Ethics and Organizational Communication) ask you to consider moral questions pertaining to the organizational communication topic being discussed. For example, in Chapter 5 we discuss methods for communicating information. As we all know one very common method for communicating in contemporary organizations is e-mail. Let's assume that you know that a particular employee rarely checks his or her e-mail. Further, let's assume that you must send information to that employee that you know he or she does not want to receive. Is there anything unethical with sending that information via e-mail so that you can claim to have communicated the message, even though you know that the employee is unlikely to have actually received your communication in a timely manner?

Throughout the text such ethical probes apppear.

PRACTITIONER'S PERSPECTIVE

Alan Barocas, Senior Vice President for Field Real Estate

Alan Barocas joined Gap Inc. in 1981 and for 6 years held several positions in field management and human resources. In 1987, Mr. Barocas joined the Real Estate department, and in the fall of 2000 became the Senior Vice President for Real Estate. He is responsible for overseeing and developing real estate strategy for over 4,200 Gap, Banana Republic, and Old Navy locations in the United States and internationally.

(continued)

My job involves communication in several ways and directions. I must communicate downward to explain our vision to corporate directors and deputy directors. I need to communicate across divisions within the Gap and be receptive to information that comes to me from persons and offices that I supervise. Also I have to communicate with our industry partners—developers and landlords with whom we work—to make sure, for example, that we can successfully launch a new store in, let's say, a particular mall in the Cincinnati area.

I supervise offices in Boston, New York, New Jersey, Atlanta, Chicago, Dallas, and here in San Francisco. Therefore, I need to contact persons in these branches and communicate efficiently with them in order to do my work as a supervisor. Interacting with the six non-San Francisco offices is more difficult, of course, since the contact there is typically not face to face. However, by using teleconferencing or e-mail or some other electronic technology for communicating you can get messages to your receivers. You miss some of the body motion, feedback, and nonverbal components when you interact that way and it is certainly a challenge to use technology effectively.

I am involved in meetings, making presentations, describing tasks and policies to subordinates and reading and responding to written communications and employee e-mail. Most of my responsibilities involve communication in some form or other. I have to be an effective communicator or I will be an ineffective manager.

When I listen to a presentation, either formal or informal, I expect some framework for the message. I want to know where she or he intends to go with this. What are the takeaways I can expect? It is frustrating to listen without context. I also like to listen to someone who has passion, energy, and some humanity. We had a CFO give a talk at a meeting a while back and he started by saying—and I'm paraphrasing, but it was something like—"Every time I make a decision I think about three things." And then he put up a picture of his wife and two kids. He said that his love for his family drives his decision making and he wanted that clear from the start. That touched me and it really engaged the rest of us in the room. We need some humanity in our communications not just facts and figures. Also we need honesty. It bothers me when I hear someone dance on a question. I would much prefer it, if the person simply said, "I don't know—I'll get back to you." Honesty is critical for anyone, but particularly for a leader in organizations. If you lose your integrity, you will never get it back. And I emphasize never. In business contexts you need people who will trust you.

A Toolbox

- Communication is central to organizational activity.
- Organizational communication is pervasive, multifaceted, and transcends the study of how to speak, write, and listen effectively.
- Effective organizational communication is not simple nor a "given" even for highly intelligent people.
- We define *organizational communication* as the study of why and how organizations send and receive information within a complex systemic environment.

1. Explain why organizational communication is central to organizational efficiency.
2. What does it mean to say that communication in organizations is *pervasive*?
3. Why is organizational communication considered *multifaceted*?
4. How has communication at your university positively or negatively affected your experience at the school?
5. Have you been in a work situation where the quality of communication

   a. Enhanced the efficiency of the organization?

   b. Created problems for employees, management, or the organization as a whole?

6. Describe your typical morning in terms of your communication contacts. How much of your day is spent communicating using new technology? Face-to-face communication?
7. Of the five myths identified in this chapter, which one do you feel is most typically embraced by organizational men and women?
8. Do you agree with the following statements? Explain why you agree or disagree.

   a. Meetings must have set agendas. Otherwise they are a waste of time.

   b. Business presentations must be accompanied with visual aids and a copy of the text needs to be provided to all participants.

   c. In today's global marketplace, company spokespersons *must be* multilingual.

   d. There's nothing wrong with leaving a meeting if your cell phone rings and you need to make another call.

   e. Broadcasting e-mails is an efficient way to get information to organizational personnel. It's the individual receiver's responsibility to review the e-mails and react to those that are pertinent.

   f. The company manual should be put on-line instead of wasting paper printing a policy and procedures bulletin.

   g. Suggestion systems are necessary for healthy organizational communication.

   h. It's wise to be vague when conveying information if the truth will hurt you or your company.

   i. Informal coffee chats and lunches outside of the office are good venues for getting a sense of what others are thinking.

9. Read Case 1.1 and address the questions that appear at the end of the case.

Case 1.1—Annette and the Inscrutable Manager

Annette is a financial analyst for a software company. She is supervised by a man, Ryan, who has difficulty communicating clearly and effectively with his employees. During the course of a conversation, Ryan constantly switches subjects without adequate transitions. He speaks almost in a stream of consciousness without organization to his ideas. Annette claims that Ryan does not use vocal inflection or any nonverbal cues to indicate that he has moved on to a new subject.

Employees have become frustrated by the difficulty and inefficiency of conversations with this manager. Often, different members of Annette's team derive varied meanings from Ryan's directions. As a result team members are basing their work on inconsistent assumptions.

Annette and her colleagues are uncertain about how to deal with the situation. Because Ryan is a superior they feel awkward about confronting him. Annette also believes that there are gender issues that affect her ability to talk with Ryan about his problem. Furthermore any such confrontation—whether initiated by a male of female—would not mesh with the corporate culture at the company. Annette has said that it simply would not be "politically correct" to tell Ryan that he is difficult to understand.

Annette has, while conversing with Ryan, asked him to stop and clarify what he is discussing. However, this can be done only so many times and Annette doesn't want to appear to be ignorant or annoy Ryan by interrupting him too often. Ryan writes well, speaks poorly, and is under the impression that he communicates as clearly when he speaks as when he writes.

- *Have you ever worked with, or for, a person like Ryan?*
- *Does it make sense that an organization's culture can affect Annette's options?*
- *How should Annette communicate to Ryan about Ryan's communication problem?*
- *What suggestions could Annette (or anyone else) make that would help Ryan improve his communication?*

ENDNOTES

[1] Management Consultant Michael Lobiondo quoted in the *Newsday* article "Talent of Learning to Talk," by Al Gordon, October 20, 1987, p. 45.

[2] Foltz, Roy, "Communication in Contemporary Organizations," in *Inside Organizational Communication*, Longman, 1985, p. 3.

[3] Barnard, Chester, *The Functions of the Executive,* Harvard University Press, 1938: p. 226

[4] Kelly, William, "Blue-Print for Employee Communication," in Elizabeth Marting, Robert E. Finley, and Ann Ward, eds., *Effective Communication on the Job,* AMACOM, 1963: p. 110.

[5] *Linking Communications with Strategy to Achieve Business Goals,* Watson Wyatt Worldwide 1999: p. 1. Page 10 in the publication has similar conclusions.

[6] Reinsch Jr., N. L. and Annette N. Shelby, *Communication Skill Needs of MBA Students.* Part 2. Paper presented at Association for Business Communication Meetings, San Diego, California. November 1994.

[7]Allen, Myria Watkins, J. Michael Gotcher, and Joy Hart Seibert, "A Decade of Organizational Communication Research: Journal Articles 1980–91," *Communication Yearbook*. Volume 16 Stanley Deetz, ed., Sage, 1993.

[8]Daly, John A. "Assessing Speaking and Listening: Preliminary Considerations for a National Assessment," *National Assessment of College Students Learning: Identification of Skills to Be Taught Learned and Assessed: A Report on the Proceedings of the Second Study Design Workshop,* November 1992: p. 19.

[9]Dowd, Karen O. and Jeanne Liedtka, "What Corporations Seek in MBA Hires: A Survey," *Selections,* Winter 1994: p. 38.

[10]Some may quibble with this designation and cite Goldhaber's 1974 book, *Organizational Communication,* as the first true textbook. Also Redding with George Sanborn actually published an earlier book called *Business and Industrial Communication* in 1964 that could be called the first organizational communication text. The Redding and Sanborn publication, however, is a reader and as an anthology is not quite the same as Redding's 1972 publication or Goldhaber's 1974 book. (*Business and Industrial Communication* is, however, comprehensive and 20–30 years ahead of its time in terms of its description of the breadth of organizational communication issues). Goldhaber, a student of Redding, published his book with WC Brown in 1974. Redding's publisher, the Industrial Communication Council, is not a textbook publisher. The book itself reflects this and has more of a self-published workbook look and feel than a conventional text. The argument has been made, however, that in terms of content this Redding publication is the first true textbook in organizational communication. Jablin, Putnam, Roberts, and Porter comment in *The Handbook of Organizational Communication* (Sage, 1987) that Redding's 1972 book is the first "comprehensive review and interpretation of the literature" (page 7).

[11]DeWine, Sue, *The Consultant's Craft,* Second Edition, Bedford, St. Martins 2001: p. vii. Redding's stature as a pioneer is further evidenced by the piece he was invited to author in *Readings in Organizational Communication* (1992) that exhaustively traced the evolution of the field. *Readings* is edited by Kevin Hutchinson. Redding's article appears on pages 11–44 and is called, "Stumbling Towards Identity: The Emergence of Organizational Communication as a Field of Study."

[12]DeWine, Sue, *Consultant's Craft,* p. xxiii.

[13]This is a theme throughout Phillip Tompkins's entire book, *Organizational Communication Imperatives.* Roxbury Press, 1993. However, comments that focus on this point in particular are found on pages 166–167 and 195.

[14]Pace, R. Wayne and Don F. Faules, *Organizational Communication,* Prentice Hall, 1989: p. 22.

[15]Quote attributed to Paul Strassmann in Tom Richman, "Face to Face: Information Strategist Paul Strassman," *INC.,* March 1988: p. 40.

[16]From a paper presented by Dr. Raymond Beaty at the Speech Communication Association annual convention in Louisville, November 1982. The paper was entitled "A Consultant's Perception of Speech Communication." The quotation appears on page 3 of the paper.

[17]Mintzberg, Henry, *The Nature of Managerial Work,* Prentice Hall, 1973: pp. 58–94.

[18]Penley, Larry, Elmore Alexander, I. Edward Jernigan, and Catherine Henwood, "Communication Abilities of Managers: The Relation to Performance," *Journal of Management,* March 1991, Vol. 17, No. 1: p. 57.

[19]Gellerman, Saul, *The Management of Human Relations,* Holt Rinehart and Winston, 1966: p. 59.

[20]This list reflects topics discussed at recent IABC meetings.

Building employee relationships through communication
Communicating your organization's ethics program
Communication auditing (Assessment. Auditing will be discussed in detail in Chapter 14)

Creating speeches with impact
Crisis communication: Ford's perspective on the tire crisis
Integrating print and on-line communication
Integrity and the ethics of "spin"
Intranet and Internet use
Linking communication to business performance and organizational behavior
Motivating employees using visual media
Persuasive communication and leadership
Upward communication
Using communication to transform culture

[21]Zaremba, Alan, "Communication in Its Entirety," *Journal of Employee Communication Management,* March 1999: pp. 24–32.

[22]Timm, Paul and Kristen Bell DeTienne, *Managerial Communication: A Finger on the Pulse,* Prentice Hall, 1995: pp. 6–7.

[23]This quote appeared in the *Wall Street Journal* on July 2, 1985 (page 1 column 5) in a section entitled "Worker Communication Programs Take Many Forms to Keep Talk Flowing." In the article there are references to how Quaker Oats, TRW, and other corporations "keep talk flowing." The specific quote cited in the chapter was made by a Mead corporation representative.

[24]Lee Iacocca with William Novak, *Iacocca: An Autobiography,* Bantam Books, 1984: p. 54.

[25]Again, as indicated in the previous note about Tompkins, this point is thematic throughout the book *Organizational Communication Imperatives.* On page 128 there is a specific reference to rocket scientists' failure to communicate based on not understanding the essence or importance of organizational communication.

[26]Tompkins, Phillip, *Organizational Communication Imperatives,* p. 144–146.

[27]The book was called *Transracial Communication* written by Arthur Lee Smith. Prentice Hall, 1973. I have paraphrased the quote for contextual readability without changing the essence of the author's sentiments. The precise quote is, "All analyses end in definition. This book is no different." The quote appears on page 9. In the mid-1970s, Arthur Lee Smith changed his name to Molefi Kete Asante. Smith/Asante was the Chair of the Department of Communication at the University of Buffalo from 1973 to 1979.

[28]Kreps, Gary, *Organizational Communication,* Longman, 1990: p. 11.

[29]This definition is attributed to William Haney in Gerald Goldhaber's book *Organizational Communication,* 1993 edition, p. 13. In fact, Haney does describe organizational communication in this manner in his book, *Communication and Organizational Behavior,* published by Richard Irwin in 1973. The distinction is that the quote comes from the Goldhaber book which distills Haney's description.

[30]Pamphlet: Communication: The Ultimate Science. Project Communication Inc.

[31]DeWine, Sue and Dan Modaff, *Organizational Communication: Foundations, Challenges, and Misunderstandings,* Roxbury, 2002. As referenced in DeWine, *The Consultant's Craft,* page 5.

[32]Op. cit., Tompkins, page 24.

[33]You may have seen other textbooks entitled Managerial, Business, or Corporate Communication. There is a distinction among these areas based on how scholars, departments, and universities have defined the subjects' domains. Annette Shelby's 1993 article, "Organizational, Business, Management and Corporate Communication: An Analysis of Boundaries and Relationships," makes a good attempt to explain the domains of each area. Yet she comments right from the start about the accuracy of SI Hayakawa's notion that the true meaning of a term is to be found by observing what a [person] does with it not by what [the person] says about it (*Journal of Business Communication*, July, 1993, p. 241). To be sure, the domains are blurry at times and will continue to overlap as the fields evolve.

There isn't anything terrible about the overlap. Writing in *The Journal of Business Communication*, Reinsch tried to make a distinction between Business Communication, Managerial Communication, and Organizational Communication. He began by comparing the topics to "three candles on a small table, providing overlapping spheres of illumination." (Reinsch, "Editorial. What is Business Communication," *Journal of Business Communication*, Fall 1991, Vol. 26, p. 306.) However appropriate the comparison, there are real problems when attempting to identify which discrete sphere is which. These problems are compounded by finding articles in *The Journal of Business Communication* about what many typically call Managerial Communication, and finding articles in *Managerial Communication Quarterly* that many would claim to be on Business Communication topics.

Therefore with the qualifier that these fields are complementary, evolving, and overlapping, below are some traditional areas of distinction for each label.

Business Communication courses typically deal with the essential "how to" areas of communication, for example, how to write business materials and make presentations. Employee skill deficiencies can retard an organization's success. The focus in business communication is on developing and improving these communication skill sets. **Managerial Communication** has more of a theoretical component than Business Communication. The focus in managerial communication is on the communication concepts and skills managers must understand and possess to successfully meet their managerial responsibilities. **Corporate Communication** is a more slippery label. In some books, corporate communication refers to the creation of informational media and in others the emphasis is on external organizational communication. The *Corporate Communicator's Quick Reference* by Peter Lichtgarn is an example of the former. The Paul Argenti text *Corporate Communication* is an example of the latter. **Organizational Communication** is the broadest of the labels. Organizational communication is a theoretically based, comprehensive approach to studying the sending and receiving of messages in a complex systemic environment. It includes an analysis of employee communication skill set needs and the discussion of how to improve these skill sets. Similarly, organizational communication involves understanding why and how managers must communicate to meet their responsibilities as well as why and how organizations need to interact with their internal and external audiences. In essence, organizational communication is a more research-based inclusive area of study. The perspective and focus of organizational communication is on the organization as opposed to individual employees or managers.

2

Management Theory and Organizational Communication

In all affairs it's a healthy thing to hang a question mark on the things you have long taken for granted.

—Bertrand Russell

If the only tool you have is a hammer you tend to see every problem as a nail.

—Abraham Maslow

Routine work, that best of all anodynes which the twentieth century has tried its best to deprive itself of—this is what I most want. I would not trade the daily trip it gives me for all the mind expanders and mind deadeners the young are hooked on.

—Wallace Stegner in the novel *Angle of Repose*

© GETTY IMAGES/PHOTODISC

Case 2.1—*Communicating to a New Staff*

Patricia Daniels was in her first week at the job. She knew she had to send a message to her subordinates but was unsure of what she should communicate to them and how she should communicate her messages.

Daniels had been hired from the outside to be a "change agent" and head of the HR department at a software company. The department had 20 employees, including five part-time workers and three administrative assistants. One of the full-timers was an associate director who had held the same position under the previous leader.

Daniels was told by the supervisor who had hired her that the former, now retired, director had been laid-back about enforcing rules. The staff had been lax, particularly about coming into work on time. Some employees were notorious for arriving as much as 30 minutes to an hour after the assigned opening time. These same persons would often take extra time before and after their lunch breaks. Lateness was just one issue. The staff wasn't professional in performance or appearance. One veteran took days off claiming they were sick days but, according to the supervisor, they were personal days. Part-time employees were similarly indifferent to their responsibilities. Also, despite being a Human Resources department, the group had a reputation of being gruff with employees who asked questions about benefits. Even the workspace wasn't as clean as it could or should be. Meetings were haphazard informal sessions without any genuine agenda. These meetings were described by the supervisor as more of a social occasion than anything else.

Some employees enjoyed the laissez-faire approach of Daniels's predecessor. Others desired more professionalism but did not want to carry the weight of that responsibility if others were not so inclined to share the burdens. The supervisor warned Daniels before she took the job that there might be some angry employees because the associate director—a friend to many employees—had applied for the position but had been rejected. It wasn't that he wasn't qualified. However, he was tainted from his association with the former director. A hire from the outside seemed to be a good idea.

During her first week a few employees—three or four—had individually stopped into Daniels's office to wish her well. Privately they had said they were glad that she was there because the department had gotten out of hand under the former regime. Yet, it was hard for Daniels to read the others as she passed them in the hall or when she met them briefly at a company-wide session. When she first met the associate director, he had been cordial. He'd knocked on her door early in the first week apparently just to chat, but the meeting was very brief. He didn't seem abrasive, but Daniels was concerned that she hadn't come across assertive enough during their short conversation.

Patricia Daniels knew she had to somehow communicate her position to the staff. But what was her position? Were these people lazy delinquents seeking to maintain a sloppy status quo or were they dedicated professionals seeking leadership that might be the catalyst for excellence? Did she need to lay down the law? If so, what was the law?

As significantly, Daniels wondered about the method and sequencing of her communication.

☐ *Should she speak to the full-time employees at a different time than the part-time employees?*

☐ *Should she write out a policy statement and distribute the document to employee mailboxes?*

☐ *Should she use the company intranet to send a "welcoming note from your new director?"*

☐ *Should she relay any messages at a social function outside the office environment instead of during work hours?*

☐ *Would she be wise to speak formally about her plans to the associate director before meeting with any other workers?*

☐ *Should she send out a formal agenda prior to any meeting or would that send out the wrong signals—as if she was too "stuffy"?*

☐ *Would it be wise to send any communications to the staffers' home addresses?*

☐ *Should she wait a while to see how things unfolded before she communicated any message?*

To complicate matters even further Daniels was the sole African-American in the department. A part-timer was from Bombay and one of the full-timers was of Japanese origin. The company population as a whole was more diverse, but at HR, Daniels was clearly a minority. She'd been dealing with issues of race since she was a child and she tried to block out the notion of potential prejudice when she entered into a new situation with whites. It wasn't easy. It seemed as if race was always there as a barrier or at least a factor. She remembered the time when, after a preliminary phone conversation, she deplaned for an interview and was met by a host who seemed to be startled that Daniels was not white. He had fumbled for a moment and nearly blabbered something like, "You didn't sound black when we talked." Would race be something she'd have to overcome in this job as well?

The task of knowing what to communicate to her subordinates and how to say it was daunting and weighed on her.

☐ *If you were Daniels, what would you assume about your audience?*

☐ *What messages would you want to convey?*

☐ *How would you convey these messages?*

ABSTRACT

Are people inherently lazy? Or are people willing and even eager to work under the right conditions? If employees are inherently lazy, what information do managers need to communicate to them? If employees are willing and even eager to work, what messages do they need to receive? Do workers only need information related to job tasks, organizational policy, and compensation? Or do they also need to hear about how well or how poorly they are doing?

Management theory provides a framework and foundation for understanding organizational communication. In this chapter we discuss several theories about management and explain why the evolution of management theory compels students of organizations to examine principles of communication.

OBJECTIVES

When you have completed this chapter, you should be able to:

- ☐ **Explain what is meant by a theory.**
- ☐ **Discuss the practical relevance of examining theories.**
- ☐ **Identify the principles of *classical theory, human relations and human resources theory, and systems theory*.**
- ☐ **Explain the Hawthorne Studies.**
- ☐ **List the differences between McGregor's *Theory X* and *Theory Y*.**
- ☐ **Explain why the evolution of management theory has changed perspectives on the importance of organizational communication.**
- ☐ **Describe the communication related challenges for managers who adopt the classical, human relations, or systems theory of management.**

DEMYSTIFYING THEORIES

The word *theory* is often misunderstood. It has the negative connotation of an abstract, impractical notion or assumption. Steven Corman documented this attitude by conducting a simple study. He asked students to complete a sentence that began with the six words, "That works fine in theory, but. . . ." Typical responses were, "Not in real life"; "In practice it doesn't happen that way"; "Reality is a different story"; and "In reality things are a lot more complicated."[1]

Theories need not be impractical and don't even need to be confusing, although some poorly articulated theories do seem complex to students, business practitioners, and professors alike. A good theory can be clearly described and can provide a very practical foundation for understanding phenomena. One could make a strong case that a theory that does not provide a practical foundation for understanding how something works could not be a good theory. In much the same way as a building needs a foundation for it to be sturdy, what we know should "sit" on some assumptions that are themselves sturdy.

In *Building Communication Theory,* Infante, Rancer, and Womack define a theory as a "group of related propositions designed to explain why events take place in a certain way."[2] Kreitner and Kinicki define a theory as "a story defining key terms, providing a conceptual framework, and explaining why something occurs."[3] *In essence, a theory is an informed, explanatory, or predictive conceptualization.* A good theory can help us think and act intelligently.

If you want to be an effective group leader and communicate efficiently in that role, you might study groups, observe how groups react to different leadership styles, try out the different styles yourself, and then formulate a theory that explains why groups behave as they do depending upon leadership. On the basis of your theory you may communicate in a particular way when you lead your group.

If you want to communicate efficiently in times of organizational crisis, you might study how some organizations successfully communicated when they were under duress. You might examine what they did that worked and what they or others did that was unsuccessful. You might read research reports on crisis communication and/or conduct some research of your own. On the basis of your exploration you may develop a theory about the best way to communicate under crisis. When your organization is faced with such a situation you'd want to apply the principles of your theory to the very real practical problems you face.

These are simplified examples of how theories are developed. However, the point is that theories need not be and should not be impractical. "There's nothing so practical as a good theory."[4] Management theories describe ideas about the best ways to manage employees for "real-world" organizational success.

EVOLUTION OF MANAGEMENT THEORIES

As we discussed in Chapter 1, one reason to study organizational communication is because scholars and practitioners point to communication as a central factor that affects an organization's success. Another reason for examining organizational communication is based on theories of management and organizations. These theories provide a framework for analysis. Exploring the evolution of these theories makes it clear that communication is essential and not peripheral to organizational success.

Classical Theory of Management

The classical theory of management is associated with theorists Frederic Taylor, Henri Fayol, and Max Weber. Taylor is responsible for the ideas of scientific management, Fayol for administrative theory, and Weber for bureaucracy theory. These theories

Does the quality of interpersonal communication in an organization affect employee motivation?

© GETTY IMAGES/PHOTODISC

taken collectively provide the underpinnings for the broader label of classical management theory.

At the heart of classical theory is the assumption that an organization is akin to a machine. The best way to maximize organizational productivity, according to classical theorists, is to consider the most efficient ways to structure the machine and control the machine's operations. Bureaucracy theory described the best ways to structure the "machine" and administrative theory described the best ways to administer the structure or bureaucracy.

Classical theorists consider employees to be parts of the machine that is the organization. Just like a tire is part of an automobile and an efficient tire will maximize that automobile's performance, an employee is considered to be part of the organization, and an efficient employee maximizes organizational performance. Therefore, management needs to consider how employees can do a job most productively.

Taylor, in his book *The Principles of Scientific Management* (originally published in 1919), describes how he witnessed workers shoveling coal at the Bethlehem Steel Corporation machine shop. He noticed that certain types of shovels and shoveling techniques resulted in greater productivity. He studied how workers should shovel coal and on the basis of his research, workers were told what shovels should be used and what techniques to use when shoveling. Productivity went up dramatically.

Taylor's general thesis was that tests could determine the most efficient way to complete a work related task. On the basis of the tests you could prescribe an approach to make the organization as efficient as possible.

Money and Motivation. A significant feature of classical theory is the assumption that employees are motivated strictly by money. Classical theorists believe that people come to work primarily because they must. Therefore should you desire that an employee work well, you would be wise to provide some financial incentive for excellent performance. Sometimes referred to as the carrot-stick approach to motivation, managers who adhere to classical theory would dangle some reward (a carrot) at the end of a stick and entice employees to work harder in order to gain the reward of the carrot or a piece of the carrot. Subsequently the remains of the carrot or additional rewards would be offered as enticements for excellence. Taylor advocated, for example, that employees be compensated not by the hour but on the basis of the work they had done. The more work accomplished the greater the pay.

It's important to emphasize that supporters of classical theory believe that employees are not inherently motivated to work by factors other than financial incentives. Interestingly Taylor argues that management needs to offer employees what he calls a "plum" for coming together with the "science." On the surface this motivation by reward is very consistent with classical theory. Yet Taylor continues to argue that there "are many plums" and includes as rewards "better treatment, more kindly treatment, more consideration for [employee] wishes, and an opportunity to express their wants freely."[5] Nevertheless those who implemented classical theory considered money and other financial remuneration the primary, if not lone, factor that motivated employees to work.[6]

So what does all this have to do with organizational communication? For classical theorists, communication responsibilities are basic and simple. A basic tenet of classical theory is that "management plans the work, and laborers follow through with the plan—workers take orders from the foreman who is in charge of [a] particular task."[7] Therefore, management needs to inform employees about what they must do and how they must do it. Employees need to know about financial incentives so that they might work hard to obtain the remuneration. Nearly all communication in classical organizations is directed downward, from superior to subordinate. Classical theorists would acknowledge few situations in which employees would need to send information to management. Nor would classical theorists believe there is any need to communicate in order to foster relationships.

In short, classical managers have specific communication responsibilities. However, these responsibilities are limited to downward descriptions of job tasks and organizational policy. Do you see any merit in classical theory?

The Hawthorne Studies

The Hawthorne Studies may be the most well-known studies ever conducted in the field of management. Almost any textbook in industrial or organizational behavior will have some reference to the studies even if the treatment is superficial.

The Hawthorne Studies were so called because they were conducted in the Western Electric Hawthorne plant in Cicero, Illinois. The studies which began in 1924 were conducted in order to examine and test certain principles of classical theory. The idea was to assess how workers would react to varied physical conditions in order to identify the optimal physical environment for productivity. Ironically, the findings of the studies compelled advocates of classical theory to reconsider their positions. In the final analysis, instead of serving to support and solidify classical principles, the Hawthorne studies actually were a catalyst for the development of an alternate and contrary theory called *human relations theory*. (Later in this chapter we will discuss human relations theory in detail.) The studies were significant because they served to change, and change radically, contemporary attitudes about how and why people worked. Also, the Hawthorne Studies were noteworthy because they altered the perspective theorists had about the importance and nature of communication as an element of efficient management.

There were four parts to the studies. The first was the most famous and the one that's likely to be familiar to readers who have studied organizational behavior previously. In this phase workers were observed while researchers varied lighting intensity. The assumption of the theorists was that increased lighting would increase productivity. If the lighting was better, people who did piece work would be better able to do their work and produce more.

As expected when lighting was increased, performance increased. However, to the surprise of the researchers as lighting was decreased, worker performance remained higher than normal. Even as the lighting was decreased to levels that forced employees to essentially squint since they were practically working in the dark, productivity went up. In the control group where lighting remained constant, productivity also went up. The variable, apparently, was not illumination.

Therefore, there had to be some other factor that compelled employees to be more productive. The researchers agreed somewhat reluctantly that this motivator was related to observation, change, and implicit recognition.

The second phase of the Hawthorne Studies, referred to as the *relay assembly* studies, began in 1927. In this phase, work conditions such as hours, coffee breaks, pay incentives, and the quality of food provided was varied. The objective of this component was consistent with the first. The assumption would be that if pay incentives went up, coffee breaks were increased in terms of frequency and duration, and if working hours were more attractive, then productivity would increase accordingly. The idea, consistent with scientific management and classical theory, was to discover the optimal conditions.

As with the studies based on illumination, varying conditions did *not* have a direct effect on productivity. Regardless of hours, even if the hours were grueling, even if coffee breaks were eliminated, workers performed better than they had previously. *The Hawthorne Effect* is a phrase used to describe the results of these two parts of the

MEET THE MANAGERS

Is there anything unethical with managers creating an illusion that they're concerned with employees' problems when, in fact, there is no such concern? For example, assume that you work as a salesperson in a department store. Assume that every 2 weeks you are invited to a session called *Meet the Managers* which has been designed to allow you to air your concerns about your job. Finally, assume that management has no intention of changing any policy on the basis of your comments. Management is simply inviting you to Meet the Managers to create the illusion that you are being heard and your voice is being considered.

Is there anything unethical about creating and holding the Meet the Manager sessions?

study. In brief, the effect refers to the fact that people tend to alter their behavior when they are observed. It may be startling to contemporary readers that the Hawthorne Effect surprised classical theorists. Nevertheless, the notion that the motivational variable was the attention, as opposed to the altered conditions, compelled researchers to reconsider their attitudes about worker behavior.

It also made astute observers acknowledge that communication was an important factor in managerial success. If observation and recognition were motivating factors for employees, then wouldn't managers need to be able to communicate effectively to their employees? Wouldn't managers have to acknowledge, either positively or negatively, performance in ways that transcended monetary acknowledgments?

The third component of the studies, which began in 1928, involved conducting interviews with employees at the plant. Some 21,000 employees were questioned about their attitudes toward work, co-workers, management, and the organization. The results of this phase of the study showed the researchers not only that the employees had gripes and would articulate their concerns, but also that employees enjoyed the opportunity to express themselves about the various issues. The employees seemed to be able to vent during these interviews in a way that made them seem happier. The findings from this third phase appear to contradict other beliefs of the classical theorists. The classical theorists were inclined to believe that communication in organizations need only go downward from management to subordinates. This third phase of the Hawthorne Studies seemed to indicate that there might be some value in allowing subordinates an opportunity to communicate upward and to initiate communication with management.

The last part of the Hawthorne Studies is called the bank-wiring phase. Researchers observed employees and found that within their units the employees established informal rules and norms that they abided by in order to complete their tasks. These norms were not necessarily consistent with the formal guidelines and procedures established by management. This again contradicted notions of the classical theory as the results suggested that informal networks were important. Classical theorists assumed employees received the only consequential messages from downwardly directed formal messages. Apparently, the real rules might be established informally by social peer-related pressure and governance.

Human Relations Theory

The findings of the Hawthorne Studies provided the foundation for a new way to think about management which has been called *human relations theory*. The tenets of this new perspective were in contrast to those identified by classical theorists. Whereas classical theorists believe that employees are motivated by money, human relations theorists pointed to the Hawthorne Studies and argued that under the right conditions work could be enjoyable and that employees are motivated by observation and recognition. Human relations theorists assume that employees want to be involved with work-related decisions and should be encouraged to express their ideas and feelings to upper management. As opposed to the mechanistic assumptions of the classical theorists, human relations theorists believe that workers are, indeed, humans, and have human needs that if met would enhance productivity. Therefore, in order to motivate employees, managers would need to communicate not only information about job tasks and policies, but also information that recognized workers' accomplishments, respected their value, and, essentially, acknowledged that they were feeling animate entities.

The human relations theory emerged in the 1930s, but there is ample contemporary evidence to support the position of these theorists.

- An independent research company conducted a study for executive personnel consultants (aka headhunters) who wanted to know why executives choose to leave jobs and seek other ones. The study revealed that 34 percent of the respondents cited *limited praise and recognition* as the primary reason for seeking other employment. Only 25 percent of the respondents cited compensation as the main reason.[8]

- A Harris poll was conducted for an organization that wanted to get a better sense of what employees wanted. The organization assumed that employees thought that job security and money was of paramount importance. The poll discovered that there was a "perception gap" since "job security" ranked "far below" more human relations related desires such as "*respect, a high standard of management ethics, increased recognition of employee contributions, and closer, more honest communications between employees and senior management.*"[9] This finding is consistent with the comment made during an interview with a high-level engineer in a large South Carolina-based organization. "Many of our employee surveys," he said, "*indicate job recognition and positive feedback are as, or more, important, than financial rewards and incentives.*"[10]

- The Institute of Higher Education conducted a decade-long study and discovered that faculty morale at colleges was not related to salary as much as faculty opportunity to participate in the governance of their universities.[11]

- A 2001 advertising campaign for Southwest Airlines is intended to recruit potential candidates for work at Southwest. The focus of the promotion is the depiction of Southwest as an organization that builds and nourishes relationships.[12]

- An eight-year study of organizations included the finding that "*effective communication relationships contributed most to job satisfaction.*"[13]

- The recent transformation of the California Public Retirement System may be the strongest current argument in support of human relations theory. In June 2001 James Burton, the head of CALPERS, accepted an International Association of Business Communicators award for excellence in organizational communication. Burton was hired to lead CALPERS at a time when performance levels were dismal. Burton hired a consultant to examine the source of the woeful morale and weak performance. The consultant found that the problem was related to employee perception of a lack of respect and recognition for job performance. As Burton documented in his acceptance presentation, CALPERS began an extensive campaign to communicate warranted recognition to employees. Within a short period of time, CALPERS improved from a dispirited underperforming organization to one that was and is highly successful. While Burton's program is recent, the success story of CALPERS could well have appeared under the headline of a 1982 *Wall Street Journal* article with a similar theme. The headline of that piece read, "To Raise Productivity Try Saying Thank You."[14]

Opposition to the Human Relations Theory. The human relations theory encountered disapproval and criticism. Critics felt that human relations theorists put too much of an emphasis on the employee.[15] Because of this, proponents were sometimes denigrated as "the happiness boys." Also, critics claimed that the managers who employed human relations theory either misunderstood or misused human relations principles and attempted to manipulate employees by communicating bogus praise to entice productivity. Essentially, while principles of the human relations theory were sound, those who attempted to apply the principles diluted the theory's impact by establishing relationships and spewing praise in ways that were superficial, not credible, and ultimately counterproductive.[16]

Human Resources Theory. Human resources theory developed as a reaction to this criticism. In 1965 Robert Miles published an article in the *Harvard Business Review* entitled, "Keeping Informed—Human Relations or Human Resources." In the piece, Miles made a distinction between the two approaches. Whereas a human relations theorist would argue that employees need to be acknowledged, a human resource theorist would extend that principle. Human resource theorists would argue that not only do employees need to be recognized for what they do, but management must recognize that employees can contribute in ways that are "untapped." Basically, human resource theorists believe that employees should be viewed as, in fact, a resource. Employees have value and, moreover, desire to be valuable.

However, the foundational principle—that employees need to be seen as humans and not cogs in a machine—is the same in both theories. One could argue that human resources theory does not contradict human relations theory but rather complements the theory by acknowledging the potential contributions of employees and encouraging management to utilize and respect that resource.[17]

Theory X and Theory Y

A good way to contrast the classical and human relations theory of management is by looking at Douglas McGregor's Theory X and Theory Y. McGregor, in his now famous 1960 book *The Human Side of the Enterprise,* suggested that there are essentially two ways managers look at employees. He called these discrete perspectives Theory X and Theory Y.[18]

Theory X tenets are similar to classical theory principles. Specifically, a Theory X manager would assume that employees do not want to work and only seek employment for the financial benefits that work provides. Given a choice between work and "play," an employee would quickly and eagerly choose to avoid work. A Theory X

TABLE 2.1   DOUGLAS MCGREGOR: THEORY X AND THEORY Y

Theory X Assumptions	Theory Y Assumptions
1. People dislike work and avoid work when possible.	1. Under the right conditions people will view work as natural as play.
2. Workers are not ambitious and prefer direction.	2. Workers are ambitious and prefer self-direction.
3. Workers do not seek responsibility and are not concerned with overall organizational needs.	3. Workers seek responsibility and feel rewarded through their achievements.
4. Workers must be directed and threatened with punishment to achieve organizational productivity.	4. Workers are self-motivated and require little direct supervision.
	5. Workers are creative and capable of organizational creativity.

manager would assume that employees would certainly not naturally seek out responsibility. If you supported Theory X you would think that

- Students who were not compelled to attend class would stay away.
- Construction workers who were not supervised would be less than diligent regarding meeting code specifications for safety.
- Office workers who were not threatened with financial punishment for coming in late would regularly be tardy.
- Salespeople who were not on commission would sell less aggressively and successfully than those who were on commission.

Advocates of Theory Y held beliefs similar to the human relations theorists. Specifically, a Theory Y theorist would argue that under the right circumstances work could be enjoyable and even desirable. Proponents of Theory Y assume that employees naturally seek out work and are motivated not only by money, but by recognition and job satisfaction. (See Table 2.1 for McGregor's Theory X and Theory Y). If you supported Theory Y you would believe that

- If a class was interesting and challenging students would come to class even if they were not required to do so.
- Unsupervised construction workers would still be diligent because people take pride in doing work well.
- Office workers would be punctual regardless of penalties because they would want to be perceived as responsible and professional.
- Salespeople will work diligently regardless of whether they would get paid per sale because selling is what they do and they would want to excel at their work for personal fulfillment.

In order to further illustrate the distinctions between Theory X and Theory Y, assume that you had an office job that required you to answer the phones for a particular department. Assume further that the phones rang infrequently and that you had little or nothing to do.

Communication and motivation

What are your opinions on the following questions?

1. In your experience what motivates people to work harder: communications that promise increased salary, or communications that recognize performance?
2. In the absence of periodic salary increments, are employees likely to be motivated by managers who say things like, "I wish I could give you more money because you deserve it. You're a terrific worker and I really appreciate you."
3. Assume that two workers earn significantly more than they need to feed/clothe/house themselves and their respective families. Assume they both perform their jobs well and both feel the other's work is adequate. Would it matter if one employee received more of a salary increment than the other when raises were distributed?
4. Assume a manager is upset because a few individuals have abused the flexible hours policy at the organization. Specifically, out of 10 employees, 3 keep coming in late and leaving early. If you were one of the diligent 7, how do you think the manager should communicate the message? If you were one of the other 3, how would you want the manager to communicate the message?

An advocate for Theory X would think that you would be delighted with this job. You would go home and tell your friends, "What a deal! I sit in this office and I don't have to do anything and I get paid for that, can you believe it?"

An advocate for Theory Y would think that you would be miserable. You'd go home and tell your friends, "I'm going crazy at work. There's absolutely nothing to do. I ask my boss what to do and she says that I just have to answer the phone. But the phone doesn't ring. I'm going to look for another job."

A proponent of Theory Y would think that while you were at work waiting for the phone to ring, you'd look around the office for something to do—perhaps clean up the bulletin board or arrange materials in the supplies cabinet. A proponent of Theory X would think that you'd be unlikely to seek other tasks and would be content to count your lucky stars.

Which theory do you think is correct?

Problems With Theory Y. As mentioned previously, the human relations theorists were disparaged. Similarly, the human resources theorists were criticized for being too focused on the employee.[19] Let's consider some of the reasons why human relations, human resources, and Theory Y approaches might not work. There are three related reasons. One of these is essential to understand for students studying organizational communication.

One problem with human relations theory is that it is too short-sighted to be sound. It makes an assumption about workers that could not be universally true. The assumption that people under the right circumstances enjoyed work as much as play might be true for the majority of us, but there are still many individuals who are

© THE NEW YORKER COLLECTION FROM CARTOONBANK.COM. ALL RIGHTS RESERVED.

"*Pendleton, as of noon today your services will no longer be required. Meanwhile, keep up the good work.*"

delighted or would be delighted by a life of absolute leisure. How difficult would it be for you to think of a few people who would be thrilled to get an easy job where they were paid for very little effort? You've probably thought of one such person instantaneously. Therefore to build a theory on the notion of the inherent desire for people to work—as much as they like to play—is to have a plank in the foundation that is not nailed securely.

A second reason why the human relations theory is flawed is related to the first. It may be true that under the right conditions people will enjoy work as much as play. However, many of us are likely not to be working "under the right conditions." I enjoy what I do. I like to teach, write, and work with students. Yet I certainly have had some jobs—both blue collar and white collar—when I did not look forward to coming to work. I'd guess that most readers have had jobs that have been challenging and exciting and have also had others which were either inherently unpleasant or were made unpleasant by some characteristic of the workplace. Therefore, the plank of human relations theory that posits that people can enjoy work as much as play is flawed. Superficially, it may seem true enough, but while people could be in a career or at a job that they like, they may also be working at jobs that are of no interest to them or have become uninteresting and stressful for them.

Most significantly, for students of organizational communication, a principle of human relations theory is that employees are motivated by recognition and acknowledgment. *In order for human relations theory to work, then, management would need to be efficient at communicating recognition.* A criticism of human relations theory is that managers are sloppy and insincere in their people-oriented messages of recognition. There may be more managers slapping backs, asking employees to "call me Pat," and effusively saying thank you, but if the messages are not perceived as credible by employees—if the employees consider the acknowledgment spurious as if it is some grand ruse for motivation—then the foundation upon which human relations theory was built will disintegrate like a house of cards.

Consider some likely factors that could interfere with successful communication of recognition.

Credibility. If all employees were to receive the same message of recognition, it's likely to assume that the message would lose credibility. A note posted on a website that thanks all employees for their hard work will be meaningless if, when you receive it, you think that an employee who is considered a slacker has been sent the same congratulatory message. For example, one general manager signed all of her written notes to the staff with her name circumscribed by a red heart. After a while, the employees—instead of finding these messages touching—considered them absurd and ridiculed the director behind her back.

Skill Level. Some people have difficulty orally expressing praise and criticism. They may have problems maintaining eye contact, finding the right words to match their ideas, or using appropriate inflection when relaying information.

Choice of Channel. If an employer posts a bulletin thanking employees, or sends out an e-mail, it may have less of an impact than a visit to that staff member's office and a face-to-face conversation. Selecting an inappropriate channel for communicating can affect the value of the message. (Chapter 6 deals in detail with the subject of selecting appropriate media for communicating.)

In brief, the human relations theory, human resources theory, and Theory Y have meaningful components. It is, certainly, an uplifting theory. People *are* important and not inanimate equipment. To be successful, management has to understand that many individuals desire to do something meaningful with their hours at work.

However, it is easy to prescribe this, but not necessarily easy for managers to respond to the prescription. Two-day workshops in communication or human relations training will not guarantee competent or sensitive communicators. Managers coached to follow human relations principles may still harbor Theory X notions of the world and be unable or unwilling to credibly communicate recognition and support to employees. In a *Harvard Business Review* article entitled, "Asinine Attitudes towards Motivation," Levinson discusses what he calls a *jackass fallacy*.[20] The jackass fallacy is the erroneous notion held by Theory X managers that employees are essentially stubborn fools or jackasses. Levinson correctly contends that if management views employees this way, human resource type overtures will inevitably fail. He argues that employees will "automatically see management's messages as manipulative and they will resist them, no matter how clear the type or how pretty the pictures."[21]

Focus on Applications

The reward for fifteen years of service

Consider this example. The woman who received this mailing was being notified that she had earned *15 minutes* extra vacation time on the basis of her 15 years of service. As you might expect, the recipient was incensed. She spent much of the day, far more than her allocated 15 minutes, deriding the source of the message.

TO: Jean Schoener Theatre Arts

FROM: Roberta White, Account Clerk Personnel/Affirmative Action Office

Employees who have completed their seventh year of service earn 20 days vacation each year until eligible to earn bonus days again. Administrative Unit is eligible again for a bonus after completion of their 15th year; Operational, Security, PEF and Institutional Units are again eligible for a bonus upon completion of their 20th year of service.

For the Administrative Unit, this equates to 5:45 hours, each payperiod with an additional 15 minutes twice a year. For the other units, this equates to 6 hours each payperiod with an additional hour four times a year. This extra time being added has become confusing in keeping your own leave accruals on the time sheets. To simplify matters, the Personnel/Affirmative Action Office is going to add this extra time once a year for all eligible, *always on the day before your anniversary date.* (Ex., if your anniversary is on 5/2 each year, and you are entitled to 4 extra hours each year, add that four hours on your leave accrual summary on 5/1 each year. If you earn 30 min. a year, add it the day before your anniversary in the same manner.)

This procedure will become effective 5/8/80. If you have already received part of those extra minutes or hours, the balance will be added on the day before your anniversary and no extra time will be added until then.

If you have any questions, please call me at 3434.

Your anniversary date is _10/19/70_.
Your date to add extra vacation is _10/18_.
The extra vacation you should add each year is _30 minutes_.
You have already earned _15 minutes_ this year.

Systems Theory

The systems theory of management assumes that an organization is a composite of interdependent units that must work cooperatively in order to effectively survive. The theory holds that organizations should be viewed as *open* systems. This means that an organization cannot live nor thrive without interacting with both its *internal* and its *external* environment.

Your university is an example of such an open system. The various units—the colleges, student affairs staff, maintenance and grounds, and senior administration—are all interdependent. What happens in one unit either directly or indirectly affects what happens in another. These interdependent units must communicate with each other in order for the organization to be efficient and thrive. In addition, in order for your university to succeed, it must interact effectively with external audiences, for example, high schools where prospective students are considering higher education, government agencies that may provide financial resources for the school, and academic associations that may publish journals that keep faculty current and active in their areas of specialty.

The conception of the organization as an entity that must link internal departments and be linked to its environment is the essence of systems theory. The relationship between systems theory and organizational communication is fairly obvious; if you believe in systems theory, interdepartmental communication becomes a prerequisite for survival.

Systems theory does not disregard principles of classical or human relations theory. In fact, it embraces components of each. In systems theory "questions of job duty, chain of command, span of control, and decision making [classical principles] are *equal* in importance to questions of attitude, morale, behavior, role and personality [human relations concerns]."[22] Therefore, the same communication challenges that exist for classical and human relations theorists also exist for systems theorists. In addition, systems theorists must undertake to create a system that links departments.

Systems theory requires that organizations be sensitive to information regarding tasks and procedure (classical) as well as information that can provide recognition and improve morale (human relations) because both can affect how units and subunits interact. Systems theorists consider communication essential because it is the method used to connect different units within organizations.

Shortly after the September 11, 2001, terrorist attack on New York's World Trade Center, it was discovered that certain divisions of the federal government had information that, if shared with other divisions, might have served to warn the government of the possibility of attack. Governmental entities like the FBI, the Department of Defense, the INS, and the Department of the Treasury operate independently. Yet, these independent units are inherently interdependent and need to share information. The Office of Homeland Defense was developed, in part, "to bring together a bunch of different government agencies that have a bunch of different information and may not have previously talked to one another about suspected terrorists."[23] This very real-world example, illustrates the practical value of theory.

A systems theorist would argue that every department of an organization needs to be linked with every other one. There is no such thing as an autonomous independent department since the organization's product is a function of the interaction between departments. If we view the federal government as a large organization made up of interdependent units (which themselves are organizations) then the parent organization is healthiest when relevant information is shared between units, because the product—in this case the protection of U.S. citizens—is affected by this interdependent interaction.

Theory can be very practical. Systems theory which includes aspects of classical theory and human relations theory explains why communication is necessary in organizations. Proponents of systems theory are compelled to examine how communication can improve organizational quality.

Now that you are familiar with classical, human relations, and systems theory, what are your recommendations for Patricia Daniels, whom we met in Case 2.1? What should she communicate to her staff?

PRACTITIONER'S PERSPECTIVE

Robert Peterkin, Former School Superintendent

Robert Peterkin was the superintendent of schools for the city of Milwaukee for 3 years. Prior to that he had been the school superintendent for Cambridge, Massachusetts, and deputy superintendent for the city of Boston. He is both practitioner and academic. After leaving Milwaukee, Dr. Peterkin accepted a job at Harvard University where he chairs a program for persons who aspire to be school superintendents. Peterkin has appeared on Good Morning America and other national media outlets. He has written on school choice, school governance, women in the superintendency, and the impact of school reform on the achievement of African-American children.

If I had to identify what typically gets in the way of effective communication, I'd say that people don't think through what they're trying to communicate. They don't think about their audiences and what's important to them. Also, most people don't listen actively nor do they read and reflect on what they read. People possess the counterproductive dynamic that they have to win when they communicate.

(continued)

Instead of advancing the cause they feel like communicating is a contest and in order to be successful they must win. Some messages and positions we take must be nonnegotiable, but some issues are negotiable and communicating about them need not be a match to see who will be the victor.

Lack of internal communication is almost a cultural norm for public schools. School systems are set up into divisions and that noun can be used in many ways, but what is created with these units *is* division, and the classic silo effect. Communication rarely flows between different organizational units because individual departments are typically not motivated to communicate interdependently. They are rewarded for doing a job in their own units. The lack of communication between levels and departments in school systems is legendary. There are many books written on superintendent and board dysfunction and the biggest issue is lack of communication. In Texas there are mediators who go to Dallas and Houston and other urban areas and try to improve communication between the school board and superintendent. In our program here we spend so much time on communication-related issues because school systems rarely think about how to communicate within their organizations. I consider it such an important issue that we have on retainer a professional communication trainer who works with our students during their time on campus.

Communication problems are exacerbated in organizations because, typically, employees are not sufficiently trained. Look, when I first was a principal I felt passionately about my mission. My wife has a videotape of a speech I delivered as a principal during that first year. When we watch this we can barely make out what I am saying. I felt passionate, but I communicated little of my passion. One must practice to become a good communicator. And one would be wise to rely on the advice from professionals. We need feedback about how well we're doing. In Milwaukee, I had a cabinet of advisers. When we plan to disseminate a message that does not make sense, we need someone to say what one of my advisers said to me one day, "No clothes today emperor."

We were able to create a positive atmosphere in Milwaukee and we did this in large part because we worked at it. When I began there, I took the board on a retreat for a weekend with a professional facilitator. We did a day and a half workshop examining communication issues. Maybe we would have worked together well anyway, but some things came out of that retreat that set up a solid foundation for our subsequent communications. We worked with a common purpose and vision. I placed board members on our major committees which is anathema for most school systems. I can't tell you how much good will and positive votes that brought us.

A Toolbox

1. Theories need not be abstract and valueless. Good theories must actually be practical.

2. Classical theories suggest that downward communication of information about *tasks* and *procedures* is essential.

3. The Hawthorne Studies demonstrated that (1) communicating information about performance was important, (2) upward networks were desired by employees, and (3) informal networks were inevitable.

4. The successful implementation of human relations approaches requires the credible communication of information about job performance and recognition.

5. Systems theories suggest that for organizations to thrive there must be (1) communication that links departments to one another; (2) communication that links the organization to its external environment; (3) effective communication of task and procedural messages; and (4) effective communication of recognition and observation.

1. Describe classical theory, human relations theory, and systems theory.

2. What are the key distinctions between Theory X and Theory Y?

3. What are the organizational communication implications of the Hawthorne Studies?

4. Why would a classical theorist consider communicating recognition unimportant?

5. Why would a systems theorist consider interdepartmental communication important?

6. Have the managers where you've worked taken a Theory X or Theory Y orientation?

7. If you were a manager would you be likely to follow classical or human relations principles? Why?

8. Analyze the following case and respond to the questions that follow the case.

Case 2.2—Trent McGuire and Systems Theory

Background. Trent McGuire works for a large mutual fund company. One division of the company is focused on improving the Internet services for shareholders. Within that division there are several departments. One department is called Internet Development. Another department is called Communications/Customer Service (CCS).

The Internet Development department works on enhancements and new applications for the company website. Currently, shareowners have the ability to view various products and offerings on the site and can access information about their accounts on-line. In the near future shareholders will be able to perform transactions on-line. Over the past 12 to 18 months, the website has gone from offering basic product information to nearly being able to perform all types of financial transactions. In this time frame there has been a great deal of cosmetic changes as well as application changes to the site.

Trent McGuire does not work in the Internet Development department. Trent works as a manager in the CCS side of the division. The CCS is in constant contact with the shareholders. The CCS has the sole responsibility of setting up new shareholders so that they will have the ability to access their specific accounts. If there are any problems or questions concerning account access or any information regarding the website, then the CCS is usually the first to hear about the problems from the external customers. CCS representatives are expected to answer customer questions and resolve any problems.

Interdepartmental Communication and Customer Service In order to best service the customers, it is vital for the CCS to be updated with any problems or changes in the site by the Internet Development team. However, communication regarding this updating has not always taken place. For example, there are times when the account access features are not functional and CCS will find out about the problems not from the Internet Development team, but from annoyed customers. On numerous occasions, new product or marketing text has been updated on the public site yet the CCS was not notified. Calls would come in referencing specific information on the site and CCS representatives would have no idea of the changes. Finally, with the rollout of new account access features to the customers, CCS was not consulted to test the application or provide any feedback prior to the application's availability for public use. Numerous issues arose from this which caused the company to be reactive to customer response rather than proactive through internal communication.

Interdepartmental communication between the Internet Development team and CCS is lacking and customer satisfaction in the Internet services, and in the company as a whole, has been negatively affected. In addition, employees in the CCS were frustrated with the lack of information being provided to them in order to best perform their job.

- How does this case relate to the systems theory of management?
- What can Trent McGuire do to facilitate effective communication between his department and the Internet Development team?
- How common are problems like those experienced by Trent McGuire and the CCS?

ENDNOTES

[1]Corman, Steven, "That Works Fine in Theory But . . ." in *Foundations of Organizational Communication,* edited by Steven Corman, Stephen Banks, Charles Bantz, and Michael Mayer, Longman, 1995: p. 3.

[2]Infante, Dominic, Andrew Rancer, and Deanna Womack, *Building Communication Theory,* Waveland Press, 1997: p. 556.

[3]Kreitner, Robert and Angelo Kinicki, *Organizational Behavior,* Fourth Edition, 1998: p. 654.

[4]Lewin, K., quoted in Corman page 9.

[5]Taylor, Frederick, "The Principles of Scientific Management," article adapted in Corman et al., p. 65. Article in Corman is an adaptation of an article from the same title by Taylor published in 1916.

6Yuhas Byers, Peggy, "The Process and Perspectives of Organizational Communication," in *Organizational Communication Theory and Behavior,* edited by Byers. Allyn and Bacon, 1997: p. 24.

7Ibid., p. 21.

8"Limited Praise Tops Reasons to Quit Job" *Laconia Citizen,* September 29, 1994.

9*Fortune,* December 4, 1989, p. 57.

10Electronic Interview with John Aiken, Project Manager at Day and Zimmerman International, September 2001.

11Magarrell, Jack, "Decline in Faculty Morale Laid to Governance Role, Not Salary," *Chronicle of Higher Education,* November 10, 1982, p. 1, 28.

12Radio advertisements encourage those interested to "check out our website." If you visit the Southwest website and click on "Careers" you read the words "Feel free to actually enjoy the work that you do." There is a picture of smiling Southwest employees. The caption reads "LUV To Be A Southwest Airlines Flight Attendant? Now Hiring."

13Goldhaber, Gerald, "Cold Flesh Beats Warm Plastic," *Vital Speeches of the Day,* September 1, 1979, p. 686.

14Falvey, Jack, "Manager's Journal: To Raise Productivity Try Saying Thank You," *Wall Street Journal,* December 6, 1982.

15Hamilton, Cheryl, with Cordell Parker, *Communication For Results,* Wadsworth, 1993: p. 49.

16Byers, p. 26.

17Human resources theory was an attempt to enforce the principles that human relations theorists could not or did not enforce. This position is supported by Kreps (*Organizational Communication,* Longman, 1990) as he discusses the development of human resources, Pace and Faules (*Organizational Communication,* Prentice Hall, 1989) and Byers (op cit) in their books. While there are some distinguishing features both theories center around the same basic premise. "The assumptions behind the human resource perspective are much like those of the human relations perspective" (Byers, p. 26). Pace and Faules do comment that there is a distinction between developing human relations and developing human resources (p. 42). In the latter case, you are recognizing "humans" as the resources that they can be.

18McGregor, Douglas, *The Human Side of the Enterprise.* New York: McGraw-Hill, 1960.

19Byers, p. 27.

20Levinson, Harold, "Asinine Attitudes Towards Motivation," *Harvard Business Review,* January 1973, pp. 72–76.

21Levinson, Harold, p. 74.

22Goldhaber, Gerald, *Organizational Communication,* Sixth Edition, Wm. C. Brown and Benchmark, 1993: p. 47.

23Fox News Network, September 21, 2001 approximately 5:50 P.M. The issue of sharing information was discussed on many post-September 11th, news reports. This specific quote came from one such report and was stated by Mike Emanuel, a Fox Correspondent. Later in the broadcast Congressman James Gibbons from Nevada made a similar statement.

Principles of Communication

The [people] who can think and do not know how to express what [they] think are at the same level of [those] who can not think.

—Pericles

Words are loaded bullets.

—Jean Paul Sartre

I have always been struck by the impact that a few well chosen or ill chosen words. . .can have on someone's political career.

—Larry Speakes, former Press Spokesperson to President Ronald Reagan

Although no phenomenon is more familiar to us than communication, the fact of the matter is that this magical word means many things to many people.

—S. S. Stevens

© GETTY IMAGES/PHOTODISC

Case 3.1—*The Non-Sweet John Babterk and the Candy Company*

Background

John Babterk was a director in the Franchise department of a large confection company. Matthew LeFleur was in Customer Marketing and worked closely with people in the Franchise department. LeFleur was surrounded by the turmoil related to the communication capabilities of Mr. Babterk. According to LeFleur, Babterk was unable to communicate feedback in a productive manner. He would often times use words such as *stupid* to describe ideas and issues brought up in meetings (with other department peers present). These actions ultimately caused the deterioration of relationships he had with his employees (he was responsible for approximately 75 associates) and caused tension in the work environment.

In spite of the fact that John communicated inappropriately, the company found itself in a difficult position. This was because John's ideas had done a great deal to improve the efficiency and effectiveness of the department. According to LeFleur, most employees would have been let go or at least sternly disciplined if they had acted like Babterk, but the combination of John's high-ranking position in the company and his otherwise excellent performance, persuaded the company to work with him.

Successful Interventions but Lingering Problems

Babterk was sent to several classes to improve his communication skills in an attempt to correct his deficiencies in this area. The classes appeared to have been a good idea. Today, John is much better at communicating effectively with his subordinates.

However, LeFleur claims that there is a communication problem that still lingers because of John's past difficulties. Many of the employees who had worked with Babterk previously had learned to tune him out because of the insults he had hurled in their direction. These insults caused his employees to lose respect for him, and therefore they were not interested in what he had to say. They would pretend to listen, but actually tuned him out. *In short, the pre-workshop problems created post-workshop communication impediments.* In this situation, correcting the initial problem was the relatively easy part. Now John and the rest of the department must find ways to overcome the damage that was done as a result of his earlier communication behavior.

☐ *Do you know people like John Babterk?*

☐ *Can pre-workshop communication problems affect post-workshop capabilities?*

☐ *Can workshops improve the long-term communication abilities of people like John Babterk?*

□ *This case was relayed by Matthew LeFleur. Is it possible that his perception of the situation is different from John Babterk's? That is, is it possible that John Babterk believes that the problem has been solved? If so, does that create other communication obstacles?*

ABSTRACT

In this chapter we explore the concept of communication in detail. As the first three quotes that precede the chapter suggest, communication is a powerful phenomenon. As the fourth quote suggests, there is a good deal of ambiguity surrounding the term **communication.**

Most people have a general sense of what the term *communication* means. We use the expressions:

> *"She's a good communicator."*
> *"We need to communicate better."*
> *"We want employees with excellent communication skills."*

However, what exactly do we mean when we use the term *communication?* What are the elements of the process? What are the factors that increase or decrease the chances for successful communication? We will address each of these questions in the following pages.

OBJECTIVES

When you have completed this chapter, you should be able to:

□ Describe and define the term *communication.*
□ Identify the elements of the communication process.
□ Define the phrase *communication noise.*
□ Explain the distinction between *message fidelity* and *message distortion.*
□ Describe what is meant by a *receiver orientation* to communication.
□ List and discuss factors that impede or facilitate effective communication.

WHAT DO WE MEAN BY THE WORD *COMMUNICATION?*

The director of Human Resources has been asked to come to speak to your department to explain the health benefits program. He walks into the room, loads a disk in the computer for a PowerPoint presentation, and collects his notes. Then he begins speaking.

- **When did he begin communicating?**
- **What did he communicate when he began communicating?**

At a meeting a newcomer to your country and to your group says not one word. When introduced she nods her head and smiles.

- **When the session is over, has she communicated?**
- **What, if anything, has she communicated?**
- **Does the fact that the newcomer is identified as a female affect your determination?**

A member of your department stops you in the hallway and informs you that he has to get to the bank to take care of some urgent personal financial business. He knows that your superior will notice his absence when she returns from her meeting and won't like the fact that he's gone. He asks you to tell her that his kid got sick in school and he had to rush to take the child home.

- **What messages have been communicated to you?**
- **Is the gender of your colleague a factor in your determination?**
- **Is the gender of the superior a factor in your determination?**

You've sent an e-mail to the technical support people at work asking someone to explain how you can fix what appears to be a program error on your computer. You get an e-mail back that "explains" the problem, but the explanation includes four words that you do not understand.

- **Has communication taken place?**
- **What messages have been communicated?**

Review your answers to the above questions. On the basis of your responses, how would you define the word *communication*?

CONCEPTUALIZING COMMUNICATION

Imagine that you are in a room with 10 colleagues who are seated around a very large round table. You decide that instead of conversing on this day you will play catch. You take out a beanbag and ask Sandy to catch the bag that you will be throwing to her. She agrees. You throw the bag.

What's your goal?

Most people would agree that your goal is to have Sandy *catch* the bag. Your goal is not simply to throw the bag—you want her to get it. It doesn't matter how beautifully you throw it, or how much others admire the toss. Your objective is to have Sandy catch the bag.

Communication in its simplest sense is about catching and throwing bags: receiving and sending messages. The objective should not necessarily be to throw esthetic messages, but to ensure that your receivers receive whatever messages you send. In essence, all one needs to do to communicate efficiently is to send messages so that others can receive them. However, the communication process is neither that simple nor easy. If it were, you wouldn't be taking this course, and hundreds of communication consultants wouldn't have regular work. Let's return to you and Sandy at the round conference table.

You throw the bag, but Sandy doesn't catch it and it falls a short distance beyond her. Why doesn't Sandy catch the bag?

It's possible that Sandy is not actually making an attempt to receive your message. She may appear to be in receiver mode, but she may not be making much of an effort to get it. Other things may be on her mind so that she doesn't concentrate on absorbing your message. Maybe Sandy isn't the problem. Maybe you do not have such an accurate throwing arm. Maybe Sandy *is* willing to go after your tosses, but after a while she stops trying because it seems to her that your pitches are nearly impossible to grab. She gets frustrated and stops chasing down your errant throws.

Communication may be similarly frustrating. "Things" get in the way of receipt. In the language of communication study, these impediments are collectively called *communication noise.* Sometimes the communication noise is relatively simple: Sandy is not paying attention or you are not expressing yourself clearly. More often, particularly in organizations, the noises are more complex.

Let's return to the original scenario. You get to the large round table. You ask Sandy to catch your bag. She agrees.

In this instance, you throw the bag to her and while the apparent goal is for her to catch the bag, the actual goal is for her *not* to be able to catch the bag. Let's assume that your actual goal is to covertly send a different message to all the others seated around the table. This message is that Sandy is incapable of understanding your sophisticated point. Unbeknownst to you, nobody at the table "gets the bag" that "Sandy can't catch your bags." Most of the people receive a different message. They "hear" that you are an obnoxious bragger who is attempting to draw attention to your sense of your own superiority.

The next time you go to send a message to the group you're surprised that no one wants to play catch. You can't understand it. You throw out very easy simple bags— "How are you Sandy?" bags—and they drop like grenades at your feet. You ask people if they enjoyed their weekend and they respond in a way that makes you think that they would prefer you don't ask. Now you're the receiver. You're catching bags. You're catching the bags that tell you that people are ignoring you. Every bag you catch and then throw and then catch seems to be affected by the weight of the previous tosses.

In organizations with hundreds of people interacting every day, there can be thousands of dropped bags—which affect the next thousand ones that are thrown, and the next thousand. Dropped bags litter the floors. Unintentionally sent bags are hauled around by receivers, confounding and burdening them, and weighing down the organization.

DEFINING COMMUNICATION

Communication is a very complex human phenomenon. We will define it as *a nonlinear process that occurs when people intentionally or unintentionally send and receive verbal and nonverbal messages. It is*

- Irreversible
- Receiver centered
- Affected by culture
- Affected by ethical perspectives

- Not synonymous with "understanding"
- Contextual

Communication Is a Nonlinear Process

Theorist Harold Lasswell developed one model used to examine communication. Lasswell argued that communication could be analyzed by looking at "Who Says What to Whom (in Which Channel) With What Effect."[1]

If you were listening to a CEO deliver a "state of the organization address" the "who" would be the CEO, the "what" the information contained in the address, the "whom" that large diverse audience who listened to the presentation, and the "effect" the reaction the various members of the audience had to the talk.

A problem with this model is that it appears to be linear.

Lasswell may not have intended it to be interpreted this way, but the model as is implies that communication goes one way and ceases when it reaches the receiver. Communication, in fact, is not linear; it is not a one-way phenomenon. Some scholars use the word *process* instead of *act* to describe communication because *act* seems as if communication reflects an isolated occurrence. Any one act of communication is unlikely to be a discrete event. It is likely to be a function of immediate and past history, and should be understood implicitly as a process—the process that occurs when we communicate.

Assume you are in a class listening to an instructor make a presentation. The presentation, let's say, is a poor one. The instructor's wording is complex, the vocal qualities of the message monotonous, and the subject, in and of itself, dry. You become bored and steal a glance at your watch to see how much longer the class has to run. However, as you look down at the timepiece, you see from your peripheral vision that the instructor notices your time check. You feel a bit embarrassed, but subsequently notice that the instructor reframes the lecture, picks the pace up a bit, and has attempted to demonstrate an application of the lecture material with an illustration to make it less dry.

The communication, in this instance, has not been linear. Any one act of communication was part of a process. You thought the class presentation was boring, you looked at your watch, the professor noticed you look at your watch, and then changed the message. Obviously the persons who are initially the "who" and the "whom" can exchange roles and react to one another. Inherently, then, the communication process is nonlinear. Of course, different communication contexts will affect the nature and frequency of the exchange in communication roles. For example, in group interaction the "whos" and "whoms" are often reversing. In public speaking the role exchange is less frequent. In mass communication it is far less frequent, but still occurs.

Communication Can Be Intentional or Unintentional

We cannot withdraw our cards from the game. Were we as silent and as mute as stones, our very passivity would be an act.

—Jean Paul Sartre

A message does not have to be intentionally sent to be communicated. For example, some colleagues may frequently be late to meetings. They may not intend to be communicating anything by their tardiness. However, other members of the group may feel that lateness reflects a lack of professionalism, or preoccupation, or disrespect. The fact that the latecomers may not have intended to relay any of these messages does not discount the reality that these messages could have been communicated. A manager who says to her group, "I want to really thank Jack in particular for his hard work on the project" may have communicated that; in general, she thinks more of Jack than anyone else when this may not, in fact, be the case. It doesn't matter.

The humorist Tom Lehrer introduced one of his topical songs in the following way:

> One problem that recurs more and more frequently these days in books and plays and movies is the inability of people to communicate with the people they love—husbands and wives who can't communicate, children who can't communicate with their parents and so on. And the characters in these books and plays—and in real life I may add—spend hours bemoaning the fact that they can't communicate. I feel that if people can't communicate the very least they can do is shut up.[2]

The remark may be amusing, but managers, employees, and executives have no choice but to disregard this advice. As we have seen in the preceding chapters, organizational men and women must communicate to be successful. Moreover, people could not "not communicate"—even if they wished to not communicate.

If your roommate decided suddenly not to speak with you, you would likely find that behavior peculiar; you'd wonder why she or he stopped speaking. You might think that you'd irritated him. Regardless of how you would react to your roommate's shutting up, she or he would *not* have *not* communicated. You'd have received some message.

Communication Is Irreversible

Once a message has been received it cannot be eradicated. Someone might say the words, "I take that back," but this does not erase the prior message. It can add on to the message and the person hearing "I take that back" or "I didn't mean that" may consider the request. However, one cannot completely purge the message. Our computers may have delete buttons, but we humans cannot delete messages once someone else has attributed meaning to them. We can all recall messages we heard when we were children that our parents, siblings, and best pals wish they'd never said and attempted to retract. They can't. Communication is irreversible.

Recently, I received two e-mails from a former student informing me (and several others on her broadcasted list) that she feared she would be fired from her job. Then I received a third message telling me (and the others) to disregard the previous messages. It seemed as if all would work out after all. If someone were to ask me about this student I'd probably think—though I might not say—that things were not all that secure at her present job. She couldn't eradicate the first message. Communication is irreversible.

Communication Is a Receiver-Oriented Phenomenon

David Mortensen in *Communication: The Study of Human Interaction* wrote that "communication occurs whenever persons attribute significance to message related behavior."[3] Similarly, Stevens commented that communication requires "the discriminatory response of an organism to a stimulus. . . .If the stimulus is ignored by the organism, there has been no communication. The test is differential reaction of some sort."[4]

The fundamental communication characteristic of receiver orientation refers to this assumption that communication is defined as occurring when a message has been

© GETTY IMAGES/PHOTODISC

Simply sending a message does not guarantee that an intended message has been communicated. The receiver may not actually receive it, or understand it, or decode it in the way the sender expects.

received, *not when a message is sent.* Hopper writes clearly, "Communication can be said to have taken place only when messages are received and interpreted."[5] Timm and DeTienne comment that communication occurs whenever someone attaches meaning to a message, and therefore that communication success is determined by the message receiver.[6] Hattersley and McJannet write, "Only what has actually been understood will have been communicated."[7]

The act of *sending* messages, in and of itself, does not mean that communication has taken place. This is a foundational and often overlooked aspect of communication, especially in contemporary times of technological availability.

If a senior administrator sends employees electronic reports, but employees do not read these reports, we cannot say that the manager has communicated the message despite the fact that a cogent message may have been broadcast. In short, *message received is message communicated.* Or as retired basketball coach Red Auerbach has commented, "When it came to communications, my rule of thumb was very simple: It's not what you tell them, [it's] what they hear."[8]

Is it truth if we describe things as they are without troubling to consider how our hearer will understand what we say?. . .[D]oes not genuine truth consist in taking the hearers into account and giving them a faithful picture of our own knowledge.

—Sigmund Freud

Communication Can Be Verbal or Nonverbal

Communication can involve verbal and/or nonverbal messages. A verbal message is one that uses words to convey meaning. The sentences in this book are primarily verbal messages.

The word *verbal* is sometimes confused with the words *oral* and *vocal*. Any message—whether spoken or read—that uses words to relay meaning contains verbal messages. A newsletter contains verbal messages, as does a briefing session. Newsletters and briefing sessions also are likely to include nonverbal messages. A nonverbal message is one that does not use words but nevertheless conveys meaning to receivers. The font and color used in a newsletter, and the gestures a speaker makes during a briefing are examples of nonverbal factors that can convey messages to receivers. If a newsletter is well-formatted and printed on thick paper, I'm likely to get a different impression than I would if the paper was translucent or the print so tiny as to make it difficult for me to read, or if the newsletter was published on-line. If a speaker uses complementary hand gestures while addressing a group I'm likely to get a different message than if the speaker were to stand stiffly in front of the group.

There are several categories of nonverbal messages that can affect communication in organizations.

Proxemics. Proxemics refers to space and distance and the effect space has on communication. A person with a larger office may be perceived as more important than someone assigned a smaller one. If an organization has several satellite offices, the distance between locations can limit the frequency of face-to-face interactions. The distance, despite the advances of new technology, will have an effect on the quality of organizational communication.

Kinesics. Kinesics refers to body motion. A thumbs-up signal, excessive pacing during a presentation, finger pointing, and distracting gesturing with hands are all kinesic behaviors. Some body motions are akin to words in that they have discrete, word-for-word relationships to meaning. These kinesics behaviors are called *emblems*. Emblems, like many nonverbal messages, are context and culture specific. Waving your hand toward your face will mean something different depending upon whether you're helping someone parallel park or are seated in a hot room. Certain positive hand gestures in the United States may be negative in different parts of the world. The thumbs-up gesture in the United States, for example, is said to be obscene in parts of Australia.[9]

Chronemics. This nonverbal factor is related to time. You may be impressed by certain persons' punctuality. Their concern for time may leave you with the impression that these persons are professional as well as sensitive to your needs.

Artifacts. Artifacts refer to things made by humans. Therefore, clothing is an artifact as is jewelry and stationery. Most people are aware of this intuitively, which is why they're likely to carefully select what they wear to an interview and consider the type of paper they use for reports and resumes.

Oculesics. Oculesics refers to eye contact and what is communicated because of how you do or do not establish eye contact. Think about the last presentation you heard. Imagine that presentation a little differently. Imagine what it would have been like had the speaker delivered the presentation while looking at the overhead screen during the talk, instead of looking at the assembled members of the audience.

> [Secretary of State George]Schultz had given us a very upbeat analysis and he tried to sound upbeat before the press, using words like "magnificent" to describe the President's performance and stating that important agreements had been achieved. But Schultz's body language and words were two entirely different things—and his talk was transmitted live to a huge audience back home, as CBS and NBC interrupted their Sunday afternoon pro foot-

ball games to put Schultz on. He was somber, downbeat, very deliberate, slow of speech, and tired. As [newscaster] Sam Donaldson said, Schultz "looked liked his dog had just been run over by a truck."

—Larry Speakes, former Reagan Press Spokesperson,
in his book, *Speaking Out.*[10]

Haptics. If your superior puts his arm around you as he explains how to do a task you might find that behavior uncomfortable, undesirable, and unprofessional. If you attempt to glean something from the way a person shakes your hand prior to an interview you would be attempting to gauge whether that handshake told you something or, in other words, communicated something to you. Haptics is the term that refers to how touch relays information.

Olfactics. If you make a determination about another person because of how he or she smells then that person's odor, a nonverbal phenomenon, has communicated something to you. If in the morning a person typically smells clean and fresh and you can detect the odor of shampoo, you may make an assumption about that person's general hygiene and health. If you detect cigarette smoke on another, you may make assumptions about that person's concern for health. Were you to do so, you would be deriving meaning on the basis of olfactics.

Paralanguage. Sometimes called *vocalics,* this nonverbal category refers to vocal factors such as rate of speech, word emphases, volume, and tone of voice. Paralingual factors complement verbal factors. Someone who speaks to your group and utters the words "I'm happy to be here" without any conviction is likely sending the verbal message that she or he wants to be there and the nonverbal message that he or she doesn't. Most people tend to find the nonverbal message more credible and therefore the paralingual message is likely to be the message that was communicated.[11] A person who presents an idea at a department meeting and speaks rapidly with a great deal of emphasis may be relaying both the idea as well as enthusiasm for the idea.

Physical Characteristics. In addition to artifacts such as dress and jewelry, physical characteristics can communicate information. A person who has a muscular physique is likely to communicate something to others simply on the basis of that physique. Height, weight, complexion, and physical attractiveness are all factors that can convey meaning. This is why people try to shed 10 pounds before they go to their high school reunions, and why some individuals decide to join health clubs. It's an unfortunate reality that people do make assumptions based on what others look like, but it is true nonetheless.

Focus on Applications

What Meaning Do You Derive When

☐ A co-worker habitually arrives late to work?
☐ A customer where you work as a salesperson touches your hand during a sale?
☐ An acquaintance takes out a cigarette shortly after you've met?

(continued)

☐ A prospective employee comes in to an interview in unprofessional clothes?
☐ A person crowds your space in an elevator?
☐ You meet someone at a dinner who is wearing strong perfume or cologne?
☐ A classmate is excessively fidgety during a group meeting?
☐ A friend takes you to her workplace and shows you her large office?
☐ A customer maintains constant eye contact when speaking with you?

Nonverbal communication is, obviously, more than just body language. Time, tone of voice, smell, dress, size, and touch all contribute to what is perceived as meaningful. In organizations and elsewhere, much of what receivers perceive is based on nonverbal information. One researcher argued that 93 percent of what receivers perceive is based on nonverbal messages.[12]

Students of organizational communication need to remember that nonverbal messages do not actually mean anything until a receiver decodes them. This is the essence of taking a receiver orientation to communication. Even verbal messages do not mean anything until receivers decode them. However, with nonverbal messages there is considerable room for misinterpretation as Manusov and Billingsley suggest:

. . .when we view another's [nonverbal] behavior we may be inclined to judge that it is a direct reflection of some aspect of the other's character, mood, feeling, or belief. We may feel that we really have access to what is really going on inside the other's mind or heart. But we are also likely to be wrong.[13]

A committee member who never speaks may be perceived as a slacker when she or he may simply be what is called a high communication apprehensive. A candidate for a position may wear a poorly pressed garment and one might assume that he or she is less than concerned about the position when, in fact, the candidate for whatever reason does not even see the creases in his or her clothes.

Communication Is Affected by Culture

In *Cultural To Dos and Taboos in the Global Marketplace* a business communication consultant makes the following comments and recommendations.

- The traditional Malay greeting is the salaam, performed only between people of the same gender. It involves lightly touching both hands to each other, then bringing your hands back to rest over your heart.

- Foreign visitors to Korea should be on time for appointments, although your Korean contact may be late. Expect business to proceed at a slow pace.

- In India, expect tea and chitchat before getting down to business. It is better to give an evasive refusal, such as "I'll try," rather than a flat-out "no."

- When you are introduced in Holland, repeat your last name while shaking hands.

- In Switzerland, don't talk with your hands in your pocket.[14]

© JOHN G. MOEBES/CORBIS

Organizations in the twenty-first century are far more culturally diverse than those fifty or even ten to fifteen years ago.

© GETTY IMAGES/PHOTODISC

The world is becoming so much smaller than it has ever been before. One can travel on a plane and be on another continent in a short period of time. Organizations are often multinational and even those that are not tend to have a staff that reflects diversity. Because of this, it is important to note that culture can affect how you process information and how you communicate with others. Assuming the perspective that the world communicates as you do—or should communicate as you do—is likely to create tension and animosity in the workplace. Since communication is, in large part, dependent on perception, it is important to keep in mind how significant culture can be in determining what we think has been communicated. In Part 4 of the text we discuss the effects of culture on organizational communication in detail.

ETHICAL PROBE

PLEASE SIGN MY LETTER

An associate comes to you with a letter that he has written to protest an increase in parking fees at your organization. Your associate is upset since he drives in daily and has to pay what he considers to be an exorbitant amount to park his car near the office. Assume that you take the train to work or ride your bike. Also assume that you don't really think the boost in parking fees is that dramatic or inappropriate. Regardless, your associate comes to you and asks if you'd be willing to co-sign the letter. He figures the letter will have more credibility with your signature on it since you *don't* drive and also because you have more seniority than he does in your company.

You read through the letter and notice the following sentences.

"You might think that the only people who are against the parking increases are motorists. In point of fact as you can see below, one of us doesn't drive at all, but is still concerned with what amounts to an unfair tax on employees."

Finally, assume that you don't imagine that anything will occur positively or negatively to you if you sign the letter, but the truth is you don't agree with it.

- ☐ Would it be unethical to sign this letter and send this message to management as if you were an author?
- ☐ Would it be worth being unethical with this communication to preserve your relationship with your associate?
- ☐ What do you communicate to your associate if you tell him that you won't sign?
- ☐ What has your associate communicated to you by bringing you this letter?

Communication Is Affected by Ethical Perspectives

Is it acceptable to lie to your friends? Is it permissable to lie in sales if you're competing with other salespeople who are themselves lying? Does omitting significant information constitute a lie, or is a lie only a stated or written claim that one knows to be untrue?

Ethical perspectives are central to what we call communication. This is particularly true in organizations, because credibility is a key factor not only in determining communication quality, but also in establishing the overall climate for communication in an organization. How you view your ethical responsibilities as a communicator affects how you communicate with both internal and external receivers. Chapter 4 in this text deals with ethical communication in detail.

Communication Is Different From Understanding

Some people think of communication as being synonymous with understanding. Occasionally, exasperated colleagues will stop a discussion and say, "We're just not communicating." This seems to imply, "We do not understand one another," or "We can't seem to explain to each other what we'd like to explain." Even when two people who are conversing have trouble understanding each other, they are still communicating. They may not be communicating effectively, but they are communicating.

As significantly, an inability to come to agreement does not necessarily mean that two people are not communicating effectively. Two adversaries may be trying to reach agreement on a new contract. They may be unable to do so, but they can very clearly understand the other's position. It's not a communication problem. They just disagree.

Communication Is Contextual

There are several levels of communication. What is meant by communication depends on these levels or communication contexts.

Intrapersonal Communication. In simplest terms, this means communicating with yourself. When we think about what we will be saying or writing to others we are engaging in intrapersonal communication. When a subordinate asks, "What do you think about my proposal?" your response is preceded by intrapersonal communication.

Dyadic Communication. Dyadic communication refers to interpersonal interactions in groups of two. These interactions may be formal—for example, a performance appraisal interview—or informal—such as two colleagues chatting by the coffee machine. While much training and attention is given to public presentations and report writing, dyadic exchanges are the most prevalent form of communication in organizations.

Group Communication. Group meetings are a common context for communication in organizations. Typically, groups are defined as bodies of anywhere from 3 to 15 people. In contemporary organizations members need not be at the same site in order for a meeting to take place. Teleconferencing is a form of meeting. Even same-site meetings can be facilitated using electronic communication. There are many factors that can negatively affect meeting interaction, and for this reason meetings are often a problematic context for communicating.

Public Communication. Presentations by senior executives and briefings by middle managers are examples of public communication. Public communication is a more linear context for communication than the dyad or group, but public communication involves feedback and, in certain situations, involves a great deal of interaction. In Part 3 of this book, we deal with dyadic, group, and public communication in detail.

Mass Communication. Whether print or electronic, mass communication involves disseminating information to large, sometimes unknown receivers. Typically the feedback in mass communication is delayed. Often the receivers do not actually receive the messages when they are mass communicated. They may get them physically, but the distribution of mass e-mails, or the delivery of the company operations manual does not guarantee that all receivers will consume the information. We will discuss criteria for evaluating organizational communication media in Part 2 of the text.

ELEMENTS IN THE COMMUNICATION PROCESS

The process of communication involves five elements. They are the

1. Source
2. Message
3. Channel
4. Receiver
5. Feedback

As mentioned earlier, an important additional factor in the process is what is called communication noise.

The **source** in the communication process is the person who intentionally or unintentionally sends a message that is perceived by a receiver. When the message is intentionally sent, the source typically conceives of, encodes, and then transmits the message. For example, during a meeting you may hear another person's comment and then decide to respond with a different opinion. In this scenario, you would likely think about what you would say, consider how you will articulate your thoughts, and then speak your message. The process is not likely to be a gradual one and the three steps of conceiving, encoding, and expressing could be instantaneous.

The **receiver** is the person in the process who decodes and perceives meaning from the message that has been intentionally or unintentionally sent. If you are watching someone who makes a face, you decode that facial expression so that it has some meaning for you. When you read this sentence you decode it so that it is comprehensible to you. In nearly all communicative interactions, and particularly in group and dyadic contexts, you take on the role of both source and receiver throughout the interaction.

The **message** is what the source, intentionally or otherwise, sends to the receiver. The message the receiver perceives has been sent through some **channel.** We can decode information using any one of our senses, or by using combinations of our senses. We can derive meaning by sound, sight, smell, touch, and taste. We hear what someone tells us; we see facial expressions that accompany the words someone uses when he or she speaks to us; we can smell smoke suggesting that we may need to look and see if there is an unattended flame nearby; we may draw conclusions on the basis of how some product feels to the touch; and we might assess a friend's cooking skills on the basis of what we taste.

A very important element in the communication process is **feedback.** Feedback refers to the response a source gets from the receiver. The feedback can be verbal or nonverbal, immediate or delayed.

- If you are conversing with a colleague and he shakes his head when you suggest coffee, that nonverbal nod is your feedback.

- If you are making a presentation and find that your listeners are spending more time reading the handout than listening to you, that feedback is significant. It may induce you to request that listeners wait until after the presentation to read the handout.

- If your organization publishes a newsletter and a survey distributed subsequently indicates that people aren't reading it, then that feedback will inform you that the message needs to be altered to engage your internal customers.

- If your company website gets thousands of hits daily, that feedback lets your webmaster know that the site is, at least, attractive.

Feedback often does, and in fact should, influence the source of the message. *Feedback-induced response* refers to a phenomenon that may alter the communication process. It means that feedback from the receiver affects the source's subsequent message. Simply put: the feedback induces a response. For example, if you discover that few persons read your department brochure, that feedback will induce a response in you—you'll need to change the content, style, or look of the publication. If, during a meeting, colleagues roll their eyes at orbit velocity when Jan suggests an idea, that nonverbal feedback should induce a response from Jan—to either clarify the proposition, defend it, or drop it. Efficient communicators are proficient at reading feedback and responding appropriately.

Some authors include **noise** as an element in the communication process. While noise is found in nearly all communication, it is actually not an element in and of itself. Noise refers to those factors that interfere with the success of communication. Noise can literally be external noise such as a train going by while one is attempting to make a speech. It can also refer to psychological noise such as being preoccupied with another matter while communicating, or having a negative attitude about the other party while engaging in interpersonal communication. In short, noise refers to any and all impediments to communication.

As we have emphasized, sources sometimes send messages unintentionally and this can create noise. Receivers who decode these unintentionally sent messages may draw conclusions about the source that could affect future relationships. Senders, of course, will be unaware that a person harbors resentments derived from unintentionally communicated messages.

Imagine walking along your campus on a particular day thinking about the various things you need to do. You have to do "in-person-drop/add" registration, call your supervisor at the restaurant where you work, check your e-mail at the computer bank, and read the first three chapters in a philosophy text. As you walk along, your thoughts are focused on how you will plan out the hours intelligently enough so that you can accomplish all of the tasks and still have time to work out in the gym.

While you're so engaged, an acquaintance from your philosophy class walks by in the other direction. The acquaintance raises a hand, gesturing hello to you while murmuring an almost inaudible "Hi." You don't see nor hear this person, because as he walks past, you are "in space" contemplating today's schedule—version four—which will permit your workout, and drop/add registration when the lines won't be too long. You can recall, all too vividly, the last drop/add period when you had been stalled on an hour-long line standing next to some malodorous bore. He had groused for the entire time with nearly toxic breath about a course he'd taken the previous semester.

Since as you walk you are preoccupied with your schedule and this unpleasant recollection, you don't even notice the philosophy class acquaintance. You walk right past him without acknowledging his presence. The acquaintance walks by and thinks to himself that you're a snob. You didn't respond to his gesture or his "murmured hi." He doesn't realize that you didn't see him, despite the fact that you had appeared to be looking right at him.

Later on in the term there's a project in your philosophy class, which requires work in teams. You find yourself in a group with this other student. You cannot understand why, initially at least, he regards you with some disdain. It may irk you when he treats you this way. It is possible that after a period this tension could dissipate. Yet, it is not impossible that the two of you will remain at odds and you will not know why.

The noise in this instance is related to the previous message your classmate received when you, apparently, walked by without acknowledgment. This example illustrates that noise is not always something generated at the time of a communication, but that there can be accrued noise that is the residual of prior intentional or unintentional encounters.

Message Fidelity, Noise, and Message Distortion

Half the world is composed of people who have something to say and can't, and the other half who have nothing to say and keep on saying it.

—Robert Frost

Message fidelity and message distortion are two phrases used to help conceptualize effective communication. When there is message fidelity, the receiver gets the message in the way the source wanted the message to be received.[15] In the cases when the sender unintentionally sent a message, message fidelity could still occur. The receiver would be able to detect some accurate meaning despite the fact that the source had not intended for the message to be sent.

As we have seen, communication noise could result in an inaccurate decoding of messages (sent intentionally or unintentionally). When this inaccurate decoding occurs we say that there has been message distortion.

Obviously, one would prefer message fidelity to message distortion. Message fidelity can exist despite the presence of noise—however, the greater the amount of noise, the less likely the chances for message fidelity.

Types of Communication Noise

Since noise can create distortion and reduce chances for message fidelity, it is important to consider types of noises and common reasons that communication noise is created. Below are examples of some common noises that can create distortion in organizational communication:

- Knowledge of, and attitudes toward, source/receiver
- Source credibility and reputation
- Literacy and language
- Selective perception

Knowledge of, and Attitudes Toward, Source/Receiver. Biases toward receivers either because of ethnic prejudices or because of existing personality tension can create communication noise. It may be difficult for communicators to "get through" these attitudes in order to accurately transmit the message. (Similarly, it may be difficult for receivers to "get through" negative attitudes they have about sources. The result is that the receivers cannot accurately hear the messages that are sent to them.)

In addition, knowing your receivers and analyzing them in terms of knowledge, culture, and attitudes decreases the chances for noise to interfere with communication. The activity of discovering all you can about your receivers in order to more efficiently communicate with them is called *audience analysis*. It is difficult to overemphasize the need for knowing your receivers and, therefore, you will see references to audience analysis throughout the text.

If your company intends to publish a booklet on how to use the intranet, the authors will have to learn about the intended receivers in order to create a booklet that is easy for readers to digest. If the intended audience is less sophisticated about computer use than the authors of the booklet, the words employed by the authors to explain how to utilize the intranet may not be understood by the end users. One organization decided to explain how to access and navigate its new intranet by posting the how-to information on the intranet itself. The instructions were clear, but several middle managers required the instructions *in order to* access the intranet, and therefore rarely, if ever, used the site. Those who posted the how-to information didn't quite understand the concerns or knowledge base of the audience.

The term *target audience* refers to the intended audience for a particular message. The success of any message depends, in part, on how well the source can identify and target that audience, and then package the message for the targeted audience. The phrase target audience may be an unfortunate one, since it can imply that receivers are "sitting ducks" and are victims of messages. Perhaps, in some cases the metaphor applies, but identifying a target audience, and the term itself, simply encourages senders to focus in on their receivers.

Source Credibility and Reputation. Who you are in terms of your reputation may be more important than what you say. Who you are and how you are perceived by your receivers can increase or decrease communication noise. Certainly it is important for the source of a message to be a credible figure. An individual with a reputation for honesty and competence compels attention and respect. One with less positive credentials makes successful transmission of messages tough to accomplish. Doris Lessing, author of *The Golden Notebook* and other best selling novels, once sent a manuscript to publishers under a pseudonym. She did this to prove the point that who you were in the writing field can be more significant than what you wrote. The novel she circulated using the name Jane Somers was rejected by many publishers. One publisher realized that Somers was, in fact, Lessing and published the book. When literary critics wondered why the publisher (Knopf) had not pushed the book more the agent allegedly replied, "I could not do this because there was nothing to sell." Lessing had proven her point. Who she was was more important than what she had to say in terms of getting her message to audiences.[16] The same could essentially be said for organizational communicators. Who you are, in terms of credibility and reputation, can facilitate or diminish the chances for message fidelity.

Literacy and Language. If receivers are illiterate there is, of course, a great deal of noise that is difficult to overcome. A very high percentage of employees are considered to be workplace illiterate.

Even if people are not illiterate, language factors create communication noise. Communication can be problematic because of the differences in vocabularies of senders and receivers. Each individual has an expressive and a receptive vocabulary. One's expressive vocabulary refers to the words that one can use when trying to communicate. One's receptive vocabulary refers to the words that an audience member can decode or understand. Your receptive vocabulary, of course, is typically larger than your expressive vocabulary because there are more words you can understand than those you can actually use.

The more words you have in your reservoir of words, the more likely you are to select a precise one to match your ideas. Effective communicators should consider the receptive vocabulary of the receivers when selecting words to create messages. Such consideration makes it easier for example, for managers to write to their employees, technical writers to present information on complicated subjects, and executives to get their message to stockholders during shareholder meetings.

The larger our receptive vocabulary, the easier it is for us to decode messages. Consumers reading computer manuals or booklets explaining furniture assembly are often frustrated and baffled by not having the vocabulary necessary to receive these messages. Problems related to receptive vocabulary are compounded because many times we think we know words, but we actually do not. Consider the following exercise.

Focus on Applications

These sentences all make sense. However, are they likely to create communication noise among an audience of your peers?

- ☐ What do the sentences mean?
- ☐ What do the bold words mean?
- ☐ Have you previously assumed that the bold words meant something different from what they actually mean?

1. It was the **duplicity** of both the CEO and CFO that was stunning.
2. At the workshop, the speaker repeatedly **transgressed**—at least as Adam viewed it.
3. The organizational challenges were going to occur **willy-nilly**.
4. In the procedures handbook, certain activities are clearly **proscribed.**

Slang, idioms, and profanity can also affect communication. Audiences may misunderstand slang terms and idiomatic expressions. As significantly, slang, which can be literally understood by receivers, may add meaning that the source did not intend. A colleague who laces his utterances with profanity does *not* run the risk of most persons misunderstanding the literal meanings of the vulgar words, but *does* run the risk of having receivers add additional meaning to the message, for example, rightly or wrongly, wondering about the character of the person who freely uses profanity.

Selective Perception. The degree to which we make choices affects how successful we will be as communicators. Choosing correctly will help reduce noise. Choosing incorrectly will create noise. The four stages of selectivity are:

1. Selective exposure
2. Selective attention
3. Selective perception
4. Selective retention

Let's assume that you were invited to a social function to be held at a local restaurant. All members of your department were invited. If you decided to join the others you would be **selectively exposing** yourself to whatever messages you might receive at this function. Once there and chatting with colleagues, you could listen to what they were saying, or focus in on what they were wearing, or become distracted by some other person in the room. You would be **selectively attending** to messages. Once you decided to listen to an individual, you would **selectively perceive** meaning from what that person was saying. If someone began to list all of his or her wonderful accomplishments you could perceive that this person was wonderfully accomplished, or an egotistical bore, or had an inadequate self concept—depending on the meanings you perceived from the message uttered. Following the social function you would remember some things and forget others. This would be referred to as **selective retention.**

The degree to which an individual makes intelligent choices is the degree to which communication noise can be reduced. If, for example, you tend to retain only those things you'd like to hear, then communication noise is likely to surface.

Craig Ingraham, Vice President and Senior Counsel

Craig Ingraham is Vice President and Senior Counsel for MasterCard International Incorporated. He supervises a department of eight people in his St. Louis office and represents approximately 1,500 people in MasterCard's Midwest operation. His comments reflect his observations not specifically at his present company, but at other organizations where he has been employed as well.

Candor and clarity of expression are the keys to effective communication in organizations. Subordinates at any level are uncannily adept at detecting deceptive, disingenuous communication no matter how cleverly disguised. To be viewed as having no credibility is the kiss of death in your role as manager.

It is not easy to train someone to be an effective communicator. However, even someone with rudimentary communication skills, with a lot of hard work and experience, can become at least marginally effective. If you're not naturally gifted, you better be prepared to work hard to get good at communicating. Still, subordinates appreciate candor and frankness over polish and facile presentations.

Communication is extremely important to what I do at work. On a weekly basis I am called upon to communicate tasks to employees, prepare written documents, occasionally deliver presentations to my superiors, run meetings when these are essential (and only when they are essential as meetings often needlessly consume valuable time), and listen to employees' suggestions, ideas, and complaints. The latter may be the single most important thing a manager has to do in terms of communication—listen attentively and give employees an opportunity to express themselves. So many problems, I've found, are resolved somehow when I just give the employee quality time, listen carefully, and ask questions. Sometimes after I hear their comments I say, "Okay. I think I understand. What can I do to help alleviate this situation?" More often than not the subordinate says, "Nothing. I feel better after just talking about this and having the opportunity to do so."

It's also important to provide feedback to employees regarding performance. Fortunately, I am not required to prepare formal evaluations for employees more than once a year. A good manager gives constant feedback and should not need the artificial discipline of annual evaluations. These formal mechanisms are, sadly, a device designed in order to address the reality that there are so many noncommunicative managers who can't be counted on to give effective, insightful, reliable feedback on their own initiative. Good managers should be able to communicate consistently with their team on a regular basis.

I have little regard for the practice indulged by some executives and managers of deliberately using deceptive or ambiguous communications, which is often done to avoid accountability or commitment.

(continued)

If you look at the highest levels in this country, you will observe the political-speak of spin doctors, where no definitive statements are ever made for fear of alienating some constituency. The result is that instead of truth we are subjected to bland messages scrubbed free of meaningful content. This is a positive development? Bring back Harry Truman. A lack of integrity and consistency will cost you in the marketplace and with your own employees.

A Toolbox

1. Communication is
   - A nonlinear process
   - Either the result of intentionally sent or unintentionally sent messages
   - Irreversible
   - Not synonymous with understanding
   - A receiver-oriented phenomenon, meaning that the messages received are the ones that have been communicated
2. Communicated messages include verbal and nonverbal elements. Nonverbal factors that affect communication include
   - Time
   - Motion
   - Space and distance
   - Vocal factors such as rate of speech, pitch, and volume
   - Physical characteristics
   - Artifacts
   - Smell
   - Eye contact
   - Touch
3. Communication involves
   - A source
   - Receiver(s)
   - Message(s)
   - Channel(s)
   - Feedback
4. Factors that retard the success of communication are collectively called *communication noise*.
5. A goal for communicators in organizations is to identify and reduce communication noise. The result will be greater chances for understanding.

1. What does it mean to say that communication is a *nonlinear* process?
2. Describe the five elements of the communication process.
3. Cite two examples of how communication noise can reduce understanding.
4. How can not conceptualizing communication as a receiver-oriented phenomenon create communication noise?
5. What noises typically interfere with your ability to communicate effectively with:

   a. Other students in classes

   b. Roommates

c. Associates at work

d. Supervisors at work

e. Family members

6. How have nonverbal factors affected your

a. Dyadic interactions with others of the same sex

b. Group interactions

c. Presentations you've given or attended

d. Dyadic interactions with others of the opposite sex

7. Please analyze the following case and respond to the questions that appear at the end of the case.

CASE FOR ANALYSIS

Case 3.2—The Financial Manager

Background. Abbie Logan is a group financial manager at a local advertising agency. In her role, she reports directly to the CFO, and is responsible for five managers who coordinate the daily financial activity for the agency's clients. She has only been employed by the agency for a few months, but communication issues surfaced soon after her arrival. This has created major problems for the agency since the pace at which the agency moves is breakneck. Requests for information are frequent and turnaround times are short. Employees need to fully comprehend requests, and information needs to be delivered correctly and on time.

Details. Abbie creates communication problems because of her inability to comprehend and retain information. When discussing issues with her, all of her verbal and nonverbal communications would indicate that she thoroughly understands the conversation at hand. She frequently nods and replies "Yes" and "Uh huh" after most phrases (which, in itself, is distracting). However, at the end of the conversation, Abbie begins to ask questions fundamental to the entire conversation just completed. Additionally, hours later she will again ask questions that indicate she has not retained information from the prior conversation.

The five managers who report to Abbie were the first to recognize the communication problems created by her behavior. Since her tenure at the agency was so short, the managers decided to wait and see if it was merely a lack of general understanding about the agency that led to the communication breakdowns. However, high-level executives within other departments are now identifying the same issues and are frustrated by Abbie's lack of comprehension and retention. Complaints are being made to the CFO as well as to Abbie's subordinate managers.

The issues described above may have been identified to Abbie in a previous job, as she insists on completing minutes for meetings and has a habit of summarizing discussions to highlight issues and action items. *However, it is in these meeting minutes and oral summaries where Abbie's lack of comprehension and inadequate communication skills are so glaringly apparent. She doesn't accurately or comprehensively summarize what's been discussed!*

- Are you familiar with people like Abbie Logan?
- How does one become an "Abbie Logan"—in terms of both her *inability* to communicate, and her *ability* to obtain management positions, given her incompetence?

- How can someone like Abbie create day-to-day problems for companies?

- If you were Ms. Logan's superior what would you do to remedy the problem?

- If you were Ms. Logan's subordinates how would you communicate to her about her (and, therefore, your) communication problem.

ENDNOTES

[1]Lasswell, Harold D., "The Structure and Function of Communication in Society," in *The Communication of Ideas,* ed. Lyman Bryson (New York: Harper and Brothers, 1948), pp. 37–51.

[2]Lehrer, Tom, *That Was the Year That Was.* 1964.

[3]Mortensen, C. David, *Communication: The Study of Human Interaction,* McGraw Hill, 1972: p. 14.

[4]Stevens, S. S., "A Definition of Communication," *Journal of the Acoustical Society of America,* vol. 22, 1950, p. 689. An interesting sidebar to this note is that Stevens prefaced his comments with this remark, "Although no phenomenon is more familiar to us than communication, the fact of the matter is that this magical word means many things to many people." Fifty plus years after uttering this statement (originally at an MIT sponsored conference on speech communication), the prefatory comment is still very true.

[5]Hopper, Robert, *Human Message Systems,* Harper and Row, 1976: p. 8.

[6]Timm, Paul and Kristen Bell DeTienne, *Managerial Communication: A Finger on the Pulse,* Prentice Hall, 1995: p. 15–17.

[7]Hattersley, Michael and Linda McJannet, *Management Communication,* McGraw Hill, 1997: p. 7.

[8]Arnold "Red" Auerbach is the author of a number of books relating to coaching and general ideas about management, including *MBA*. *Management by Auerbach.* This quote is from a book he wrote with Joe Fitzgerald entitled *On and Off the Court,* published by Macmillan in 1985. The quote appears on page 59.

[9]Baraban, Regina, "Cultural Protocol Tips," in *Cultural To Do's and Taboos in the Marketplace. Cultural To Do's and Taboos in the Marketplace* is a reference and resource guide compiled by Karen Tucker and published by the meeting services connection. Baraban's article was originally published in *Beyond Borders* in 1999.

[10]Speakes, Larry, with Robert Pack, *Speaking Out,* Avon, 1988: p. 184.

[11]Harris, Thomas and John Sherblom, *Small Group and Team Communication,* 1999: p. 93.

[12]That researcher was Albert Mehrabian who is the author of *Silent Messages* (Second Edition, Wadsworth, 1981) and other books. He made the claim in a 1968 *Psychology Today* article entitled "Communication Without Words," vol. 2, no. 4, p. 53. Other authors have indicated that the figure is somewhat lower, but still sufficiently high to recognize the importance and pervasiveness of nonverbal messages. See Dale Leathers, *Successful Nonverbal Communication,* Third Edition, Allyn and Bacon, 1997, pp. 5–6.

[13]Manusov, Valerie and Julie Billingsley, "Nonverbal Communication in Organizations," in *Organizational Communication: Theory and Behavior,* ed. Peggy Yuhas Byers, Allyn and Bacon, 1997: p. 66.

[14]Op. cit., Baraban.

[15]Krone, Kathleen, Fredric Jablin, and Linda Putnam, "Communication Theory and Organizational Communication: Multiple Perspectives," in *Handbook of Organizational Communication,* eds. Jablin, Putnam, Karlene Roberts, and Lyman Porter, 1987: p. 23.

[16]Klein, Carol, *Doris Lessing: A Biography,* Carroll and Graf Publishers, Inc., New York, 2000: pp. 234–235. See also, Arthur Asa Berger, *Media USA,* Second Edition, Longman, 1991: p. 78.

4

Ethics and Organizational Communication

He who slings mud generally loses ground.

—Adlai Stevenson, American politician

Trust and integrity are precious resources, easily squandered hard to regain.

—Sissela Bok in *Lying*

The cruelest lies are often told in silence.

—Robert Louis Stevenson

Outside [the Heavenly City] are the dogs and sorcerers and fornicators and murderers and idolaters, and every one who loves and practices falsehood.

—Revelation 22:15

© GETTY IMAGES/PHOTODISC

Case 4.1—*Lying to Rachel Adams*

n the fall of 1999 Rachel Adams was a hot commodity. The job market was excellent for someone with her computer-related skills. During 1 week in October three headhunters had contacted her trying to woo her away from her present position at Ballinger Systems. However, Adams liked her job, was compensated well, and had just bought a new home with her husband that was within a 15-minute drive of her Ballinger office. Adams's husband was happily employed. With their two incomes, life was very comfortable. Adams was a computer design specialist and part of her responsibilities involved managing other such specialists. She had an MBA and when she was initially hired by Ballinger Systems she had four other job opportunities.

Rachel Adams decided not to encourage the headhunters. Times were good; if they turned bad she figured she could still get another job easily.

Times did turn bad. By November of 2000 Ballinger Systems's stock was plummeting. Not only was Ballinger stock plummeting, but so were several other similar operations. Through the grapevine Adams heard that Ballinger was considering merging with a competitor. Adams set up a meeting with her superior to ask if there were, in fact, merger talks. Her superior assured her that there were no such conversations. As far as she knew, claimed the boss, Ballinger would be independent forever. "I promise you, Rachel, we're not going anywhere."

This was reassuring to Rachel Adams. She was no longer as marketable as she had been. Nevertheless, one headhunter had very recently contacted her. The job he proposed was for a similar position in a nearby location. Rachel and her husband could stay in their home. The salary was a little less than what she was making with Ballinger, but the company was, certainly, not going anywhere. They were a major player and were not about to be merging. The headhunter reminded Rachel that times were not like they used to be. Adams, of course, knew this. The headhunter also commented about the possible merger of Ballinger that Adams herself had heard through the grapevine. "Consider this opportunity Rachel. Listen to me. Times are not good and they will get worse. Anything could happen. I know you'll get this job I've lined up for you."

Adams weighed the idea of applying for the other job and decided against it. Her boss had assured her that the merger talks were nothing but hyperactive grapevine rumors. She wanted to stay put and decided to do so.

Her subordinates, who had also heard of the possible merger, asked Rachel about it. "Look," she told them, "I was concerned, but I was assured by Janet that there will be no merger. Janet told me this point blank and I believe her."

In January 2001 all employees at Ballinger received a happy mailing announcing the successful merger with Wellington Inc. Adams quickly set up a meeting with her superior. Janet apologized but said she had been under strict orders not to comment on any of the merger negotiations.

"I thought we had a good relationship. I trusted you."

"Look Rachel. I work for Ballinger. I have to be concerned for Ballinger. If I tell you about the merger, you might jump ship. If you jump ship, others might leave. This could jeopardize our day-to-day operations and also might make it difficult for us to close on this merger. You may think I had a moral obligation to tell you the truth, but I have a moral obligation to Ballinger to do my job. In this case doing my job means keeping you here. Keeping you here requires that I omit certain information."

"Omit certain information? You promised! You said, 'I promise you Rachel. We're not going anywhere.' That's what you said."

"I didn't lie. We're not going anywhere. There will be some downsizing as obviously there will be duplication of responsibilities with the merger. However, Wellington and their people are moving in here. We're not going anywhere. I didn't lie."

Adams was incredulous. She nearly screamed, "I cannot believe you would do this."

"Welcome to the real world."

"You know I told my subordinates that there would be no merger. I trusted you. I told them I trusted you. What should I tell them now?"

"Tell them what I just told you."

In February 2001 Rachel Adams lost her position at Ballinger-Wellington. As of November 2001 she remains unemployed.

☐ *Did Ballinger administrators have the responsibility to honestly inform all employees about the proposed merger?*

☐ *Did Adams have no excuse since she opted not to pursue other leads when she had the opportunity?*

☐ *Janet claimed that she did not lie when she made her promise. Did she?*

ABSTRACT

In a March 2002 business publication, a photo of Enron CEO Kenneth Lay appears on the cover. The word LIAR is written in large yellow letters next to his image. The picture itself has been doctored so that the executive appears to have a Pinocchio nose. Beneath the elongated extremity is an excerpt from an e-mail that Lay had sent to all his employees on August 14, 2001. It read, "Our performance has never been stronger; our business model has never been more robust; our growth has never been more certain. . . ."[1]

Researchers in the field of organizational communication have discussed the merit of honesty, credibility, and openness as imperatives for effective organizational communication. Some writers have claimed that not meeting this imperative can result in insidious if not devastating consequences for organizations.[2] In the early months of 2002 few former employees of Enron would disagree with such claims.

If those who believe in the imperative of open, honest, and credible communications are correct, and moreover, that the absence of honesty can be devastating for an organization, then employees and employers who are dishonest, and an organizational culture that condones dishonesty, is inevitably toxic to the health of an organization. This chapter examines ethics as it pertains to communication within the organization.

When you have completed this chapter, you should be able to:

☐ **Explain why ethical considerations are foundational for organizational communication study.**

☐ **List several ethical decisions that communicators must make in organizational contexts.**

☐ **Explain the perspective of those who support, and those who reject, *strategic ambiguity*.**

☐ **Compare your own personal criteria for what constitutes ethical organizational communication with others who have been surveyed.**

☐ **Identify methods that can be used to improve ethical decision making.**

EXAMINING ETHICS

Nearly 15 years ago I published a controversial article about an issue related to college education.[3] Some time later, in the summer of 1988, I was invited to speak about the issue on a local talk show magazine program. During the program both the host and phone callers would ask me questions about my positions.

There were to be three other guests on the hour-long program and each of us would be interviewed independent of the other. Before the show began the guests sat in the "green room" and we introduced ourselves. On that day's program there would be a mayor of a local municipality, a female bodybuilder, a psychic, and me.

The mayor was on first and discussed how his community had been wronged by a recently published book. Then I was brought in and talked about my article. Then the bodybuilder entered and, dressed in appropriate garb, lifted astonishing amounts of weight to the beat of some bouncy music. Each of us handled a few softball questions from the host and took one or two calls from viewers.

Then the psychic entered. The psychic was, without doubt, the most popular of the four guests. She sat with the host and spewed predictions on every subject from foreign affairs to the stock market. While she was able to "see all," her specialty, she said, was predicting what would happen in individuals' romantic futures.

The phones rang off the hook. A caller wanted to know if he would ever meet the woman of his dreams. The psychic said that from "what she was feeling from what he was saying" there was a "positive surprise" in the future, but he "should be careful."

Another caller asked—frantically it sounded to me—if her husband would ever come back to her. This, the psychic said, was a tough one since "there were some clouds around it" but after she closed her eyes for a few seconds she began to nod her head. She said "Yes, yes, this is not beyond the realm of possibility," but that the caller might want to consider whether the return of the spouse would indeed be a good idea.

The next caller said that she missed her cat, now deceased from a traffic accident. She wondered if she should replace her cat or if perhaps the death of the pet was a sign that she needed to seek some human companionship instead. The psychic responded that it "could very well be" that this was "a spiritual signal."

If the show did not have to end the psychic would still be sitting on the guest stool taking questions. However, eventually the psychic returned to the green room with the mayor, the weightlifter, and me. After she settled down, she noticed me and said that she had enjoyed my segment. "Education is very important," she said. I concurred and mentioned that even then-Vice President George H. W. Bush was making it a campaign issue in his battle with Michael Dukakis for the presidency.

"Oh yes," she said with interest—no longer the psychic but an interested citizen. "It's going to be something: Bush and Dukakis. *Who do you think is going to win?*"

I couldn't avoid seeing the irony in her question. Who did *I* think was going to win? Here she was, a self-described contemporary soothsayer advising hungry, needy strangers about what she "sees" in their futures, and she had to ask me who was going to win the election.

"You're the psychic," I said. "You tell me who is going to win."

"Oh, oh," she stammered trying to recover, "Yes, well, uh, we in the psychic community think it will be Vice President Bush, but there are still some clouds around the issue."

ETHICAL DECISIONS AND ORGANIZATIONAL COMMUNICATION

All persons make ethical decisions when they communicate. Those decisions may be conscious or subconscious decisions. It struck me when I met the psychic that she had made some poor decisions.

Perhaps there are those who are psychically gifted but this person did not appear to be so blessed. Her career as a romantic seer was a lucrative one. Yet her musings on others' emotional predicaments could have insidious consequences and, it seemed to me, there were some moral responsibilities that she neglected as she plied her trade. Certainly the callers were responsible for their willingness to participate, but by posturing as omniscient—occasional "clouds" notwithstanding—the psychic was violating a very basic ethical principle. She was being disingenuous.

Does it matter if she could get away with it? Does it matter if such psychic advice is often dispensed or that there are willing and voracious receivers waiting for the message?

Organizational communicators are not sleight of hand psychics. Yet organizational communication requires making ethical choices. While the repercussions may be less dramatic, the effects of unethical communication can be both dramatic and significant, or at least be perceived as such by employees. Whether one works in an office of corporate communication, is a manager who must relay information to subordinates, or is a nonmanagerial employee who regularly needs to communicate intra- or interdepartmentally, one makes ethical choices that can affect interpersonal relationships and organizational quality.

It seems apparent that ethical attitudes are foundational to the study of organizational communication. To illustrate this point, please take a few moments to complete the survey in the Focus on Application section that follows.

Focus on Applications

Effects of ethics on organization communication

Below you will see a numbered list of communication-related activities. For each item:

- ☐ Explain how ethical decisions can affect these activities.
- ☐ Identify the repercussions, if any, of communicators not being concerned with ethical factors that pertain to the item.

1. Creating job descriptions
2. Constructing mission statements
3. Evaluating employee performance
4. Describing organizational achievements
5. Describing departmental achievements
6. Orienting incoming employees
7. Conducting informational interviews
8. Expressing concern for individual employees' welfare
9. Articulating personal achievements
10. Responding to personal performance evaluations
11. Persuading colleagues to agree to policy changes
12. Phoning in "sick"
13. Persuading customers
14. Constructing advertising copy
15. Providing information to investment companies
16. Updating project status
17. Identifying product virtues
18. Discussing changes to health and retirement benefits
19. Claiming responsibility for successes
20. Accepting responsibility for problems

As you probably discovered as you completed the exercise, many communication-related activities can be affected by ethical decisions.

IS HONESTY OVERRATED?

Recently an MBA student made the following comment during a discussion of ethics and organizational communication:

"What's so wrong about lying in certain situations?" she said. "Isn't honesty overrated?"

Organizational communicators should respond negatively to the student's second query if for practical reasons alone. W. Charles Redding, the research pioneer in organizational communication, made it clear that the communication climate of an organization was far more critical than individual communication skills in determining the overall communication quality in an organization.[4] As we will see in more detail in Chapter 7, Redding identified five criteria for what he called the ideal communication climate. One criterion was organizational *credibility*. Another was *openness*.

Remove credibility and openness as organizational trademarks and you have eliminated important planks from the foundation of your enterprise. Individual communication skills are relatively insignificant in an environment where organizational communications are distrusted by default. If honesty is devalued by those who disseminate information, organizational credibility and communication will inevitably be damaged and be difficult to repair or restore. Honesty is not overrated if only for the practical reason that dishonesty can be insidiously corrosive.

STRATEGIC AMBIGUITY

There are those who disagree with Redding and who have written in defense of what is referred to as *strategic ambiguity*. In this section we will discuss

- What is meant by strategic ambiguity
- The purported value of strategic ambiguity
- Problems with strategic ambiguity

What Is Strategic Ambiguity?

In 1984 Eric Eisenberg authored an article in *Communication Monographs* entitled "Ambiguity as Strategy in Organizational Communication."[5] In essence, strategic ambiguity refers to purposefully being vague in order to derive personal and/or organizational benefit. Eisenberg's article gained "an appreciative audience."[6] He questioned the notion that open communication is inherently desirable in organizations and argued that "at all levels, members of an organization stand to gain by the strategic use of ambiguity."[7]

There is both political and academic evidence of the acceptance of strategic ambiguity. For example, the United States foreign policy in regards to Taiwan and China has been described as one of strategic ambiguity.[8] Paul and Strbiak in a special *Journal of Business Communication* issue devoted to ethics, published "The Ethics of Strategic Ambiguity," which discussed under what circumstances strategic ambiguity could or would be ethical.[9] Organizational communication textbook anthologies include Eisenberg's article or related articles.[10] Another indication of the acceptance of strategic ambiguity is found in Contractor and Ehrlich's article in *Management Communication Quarterly* which discusses the benefits of strategic ambiguity for certain types of emerging organizations.[11]

Purported Values of Strategic Ambiguity

Eisenberg and Goodall Jr. digest the concept of strategic ambiguity and list its advantages. The authors write that strategic ambiguity

- Promotes *unified diversity*
- Facilitates organizational change and creativity
- Preserves privileged positions
- Is deniable[12]

Unified Diversity. *Unified diversity* appears to be an oxymoron. If an organization is unified how can it be concurrently diverse? Eisenberg and Goodall Jr. argue that "strategic ambiguity takes advantage of the diverse meanings that different people can give to the same message."[13] They argue that strategically ambiguous messages can result in employees "giving diverse meanings to the same message" while, concurrently, the organization is creating a sense of unity.

Consider Avis's long-standing slogan, "We Try Harder." The slogan will mean different things to different members of the organization. "We Try Harder" applies to the people who clean the cars as well as those who rent the cars. If the slogan was, "We are the car renting specialists" it would be less inclusive. Thus if an organization generates an ambiguous message, receivers may interpret the message variously, yet the message may result in receiver perception of organizational unity.

Eisenberg uses the specific example of *academic freedom* as an ambiguous phrase that promotes unity. Professors and students may have divergent and even contrary conceptions of what is meant by academic freedom. Nevertheless, the ambiguity of the phrase *academic freedom* can create a sense of unity within colleges and universities. Such unity would disappear if the phrase academic freedom was to be defined specifically.

This ability to create the illusion of unity when, in fact, there is—or may be—diversity is considered by proponents to be an advantage of strategic ambiguity.[14]

Facilitation of Organizational Change and Creativity. The advocates for strategic ambiguity claim that by being vague, organizational communicators can facilitate change and creativity. For example, if a manager tells an engineer to design a chair but is ambiguous regarding what type of chair, the resulting design may be for an innovative product that would never have been created had the directive not been ambiguously communicated. If you tell employees precisely what to do they may do precisely that, and only that which is prescribed. If you are strategically vague then you might receive work that reflects creativity and innovation.

The cruise ship industry is cited by proponents as an example of how strategic ambiguity facilitated organizational change. At one time ships were used primarily for transportation. When the airplane became the dominant means for international travel, the shipping industry had to make some changes. They did so by defining themselves ambiguously. Instead of thinking of ships in terms of transportation, the industry survivors defined themselves ambiguously as "entertainment or hospitality" vehicles. This ambiguity allowed for the evolution of cruise lines that became floating hotels, casinos, and restaurants.[15]

Preserving Privileged Positions and Deniability. Eisenberg and Witten, in "Reconsidering Openness in Organizational Communication," comment that by using strategic ambiguity "organizational participants can express their feelings and can deny specific interpretations, should they arise."[16] In essence, supporters of strategic ambiguity argue that persons in authority can use ambiguity to "plausibly deny" blame and maintain their privileged positions. This, as we will see shortly, is a controversial advantage. Yet it is identified as something positive by those who support the notion of strategic ambiguity.

STRATEGIC AMBIGUITY: DID THE HUMAN RESOURCES DEPARTMENT DO ANYTHING WRONG?

ETHICAL PROBE

The members of the Human Resources department within a large college of business feel as if other units are not giving them the respect that they are due. They suspect that other departments—Finance, Marketing, and Accounting to be specific— believe that the Human Resources unit has a weak faculty, weaker students, and unsuccessful alums. For years the Human Resources department has been getting less financial support from the college in terms of additional faculty, computers, and research equipment. Also, faculty members feel that their chances for promotion and raises are diminished because of the collective departmental reputation. In brief, the faculty feels disrespected by their colleagues and college administrators.

(continued)

CONTINUED

Each year the college publishes a bulletin that presents information on the units within the college. The bulletin includes the following information on each department:

☐ Faculty and staff profiles
☐ Mission statement
☐ General student descriptions in terms of academic qualifications (average test scores, for example)
☐ Alumni success (the alums are profiled in terms of their salary levels)
☐ Criteria for maintaining active student status

For the last 3 years, in addition to the bulletin, all of the information found in the bulletin is also available on the web. An interested visitor could go to the college website, click on a particular department and then, by navigating that unit's pages, find out about the program. While the publication is sent out primarily to people within the university and, on occasion, to prospective students and faculty who visit the campus for interviews, the website is accessible without any kind of password by anyone so inclined to visit the site. *The departments themselves create the information that will be placed in the publication and on the website.*

An agenda item at a spring meeting of the Human Resources department was to update material for the following year's bulletin and website. At the meeting several faculty members suggested that revising the bulletin/website was an excellent way to boost the sagging perception of the unit to external audiences. These persons suggested that the department *inflate* the SAT score statistics and grade point averages of current students, and *the income level* of the graduates. The specific arguments in support of falsifying the data were these:

☐ Every other unit does essentially the same thing. It's time that the Human Resources department stopped getting kicked around. They need to play by the real rules. And the real rules, euphemistically, are "to put your best foot forward."
☐ The department can put its best foot forward by being **strategically ambiguous** and can avoid overtly "lying." For example, when describing the salaries of alums they could write: "The average salary of our alums *in Human Resources* is. . . ."

Using this phrasing they could justifiably calculate the average salary by *excluding* any alumnus who had been unable to land a job *in Human Resources.* The proposed language could be seen as meaning either that the students *were working in Human Resources,* or that they had *studied in Human Resources.* By using figures pertaining to the former interpretation the department could easily inflate the salary figures without "really lying" by excluding any low-salaried alums who were either not working in HR or had taken menial jobs. Also by defining positions *in Human Resources* narrowly they could exclude even some HR jobs that were low-paying ones.

Playing with the language similarly would allow the department to inflate the statistics about student SAT scores. Some students were admitted to the department on a probationary basis because their high school test scores were low. If they achieved in classes they could remain in the department. The probationary students took all the same classes as the other students so, in essence, they were part of the department's student population. However, by excluding the probationary student's SAT scores, they could elevate the "average SAT score" published in the bulletin and on the web. This would elevate the perceptions that other units would have about the HR department.

☐ The end result of gaining greater respect justifies the deception. Once they became better respected then they can go back to what they'd done before.

The opponents to this proposal made the following counterarguments:

☐ If we're caught our image could be even worse than it is now.
☐ It might not affect our image positively anyway.
☐ It's lying no matter how you finesse the language.
☐ It doesn't matter how many other departments are doing it.
☐ Given the web, the information could go to many external audiences now as well as internal audiences.

Despite the opposing arguments the department decided to make the adjustments to the language in the publication and on the website.

☐ Did the HR department do anything wrong?
☐ Did the HR department lie or were they just being strategically ambiguous?
☐ Are the three arguments they used to justify the behavior valid arguments?
☐ What are the merits of the five counterarguments?

Problems With Strategic Ambiguity

One of the advantages of a free society is that it allows disparate ideas to surface. People can express their opinions and others can assess the merit of these positions. As you might imagine the idea of strategic ambiguity has been debated and criticized. I have and will continue to be one of the critics. It is difficult to reconcile the purported advantages of strategic ambiguity with its ethical problems and the practical consequences of advocating for ambiguity.

The identification of strategic ambiguity as an academic theory is discomforting. Journal article titles like "Reconsidering Openness" or "The Ethics of Strategic Ambiguity" create a membrane of legitimacy for behavior that is morally indefensible, individually (as opposed to organizationally) self-serving, and incontrovertibly dangerous. Arguments articulated *in support of* strategic ambiguity seem to be contrary to ethical principles. Below are a number of examples.

• "The use of strategic ambiguity complicates the task of interpretation for the receiver."[17]

• "By complicating the sense-making responsibilities of the receiver, strategically ambiguous communication allows the source to both reveal and conceal, to express and protect, should it be necessary to save face."[18]

- "Ambiguity can be used to allow specific interpretations of policy which do more harm than good, to be denied, should they arise."[19]
- "Strategic ambiguity preserves privileged positions by shielding persons with power from close scrutiny by others."[20]
- ". . . strategic ambiguity is said to be deniable; that is the words seem to mean one thing, but under pressure they can seem to mean something else."[21]

Eisenberg and Goodall Jr., as well as Eisenberg, do acknowledge the ethical problems with strategic ambiguity.[22] However, the theory has been advanced despite these acknowledgments. Essentially, proponents argue that the ethical problems are not significant enough to outweigh the advantages of strategically ambiguous communication.

Consequences of Strategic Ambiguity. Tompkins refers to the dangers of strategic ambiguity in *Organizational Communication Imperatives*. Writing about the Space Shuttle Challenger disaster he remarks

> Those who find the concept of "strategic ambiguity" appealing should read the addendum to Chapter V of the Roger's Commission Report. They will be sobered by the possible consequences of ambiguity, strategic or not. Ambiguity was a factor in the Challenger accident.[23]

Commenting on the Clinton administration's use of strategic ambiguity, Cox states

> . . . [I]t is ironic that the Clinton administration described its own policy as "strategic ambiguity" because that is exactly what I would say about it in criticism. . . . Strategic Ambiguity is a dangerous policy because uncertainty risks war.[24]

The problem with fostering the idea of strategic ambiguity is that the theory provides a license for people to be misleading. Strategic ambiguity promotes the notion that deception is defensible. Deception, simply, is dangerous. Deceit is corrosive to the organization and to the people who comprise the organization. The advantages of strategic ambiguity are not organizational advantages but individual advantages—and even these are short term. In the chapter on Crisis Communication we will see that most experts in crisis communication argue for transparency and openness when dealing with organizational crises. Deliberate ambiguity militates against transparency and openness.

Bok argues that those who are deceived become "resentful, disappointed and suspicious. . . . They see that they have been manipulated, that the deceit made them unable to make choices for themselves according to the most adequate information available."[25] She comments that even those who are inclined to deceive others desire to be treated without deceit.[26] Further, she argues that the damage of deceit transcends the effects on the deceived and includes the erosion of societal trust.[27]

In organizational communication terms, deliberate dishonesty is likely to result in bruised interpersonal relationships that will affect the organization's communication climate. The affected relationships and damaged climate can undermine organizational communication and efficiency. Dalla Costa in *The Ethical Imperative: Why Moral Leadership Is Good Business* comments that the reason for developing an ethical orientation in organizations comes "not just [from] what we gain from being ethical, but in realizing what we lose—in economic, social, natural, and personal terms—by succumbing to irresponsibility."[28]

ASSESSING ATTITUDES TOWARD ETHICAL COMMUNICATION

Individual attitudes toward honesty in communication are important to assess. Merrill points out that "the only valid ethics is that which is within each person."[29] This seems self-evident. Individual ethics, as a practical matter, transcend institutional codes of ethics in that personal convictions, more than company policy, fuel what becomes the amalgam of corporate philosophy. Of course the reverse can occur. Individuals can adopt behaviors that are the attitudes of the organization. In either case it is valuable to examine how those with whom we work feel about ethical issues. If organizational communicators are compelled to make ethical decisions, and if those decisions can affect the performance of an organization, it is wise to explore the range of attitudes employees have that pertain to ethical considerations and organizational communication.

In the May/June 2000 issue of the *Journal of Employee Communication Management*, I reported the results of a study I conducted on attitudes toward ethical organizational communication.[30] Fifty-six participants, all of whom were part-time MBA students (who were concurrently full-time employees), were asked to rate 18 communication actions, policies, or tendencies in terms of the ethical nature of each of the behaviors.[31] The specific 18 items that the respondents rated are listed below.

Before reading further, please take a few moments and respond to the questions in the survey.

Focus on Applications

Survey on ethical attitudes

The following statements refer to various communication behaviors. Please assess the statements by placing a number, 1–5, next to each item using the following scale. This statement is

  1 = highly unethical
  2 = somewhat unethical
  3 = neither ethical nor unethical
  4 = ethical, for the most part
  5 = there is nothing unethical about this at all

Statements

  1. Articulating a department or organizational policy that cannot and will not be enforced in order to make the department or organization look good to outsiders.
  2. Responding to a crisis by denying allegations that you know to be true, but you know you can get away with the fabrications.

(continued)

3. Not overtly lying, but omitting key facts when communicating to the media about a crisis within your organization.
4. Deliberately lying to employees about layoffs because the truth will demotivate them.
5. Telling employees that they are empowered in order to boost their willingness to work when you have no intention of so empowering them.
6. Deliberate vague wording on job descriptions to allow management more flexibility in assigning tasks.
7. Deliberately communicating a high evaluation for employees when lower evaluations are more appropriate in order not to create tension among employees.
8. Deliberately communicating a low evaluation to employees who deserve higher evaluations in order to get more out of them.
9. Using e-mail to communicate bad news to employees when you know the employee never uses e-mail. This way you can have a record of the message and never have to face an angry employee.
10. Not answering your phone and allowing the voice mail to pick up when you know who is calling and don't want to speak with them.
11. Deliberately calling someone when you know they are not in so that you can speak to a machine and avoid the person.
12. Placing the names of all members of a committee on a report supposedly generated by the committee when only one or two persons had anything to do with the document—either the actual writing of it or the ideas therein.
13. Requiring employees to sign an "I have read the Policy Manual" statement when you know they are unlikely to have read it, but you can later hold them responsible for having read it.
14. Deliberately telling two employees to do the same task without informing the employees that they are both doing it independently. The goal here is to get the best product.
15. Excessive use of e-mail for personal use as opposed to business use. Excessive here means you use e-mail more for personal use than for business use.
16. Having a suggestion box and not reading the suggestions.
17. Having a better external network for customers with complaints than an internal network for employees with complaints.
18. Using the informal grapevine to spread inaccurate information that will tarnish the integrity of a rival within the organization.

What Constitutes Ethical Communication?

There were three groups of respondents that participated in the study. After the individuals within each group had completed the survey, the members of that group discussed their positions on the items. The discussions were revealing for a number of reasons.

Different Value Systems. Attitudes on what constituted ethical communication varied dramatically. What some persons considered inappropriate or amoral was deemed perfectly legitimate by others. These differences led to several bouts of incredulous

CORBIS

Is it unethical to tell employees they are empowered in order to boost their willingness to work when you have no intention of so empowering them?

staring, head shaking, and less than dispassionate arguments. Both the polarity and the disbelief are worth noting. The respondents seemed stunned to discover that others with whom they could be working would have such disparate values and might behave according to their principles.

One person commented that

> Unless I preface what I say with, "This is the truth," then it is the receivers' obligation to discover whether what is being said is the truth. It is not the source's responsibility to be truthful. Therefore there's nothing unethical about deception unless a falsehood is prefaced with "this is the truth."

While several participants visibly shuddered when hearing this person's perspective on honesty, there were others who nodded their heads in agreement. The reality is this: There is a great range in attitudes on what constitutes ethical or unethical communicative behavior.

Ethical Behavior Is Justified on the Basis of Personal Experience. Participants often defended communication activity as ethical *not* on the basis of the action's inherent integrity, but because they themselves had communicated similarly or because such "things are done." This indicates that what prevails becomes ethical to some by virtue of the fact that it prevails. It was remarkable how often respondents, without hesitation, would say, "That's perfectly fine. I do that all the time."

On occasion there would be some contextual justification, but often the fact that it had been done, in and of itself, served as evidence of the legitimacy of the activity.

Victimization as Criteria for Ethical Communication. Items were often considered unethical when the respondents had been victims, or perceived themselves to be victims, of the particular act. This became apparent in discussion over item 4,

> Deliberately lying to employees about layoffs because the truth will demotivate them.

Those who had been victims during layoffs considered "deliberately lying to employees about layoffs. . ." unethical communication. Those who had experience communicating to subordinates during layoffs felt differently.

Organizational Responsibility as Justification for Ethical Behavior. Ethical legitimacy was often assessed in terms of organizational pragmatics. Some persons defended what others called unethical behavior on the basis that questionable behavior is not unethical if it, in fact, could be considered good management. In other words these respondents claimed that if an act was considered to be in the best interests of the company then the act was ethical because it is right to do what is good for the company. Similarly, if an act was perceived to be a waste of company resources, then it was considered unethical. The communication act was considered unethical because it would reflect poor management and, it was reasoned, it is unethical to manage poorly when one's job is to manage well. Other discussants found this reasoning to be meaningless when examining ethical issues.

Highs and Lows

Table 4.1 provides a breakdown of the results from the study. As indicated previously there were great differences in terms of attitudes about ethical communication. However, the items considered most unethical were those which involved deliberate malice, overt lying (as opposed to deception by omission), and promulgation of spurious policies and evaluations.

The specific items were

- Lying about potential layoffs (item 4)
- Using the grapevine to unofficially damage others (item 18)
- Denying accurate allegations during crises (item 2)
- Disseminating bogus messages about empowerment (item 5)

Items considered relatively benign included those that involved ambiguity, omissions (as opposed to overt lying), and avoidance. The specific items were

- Deliberately writing job descriptions vaguely to allow subsequent "flexibility" (item 6)
- Exacting unrealistic pledges of familiarity with company policy (item 13)
- Deliberately phoning others when the caller is aware of the absence of the receiver (item 11)

How did your individual responses to the survey questions correspond to the survey responses reflected in Table 4.1?

MAKING ETHICAL DECISIONS

Honesty in organizational communication is not overrated nor is it an ethereal concept only suitable for after-work musings. It is central to the job of communicating with and to employees and clients. We all are offended when we have been misled and it's difficult to justify misleading others. Even for those who have little patience with "golden rule" logic, the practical consequences of dishonesty can be significant.

Not everyone cares about ethical considerations. For some, ethics is an academic enterprise with no place in a practical world. In your class discussions you may have already discovered this. However, as we have seen, ethical factors can affect what is communicated in your organizations. This section is intended to suggest some guidelines for making the difficult decisions regarding ethics in organizational communication.

TABLE 4.1 *RESULTS OF ETHICAL ATTITUDES SURVEY*

Average scores for each item: 1 = highly unethical, 5 = there's nothing unethical about the behavior.

Ten of the items were considered more *unethical* than *ethical*. In rank order they are presented below.

Item

18.	Using the grapevine to spread damaging information	Avg. = (1.33)
8.	Evaluating negatively to motivate employees	(1.53)
4.	Deliberate lying about layoffs	(1.6)
2.	Denying allegations during crises despite charge authenticity	(1.63)
5.	Disseminating spurious messages promising empowerment	(1.82)
9.	Communicating bad news via e-mail to persons who don't use e-mail in order to have a record of the act and avoid confrontation	(1.96)
16.	Operating spurious suggestion programs	(2.14)
1.	Articulating spurious policies for window dressing	(2.15)
7.	Evaluating positively in order to decrease tension	(2.45)
12.	Crediting nominal participants in project submissions	(2.71)

Eight of the items were considered more *ethical* than *unethical*. In rank order they are presented below.

Item

10.	Screening out undesired phone callers	Avg. = (4.41)
11.	Calling when you're aware that the receiver is not present	(3.75)
6.	Wording job descriptions vaguely for subsequent flexibility	(3.64)
13.	Requiring unrealistic pledges of familiarity with policy	(3.46)
14.	Telling two persons to perform the same task to get a better result	(3.35)
17.	Having better external than internal network for complaints	(3.14)
3.	Omitting key facts when speaking to the media after crises	(3.1)
15.	Using e-mail for personal use more than business use	(3.07)

Establish Codes of Ethics

Individual, unit, or industry Codes of Ethics can, but not always do, set a meaningful guideline for ethical organizational communication (See sample in Table 4.2). These codes will work only if the individual, unit, or industry is serious about making them work. Four requirements are essential.

1. There needs to be a well-thought-out list of guidelines. This includes a clear definition of any gray terms. A good way to hammer out a code of ethics is to try to respond to ethical cases using the code. In short, the code must be functional.

2. The guidelines need to be published or otherwise disseminated in a manner that makes access to them easy. The guidelines must be familiar to all who work in the organization. Sometimes an organization has published a code of ethics, but some members of the organization are not even aware that such a code exists.

3. There needs to be a commitment from top management to enforce the code. If the code is merely window dressing then the charade should be eliminated.

4. A meaningful method for enforcing the guidelines has to be a component of the code. If there are no punishments for violations then the code becomes valueless.

TABLE 4.2 *SAMPLE CODE OF ETHICS: INTERNATIONAL ASSOCIATION OF BUSINESS COMMUNICATORS*

Professional Communicators

---

1. Uphold the credibility and dignity of their profession by practicing honest, candid, and timely communication, and by fostering the free flow of essential information in accord with the public interest.
2. Disseminate accurate information and promptly correct any erroneous communication for which they may be responsible.
3. Understand and support the principles of free speech, freedom of assembly, and access to an open marketplace of ideas—and act accordingly.
4. Are sensitive to cultural values and beliefs and engage in fair balanced communication activities that foster and encourage mutual understanding.
5. Refrain from taking part in any undertaking that the communicator considers to be unethical.
6. Obey laws and public policies governing their professional activities and are sensitive to the spirit of all laws and regulations and, should any law or public policy be violated, for whatever reason, act promptly to correct the situation.
7. Give credit for unique expressions borrowed from others and identify the sources and purposes of all information disseminated to the public.
8. Protect confidential information and, at the same time, comply with all legal requirements for the disclosure of information affecting the welfare of others.
9. Do not use confidential information gained as a result of professional activities for personal benefit and do not represent conflicting or competing interests without written consent of those involved.
10. Do not accept undisclosed gifts or payments for professional services from anyone other than a client or employer.
11. Do not guarantee results that are beyond the power of the practitioner to deliver.
12. Are honest not only with others but also, and most importantly, with themselves as individuals; for a professional communicator seeks the truth and speaks that truth first to the self.

Employ Ethical Yardsticks

Philosophers have long discussed ethical issues. Some of their approaches to resolving these matters are presented below.

The Categorical Imperative. Often associated with Immanuel Kant this approach assumes that there are universal absolutes regarding what is ethical and what is not. In assessing any particular act, what one needs to do is use the absolute as a guideline. This philosophy is actually clarified by defining the Utilitarian approach with which the Categorical Imperative is often contrasted.

Utilitarianism. John Stuart Mill wrote of something referred to as "The Greatest Happiness Principle." Essentially Mill's argument was that what made an act moral was whether the action benefited the greatest numbers of those affected by it. Obviously, the Categorical Imperative is at variance with Utilitarianism. The former argues that receivers' collective happiness is no yardstick. The yardstick is hard and fast. The latter argues that collective benefit is the primary yardstick.

Veil of Ignorance. Philosopher John Rawls argues that justice should be blind, and this approach suggests that ethical arbiters go behind a veil to make decisions that do not take into consideration role, financial influence, or political power. The veil of ignorance, if people legitimately accept the challenge of standing behind it, guarantees dispassionate assessments and is likely to increase the chances of quality decision making.

Aristotle's Golden Mean. This refers to Aristotle's approach that between two poles in decision making there is a golden mean which would make for an optimal decision. The mean, a statistical term referring to the arithmetic average of any sum, would be that decision that falls between the extremes. Such a mean, according to this approach, is a golden resolution to ethical dilemmas.

Would These Yardsticks Help Janet in the Rachel Adams Case?

Obviously, these approaches are only useful if the individuals, units, or industries care to employ them. Even so, the applications of any of the principles are a complex matter. To see how difficult it is I suggest that you attempt to apply any one of the yardsticks or methods to either the Ballinger case (Case 4.1), the Ethical Probe about the Human Resource Department on pages 77–79, or Case 4.2 that appears at the end of this chapter.

It is relatively easy to contemplate morality. It's more difficult to be moral and ethical. The dollars and cents issues that surround organizations are catalysts for questionable ethical practices. If an employee believes that she or he can get a raise, or credit, or perhaps a promotion by being unethical then perhaps at that point to that employee, ethics takes a back seat to the financial considerations. People are quite capable of justifying borderline behavior when unethical behavior provides some political, economic, or personal reward.

We have discussed the reality of disparate value systems. One of the problems with Kant's Categorical Imperative (or other ethical guidelines) is that few can agree on terms. What ethics means to me may have no meaning to you. Also, many of the absolutes that have been agreed upon have been codified into law. Therefore many of the issues not so codified become areas of disagreement without any real procedures for enforcement.

It's difficult to apply ethical yardsticks when people disagree on the number of inches to a yard, or whether a situation needs to be measured at all. What is racist to some is egalitarian to another. What is obscene to some is benign to another. Defining and controlling ethical behavior is like trying to add two numbers when the parties involved cannot agree on numeric values and give lip service to the rules of arithmetic.

Focus on Applications

Disparate value systems

A young boy comes home from school one day and approaches his father who is a co-owner of a hardware store.

"Dad," the boy says, "In school we were talking about ethics. What is ethics anyway?"

"Son, sit down," says the father. "Let me explain ethics to you. Let's say a man comes into the store and buys a hammer. The hammer costs five dollars and the man hands me a five-dollar bill. But, aha, I notice that the man has handed me two fives, but he thinks he's giving me just one five. One bill is simply stuck to the other.

"Now," the father continues, "ethics revolves around one key question: 'Should I, or should I not tell my partner about the extra five dollars.' "

Ethics is part of the fabric of organizational communication. Individuals, departments, and the collective that is the organization are affected by ethical decisions pertaining to how and what is communicated in organizations. The question becomes to what extent is an organization and those within it willing to work to ensure that communications are characterized by honesty and integrity.

Working to ensure that communication is ethical is worth the effort. The bottom line is that ethical communication affects the bottom line. The residual of open, honest, transparent communication is an environment that is characterized by trust. Ciancutti and Steding in *Built on Trust: Gaining Competitive Advantage in Any Organization* write that "we are a society in search of trust. An organization in which people earn one another's trust . . . has a competitive advantage."[32]

Dalla Costa lists several tangible benefits of what he refers to as "an ethical corporate character":

- A trusted company attracts and holds onto good people.
- A trusting work environment creates the support that fuels creativity.
- A trusting company is motivated to produce excellence in both revenues and social results.[33]

The challenge for organizational men and women is to realize these benefits by communicating ethically. The challenge for organizations is to seek out those employees who are willing to accept the responsibility to communicate ethically.

On December 14, 2001, the University of Notre Dame, in essence, fired football coach George O'Leary. O'Leary had been named head coach only weeks before. The university "accepted his resignation" because, it was discovered that O'Leary had included inaccurate information in prior biographical releases. The coach's bios had stated that he'd earned letters for playing college football when, in fact, he had not. He'd also indicated in these bios that he had earned a Masters degree, and he had not. O'Leary had been a successful football coach at other institutions. Neither the "letters" nor the graduate credential had been prerequisites for the Notre Dame job. What had, apparently, been a prerequisite was honesty.

> How will this episode affect communication at Notre Dame?
>
> How will this episode affect the health of the organization that is Notre Dame?
>
> On the basis of the university's decision, would you be more or less inclined to work or study at the University of Notre Dame?

Victoria Kohlasch, Managing Director of Marketing

Victoria Kohlasch is the Managing Director of Marketing for CRIC Capital. CRIC Capital purchases real estate from, and leases it back to, companies through a variety of customized net leases. These leases allow the organizations to free up capital for their core businesses. Ms. Kohlasch is responsible for CRIC's marketing and advertising programs. She has more than 12 years of experience in brand development and strategic marketing and has worked with several organizations to improve both their internal and external communications.

The benefits of deceptive communication are, at best, short term. In the final analysis dishonest, misleading communication has a corrosive effect on the organization. When you lie you are not creating a new truth. You may think you are, but what you are creating is a foundation for pervasive deception in your organization. You're not convincing people that *x* is *y*, you're convincing people that it is okay in your organization to say that *x* is *y*, even though *x* may not be *y*.

Now, the people who run a business have a responsibility to know their internal audiences. Being honest does not mean flooding audiences with irrelevant information. There are some people who do not need nor want to be swamped with details about a particular transaction. To give people all information about some matters is likely to make communication more, not less, difficult. There are some things to share with employees and other things to not share—not because you want to deny people information, but because some people can't or don't want to process that information, or because releasing such information could jeopardize the company from a legal standpoint.

You have the responsibility not to intentionally mislead your audiences. And this responsibility is practical as well as moral. Here at CRIC Capital, for example, Adam King developed a wonderful internal newsletter called *Footprints. Footprints* has been a very valuable communication tool. People, even people who provided information to Adam for *Footprints*—who know what's in a particular edition—look forward to getting the newsletter. How eager will people be to read information about a company if the organization has a reputation for being deceptive with its communication? Do you want to read about a company's financial status if it's common knowledge that the top brass tacitly approves of misrepresentation? *Footprints* is valuable here not only because it is handsomely and intelligently put together, but because people trust the information that's in it.

If a company lies about what its product can do, the employees say to themselves, "Can our product really do this?" and when they say, "No, it really can't," you lose their passion and their commitment. You lose work productivity. You lose a lot of things that are not easy to measure. You would have high turnover and would have a hard time

(continued)

maintaining consistency because with high turnover it's difficult to maintain your institutional history. All of these things affect bottom line profit.

There's no place for lying in business. However, there are many places where businesspeople routinely lie. This is, unfortunately, life. If you were to go to every office in this building complex and ask the people if they thought lying is wrong, 70 percent would tell you that lying is wrong. However, I'd estimate that only 10 percent of those offices would be telling you the truth. That's the irony. Ninety percent of the people who tell you that they value truth, either are lying or are kidding themselves because—as their behavior demonstrates—they are at times deceptive or purposefully vague to cause confusion. That's life. But, just because it's life doesn't make it right or bright. Codes of ethics are valuable if, and only if, they are adhered to and enforced. Otherwise the codes become another type of deceptive communication.

A Toolbox

1. Researchers such as Redding and Tompkins have argued that credibility, honesty, and openness are essential for effective organizational communication.
2. Most organizational communication activities are affected by ethical decisions.
3. While *strategic ambiguity* has been advanced by some writers the value of deliberately being vague is suspect.
4. Perspectives on ethical behavior are wide-ranging. Criteria used for determining ethical communications vary.
5. Techniques can be used as guidelines for ethical communication, but they require dedication and work.

1. Identify five communication activities in which you engage that require making ethical decisions.
2. What are the criteria you employ when making these decisions?
3. In your opinion, "Is honesty overrated?"
4. What are the advantages and disadvantages of *strategic ambiguity*?
5. Which of the ethical yardsticks identified in this chapter is most valuable for the ethical decisions you need to make when you communicate?
6. What does the phrase "Put Your Best Foot Forward" mean to you?
7. Assume that an instructor announced that she or he would be administering an exam on the following Friday. Assume that you asked what would be on the exam. Would it make sense for the instructor to be vague about the nature of the test so that you would be encouraged to study comprehensively and not just focus on identified question topics?
8. Analyze the case that follows. Please respond to the questions at the end of the case.

Case 4.2—Did Janet Smith's Boss Communicate Unethically?

Janet Smith worked in a hospital and was familiar with a piece of hospital equipment. She'd worked with it, knew how to use it, and management thought she could teach others to use it. Smith was not a trainer, but she was called into her superior's office and was asked to train 12 other individuals to use the equipment. Her superior was very supportive. She smiled and said, "I know you can do this and we really need your help."

Smith was unsure, but decided to accept the responsibility. In a way, she was excited by the challenge. She had never had to explain how to use the equipment before and thought it might be enjoyable in the way that work can sometimes be fun. Smith carefully planned a training program that included an assessment mechanism.

Janet Smith implemented the program. She followed her plan and orally explained how to use the equipment. She demonstrated some techniques and asked the others to watch and follow her. Afterwards she took any questions the trainees had. Finally, after a digestion period, she observed each of the 12 as they successfully completed the test.

Smith was elated. She had gotten the message through to all of them.

She phoned her superior to relay the news of the trainees' success and was disappointed when the boss was not in. She left a voice mail message indicating that all 12 had completed the training. Smith didn't hear back from her boss that day and that bothered her a bit, but a day later she informally bumped into her superior as they both passed in a hall way. The boss seemed to be in a hurry, but as they came close the boss winked at her and gave her a thumbs-up. Smith gave her the thumbs-up sign in return and went on her way. The boss's thumbs-up was the only acknowledgment Smith ever received from her superior about her training effort.

Weeks later, a thirteenth person needed to be trained and management came again to Janet Smith and asked her to explain the operation to the thirteenth employee. This time the request was unwelcome and that was made clear by the way Smith sighed and then nearly gasped when she was asked, face to face, to take on the responsibility. While she had enjoyed the work, she had other tasks to do. What's more, it would have been nice to receive some type of acknowledgment for her initial effort. After a moment, Smith agreed reluctantly and indicated her agreement by tersely saying, "Fine, get me his e-mail and I'll do it."

The thirteenth person, Tom, couldn't get it. No matter how hard or how many times Smith attempted to explain how to use the equipment, he simply could not get it. She told him to do one thing and he would do another. She told him to watch her and do what she did. Tom watched and then didn't follow Smith's lead. Exasperated this time, and not exhilarated, Janet Smith left a voice mail message for her superior explaining that the trainee seemed to be unable to understand the information. She didn't want to talk to her boss, so Smith made the call at a time when Janet knew she wouldn't be around. After leaving the voice mail message Smith figured that was the end of it.

The hospital, however, needed another person to perform the operation. Without Smith being aware of it, her manager approached the thirteenth person and asked him if he could operate the equipment. The unsuccessful trainee commented that he, in fact, could work the equipment. Janet Smith was not consulted.

When she discovered that Tom was operating the equipment, Janet Smith was livid. She approached her superior and literally shouted her objection. Her boss said that Janet's tone of voice was inappropriate. The boss also commented that Smith was now "out of the decision-making loop. I thought Tom could handle it and I made the call."

"On what basis?" shouted Smith. "Tom is an idiot."

"Why are you so upset?"

"You know exactly why I'm upset."

The boss tried to placate Smith. "Maybe you did a better job than you think you did." Smith was implacable and repeated, "He was incompetent!" Then, very sarcastically, she added, "it's nice to know that what I communicate to you is valued and respected, thanks a lot."

Subsequently, communication and relationships between Janet Smith and her superiors were strained. Conversations were typically short and solely focused on business issues. When her superiors attempted to lighten the mood, Smith frowned, got back to the point, and then moved away.

Smith eventually left the hospital.

In her exit interview she said, among other things, that it was never communicated to her that she was a valued employee despite her extra efforts. The only message of appreciation she received was the nonverbal thumbs-up. She said that the absence of communication when hiring the thirteenth person to operate the equipment was one of the worst things that had ever happened to her while working in an organization. She implied, but did not say outright, that if she were a man and the thirteenth trainee were a woman, this never would have happened. "I wonder if I would have been consulted if *my* name was Tom and the trainee's name was Janet," she said.

- Did Smith's boss behave unethically when she did not consult with Smith before assigning the job to Tom?
- Did Smith communicate unethically when she

  1. Deliberately avoided a conversation with her boss?
  2. Referred to Tom as an "idiot?"

- Did Smith's boss communicate unethically when she urged Smith to train for the second time when it was clear from her nonverbal reaction that Smith was not interested?
- If you were Smith, how would you have responded to the boss's hiring of Tom?
- Can someone be held accountable for being unethical when they are unaware that what they are doing may be unethical?

ENDNOTES

[1] *Business 2.0*, March 2002, Cover.

[2] Tompkins, Phillip, *Organizational Communication Imperatives*, Roxbury Press, 1993: p. 137.

[3] The article was entitled, "The Emperor Is as Naked as a Jaybird" and was published in the Winter 1987 edition of *Educational Horizons*, pp. 71–74. The article argued that the emphasis placed on learning in colleges and universities was insufficient despite claims to the contrary made by colleges and universities.

[4] Redding, Charles, *Communication Within the Organization*, New York, Industrial Communication Council, 1972.

[5] Eisenberg, Eric, "Ambiguity as Strategy in Organizational Communication," *Communication Monographs*, vol. 51, 1984, 227–242.

[6] Tompkins, Phillip, *Organizational Communication Imperatives*, p. 137. Interestingly, graduate students and undergraduate students who have read Eisenberg's 1984 article and who have been asked to either support or reject his perspective have almost uniformly supported the idea that strategic ambiguity can be valuable.

[7] Eisenberg, Eric and Marsha Witten, "Reconsidering Openness in Organizational Communication," in *Readings in Organizational Communication*, editor Kevin Hutchinson, Wm C. Brown, 1992: p. 127. Originally published in *Academy of Management Review*, vol. 12, no. 3, pp. 418–426, 1987. Eisenberg and Witten reference the 1984 Eisenberg article as support for the excerpted claim.

[8] Cox, Chris, "A Policy for Freedom in China" (excerpts from a speech), October 31, 1997. Publication of the Center for Security Policy No. 97-P 162.

[9]Paul, Jim and Christy Strbiak, "The Ethics of Strategic Ambiguity," *Journal of Business Communication,* vol. 34, pp. 149–159, 1997.

[10]For example, Corman, Banks, Bantz, and Mayer, *Foundations of Organizational Communication,* Longman, 1995: pp. 246–257, and Hutchinson, *Readings in Organizational Communication,* Wm C. Brown, 1992: pp. 122–132.

[11]Contractor, Noshir and Matthew Ehrlich, "Strategic Ambiguity in the Birth of a Loosely Coupled Organization: The Case of the $50-million experiment," *Management Communication Quarterly,* February 1993, p. 258.

[12]Eisenberg, Eric and H. Goodall Jr. *Organizational Communication: Balancing Creativity and Constraint,* Third Edition, Bedford/St. Martins, 2001: p. 24.

[13]Ibid.

[14]Op. cit., Eisenberg, "Ambiguity as Strategy," pp. 230–232.

[15]Ibid., p. 233.

[16]Op. cit., Eric Eisenberg and Marsha Witten, "Reconsidering Openness in Organizational Communication," in *Readings in Organizational Communication,* p. 127.

[17]Op. cit., "Ambiguity as Strategy," p. 236.

[18]Ibid.

[19]Ibid., p. 235.

[20]Op. cit., Eisenberg and Goodall Jr., p. 25.

[21]Ibid.

[22]Eisenberg and Goodall Jr., p. 25; Eisenberg, p. 239.

[23]Op. cit., Tompkins, p. 137.

[24]Op. cit., Cox.

[25]Bok, Sissela, *Lying: Moral Choice in Public and Private Life,* Vintage Books, 1999: p. 23.

[26]Ibid., p. 20.

[27]Ibid., p. 23.

[28]Dalla Costa, John, *The Ethical Imperative: Why Moral Leadership Is Good Business,* Addison Wesley, 1998: p. 11.

[29]Merrill, John, *Existential Journalism,* New York, Hastings House Publishers, 1977, p. 132.

[30]Zaremba, Alan, "Is Honesty Overrated: Employee Attitudes Toward Ethical Communication," *Journal of Employee Communication Management,* May/June 2000, pp. 38–47.

[31]For the purposes of the survey unethical behaviors were defined as those that were perceived by the respondents as "not right regardless of the legal aspects" of the action. The survey items themselves were "real world" as opposed to hypothetical. Over several years I collected descriptions of issues reported as work-related communication concerns. In order to create the survey, I reviewed the collected descriptions, selected communication problems that had ethical dimensions, and then digested the problem into a statement of behavior to which someone could react.

[32]Ciancutti, Arky and Thomas Steding, *Built on Trust: Gaining Competitive Advantage in Any Organization,* Contemporary Books, 2001: p. ix.

[33]Op. cit., Dalla Costa, p. 204.

Part

2

COMMUNICATION IN A COMPLEX SYSTEM

5   Managing Information

6   Communication Networks

7   Communication Climate and Organizational Culture

© PHOTODISC

95

5

Managing Information

Information Means Money.

—Forbes

Men have become the tools of their tools.

—Henry David Thoreau

The computer is a moron.[1]

—Management expert Peter Drucker

© GETTY IMAGES/PHOTODISC

Case 5.1—*Williams: Too Much E-Mail*

Ken Williams is a salesperson who is often on the road. His group is a loose confederation of other salespeople who are also most often traveling. They check back into the main office sporadically to touch base, but for the most part each salesperson is traveling from city to city selling the product.

Ken's organization uses e-mail as the primary method for communicating. Messages are sent by his manager to all salespeople. They check their e-mails on the road or when they return to home base. Then they respond to the e-mails via e-mail. Ken has two problems with this.

The first problem is that he finds that the e-mail messages are often not elaborate enough for him to get the details pertaining to the message. He'll receive what he knows is an important electronic message, but when he reads it, it appears to be incomplete. It's difficult for him to get in touch in real time with the sender of the message because he or she is also out traveling. Occasionally, he can connect with the senders on their cell phones, but even then he's typically leaving messages and getting messages in return—not interacting concurrently with the other party. Most often he finds that he's forced to act on the incomplete information he receives via e-mail.

The second problem is related to the first. Occasionally, Ken gets information via e-mail too late for him to do anything about it. He'll access his e-mail when he can, but sometimes when he can is too late.

He presents the concern (via e-mail) to his colleagues that e-mail may not be the best way to communicate. Apparently others either do not share his concern or are too busy to offer alternatives since no person responds to his comments. When the occasions are such that he runs into someone at the home office and brings up the matter, his colleagues typically agree but seem too busy to stop and think about alternatives. Their attitude is "What can you do?" and then they are off to their next sales call.

☐   *Is Ken's concern legitimate? That is, are there sufficient reasons for the organization to reconsider its usage of e-mail as the primary or sole method for communicating? Explain.*

☐   *Assuming that your answer to the question above is "yes," how could Ken's organization more efficiently deal with organizational communication?*

ABSTRACT

People in organizations have more alternatives now than ever before when they select media for communication. There is e-mail, intranets, voice mail, corporate video, tele-conferencing, and the conventional methods of using print or face-to-face communication. Managing information requires the intelligent use of the various communication alternatives available. Another aspect of information management involves understanding what types of messages need to be communicated in organizations. Most people would agree that employees need information about safety, benefits, job tasks, and organizational policies. However, do employees need to know about the successes of other workers? Do employees need to know that Tom over in Sales is now the proud father of twins? Should management bother to send out a formal appreciation to the custodial staff who decorated the cafeteria beautifully for the annual Christmas party? This chapter examines what needs to be communicated in organizations and what methods can be used to communicate these messages effectively.

OBJECTIVES

When you have completed this chapter, you should be able to:

- ☐ Define *task, maintenance,* and *human messages.*
- ☐ Explain the importance of *task, maintenance,* and *human messages.*
- ☐ Identify five characteristics of effectively communicated information.
- ☐ Describe what is meant by media *richness.*
- ☐ Describe the distinction between first- and second-level effects of technology.
- ☐ Explain the perspective of those who support the need for *human moments.*
- ☐ Discuss the advantages of *print, face-to-face,* and *electronic* methods of communicating information.
- ☐ Evaluate the way information is managed in an organization with which you are familiar.

IDENTIFYING MESSAGE NEEDS

Why Information Needs to Be Communicated

Daft and Lengel begin and end a *Management Science* article with a simple question: "Why do organizations process information?"[2] The answer, they conclude, is to "effectively manage uncertainty and equivocality."[3]

Uncertainty refers to the absence of information in organizations. *Equivocality* refers to the existence of conflicting or ambiguous information. Organizational men and women need to receive messages so that they will be able to function as the valuable organizational resources that they can be. In the absence of knowledge, or the presence of ambiguity, not only will employees be frustrated, but the organization as a whole will be frustrated. For example,

- Without information about a product's specifications, a salesperson cannot effectively sell the product.
- When two messages about organizational policy seem to conflict, an employee may select the wrong information and follow a counterproductive course.

An organization can *survive* with uncertainty and equivocality but the absence of important information can reduce organizational efficiency. Consider the following metaphor. Think of information as oxygen in our respiratory systems. That is, imagine information to be that which facilitates the physical operation of the organizational system. Organizations that communicate poorly can "live," but like the ingestion of unclean and perhaps toxic air, equivocality and uncertainty will result in a system that does not function as well as it might. At some point, the system might even "get sick," malfunction, and become significantly less productive. Uncertainty and equivocality can affect the fiber of the organizational foundation.[4]

Not all managers acknowledge the merit of this fundamental principle. Tompkins writes about a perspective some administrators hold about managing information. This perspective assumes that the organization is better off when employees do not receive information pertaining to the organization. Tompkins reports that "too often" managers keep employees in the dark and periodically shower them with valueless information in order to keep them uninformed while concurrently creating the illusion that information is being relayed.[5] The notion that good management is facilitated when useless memos, bulk e-mailings, and reports are sporadically dumped on employees is inconsistent with any credible management theory. Uncertainty and equivocality are deleterious to organizational health. Therefore the two-fold question becomes this: What types of messages need to be communicated in organizations and how should these messages be relayed?

Types of Messages

In order to be efficient, organizations must be adept at communicating three types of messages to their internal audiences. These types of messages are labeled *task*, *maintenance*, and *human* messages.

Task Messages. Even classical theorists would consider task messages important. Task messages refer to those communications that explain employee jobs or responsibilities. For example,

- If you need to write a draft of a speech for your CEO by Wednesday at 4 P.M. then you need to be informed that that is, in fact, a job task.
- If you are a manager in a convenience store and you inform an employee to move the soup from aisle A to aisle B, you are relaying a task message.
- When your instructor announces a reading that will be due for the next session, she or he is communicating a task message.

Task messages seem very basic. However, because of inattention to detail or unwise choice of communication media, even task messages can result in communication distortion. Consider the following examples.

1. I manage 35 full-time and 15 part-time staff members. Each of my subordinates is responsible for specific tasks that require accessing accounts via a PC. The users have varying levels of computing knowledge and therefore the degree of assistance they need from the Systems people varies. In November 1999 my office received 40 new computers to run Windows NT. Each staff member attended a short training session on the basic operations of NT.

The communication problem occurred 3 weeks after the computers were installed. Due to the nature of the system, any errors that occur on the network server would now be observed by all end users. There was a problem with a product called Chameleon and therefore all of my people were unable to access accounts. This halted work in the office. I was notified of the problem and was told how users could fix the problem.

As I mentioned, there are 50 people who work for me. I broadcast an e-mail explaining *precisely* what they had to do in order to rid the computer of the Chameleon problem. Only an idiot wouldn't have been able to complete the task. Some users followed my directions and fixed the problem. A large number, however, didn't read my e-mail. One by one an army of these people paid a personal visit to my office. When I told them that I'd sent them comprehensive step-by-step instructions, I heard a host of incredible responses that included:

- I deleted it.
- I didn't know it pertained to me.
- I didn't have time to read it.

I'm busy. I don't have time for this kind of thing. After the fourth or fifth visitor approached me I lost patience. The sixth or seventh met a very unhappy camper. Believe me, I couldn't have explained what they had to do more clearly.

2. I'm a salesperson and our store recently changed managers. The replacement manager came from a different branch of the same nationwide chain. He was well experienced in management, but not in communication. For instance, I think he was intimidated by the salespeople. He is a relatively shy and quiet person who doesn't say much—even in conversations that are not job related.

When he came to us he noticed that our store wasn't as tidy as his other unit had been. He wanted to tell us about his dissatisfaction. He wanted to tell us to clean up more, but he just couldn't do it.

Instead he wrote a small note addressing the problem and placed it on a tiny bulletin board in an obscure spot in the back office area where no one spends any time at all. Of course, the tidiness of the store stayed the same. I really lost a lot of respect for the new manager, and I believe he turned the situation into a larger problem than it had been originally.

3. I'm a manager. About 10 people work under me. On a Monday I assigned a worker to a project that absolutely had to be taken care of within a week. I explained this in detail—face to face. I asked on a number of occasions if he understood the assignment and I was adamant about the need for the work to be completed after the following weekend.

On Friday, this particular worker came to the office with a bad cold. He was sneezing and coughing and looked under the weather. I knew that he'd been working hard on the project so I figured if I let him go home a bit early, he could rest up and bang it out at home over the weekend when he felt better. People work at home all the time in this business. I told him to take the rest of the day off, but to make sure that he got the work done when he felt better. He told me, "No problem" and left. On Monday, after he got settled, I asked for the completed work. He looked at me like I was crazy and said that I'd told him that I could complete it on Monday. I nearly went berserk. He saw me getting angry and said almost indignantly that I had told him that he could take the day off on Friday, so he assumed that that meant he could work on it for an extra day. I was very upset at the irresponsibility because now I had to either go to my superior and explain why the work was late, or complete the whole thing myself within an hour.

These examples illustrate that communicating task messages may be more difficult than we might think it would be. Each instance reflects a different problem. In case 1 the choice of media, and receiver responses to e-mail, affected the communication of information. In case 2 the interpersonal skills of the manager and media choice affected the process. In case 3 the manager did not recognize a phenomenon we discussed in Chapter 3—selective perception. In each instance, the result of the poor communication transcended inaccurate receipt of information and resulted in negative attitudes.

Maintenance Messages. Classical theorists would also support the need for disseminating maintenance messages. These messages explain guidelines, rules, policies, regulations, objectives, and any related procedural information. The word *maintenance* is used to describe this category of messages because these communications help *maintain* the operation of the organization.

The list of courses for your next semester, whether presented in a brochure or on your university's website, is an example of a compilation of maintenance messages. An e-mail that lets you know when the computers will be down, or who the new vice president will be, or what the procedure is for requesting a salary increment are all examples of maintenance messages. Sometimes maintenance messages can be used in conjunction with task messages. If a task message informs employees to record all incoming client calls, the maintenance messages would include the procedures for recording client calls.

Maintenance messages may also seem simple to communicate, but as was the case with the task examples, there are instances when poorly conceived approaches are used to relay this information.

1. Three weeks ago, I joined a small biotech firm where I oversee all financial activity for two of the company's five manufacturing facilities. Since I started working at this new company, my boss has spent little time with me. He is extremely busy and under a lot of pressure. He has given me assignments and quickly rushed through instructions about how to do them. I ask as many questions as I can about the procedures for an assignment before he gets called to a meeting or receives an urgent phone call and I am left to fend for myself.

While I do have experience in financial matters and can sometimes figure out the procedures that govern a particular task, I frequently need information that only my boss possesses. Different organizations have varied policies on how to process financial information. When my boss vanishes, I'm forced to wait "in limbo" until I can again speak with him and clarify questions so that I can obtain the information I need.

While I am "in limbo," I have attempted to ask my boss's other subordinate for the information. While this sometimes remedies the problem, it frequently complicates it. Often the information I receive from this subordinate contradicts what my boss has told me. This is because my boss and this subordinate do not communicate either because of their busy schedules, and moreover, are apparently following different procedures when doing the same tasks! The bottom line is this: I know what I'm supposed to do, but need information to understand the guidelines. I can't get it.

2. I work as a cocktail waitress. Right in the middle of a shift on a Saturday night my manager approached me with the new updated employee handbook of rules and regulations. He also had with him a clipboard with signatures on it. The following words were written at the top of the sheet on the clipboard:

I have received and read my copy of the employee handbook, and am fully aware of the regulations and penalties therein.

Human messages are every bit as vital as task and maintenance messages. According to the practitioner interview presented at the end of this chapter, human messages are "99% of the game."

© GETTY IMAGES/PHOTODISC

I had a whole section of people waiting for drinks and absolutely no time to read the handbook, which was about 30 pages long. I thought that since he approached me with the handbook at such a hectic time, it didn't matter that much to management whether I read the handbook or didn't read the handbook. I signed the clipboard and tossed the handbook behind the bar where it is probably still sitting. I don't know of any waitress who read it. For the most part, people just laughed when they saw it. I think that the reason for the whole thing was to make it easier for the management to fire us if we screwed up.

In the first example we have an instance where there is both uncertainty and equivocality. What is the problem in the second instance? Media choice? Source credibility? Audience analysis? Ethical factors? Which of these factors (or what others) create the noise in the second instance?

Human Messages. A classical theorist would not be concerned with human messages. However, both systems and human relations theorists would be concerned with these messages. Human messages, as the name suggests, are concerned with the human needs of employees. Messages pertaining to performance evaluation, employee morale, attitudes, gripes, and relationships would all fall into the category of human messages.

Inquiring about a colleague's baseball-playing child, commiserating with someone who'd lost a loved one in the attack on New York's World Trade Center, congratulating a subordinate on an excellent submission, and contributing during a "good of the order" session at a department meeting all would be considered human messages.

Human messages are every bit as vital as task and maintenance messages. Some people might even argue that human messages would be more important than task and maintenance messages since human messages help create an environment that makes it easier for receivers to be interested in task and maintenance messages.[6] For example,

- The head of a department may be quite clear about what you need to do and what regulations govern your work, but if you never hear a word from this person about how you're doing, you may begin to wonder about whether your work is meeting expectations and may be reluctant to listen to task assignments.

- If you've never had an opportunity to voice your opinions regarding certain policies you might be reluctant to follow them as religiously as you would if you had participated in the decisions that resulted in the policies.
- If after you've lost a loved one, a manager does not extend an expression of sympathy, you may balk at responding to task messages that may be just marginally beyond your job description.
- You could become displeased if after submitting an assignment that you labored over, your instructor decides to congratulate all students similarly—regardless of effort or quality of submission. Perhaps you'll work less diligently on the next task.

As we saw in Chapter 2, it is not uncommon for employees to remark that messages of appreciation mean a great deal. Faculty colleagues, for example, will often pull student notes from their desks and comment that the sentiments were as meaningful as monetary rewards. A cleaning woman once told me that a stuffed animal she received from a grateful administrator meant "the world to me." Everyone likes to have their work acknowledged regardless of income bracket.

One could argue that there are times when employees' needs in this area are excessive. One cannot argue, however, with the general premise that managers need to communicate these messages when situations warrant it.

Focus on Applications

How well does your organization manage information?

Select any one of the organizations in your life, for example, your school, a club, your most recent job, a fraternity or sorority. Then complete this exercise by following the steps listed below.

(a) Review the bulleted questions listed below and write a 1, 2, 3, 4, or 5 next to each item. A "1" indicates that you do not receive enough information on the subject. A "5" indicates that your manager or organization is very efficient at disseminating this information to you.

(b) Return to each question and write a second number. In this case a "1" would indicate that it is very IMPORTANT that you receive this information. A "5" would indicate it's not at all important.

(c) Determine whether each item refers to task, maintenance, or human messages.

(d) What types of messages does your organization most effectively communicate?

(e) What types of messages are most important to you?

How satisfied are you with information you receive about

☐ What you have to do each day?
☐ Organizational policies?

(continued)

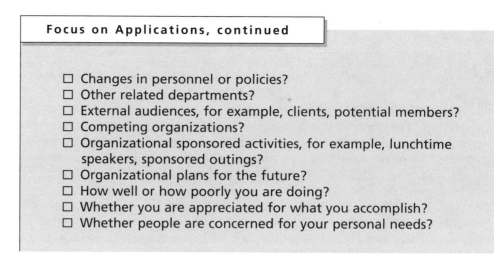

Focus on Applications, continued

☐ Changes in personnel or policies?
☐ Other related departments?
☐ External audiences, for example, clients, potential members?
☐ Competing organizations?
☐ Organizational sponsored activities, for example, lunchtime speakers, sponsored outings?
☐ Organizational plans for the future?
☐ How well or how poorly you are doing?
☐ Whether you are appreciated for what you accomplish?
☐ Whether people are concerned for your personal needs?

Five Criteria for Effectively Communicated Messages

As we have seen, task, maintenance, and human messages have to be communicated in organizations. Those who send this information should be concerned with meeting five communication-related criteria. Specifically, the messages that are communicated should be

1. Timely

2. Clear

3. Accurate

4. Pertinent

5. Credible

The first criterion relates to *timeliness*. Receivers must get messages at a time when the information is meaningful. The message is meaningless if it arrives too late for the receiver to do anything about it. If you receive a notice about a report due on Wednesday on late Tuesday afternoon, the notice that you receive may reduce uncertainty but will not allow you the opportunity to complete the assigned task. As significantly, you might be angered by the short notice and this anger may affect how you perceive subsequent messages from that same source. Therefore, one must choose a method that will ensure that messages will reach the receiver in a timely fashion.

Focus on Applications

Was United's message not timely? Was John at fault?

After booking a flight to Chicago on United's website and getting an electronic confirmation for that flight, John was stunned to arrive at the airport and be told that he did not have a ticket. There was a lengthy heated discussion with the agent who, despite seeing the printed version of the confirmation, maintained that John had no ticket. Rather than pay over four times the cost of his Super Saver fare to buy a new ticket, John was forced to travel to a different airport and fly on Southwest, a carrier with which he had a free Rapid Rewards coupon. When he returned home, John checked his e-mail correspondence to see if he had received any notification from United indicating that his ticket had been cancelled. He noticed that in his electronic in-box there was a message from Technical Support. The subject line was "Message from UN." Technical Support was the Subject line for all messages John received internally at work from the computer staff. Typically, information about computer downtimes would be listed in messages from Technical Support. Often, as was the case in this instance, John would not open Technical Support messages since they rarely pertained to him. Now, he clicked on the "Technical Support" with the subject line "Message from UN" and saw that "Message from UN" was an abbreviated version of "Message from UNITED." The message from United informed John that there had been some problem with his credit card electronic purchase and that if he did not respond by a date (which had come and gone weeks before) his e-ticket and reservation would be cancelled.

John investigated and found out that the problem with his credit card was that he'd provided a new ZIP code number with his payment. His credit card company, however, still had the old zip code address on file. The disparity caused the computer to spit out his reservation and generate the "Message from UN."

John was furious with United and wrote an angry letter. They responded by saying that they'd communicated the message and could not be held responsible because John had not checked his e-mail.

☐ Was John responsible for the snafu?
☐ Should United Airlines have communicated differently?
☐ What is the source of this communication problem?

A second criterion is *clarity*. Whatever method used must be one that will likely result in the message being received clearly. Face-to-face methods allow for immediate feedback and include nonverbal cues that improve the chances for a clearly received message. A problem with face-to-face methods is that the sender may be unable to articulate orally as clearly as he or she might be able to in writing. When we write a document we can write it and rewrite it before distributing it to make sure we express what we'd like.

It's a good idea (but not always possible) to complement a written message with an oral communication to ensure clarity. Often, business persons will distribute a written document to employees who will later meet and discuss the documents. After reading the materials the employees can ask questions for clarification.

The third criterion is *accuracy*. Accuracy and clarity are closely related but there is a difference. Assume that you receive a very clearly written notification about an upcoming assembly. The message includes the following information. You are invited to attend a meeting. It is to begin at 5:15. The meeting is to be held in Blackman auditorium. The agenda will include four speakers. The session will end at 6.

The written message could not have been more clear. Assume, however, that the information is inaccurate. Assume that the meeting will actually be held at 4:45 and convene in Richards Hall. Even if everyone who received the mailing subsequently receives a follow-up e-mail that corrects the error, a good portion of the attendees will go to the wrong place at the wrong time.

A fourth factor relates to *pertinence*. The receiver of a message should view the message as relevant to him or her. Otherwise messages that are irrelevant may begin to taint the value of those that are relevant. Sometimes managers must mass communicate messages for reasons of timeliness. However, if, as a matter of course, all messages are broadcast to all receivers, eventually the value of any one of these messages will be reduced. It has been argued that receivers in organizations have the responsibility of reading all their messages, that such activity is part of the job. This may be a legitimate claim. A reality, however, is that organization members will not consume all messages sent their way. As we discussed in Chapter 3 people selectively receive information. Mass communicated printed messages addressed to *Staff* may be skimmed, or discarded altogether. Marking them URGENT will only work if the URGENT indicator turns out to be credible.

This leads us to the fifth criterion which is *credibility*. Messages received must be believed or they will be disregarded. Will a printed appreciation, sent to all internal receivers thanking them for hard work, make sense? To a large extent the credibility of the message is dependent on the source as opposed to the method used for dissemination. However, the method can play a part in how a message will be received and, therefore, one should consider whether a particular method will increase or decrease the credibility of the message.

SELECTING MEDIA OPTIONS

Disseminating task, maintenance, and human messages to reduce uncertainty and equivocality is an important aspect of organizational communication. It is necessary then to consider how to send information to meet these three message needs and to ensure the timeliness, accuracy, credibility, pertinence, and clarity of receipt. There are various options available. Managers can write memos, send e-mails, use the intranet to post information, phone employees, use bulletin boards, send faxes, employ "corporate video," call a department meeting, teleconference, or meet with employees interpersonally. Since how you send information may affect the nature of receipt there's reason to intelligently identify criteria for using one method over another.

Media Richness

Daft and Lengel define *media richness* as a medium's capacity to change understanding.[7] If a medium is rich then it has a better chance of reducing equivocality and uncertainty and therefore "change understanding." Daft and Huber, as well as Sullivan, identify three criteria for determining richness. A medium's richness is dependent upon the

- Opportunities for immediate feedback

© GETTY IMAGES/PHOTODISC

- Presence of multiple communication cues
- Capacity for the medium to tailor a message to personal circumstances.[8]

Opportunity for Immediate Feedback. A medium becomes richer if, in order to decrease equivocality, a receiver can respond immediately to gain a clearer understanding of any message sent. The absence of immediate feedback reduces the chances for decreasing equivocality. Print, as it relates to this criterion, would be less rich than face-to-face communication.

The term *asynchronicity* is sometimes used to describe a medium that does not require that source/receiver be present at the time of communication. E-mail is asynchronous and that is both advantageous in that messages can be transmitted for subsequent receipt, and disadvantageous because feedback that could reduce equivocality is not instantaneous.

Presence of Multiple Communication Cues. This criterion for richness refers to the perspective that the more communication cues there are when a person communicates with another, the greater the chances of reducing equivocality and uncertainty. A message can be communicated verbally (with only words), nonverbally, or both verbally and nonverbally.[9] If you see me when I speak to you, you can observe my facial expressions, hear the tone of my voice, and notice any complementary gesturing. If you read a brochure you may have words and visual components, but will not have any vocalic cues. If you participate in video conferencing you have some visual and some vocal cues, but you will not have any haptic (i.e., touching—e.g., handshaking, pats on the back) cues and the range of your visual cues will be reduced by camera angles and directors' or camera persons' decisions.

Capacity to Tailor a Message to Personal Circumstances. A broadcasted e-mail is, of course, less likely to address personal circumstances than a face-to-face meeting. Print, in general, is less "able" to tailor to particular circumstances unless it is a personal memorandum or letter. Messages in company brochures and manuals cannot be easily tailored to literacy levels of large diverse populations.

Ranking Media in Terms of Richness

Huber and Daft ranked six media options using the criteria for media richness. The list reflects their rankings with the richest media appearing at the top of the list:

1. Face to face
2. Videophone and Videoconferencing
3. Telephone
4. Electronic mail
5. Personally addressed documents (memos and letters)
6. Formal unaddressed documents (brochures, pamphlets)[10]

Can you understand the rankings given the criteria?

Where would you place *voice mail* on this list?

Where would you place maintenance messages communicated *via the intranet*?

How significant do you feel richness is as a determinant for media selection?

Additional Criteria When Evaluating Media

Side Effects—Information Overload. When evaluating media choices it is important to consider the derivative effects of the use of that medium. To some extent this factor is addressed in the section on page 109 that describes first- and second-level effects of new technology. However, as we discuss media options here, the issue of overload is important to consider.

In organizations, communication is not an isolated event that happens once or twice a day. Organizational men and women are bombarded with messages. The use of particular approaches for communicating may result in the receipt of so many messages that any one message becomes less likely to reduce uncertainty. The accrual of many messages may render electronic mail, for example, less rich because while it *could* change understanding it may never do so, because recipients may not, in actuality, ever get the message.

In a *Fortune* article entitled "Surviving Information Overload," Mark Rosenker, a vice president of Public Affairs for the Electronic Industries Association, was quoted as follows:

> Let me put it this way. E-mail is an incredibly valuable service, but when you become inundated, it gets to be just like junk mail. I wonder if we're not getting e-mail trashed. It's reaching the point where I'm spending an hour a day going through junk, or using a key board to respond to junk, or thinking about junk, or reading junk.[11]

When considering a medium's potential for reducing uncertainty, a consideration has to be whether the receivers will have accrued so many messages from this medium that they will not likely attend to any individual message.

Permanence. Permanence refers to the enduring qualities of a message. Print is a permanent medium. This means that a person has the opportunity to keep, get, or review a copy of the communication after the initial receipt. There are two valuable advantages of permanence. The first is that you can have a record of communications. The second is that you can return to the message subsequently when convenient. Complex procedural manuals can be reviewed by the receiver when necessary. A

COMMUNICATING TO IMMIGRANTS

Assume that you know that a group of immigrants who work in your company cannot easily read English. Assume that you are told to provide health benefit information to all these employees. Also suppose that hiring a translator who would orally explain these benefits to the non-English-speaking population will cost a great deal of money, and that printing a translation of the benefit publication will be similarly expensive.

Is there anything unethical about distributing a copy of the English language benefit publication to those who have trouble reading English—and then claiming that you've met your obligations?

compendium of all organizational rules is not intended to be read cover to cover, but it can be used as a resource when a user needs to access particular information.

Speed. Speed refers to how quickly a message can get to, and will be received by, the receiver. In order to deal with issues of timeliness when reducing uncertainty or ambiguity, speed of transmission has to be considered a factor.

Cost. Cost is a consideration in nearly all organizational contexts. It does *not,* however, directly affect media richness. That is, a medium isn't rich or effective *because* it's inexpensive. For example, it may be cheaper to train hundreds of employees at once using videotape than having trainers conduct several orientation sessions. Using the videotape may be cost effective, but it reduces the value of the communication. One doesn't reduce a whole lot of uncertainty if receivers who watch poorly made videotapes snooze through the mandatory viewing.

New Technology: Examining First- and Second-Level Effects

Two professors, Lee Sproull and Sara Kiesler, make a distinction between first- and second-level effects of communication technology.[12]

First-level effects of technology refer to the "efficiency effects" or in other words what the technology was designed to accomplish. The first-level effects of the telephone enable us to speak to persons regardless of our receivers' locations as long as those persons have access to a phone and are present at the time when we make the call. The first-level effects of voice mail include our ability to leave messages for those who are not present when we phone.

Second-level effects of technology refer to the derivative effects of using the technology. Some may argue, for example, that increased telephone use resulted in a decrease in literacy. As more people stopped writing and began using the phone for conversation, fewer people became adept at writing and reading.

A second-level effect of the intranet and the use of electronic mail has been that face-to-face encounters have become relatively infrequent. It's possible to stay in your cubicle all day and "talk" to colleagues. Organizational "friends" may be people that you have never seen. Relationships develop without face-to-face interaction and a new informal network develops among those who use the intranet. Typing proficiency has increased among the average worker. Whereas 25 years ago most business

© 2002 THE NEW YORKER COLLECTION FROM CARTOONBANK.COM. ALL RIGHTS RESERVED.

"The E-mail isn't functioning—pass it on."

people gave their handwritten notes to assistants for typing, now nearly everyone is capable of using a keyboard for a first draft of a document.

Flaming and Self-Disclosure. Other second-level effects of e-mail relate to the relative anonymity associated with the technology. E-mail allows for communication without complete source attribution. You may know that a message came from ajones@aol.com, but you may not know what ajones looks like, where ajones is located, or even if ajones is a male or female. Sproull and Kiesler claim that a second-level effect of this relative anonymity is flaming—the tendency for employees to write bruising comments via e-mail that they probably would not express in face-to-face situations.[13] Similarly, in a 1996 article in the *International Journal of Technology Managment,* I reported results that suggest that the relative anonymity of e-mail can increase the number of messages sent and the self-disclosing nature of these messages.[14]

"Throwing Automation at Them." In a piece entitled "Planning for Information Effectiveness," Valdis Krebs, a project leader for Toyota's computer systems, writes that organizations often deal with communication needs by "throwing automation at them. . . . This often results in doing the wrong things faster."[15] The perspectives of Sproull and Kiesler explain to some extent why Krebs's declaration is very true. If organizational men and women focus on the first-level effects of any method for communicating and ignore the likely second-level effects, then inaccurate and/or unintended messages may be communicated—rapidly or otherwise.

Sproull and Kiesler argue that second-level effects of e-mail include reduction of authority and perceptions of "who is important, what is legitimate, what is prestigious."[16] They argue that second-level effects of intranet use are such that the culture of an organization can change. While an intranet may have been implemented in conjunction with its first-level effects—for example, the intranet's capacity to provide a vast amount of information that otherwise would have had to be more slowly distributed—a second-level effect is that the intranet has created a society of haves and have nots. Those with easy access to the intranet are in a different bracket from those who have less accessibility. Also, those who are computer intelligent are in a different category from those who remain techno-phobic or those who simply are less than expert about inter/intranet use. If "information is power" as some would claim, then employees who can access, and know how to access, information are more powerful than those with relatively less accessibility and knowledge.

The ramifications of second-level effects are significant and relate to our choice of message sending alternatives when we communicate. The idea that we can have a meeting spanning time zones using videoconferencing equipment is incontrovertible. We can share information and see the other participants who may be residing in other countries.

However, if teleconferencing results in the reduction of after-hours informal social relationships that typically develop during conventional meetings, and if those social relationships have an effect on the success of our persuasion during our formal meetings, then while we may have eliminated the time barrier and costs, we may have also eliminated a catalyst for successful interaction. If some persons are camera shy and participate infrequently in videoconferences, whereas they might have participated regularly during a conventional meeting held in the office conference room, then the first-level benefits of videoconferencing are undermined by the second-level effects.

In sum, when making media choices, we need to consider the second- as well as first-level effects of communication technology.

Human Needs: The Human Moment

Edward Hallowell, a practicing psychiatrist, published a 1999 article in the *Harvard Business Review* entitled, "The Human Moment at Work."[17] Hallowell's argument in the piece is that essential face-to-face communication is being reduced by the proliferation of communication technology. Moreover, he suggests that there are serious negative consequences of not having human contact.[18]

Human moments are defined as communications requiring (1) the physical presence of the two communicating parties and (2) emotional and intellectual attention. Hallowell states that organizational men and women need these moments to "maintain their mental acuity and their emotional well-being." He does not suggest the elimination of technology, but rather the complementing of electronic interaction with communications that include these human moments. As an unidentified executive quoted in the article comments, "You cannot have high tech without high touch."[19]

In a special issue of *Human Resource Management,* Argenti expresses related sentiments when he writes: "With all of the sophisticated technology available to communicate with employees today, such as electronic mail, newsgroups, desktop publishing, and satellite meetings to far flung places, the most important [managerial responsibility] . . . is to listen to what [employees] have to say and get to know who they really are as human beings." [20]

What do you think of Hallowell's position? Are there tangible consequences of not having human moments? Is an inherent weakness in online education related to an absence of human moments? Is Argenti's perspective accurate?

Not until a machine can write a sonnet or compose a concerto because of thoughts and emotions felt—and not by chance fall of symbol—could we argue that machine equals brain. No mechanism could feel pleasure at its successes, grief when its values fuse, be warmed by flattery, be made miserable by mistakes, be charmed by sex, be angry or miserable when it cannot get what it wants.

Sir Geoffrey Jefferson, June 9, 1949

Shoveling Coal and Human Moments. As it relates to human moments it might be appropriate to recall the observations of classical theorist Frederick Taylor and the results of the Hawthorne Studies. If you remember from Chapter 2, Taylor was the originator of scientific management—the idea that job tasks could be measured and examined in order to ascertain what was the best possible way to complete a job. Taylor observed employees shoveling coal and noticed the best way for employees to shovel coal. He advocated that all organizations test to see the most effective way for employees to complete tasks and then prescribe these methods as policy. As we discovered in Chapter 2, the Hawthorne Studies proved that the mechanistic notions of the classical theorists were flawed. People are unlike machines. Managers might be able to discover the most efficient way for a machine to shovel coal, but unless they factored in human needs and desires they couldn't compute the best way for humans to shovel coal—at least in the long run. (As we discussed, Taylor's proposals for coal shoveling were successful initially.)

When considering media options, it's important to remember the lessons of the Hawthorne Studies. When we identify the factors that affect media richness we need to consider not only the richness of a particular medium, but the residual effects of communicating information using that medium. In the human organization we may need human moments now and again to make us effective organizational players, and to facilitate receipt of future messages however they may be sent.

In an October 2001 article, "The Guru's Guru," management expert Peter Drucker comments that the "computer is a moron."[21] Maybe so. Computers cannot think and feel like humans can, so perhaps machines should be excused for being moronic. Humans, however, who have the capacity to acknowledge what separates the animate from the inanimate, have no such excuse. We cannot use machines intelligently without acknowledging what distinguishes us from the machines we use.

Focus on Applications

The "intelligent use" of technology—communicating the bomb threat

In the summer of 1999, the administrative office of a Boston-area therapeutic counseling center received a phoned-in bomb threat. The administrators took the threat seriously and decided to notify the therapists and tell them to leave the building immediately. They did notify the therapists. They notified the therapists by sending out a mass e-mail informing all to evacuate the building. At the time of the broadcasted e-mailing, the therapists were convening in a conference room and were not near their computers. Even if they had been at their computers they might not have accessed their e-mail in enough time to read the notice and exit immediately. Fortunately, this bomb threat was a false alarm, but the incident reflected an uninformed notion about how to communicate information in organizations. Stunning enough for this to have been done once, a month later the same "strategy" was employed when another bomb threat was phoned in. Again, fortunately, this threat too proved to be a false alarm.

INFORMATION NEEDS AND SELECTING MEDIA: A RECAP

Let's recap our discussion. Below is a list of 10 principles related to information management and selecting media. The principles are based on the previous sections and what we've learned about communication in prior chapters.

1. The objective when communicating is to get information to receiver(s), not simply to send information. Therefore, a method for communicating should not be selected primarily because of the sender's comfort level with the medium or how easy it is to generate information using the medium.

2. There are three types of messages that need to be communicated to employees: task, maintenance, and human messages.

3. Receipt of information must be timely. Information must be perceived as credible and pertinent. Information received must be clear and accurate.

4. The method used for communicating can affect the quality of communication. There are different strengths and weaknesses for each media choice.

5. The "richest" media are those that provide multiple cues, opportunities for instantaneous feedback, and can be used to personalize messages.

6. When selecting media, communicators need to consider the possibility of information overload, speed of transmission, and whether the message communicated needs to be "permanent."

7. New technology is not a panacea and must be viewed in terms of both first- and second-level effects.

8. There is nothing wrong with using complementary media when communicating.

9. The lessons of the Hawthorne Studies suggest that there may be a need for human moments.

10. Understanding your audience and respecting your audience is an essential factor, if not the essential factor, in determining communication methods to employ.

PRACTITIONER'S PERSPECTIVE

Jules Polonetsky, Chief Privacy Officer

Jules Polonetsky is the Chief Privacy Officer for DoubleClick, Inc. Prior to March 2000, Mr. Polonetsky served as the New York City Consumer Affairs Commissioner under Mayor Rudolph Giuliani. Jules Polonetsky practiced law from 1989–1990. The comments below do not reflect his observations at DoubleClick specifically but are based on his various organizational experiences.

The primary source of communication breakdown is that people don't take the time to do it well and are not proactive about communication. Often managerial employees will wait

(continued)

until there is a clamoring for information and then they rush to get it out. Communication is integral to the operation and one needs to consider it as part of the plan and not as an afterthought. A secondary problem relates to employers not being aware of what employees need, and not being familiar with the various organizational audiences in order to communicate appropriately with these different audiences. Not everyone needs or wants the same information, and employers must understand this.

Communicating appreciation is 99% of the game. It's probably more important to communicate this than anything else. People become ineffective in a company when they don't feel as if their end product is appreciated. Employees want to feel as if they have a role and they are recognized for contributing to the overall goals of the company. Good managers are good at relaying recognition and bad managers are not. Sometimes managers are too critical. An employee brings a suggestion forward and the manager just identifies the flaws. That manager may think that implicitly she or he is applauding the other components of the suggestion, but perhaps the receiver who only hears the criticisms does not understand that.

The reduction of face-to-face communication and reliance on e-mail is a problem. I receive 1,000 e-mails a day and can sit and respond to e-mail as a full-time occupation. People are overwhelmed with the volume. E-mail certainly has benefits. I can interact with colleagues in Japan and Ireland and other countries in a time-efficient way. However, e-mail can drive your agenda. You wonder if someone who spends 2 hours a day on e-mail and is employed to do x, y, z, is using e-mail to create an agenda that is inconsistent with his or her organizational obligations. E-mail is a blessing but it creates problems—one of my colleagues only allows certain people to e-mail him during the workday.

Written communication needs to be concise and to the point. Give me the facts. I don't want a chart that compels me to decipher it in order to get my answer. I learned in law school that you had to frame the answer with the question when you spoke to the judge. In other words you had to make it clear to the receiver what it was that you were addressing, and then go ahead and address it. Written documents sometimes are filled with numbers and charts, and look impressive, but occasionally I have to go and contact the source and get the information I need that hasn't been communicated in the written document. Similarly, effective presentations need to be brief and to the point. Don't rely heavily on slides and PowerPoint processes, but argue a point of view and bring only relevant information to your argument. People are in love with PowerPoint, but then speakers and audience members become slide show readers. The speakers don't argue a point; they simply read the slides that the audience members can read as well.

A Toolbox

1. Information is communicated in organizations to reduce uncertainty and equivocality.
2. Employees require information pertaining to job responsibilities, organizational policies, and individual performance.
3. The various options that are available for communication (for example, e-mail, oral communication, print) have distinct characteristics.
4. Selecting the best media option for communicating any particular message is an organizational communication responsibility that should be taken seriously.
5. When evaluating methods for disseminating information, it is wise to consider both first- and second-level effects of the method for communicating.
6. Technology in and of itself is not a panacea for organizational communication problems.

1. Describe the distinction between *task, maintenance,* and *human messages.*
2. What does it mean to say that a medium is "rich?"
3. What is the difference between *uncertainty* and *equivocality?*
4. What is a first-level effect of fax machines?
5. What is a second-level effect of teleconferencing?
6. Please respond to the following questions. Answer by indicating whether you *Strongly Agree, Agree, Neither Agree or Disagree, Disagree, or Strongly Disagree* with the statement. In addition, write your rationale for your reasoning in each case.

   a. Videotraining is a good way to inform new employees about their job responsibilities and the nature of the organization. It's more beneficial to watch a training video describing your new company than to receive a printed manual or listen to an oral presentation.

   b. Instead of convening in Chicago or some other major city, executives can accomplish the same work by having a videoconference—a meeting via video where the executives see and talk to one another on television.

   c. Employers should use e-mail to communicate information to employees about changes in organizational policies.

   d. E-mail should be restricted to use for business purposes only. Employees should not use e-mail to discuss social activities, book clubs, or just to "talk" as one might on the telephone.

   e. If you want to distribute social news to employees the best way to do it is to use the company hard copy newsletter. Don't use the intranet for this.

   f. Typically operation manuals that explain how equipment works or how to assemble equipment are easy for the lay person to understand.

   g. When you place a call to a business, you would prefer to hear an automated receptionist that gives you options, rather than to speak with a human being who would subsequently forward your call to the correct party.

h. A large organization should require managers who work off-site to carry and wear beepers. Beepers in the new millennium are like phones in the 1970s, 1980s, and 1990s. They're essential for business communication.

7. Analyze the following case. Please respond to the questions that are listed at the end of the case.

CASE FOR ANALYSIS

Case 5.2 — Perceptions of the Conference Call

Background. The Home Office Property Team consists of 17 individuals who have the responsibility to guide and support the 13 regional field claim offices of Garrett Auto & Home. The company is in the Personal Lines Insurance Industry specializing in settling automobile and homeowner insurance claims. The structure of the team includes an assistant vice president (AVP), a director, five team leaders, and nine direct reports. The team members are housed all over the United States. Once every month the AVP conducts a "what's new" conference call in which all the team members discuss whatever is current in their area of responsibility.

Problem Details. The monthly conference calls have lost their effectiveness. Each month they take on the same format starting with a roll call and then each team member talks about all the new initiatives they have started each month. There are three major problems affecting these conference calls. These issues concern the format of the conference call, lack of feedback, and content of the session. There is a great deal of wasted time as each person listens to others talk about subjects that (in some instances) have no bearing on what the rest of the team members do. Each speaker can talk about whatever he or she want and sometimes individuals go off on tangents that are very unproductive and time consuming. Everyone then waits for the AVP to intervene so that we can get on to the next person and get through with the call. The feedback given by the AVP is always positive, recognizing the efforts of each individual. The problem with the feedback is that it lacks direction and depth. It does not focus on the actual initiative, but only the effort given by the individual. No problems or issues are ever raised or debated. When the call is over, participants wonder if anything of value has been accomplished.

This problem needs to be addressed proactively, yet with an element of tact. Any changes have to begin with the AVP. This is a problem in itself as the AVP is difficult to read. He portrays himself as a classic human relations theorist in public; often giving public displays of recognition, but he is very opinionated about those same individuals in private. He does give complete access to a small group of individuals who are part of the property team. These members have had an impact on decisions he has made in the past when he has consulted them.

- Should the company eliminate the conference call system?
- What needs to be communicated to the AVP?
- How should that information be communicated?

[1]Schonfeld, Erick, "The Guru's Guru," *Business 2.0,* October 2001: p. 67.

[2]Daft, R. L. and R. H. Lengel, "Organizational Information Requirements, Media Richness, and Structural Design," *Management Science,* vol. 32, no. 5, 1986, pp. 554–569.

[3]Ibid., p. 567.

[4]The idea that uncertainty is deleterious to organizational health is presented in several sources including the previously cited Daft and Lengel article (see prior endnote). The clean air metaphor is adapted from Zaremba, *Management in a New Key: Communication in the Modern Organization,* Second Edition, pp. 6–7.

[5]Tompkins, Phillip, *Organizational Communication Imperatives,* Roxbury Press, 1993: pp. 18, 21. Tompkins refers to this phenomena while discussing the "Mushroom Anecdote." In this section of the book, the author explores four anecdotes germane to organizational communication. The mushroom anecdote pertains to a conversation Tompkins had with a laboratory director who was discussing organizational communication problems. The director comments that the way mushrooms are grown reflects a common problem with organizational communication. "You put them down in the basement and keep them completely in the dark. Every once in a while you open the door and throw some horse manure on them." (Neither the director nor Tompkins supports this approach to organizational communication.) Tompkins writes that "too often top management keeps employees in the dark" in ways akin to how one cultivates mushrooms.

[6]Goldhaber, Gerald, *Organizational Communication,* Sixth edition, 1993: pp. 148–149.

[7]Daft and Lengel, 1986, p. 560. The appropriate attribution for this statement is difficult to identify with certainty. Daft and Lengel in the cited piece define information richness as "the ability of information to change understanding within a time interval." They go on to discuss media richness in terms of a medium's capacity to generate information that would be rich because the information that would be sent using the medium would result in changed understanding. It is on this basis that the authors rank the media in terms of richness. However, it is in Huber and Daft's article cited in Notes 8 and 10 where the authors, referring to the Daft and Lengel piece, define richness as a "medium's capacity to change understanding." Huber and Daft also rank media in terms of richness. See Note 10.

[8]Daft and George Huber, 1986, referenced in Huber and Daft, "The Information Environments of Organizations," in *Handbook of Organizational Communication,* 1987: p. 152; Christopher Sullivan, *Journal of Business Communication,* vol. 32, no. 1, p. 49, January 1995. The lists from the two sources are not exactly the same. Huber and Daft include "language variety" whereas Sullivan does not. Huber and Daft refer to "timely" feedback, whereas Sullivan refers to immediate feedback.

[9]Mark Knapp and Judith Hall present the position in the early pages of their book *Nonverbal Communication in Human Interaction* that messages can be seen as *always* being both nonverbal and verbal. They write that while messages may be nonverbally sent, words are used intrapersonally to decode the message. Therefore since communication requires receipt of messages, no message however nonverbally uttered could be purely nonverbally communicated. Harcourt Brace College Publishing, Fourth Edition, 1997: p. 11.

[10]Huber and Daft, p. 152.

[11]Mark Rosenker quoted in Tetzeli, Rick, "Surviving Information Overload," *Fortune,* p. 60, July 11, 1994.

[12]Kiesler, Sara and Lee Sproull, *Connections: New Ways of Working in the Networked Organization.* Cambridge MA: The MIT Press, 1991.

[13]Ibid., p. 49.

[14]Zaremba, Alan, "Effects of E-mail Availability on the Informal Network," *International Journal of Technology Management,* January, 1996, pp. 151–161.

[15]Krebs, Valdis, "Planning for Information Effectiveness: A New Opportunity for Human Resources and Organizational Effectiveness," unpublished paper copyrighted by Valdis Krebs, 1988: p. 1.

[16]Kiesler, S. and L. Sproull, *Computing and Change on Campus*, Cambridge, Cambridge University Press, 1987, p. 34.

[17]Hallowell, Edward, "The Human Moment at Work," *Harvard Business Review*, January/February 1999, pp. 58–64.

[18]Hallowell, p. 59.

[19]Ibid. Quote appears on page 64. Reference to requirements of "human moments" appears on page 59. Reference to mental acuity appears on page 61.

[20]Argenti, Paul, "Strategic Employee Communications," *Human Resource Management*, Fall-Winter 1998, p. 205.

[21]Op. cit., Schonfeld.

6

Communication Networks

Just remember this, organization means communication, communication means connectivity, connectivity means knowledge, that's the mantra.[1]

—Business consultant Paul Strassmann

A lie can be halfway around the world before the truth has its boots on.

—James Gallagher, British politician

© GETTY IMAGES/PHOTODISC

Case 6.1—*Sales Department, Service Department, and Customers*

Background

The Sales department of a small software company was a group that prided itself on being able to party all night and still close a deal at 8 A.M. the next day. This play hard but work hard attitude was fostered by the management of the department who had never missed a quarter of achieving the quota and would do virtually anything to close a deal before the deadline of a quarter or fiscal year.

Between 1997 and 1999, the company was acquired twice. The 200-person software company that had enjoyed beers on Friday afternoons and concerts by the company band was quickly enveloped in a tornado of cultural changes and customs that seemed entirely too rigid and "corporate." The Sales department suddenly realized that the days of special treatment for being the company breadwinners were behind them. The salespeople were now part of a national sales force, selling only a fraction of the products under the umbrella of a new parent company. Integration into the larger company was also accompanied by countless new political roadblocks that needed attention during each six- to nine-month sale's cycle. *One of the most frustrating new challenges for the salespeople was communicating with the corporate Services department.*

Service Department Responsibilities

The corporate Services department implemented and properly configured the software for each new customer. As soon as a sale was complete, it was Services's responsibility to step in and ensure that the product met each customer's exact specifications. It was not unusual for product configuration and customer training to last up to a year.

The Services department was understaffed and overworked. Therefore, the Services department felt that they had the authority to step in and stop or, more likely, postpone a sale because of a potentially complicated post-sale implementation process.

For a group of salespeople who were compensated based on the quantity and dollar value of their sales, this type of interference was unacceptable. As the Services department became more stubborn, the sales force became more "creative" and resisted communicating with Services in the sales process.

Results

The result of this was somewhat disastrous for customers. For the sake of closing deals, commitments were made to customers by the sales force, guaranteeing short and unobtrusive Service implementation periods. *When contracts were signed, the Sales department often neglected to inform Services. Therefore, Services would discover a sale had taken place when an angry customer called asking why he or she had not received a phone call from Services since signing their contract weeks prior.* This type of chaos was possible because the integration into the new parent company had been so haphazard that no formal governance had yet been established. The new parent had been communicating only through the HR department because the parent was so busy deciding how to run the division and determining which departments to eliminate. This resulted in a local management team that felt unsure of their tenure, resentful of this fact, and were thus determined to reap as much in sales commissions and quota credit as possible before looking for a new job.

☐ *How might the acquiring company have acted to create a formal network between the two units and its customers?*

☐ *Given the present situation, can anything be done to improve future communication between Sales and Services?*

ABSTRACT

Organizations require networks to facilitate the transportation of information. Organizations must create, cultivate, and nourish these networks in order to facilitate the flow of task, maintenance, and human messages. This chapter discusses the types of networks organizations need to have, the advantages of using these networks, and the characteristics of particular communication networks.

OBJECTIVES

When you have completed this chapter, you should be able to:

☐ **Explain the distinction between messages and networks**
☐ **Define** *internal and external networks; upward, downward, and horizontal networks;* **and** *formal and informal networks.*
☐ **Describe the importance of each type of network.**
☐ **Explain the problems related to using each type of network.**
☐ **Evaluate the quality of communication networks that exist in an organization with which you are familiar.**

WHAT ARE COMMUNICATION NETWORKS?

In order to drive from one place to another, motorists need highways. Without Interstate 70 or other alternate routes, it would be difficult to drive from Kansas City to St. Louis. It does not matter whether motorists drive beat-up Chevrolets or state-of-the-art Porsches, they still would have trouble getting to St. Louis by car if there were no viable routes. Similarly, organizations require routes to facilitate the transportation of information. Managers must create, cultivate, and nourish these networks in order to permit the flow of information.

Networks do not refer to specific messages such as an interoffice memo or a broadcasted e-mail. These examples are analogous to the Chevrolets and Porsches that use the highways. The networks refer to the highways themselves. The networks refer to the existence of navigable channels that permit the use of communication methods like interoffice memos and e-mails. The roads need to be open before motorists can use them.

To some, the distinction between networks and message strategies may seem to be minor and not particularly meaningful. The distinction, however, is not insignificant. There is a foundational difference between messages and communication networks. To illustrate this, analyze the following two examples. The examples point out that the root of the communication problems in both cases is *not* the method of sending information, but the absence of any way for important messages to get from one place to another within the organizations.

Example 1: Buckley, Marshall, and Keyes

John Buckley, a newly hired middle manager, noticed that his department was wasting a great deal of money. Since he had worked in a similar capacity previously, he was aware of a cost-saving method for production that would reduce expenditures by 30 percent.

Buckley was excited by the prospect of contributing to the department so early in his tenure and was also eager to improve his own personal stock with his superiors. He approached his immediate supervisor with the suggestion and was informed that such changes were out of her hands. It seemed as if the only person who could authorize that type of move was a vice president named Marshall.

Buckley attempted to make an appointment to see Marshall and was told by Marshall's assistant, Keyes, that as a general rule Marshall did not meet with middle managers. Buckley tried to impress upon Keyes the importance of a meeting with Marshall, but Keyes insisted that no interviews would be granted and became annoyed at Buckley's tenacity.

Buckley did not give up. He wrote a three-page explanation of the cost-saving measure and sent it to Marshall through e-mail with a hard copy sent through interoffice mail. Two weeks later, after hearing nothing, he phoned Marshall and was intercepted by the assistant, Keyes. Buckley inquired about the proposal and was told, peremptorily, that Marshall was a very busy person and it was unlikely that the proposal would be reviewed in the near future.

Buckley discovered afterwards that Marshall's mail—electronic and hard copy—was always screened by the protective Keyes and that it was unlikely that Marshall had ever received the proposal. At this point Buckley decided to forget the matter. His enthusiasm faded to indifference. "Let the company continue to lose money," he thought. "It doesn't matter to me."

Example 2. The Patel CDs

A retail CD and tape company sold CDs, tapes, and audio accessories out of several retail outlets as well as through mail order. The mail-order division consisted of a sales department, a billing department, and a credit department that pursued customers with debts.

A Mr. Patel purchased two CDs via mail order and received the merchandise and billing simultaneously. He played the CDs upon receipt and discovered that one was damaged. He proceeded to send a package by mail to the company. In the package he placed the damaged CD, the original order form, a check for the good CD, and a simple note requesting a replacement copy for the defective product. On the note, Patel indicated that he would pay for the defective CD when he received the replacement.

Two weeks later, Patel received a second bill from the company with *Second Notice* stamped on the form. The bill contained a placating message that read, "If you've already paid your bill, please disregard this message." Patel assumed that the sales office would soon be in contact with the billing department and did nothing. This assumption proved to be incorrect. Three days went by and Patel received a package from the CD company. In the package Patel found another copy of the good CD he had previously received, two copies of the defective CD he had returned for replacement, and a bill for the three CDs.

Patel rifled a letter to the company indicating that he had not wanted to order two copies of the damaged CD and that he had no use for another copy of the CD that had arrived in good condition. The letter was caustic, and Patel demanded that the matter be cleared up immediately. He found the company website and wrote a shorter note to the "contact us" address, similarly demanding resolution. There was an immediate response to the electronic note that was not reassuring. It contained a standard message: "Thank you for contacting us. Your comments are very important and we will take them into consideration. We appreciate your interest and concern." Patel hoped for a more personal reply in the U.S. mail.

He didn't get one. Ten days later Patel returned from work to find a Third Notice billing from the company for the original order, and a Second Notice billing (complete with placating message) for the second package he had received.

With the Third Notice in his angry fists, Patel drove to the nearest retail outlet of the CD company. He approached the manager and demanded immediate intervention. The manager told Patel that the retail outlets had absolutely nothing to do with the mail-order division and that there was no way the manager could or would communicate with the mail-order people. If Patel wanted to resolve the matter, he was told, he would have to write to the mail-order division directly.

Patel asked for a phone number, and he was told again that the retail outlets had nothing to do with the mail-order division. Patel attempted to obtain a phone number for the mail-order warehouse through the telephone directory and was unsuccessful.

One more time Patel wrote to the mail-order division explaining the situation, sending a similar letter to the "contact us" address on the website. The electronic contact resulted in the same immediate, now infuriating, response: "Thank you for contacting us. Your comments are very important and we will take them into consideration. We appreciate your interest and concern." He did not receive any more CDs. He did receive a letter from the credit department, however, indicating that his "case" had been brought to the attention of that department for appropriate action. The letter was admonishing and sternly warned of repercussions if the matter was not addressed immediately.

It took Patel 3 months to straighten out the situation. During the course of Patel's investigation, he discovered that there was very little interaction between the sales, billing, and credit division. They perceived themselves as autonomous units within the larger organization, and there were no systematic channels available to facilitate the movement of information on matters like his problem. Simply, the left hand did not pay much attention to what the right hand was doing.

The Patel and Buckley cases are, unfortunately, not uncommon situations. Organizations must be concerned with developing channels that facilitate the flow of information. The Patel case, especially, is so typical that it is doubtful that many readers would not have experienced a similar situation as consumers. Patel's situation, in fact, was easy. It can take more than 3 months sometimes to sort out similar confusion.

Because we are aware of the frustrations that Patel experienced it makes sense as organizational communicators to recognize the problem and take proactive measures to eliminate the chance that we will alienate our own external audiences in the same way that Patel was alienated. The Patel matter could have been easily remedied if the organization had a system of networks connecting the different units of the organization.

There are three basic network systems that operate within an organization:

1. External and internal
2. Formal and informal
3. Upward, downward, and horizontal

EXTERNAL AND INTERNAL NETWORKS

In organizations *external networks* refer to those channels that carry information from within the organization to outside the organization, or those networks that carry information from outside the organization to inside the organization. Typically, external networks carry advertising messages, messages related to public relations; and messages relaying information about consumer complaints, concerns, and recommendations. The phone numbers and website addresses you find on many edible products are examples of external networks.

Celestial Seasonings Echinacea Cold Season Tea has a message on its container that reads "Thanks for Buying Our Tea! Please write to us in Boulder or call us at 800–351–8175 and let us know how we can serve you better. . .or visit our website at *www.celestialseasonings.com*." Contadina Tomato Paste's label includes the words, "We'd like to hear from you! Please write to Contadina Consumer Services at. . . ." The label on Near East Curry Rice lets consumers know that "If you have questions, comments, or would like recipes, call us at 1–800-. . ., weekdays 10 A.M. to 5 P.M. Eastern Time."

These companies are each establishing external communication networks with their customers. If your university schedules regular informational meetings with area high schools to explain the merits of your institution to prospective students, those questions and answer sessions are external networks for communication.

External networks do not function independently. In order to communicate to external audiences, internal agents must be connected to other internal populations. As is the case with most organizational interaction, there is an interdependent relationship between the external and internal communication networks. Consider the next example, which illustrates how poor internal management can affect the functioning of the external network.

A student intern, Stuart Markwardt, was working in the Public Relations department of a large high-tech company in San Jose. Interns were favored by this company because, frequently, high-tech magazines would call the company in need of information for articles regarding new products. The Public Relations department was understaffed and swamped with these inquiries. Since most of the time these callers asked simple questions that any employee with some information about the organization could answer, the student interns satisfied a real need for the department.

On a particularly busy day, a writer for a nationally known financial periodical phoned because she wanted to write a story about a word-processing package that had recently been introduced. The full-time employee she reached was swamped with work and passed the writer along to Markwardt.

Markwardt took the call and answered the journalist's questions. At the end of the interview the journalist asked for, and was given, Markwardt's name.

Three months later, the magazine came out with a positive review of the new product. The review concluded with the information that Stuart Markwardt was the product manager for the new software and the contact person for questions regarding the product.

This, of course, was not true, but to the more than 250,000 readers of the magazine it certainly seemed like Markwardt was the person to call with questions. By the time the article was published, Stuart Markwardt was back in school and no longer working for the corporation. Nevertheless, the company received hundreds of phone calls from persistent customers who insisted on speaking to Stuart Markwardt and to no one else. Some people will not settle for second fiddle and would not be put off in their quest and clamoring for Markwardt.

The company president was flabbergasted. After he read the article he allegedly shouted, "Who is this guy, Markwardt? What's a Markwardt anyway? I don't remember us hiring any Stuart Markwardt."

One year later, the company was still receiving phone calls and letters addressed to the intern. Over 2,000 calls have come in asking for Stuart Markwardt. More importantly, nothing has been done to improve the networks in order to keep such an event from happening again.

Any channels *within* the organization that carry information are called *internal networks*. This can refer to *intra*departmental routes and *inter*departmental routes. The systems theory of organizations described in Chapter 2 suggests the necessity for organizations to establish channels for interdepartmental interaction. If an organization is a system with interdependent parts, the organization must have a way to link the interdependent parts. As was the case with Mr. Patel and the CD company, the lack of such conduits can result in customer frustration.

Often the internal channels exist, but they are crudely constructed and therefore impede traffic, as was the situation with Buckley. Organizations have traditionally spent little time engineering the internal networks and ineffective internal communication is an inevitable result.

FORMAL AND INFORMAL NETWORKS

Formal networks are those that are prescribed by the organization. These are the official, appropriate channels for people to follow when relaying information. Most often these official channels have not been described as "communication networks." They have come to be the appropriate channels because they conform to the corporate organizational chart. These charts indicate who is to report to whom and what the appropriate chain of command is in an organization. The fact that a network is a formal network does not guarantee that communication "traffic" can

Figure 6-1   Types of grapevine chains

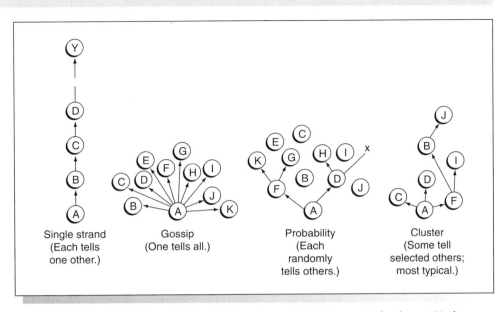

Single strand
(Each tells
one other.)

Gossip
(One tells all.)

Probability
(Each
randomly
tells others.)

Cluster
(Some tell
selected others;
most typical.)

Source: Keith Davis, Ph.D., and John W. Newstrom, Ph.D., *Human Behavior at Work: Organizational Behavior,* Eighth Edition (New York: McGraw-Hill Book Company, 1989), p. 373.

utilize the particular channel. In the Buckley case, for example, Buckley was supposed to see Marshall, but he had to go through Keyes to do so. Keyes proved to be an unyielding roadblock.

To continue the highway metaphor, there are roads that appear to exist on a highway map, but for sometimes curious reasons, these roads are closed to motorists. Similarly, there are networks that appear to exist on the organizational chart, but these networks are in actuality closed to subordinates or organizational peers. Of course, there are times when "roads" might need to be closed. Vice presidents cannot be at everyone's beck and call. However, if the formal policy implies that a network is open, it can be frustrating not to be able to use that network. If the conduit is simply superficial and, as a practical matter, is not available, the company runs the risk of not receiving valuable information. Managers need to make sure that the formal networks are indeed available for the sending and receiving of organizational messages.

Informal networks are those channels that carry information on routes that are not prescribed by the organization. Typically, these informal routes are referred to as the grapevine, and for a number of reasons the grapevine is an important network. Keith Davis is the researcher most associated with the grapevine. Since 1953 when he wrote a groundbreaking article in *Harvard Business Review,* Davis has been in the vanguard in terms of studying the informal network.[2]

Davis identifies several types of grapevine patterns (see Figure 6-1). They are

- **Single Strand.** One person tells another who then informs a third in a single linear format.
- **Gossip.** One person tells a host of others.

- **Probability.** Individuals randomly inform others.
- **Cluster.** Of those individuals informed, one tells others. Of those others informed, one tells others, and so on.

Development of Informal Networks

By definition, the grapevine is not prescribed. While prescient managers might attempt to engineer its development, the informal networks usually generate on the basis of factors that are only peripherally related to corporate policy.

The nature of the grapevine will be affected, for example, by the physical layout of the buildings and offices within the buildings. If production and advertising share a common lounge area and restroom facility, it is likely that an informal network will develop among those people who populate the departments of production and advertising.

Common hobbies and activities play a large part in the development of the grapevine. If seven employees from different departments jog together at lunch, information is likely to be passed along in the course of the run. The friendships that develop because of the common activity will result in social gatherings outside of the organization during which information about the organization will be passed along as well. If Liu in Production wants to find out about a policy in Engineering, Liu may not call the Engineering manager as prescribed on the formal network, but contact Resnick, her jogging buddy.

It is not difficult to list the factors that contribute to the growth of this important network. Lunch schedules, family ties, social relationships, and common hometowns can affect the growth of the network. Even the formal network can affect the growth of the informal network. If you participate on a committee and in the course of your conference sessions become friendly with a person who previously had been a stranger, that budding friendship creates a part of the informal network.

On the basis of grapevine development individuals assume certain characteristics. Hellweg and others refer to these as "roles" we "play as a function of our positioning and the structure of the network."[3] These roles include

- **Isolates:** Individuals who are essentially "out of the loop" of grapevine communication.
- **Bridges:** People who are members of a department and serve as links between their department and others.
- **Liaisons:** Persons who link one department with another but are not members of either department.

Think about the various organizations of which you are a member. Are you in the grapevine loop? Are you a bridge? Isolate? Liaison?

Traffic, Speed, and Accuracy of Informal Network

Many messages travel along the grapevine and do so relatively quickly. That is, information moves more rapidly on the grapevine than it moves on the formal network.

The existence of the grapevine and its innate speed can pose some serious organizational problems. Rumors spread speedily and inaccurate incendiary news can move throughout a large organization in hours. Incorrect information is difficult to stall once it begins to travel on the informal networks. As the British politician James Gallagher once said, "A lie can be halfway around the world before the truth has its boots on."

Although the grapevine can and does distort information, the grapevine can be, and often is, a rapid conveyor of *accurate* information as well. Often this accurate grapevine information reaches its destination before the chugging formal network can relay the message. The obvious result is employee anger and organizational embarrassment. Organizational communicators are occasionally placed in positions where they have to deny the accuracy of information employees have received via the grapevine until such time as the formal networks, dawdling along at a glacierlike pace, can officially inform the receiver of the information. Because of the swiftness of the informal network, the relatively slow formal network, and the occasional denials issued until the formal network catches up with the grapevine, the credibility of the formal network and those who operate it can be damaged.

Resilience. It is important to remember that the grapevine is not only fast and often accurate but that it exists willy-nilly. No amount of plumbers units, directives from senior executives, or threats will stop the informal network from operating. As long as there are cocktail parties, racquetball courts, lunchroom cafeterias, water coolers, bathrooms, coffee machines, two chairs in an office, and sexual energy, there will be informal networks. Therefore, managers must try to manage the informal network and not attempt to eliminate it. The latter is only an exercise in frustration.

Management. Managing the informal network is difficult. The tendency is to try to eliminate the grapevine, because the grapevine is so troublesome. Its very existence makes it hard for employers to manage information. Management will occasionally issue directives in order to curtail or eliminate the informal network. Such attempts are likely to be futile. They will either not work or will not work for long. Grapevine communication is a reflection of natural human behavior.

Consider this memo that was distributed in a major international organization in an attempt to curb the grapevine.

TO: *Personnel Relations Directors*

FROM: *(a corporate Vice President)*

SUBJECT: *Employee Networks*

*There have been questions about how we feel about **employee networks** and how management should react to them. (emphasis added) The attached statement describes our corporate position on employee networks. Please share this with managements and staffs.*

Employee Networks

A network is made up of individuals who interact in a formal or informal structure for the purpose of self improvement, and the exchange of ideas and information intended to enhance their ability to successfully pursue their careers. The company realizes that networking and employee networks exist within [the company]. It is the company's desire to encourage self-improvement and the exchange of ideas and hence, there is an expectation that any such networking activities will make a positive contribution and not be negative. Of course, company management cannot overlook activities that violate company policies or are contrary to our business purposes or employ company resources or property for purposes other than [the company] business. . . .

This note contains a veiled threat. It suggests that some networking "activities that violate company policies or are contrary to businesses purposes" would not be "overlooked."

In some quarters this memorandum might have had the desired effect. In others, the memorandum may have had the opposite effect and may have fueled the proliferation of "employee networks" and the grapevine. I have this memorandum, in fact, because of the grapevine. A manager whom we'll call Doris received this "Employee Networks" memo. She read it and sent it to a high-ranking company official with a note attached. The note read:

"Anne:

What is this about?

Doris"

Anne received Doris's note and then sent the memorandum along to a colleague of hers who is an acquaintance of mine and knows of my interests in organizational communication. Anne also attached a note. It read,

"Richard,

Do you believe this? Send this to Alan.

Anne"

Richard, my acquaintance, then mailed the memorandum to me: the grapevine at work. Instead of stifling the employee networks, the attempt to curb the interactions was a catalyst to use the informal networks.

Although the grapevine—and the problems endemic to the grapevine—are realities, there are ways to deal with them.

Get Information Out. Rowan reports that it's essential to "get the facts and get them out fast."[4] Hellweg argues that management "needs to provide important information to employees openly, honestly, and quickly to reduce speculation."[5] Kreps writes that employees "have an insatiable appetite for meaning" and naturally will seek out information.[6] Pace and Faules make three specific recommendations for grapevine management:[7]

- Keep downward, horizontal, and upward networks open
- Maintain supportive supervisor–subordinate relationships
- Communicate awareness and acceptance of grapevine information

Use the Informal Network. As it pertains to the second and third bullet above, remember that the informal network is natural and inevitable.[8] One can, as indicated, curb its proliferation by using the formal network. However, some of the grapevine will, and even should, remain. Davis writes that the grapevine ". . .cannot be abolished, rubbed out, hidden under a basket, chopped down, tied up, or stopped. If [it is] suppressed in one place, it will pop up in another. . . .It is as hard to kill as the mythical glass snake which, when struck, broke itself into fragments and grew a new snake out of each piece."[9] He argues that management should acknowledge that it "accepts and understands the informal organization."[10]

Figure 6-2 Types of networks

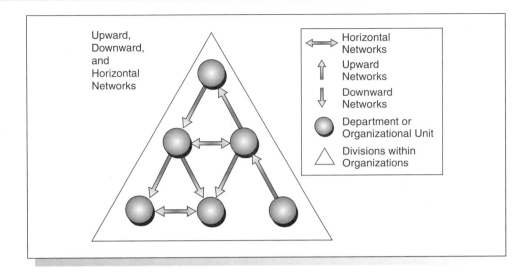

The informal networks will exist and do work. Use them. Complement the usage of the formal networks with the informal network. Concede that the grapevine exists, attempt to find out how it operates and, when appropriate, use the grapevine to communicate information.

UPWARD, DOWNWARD, AND HORIZONTAL NETWORKS

Messages in organizations, whether they are formal or informal, travel in one of three directions. Either the messages travel *upward* from subordinate to superior, *downward* from superior to subordinate, or *horizontal* between employees on the same level, as shown in Figure 6-2.

Upward Networks

Without question, the formal channels that are used the least are those that carry messages from subordinate to superior. Even when these networks exist, they often are spurious.[11] That is, often the upward communication routes appear to be an existing channel for subordinate-to-superior communication, but in reality the routes are not extant or are used infrequently.

Consider the following example. It took place within a federal agency and is a prime example of bogus upward networks.

One day, all the employees of a federal agency received the same letter. It was hand-delivered by their immediate supervisors. The letter indicated that a $50 reward would be offered to any employee who could present an idea to management that subsequently would be implemented by the organization.

A new employee received the letter and immediately began to contemplate a series of $50 checks being made out in his name. The employee could think of dozens of *organizational* problems and saw this as an opportunity to make some reward money and also to impress management. Almost immediately, he began scrawling down ideas that he intended to refine and later submit as recommendations for his reward.

A veteran of the agency watched this scenario unfold and while the newcomer feverishly scrawled, the old timer issued the following advice: "Make sure you put that idea on a soft piece of paper."

The newcomer was surprised, but continued writing. Again came the warning, "Make sure you put it on a soft piece of paper."

Again, the new employee paused only momentarily from the lists. Finally there was a third, "Make sure you put it on a soft piece of paper."

"Okay," said the rookie, "Why should I put it on a soft piece of paper?" "Cause that way," said the old timer, "it won't leave a scar when they throw it back in your face."

The beginner was momentarily stunned by this cynical advice. He began to ask around and discovered that the organization issued similar "calls for suggestions" on an annual basis. However, no one could identify a single employee who had ever received any monetary reward for any idea submitted. The grapevine information was that no one even read the suggestions. Requests for suggestions were issued to create an illusion of participatory decision making, but it was nothing short of a ruse.

Any such disingenuous attempt will not only retard the flow of information in the subordinate-to-superior network, it will also help demoralize the workforce.

An examination of upward networks requires an understanding of the

- Specific values of upward networks
- Problems related to creating genuine upward networks
- Ways to manage and implement the upward network

Values of Upward Networks. The upward networks are very important to the organization. If administered effectively these channels carry valuable information from subordinates to superiors. People on lower levels of the organization are often aware of problems that people on the top levels of the organization could not possibly be privy to. If a machine is malfunctioning on a certain level, it might take an unnecessarily long time for that malfunction to come to the attention of the appropriate manager, if not for a subordinate-to-superior network.

In addition, subordinate-to-superior networks provide a vehicle for obtaining feedback for messages that have been sent downward. When a superior sends a message to subordinates, that superior should want to get some reaction. Subordinate-to-superior communication networks facilitate the acquisition of this feedback.

Upward networks allow the employees to feel like they are valuable resources—as if they have "a piece of the rock" and their opinions matter. This opportunity, all other things being equal, is likely to improve morale.[12]

Employees may have suggestions that can be valuable for the organization. For example, McDonald's *Egg McMuffin, Filet O' Fish* sandwich, and *Big Mac* were all ideas that came from McDonald's franchisees.[13] It's almost difficult to imagine the fast food giant without these offerings, yet had top management been resistant to accept recommendations from subordinate levels, these sandwiches (and their clones) may never have been part of fast food menus.

Finally, subordinate-to-superior networks can be valuable because employees on different levels of the organization have specialized knowledge and expertise. It is in the best interest of the organization to allow this esoteric knowledge to be ventilat-

© 2002 THE NEW YORKER COLLECTION FROM CARTOONBANK.COM. ALL RIGHTS RESERVED.

"Mr. Smith's office doesn't have a door. You have to batter your way through the wall."

ed to upper management. Even the brightest manager is unlikely to know as much about a particular operation as that person who performs the operation daily. It is wise to solicit and tap the knowledge that is available from experienced and knowledgeable employees.

Problems With Upward Networks. Despite the value of upward communication networks, a common and valid complaint among employees is that there are not appropriate vehicles available to carry messages from subordinate to superior. Once again, upward communication networks are rarities and are often not authentic when they do exist. This is due more to human nature than to ignorance of the value of these networks.

People, no matter who they are and no matter how confident they might be, are reluctant to solicit rejection. When managers use the upward network, they invite criticism. Occasionally, that criticism will not be constructive. Sophomoric and destructive criticisms may surface only once in a great while, but they will still be painful regardless of their relative infrequency.

For example, department heads in many organizations are required to solicit evaluations from their subordinates. After reading many positive comments, these managers are still bothered when they read caustic negative comments. They would be less than human to react differently. After reading a particularly caustic evaluation it is unlikely that a manager will say philosophically, "Well this troubled employee represents a mere .05 percent of the subordinate population. I shall not concern myself with this silly and apparently bitter comment."

Likewise, if top management solicits feedback and encourages suggestions from subordinates, these managers will run into similar problems. Imagine a manager reviewing a number of subordinate comment cards:

Comment Card (1): There are not enough workstations for us over in Development. It is, it would seem, a minor investment to address this need and it would improve not only productivity, but morale as well.

The manager might react to this message by thinking, "I didn't realize there was a problem with inadequate work space. How come I wasn't aware of this? I'll check on the cost of getting more equipment and contact LaFlamme to see if this could be done. This idea of encouraging subordinate input is a good one." The manager continues to review the material.

Comment Card (2): We would appreciate more meaningful and frequent evaluative sessions. As it is, and I think I speak for many, we often don't know how top management is reacting to our work until it is too late. Also, the evaluations we do have seem to be meaningless formalities. Thank you.

Again the manager might think that the suggestion process is a good idea. The manager may decide not to do anything about the particular evaluation issue but may discuss the matter with others. At the very least, the manager has learned something that could, at some point, be important for the health of the organization. The manager picks up the third recommendation and reads:

Comment Card (3): You are the worst kind of manager. You run this place like some kind of Napoleonic tyrant. I want you to know that I hate coming to work each and every day because of you. You think you're a class act, but I assure you that there is nothing and no one that I disrespect more. Thanks for making my life miserable.[14]

Even though this comment might be the only one of its kind, it may be difficult for the manager to continue to think of soliciting subordinate recommendations as a good idea. In fact, the manager may want to know who wrote the "suggestion" and attempt some type of retribution. The manager might disregard the legitimacy of the other suggestions because of this caustic one, or may try to purge the negative comment card from the others, fearing that it could besmirch the manager's status if someone else were to come across it.

A simple reason for the underutilization of upward communication networks is that few people like to hear bad things. There is a basic self-defense mechanism that operates, and there is the concomitant feeling of, "If they knew what I know, they'd be where I am."

Earthquake Prediction Business. Another problem with upward networks relates to what Dr. Wernher von Braun referred to as the *earthquake prediction business*.[15] When von Braun was the director of NASA's Marshall Space Flight Center, he commented that senior people at the center were in the "earthquake prediction business" in that they needed to "put out sensors" to detect tremors that would reflect upcoming "earthquakes" (i.e., potential disasters). The problem, von Braun suggested, is that when one is in the earthquake prediction business one is likely to hear of many potential "earthquakes." Some people "are too sensitive; they overact. Someone else might underestimate. . . .Others make a lot of noise just to get the mule's attention."[16]

A problem with upward networks is that a great deal of information can travel on a well-cultivated and receptive upward network. Managers have to address all these messages in a timely manner. Sometimes the information will be valuable. Administrators do need, and should want, to hear about impending earthquakes. But the challenge of knowing which messages are important to consider can be daunting—so daunting and exhausting that a manager might not attend to the messages that come up from the upward network.

Feynman's Theory and Upward Networks. The late physicist Richard Feynman was a member of the Roger's Commission that studied the 1986 Space Shuttle

IS THERE ANYTHING UNETHICAL ABOUT DELIBERATELY DISCOURAGING UPWARDLY SENT MESSAGES?

Assume that for several years you've run a summer soccer camp for grade schoolers. Further assume that several high school players serve as counselors at your camp and that the soccer camp is funded by the local school district.

Each year you need to make a presentation to the school board explaining why you should receive money for the program. In your presentation you are required to list the benefits that campers who enroll will derive from the activity of participating in the program.

You prepare for your presentation and do intend to list the various benefits to the campers. However, in your heart of hearts you suspect that these skills are *unlikely* to be realized. Given the numbers of campers that you need to run the program, the time allotted, your prior experience running similar camps, and the low athletic skills of many of the prospective campers, you actually feel that it would be a miracle if all of the kids would derive the benefits that you plan to list in your presentation.

Are you likely to give a "dry run" of your presentation to the high school athletes who serve as counselors? Are you likely to discourage the counselors from telling you, before you make the claims to the board, that the list of outcomes for the camp is unrealistic?

Challenger disaster. Feynman is most famous for his work as a Harvard Physics professor. He also wrote some best selling nonacademic books including *Surely You're Joking, Mr. Feynman* and *What Do You Care What Other People Think?*[17]

In a *Physics Today* article Feynman recounted his experience working on the Roger's Commission and discussed some perspectives he had regarding upward communication. Feynman observed that subordinates often had valuable information that had not been communicated to managers. In one instance he attributed this lack of upward communication to the fact that workers had poor written communication skills:

> They had a lot of information, but no way to communicate it. The workmen knew a lot. They had noticed all kinds of problems and had all kinds of ideas on how to fix them, but no one had paid much attention to them. The reason was: Any observations had to be reported in writing, and a lot of these guys didn't know how to write good memos.[18]

In another instance Feynman documented that the engineers at the Marshall Space Flight Center and the managers at the center were not "on the same page." He asked three engineers to write down the chances of flight failure on the basis of *engine* failure. He also asked a manager to approximate the chances of failure. The engineers all predicted a rate of about 1 in 200. The manager predicted 1 in 100,000![19]

This glaring inconsistency flabbergasted Feynman and the engineers.[20] Feynman advanced a theory of organizational communication in an attempt to explain how it was possible that the managers could be so out of touch with the engineers. He conjectured that what happens in organizations is that, at times, managers feel compelled

Figure 6-3 Types of upward networks

☐ Opinion surveys
☐ Question and answer sessions
☐ Suggestion programs
☐ Electronic or telephone systems (see sample below)
☐ Advisory boards
☐ Ombudsman—the organization has a representative whose job it is to seek out employee attitudes and convey them to management
☐ Skip Level Interviews—Senior management meets with employees who are levels below them.[22]

to exaggerate the capabilities of the units they manage. He argued that in order to ensure that resources continue to flow into a department, managers feel as if they must highlight the accomplishments of the department and downplay the problems. Managers might, therefore, claim that their units can do various things that they may not be able to do in order to guarantee that the unit will continue to be funded.

What happens in these instances—according to his theory—is that upward communication gets "clogged." Employees who are aware of information that would refute the exaggerated claims of managers are discouraged from communicating this information. If managers were to receive this information they would be unable to continue to exaggerate the accomplishments of the department. In other words, Feynman contends that managers *don't want to know* certain types of information and actually discourage it from coming up the line:

> I believe that what happened was. . .that although the engineers down in the works knew NASA's claims were impossible, and the guys at the top knew that somehow they had exaggerated, the guys at the top didn't want to *hear* that they had exaggerated. . . .It's better if they don't hear it, so they can be much more "honest" when they're trying to get Congress to Okay their projects.[21]

What do you think of Feynman's theory? Have you ever been in a leadership position when you "didn't want to know" certain information?

Suggestion Systems. Despite the problems, subordinate-to-superior networks are extremely important for organizational health. However difficult, they must be dealt with to improve the functioning of the organization.

If the upward networks are suggestion systems of any sort the network should meet four specific criteria. The program should have:

1. Support from top management
2. A program administrator who has this responsibility as a primary or sole job responsibility
3. Efficiently communicated instructions regarding the procedures, rules, and rewards
4. Timely and meaningful feedback for all those who participate in the program.

Sample of an upward network

A major health care provider uses the following voice mail system to facilitate the generation of upwardly directed communications.

Step 1. Employees call a specific number in the voice mail system. This number is advertised in the internal newsletter and can be found inside most formal publications disseminated by the organization.

Step 2. Employees who make the call hear a recorded message from the President of the company:

> This is Gwen Osterbrook, chairman of. . . .Thank you for your call. Your call is very important to us. Please leave us a message with your name and phone number if you wish to receive a return call. We will address your concerns and return your call within 48 hours. Thank you again.

Step 3. At the end of each day an assigned employee retrieves each of these messages. In order to do this, he or she follows a specific accessing procedure that requires the use of a confidential, and regularly changed, password.

Step 4. The assigned employee listens to, saves, and forwards the messages. The employee completes a form to record each and every suggestion. Then, depending on the nature of the suggestion she or he forwards the suggestion to the relevant department. In addition, all messages are concurrently sent to the CEO Osterbrook. The messages are sent out with an introduction. For example,

> Hello, this is Ann Williams forwarding a message to you that we received today November 6, 2001 on the Employee Communication hotline. This message concerns Jim Rogers who did not receive a pay check last week. This message is also being forwarded to Marty Peters, in HR, and Wendell O'Malley, Rogers's immediate supervisor. As you know the company policy is to respond to our employees who use the hotline within 48 hours. Thank you very much. If you have any questions, please call me, Ann Williams, title, at. . .

Step 5. The relevant department responds to the employee and concurrently communicates to Ann Williams explaining the nature of the follow-up.

Step 6. All hotline calls and responses are recorded on an Excel spreadsheet including

- ☐ Name of the caller
- ☐ Location within company
- ☐ Contact information of caller
- ☐ Nature of the problem
- ☐ To whom the problem was forwarded
- ☐ Problem resolution

Downward Networks

The downward networks are the channels that are most likely to be formalized. They carry a great deal of the official superior-to-subordinate information. Formal downward networks travel relatively slowly.

It is important to emphasize that downward networks should not be "one-way streets." Messages sent along the downward networks are only valuable if they reach their destinations. If conceived and perceived as one-way streets, downward networks are not likely to encourage feedback. Without some form of feedback, senders will not know if information they sent was received or how it was received. Certainly, information has to travel downward for all the reasons we identified in Chapter 5, but what is the value of the voyage if the information winds up in a cul de sac and the source is unaware? Therefore, downward networks should be utilized in conjunction with upward networks.

In addition, the effective utilization of downward networks requires an understanding of the organizational communication phenomenon known as serial distortion.

Serial Transmissions and Serial Distortion.

> I work for a large paint company. At one point the organization advertised an incentive plan for employees. The plan called for monetary rewards to those who sold the most paint and paint accessories. In addition to salary increments, prizes like television sets and stereos would be distributed to employees who were successful at selling.
>
> Although this promotion had the potential to be a big success, it was not, due to the fact that the information never reached the employees. My manager had received a newsletter explaining the incentive program but had failed to relay the information to the salespeople or post the newsletter in a public area where it could be read by employees.

Messages traveling on downward networks in organizations are frequently transmitted serially. That is, often there are intermediary stopping points between the original source of the message and the desired receiver of the message. Serial transmissions can and do occur on other networks as well.

Consider the diagram below:

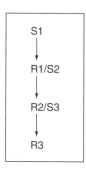

A message might emanate from a CEO (S1) intended for all employees (R3). The message might be orally diffused at a meeting of the CEO and all organizational Vice Presidents (R1/S2). The appropriate Vice President might phone the department heads (R2/S3) and ask the department heads to relay the information to the employees (R3). The department head might write a memorandum to be distributed to all employees. See Figure 6-4.

Such serial transmission can result in serial distortions that go beyond those that occur when children engage in the game *Telephone*. Some distortions may, as is the case in the Telephone game, be caused simply because of the frequency of encoding and decoding. However, some distortions occur due to reasons that are related to organizations and the relationships that develop within organizations.

There are four categories of serial distortions: (1) adding, (2) leveling, (3) sharpening, and (4) assimilating.

Figure 6-4 Serial transmission

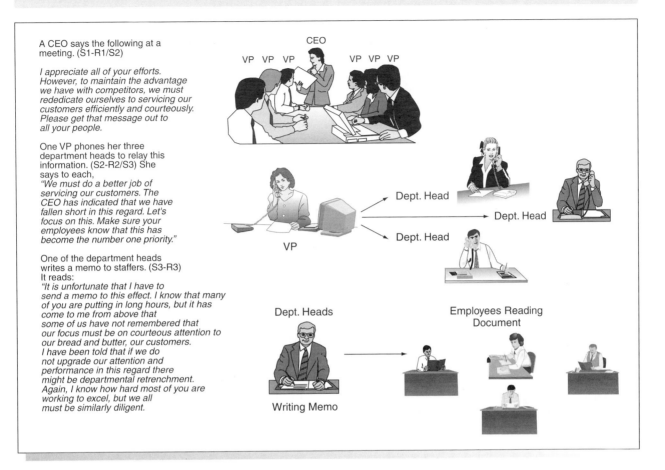

A CEO says the following at a meeting. (S1-R1/S2)

I appreciate all of your efforts. However, to maintain the advantage we have with competitors, we must rededicate ourselves to servicing our customers efficiently and courteously. Please get that message out to all your people.

One VP phones her three department heads to relay this information. (S2-R2/S3) She says to each,

"We must do a better job of servicing our customers. The CEO has indicated that we have fallen short in this regard. Let's focus on this. Make sure your employees know that this has become the number one priority."

One of the department heads writes a memo to staffers. (S3-R3) It reads:

"It is unfortunate that I have to send a memo to this effect. I know that many of you are putting in long hours, but it has come to me from above that some of us have not remembered that our focus must be on courteous attention to our bread and butter, our customers. I have been told that if we do not upgrade our attention and performance in this regard there might be departmental retrenchment. Again, I know how hard most of you are working to excel, but we all must be similarly diligent.

CEO
VP VP VP VP VP VP
VP
Dept. Head
Dept. Head
Dept. Head
Dept. Heads
Writing Memo
Employees Reading Document

Adding. Adding takes place when an intermediary adds onto the original information. Some people are more verbose than others and speak or write more elaborately than others. This may seem relatively harmless, but the result of adding can be serial distortion. "Tell Angela we appreciate her efforts," changes meaning when an intermediary writes a lengthy message congratulating Angela on work well done and intimates in the mailing that there might be a monetary reward forthcoming.

Leveling. Leveling is the opposite of adding. In leveling, the intermediary abridges the message. Just as some intermediaries are verbose, others are reserved and therefore shorten messages because it is not their style to speak or write a great deal. Sometimes messages are leveled not because of speaking tendencies, but because there are strained relationships between the intermediary and a receiver.

Sharpening. Sharpening refers to distortions that occur when intermediaries make information they're relaying more sensational than the news needs to be. For illustration assume that Richard Duncan, a middle manager, receives a phone call from his supervisor, Jane McCoy. McCoy tells Duncan that two workers will have to be temporarily laid off due to some budget cuts. McCoy gives Duncan the names of the two employees who will be laid off and asks that Duncan take care of the matter immediately. Duncan calls a meeting of his employees and somberly informs the group that two people will have to be temporarily laid off. Duncan, concludes his speech with the following, "Right now it's only two. Who knows what's going to be? Times are tough. This could be the start of something major. I get that feeling." In this illustration, the message has been sharpened.

Assimilating. Messages are assimilated when the intermediary alters the message to make it more palatable to the person who is to be the recipient of the message. This is a very common kind of serial distortion. Few people like to convey devastating news to individuals. Some may want to startle groups, but it is not enjoyable to have to tell a friend or even an acquaintance that a superior is furious with performance or that one's employment is terminated. If one is told to relay such negative messages to individuals, it is not unlikely that the intermediary will attempt to make the message more palatable to the receiver. For example, consider the following message traveling on a downward network.

> Tell Schober that in a service industry we cannot tolerate mistakes like the one he made last week. Our customer base must remain strong and that kind of error, however unintentional, can dilute that strength. Frankly, I would be inclined to terminate him immediately given the magnitude of the transgression. However, I am willing to give him another opportunity to prove his worth to our organization. Make sure you impress upon him how close he is to termination. Are we clear?

If assimilated, the message may be conveyed in this way,

> The boss was unhappy about last week. She was upset, but you know how they all are upstairs. She'll get over it, trust me. I know your worth. However, I wanted you to know that she registered some concern when we last met. Let's just be more careful next time.

As we discussed in Chapter 3, any interaction between a single source and a single receiver is subject to communication noise and message distortion. The serial nature of communication on downward networks creates additional noise and the chances for serial distortion. It is not possible to eliminate all intermediaries when communicating information downward in organizations. However, it is the responsibility of organizational men and women to be aware of the potential for serial distortion and be careful and vigilant as they relay information.

Horizontal Networks

Horizontal networks transport information along the same strata in an organization. Katz and Kahn in *The Social Psychology of Organizations* comment that "Organizations face one of their most difficult problems in procedures and practices concerning lateral communication."[23] Formal horizontal networks are rarities, particularly at the lower levels of the hierarchy. Top managers may meet periodically to discuss the nature of each manager's division. At the lower levels, however, employees are unlikely to have many formal horizontal contacts. There tends to be what is referred to as a "silo mentality" in organizations. This means that units within organizations perceive themselves as discrete entities that perform independently. As we discovered when we discussed systems theory, such a silo mentality is counterproductive since departments in organizations are inherently *interdependent* and not independent. See Figure 6-5.

Organizational Penetration and Horizontal Networks. Tompkins discusses the value of "consciously-created redundancy of communication channels."[24] He strongly supports the idea that a systems orientation requires horizontal networks linking departments to ensure that relevant messages get from one unit of an

Figure 6-5

A silo mentality is counterproductive since departments in organizations are inherently *interdependent* and not independent.

organization to another. He extends horizontal networking to include what he refers to as "organizational penetration." Tompkins contends that if an organization hires external contractors it is the responsibility of the organization to "penetrate" the contractors so that the external unit becomes, temporarily, like a unit of the organization. As a temporary unit of the organization, horizontal networks need to be created to facilitate interdepartmental communication and reduce the deleterious effects of silo mentalities.

The aforementioned Feynman conducted an experiment while on the Roger's Commission that reflects problems that can occur when there is neither penetration nor horizontal networks. Feynman dipped a "model of the [Space Shuttle Challenger] field joint complete with the inserted O-ring" into some ice water and demonstrated conclusively that the O-rings on the Challenger were not resilient enough to withstand freezing temperatures.[25] The contractor, Morton Thiokol, was aware that the O-rings were not resilient below certain temperatures. However, when Thiokol recommended delaying the Challenger launch, the Marshall representatives were unwilling to accept the recommendations from Thiokol. Eventually, Thiokol relented. Had the MSFC established horizontal networks and, in fact, penetrated Thiokol, they would have known to the same extent as the Thiokol representatives knew— just as Feynman demonstrated that any casual observer would have known—that the O-rings were not resilient under the launch conditions. Yet effective horizontal networks had not been established, penetration had not occurred, and a disaster was a result.

Similarly if units within the same organization do not establish horizontal linkages, important information that must be shared will not be shared. It's unlikely that there will be an explosion as spectacular as that which shattered the Challenger and NASA, but an organization could be devastated nonetheless.

The importance of communication networks for organizational effectiveness can not be overstated. The problems associated with inadequate networks are exacerbated because management often views communication parochially and as a back-burner issue.

What may be the most powerful argument in support for the conscious development and nurturing of communication networks is this: Fourteen years after the Roger's Commission and Richard Feynman described the communication problem at NASA, seven years after Tompkins wrote about the significance of horizontal and upward networks specifically at the MSFC, two panels concluded that NASA's 1999 Mars Polar Lander failure was a function of poor interdepartmental communication. As the *New York Times* reported,

> The reports issued today found failures in communication between project officials and managers at the Jet Propulsion Laboratory, which oversees interplanetary missions, as well as between these managers and Lockheed Martin.[26]

Thomas Young who chaired the team reviewing the agency commented, "People were trying to do too much with too little and not adequately conveying their concerns to others, particularly upper management. . . .No one had a sense of how much trouble they were actually in."[27]

PRACTITIONER'S PERSPECTIVE

Bob Greim, Pressroom Superintendent

Bob Greim manages the printing production end for the Boston Herald. *The* Herald *is a daily newspaper with a circulation of 263,000. It competes directly with the* Boston Globe *for readership. Mr. Greim supervises seven foremen and 70 to 80 other print production employees. His unit prints and, literally, produces the newspaper that is subsequently delivered to the doorstep of subscribers and to the newsstands. Mr. Greim reports to the vice president of production.*

A newspaper is on a daily cycle. It's not like other industries where a project can take a month or three months or years. Our projects are a day long, and there is a very tangible outcome, the newspaper. Every 24 hours we must communicate with other departments, or else the product for that day—or the next day—will suffer. Other organizations have to share information too, I know, but here because of time issues. The importance of communicating well is magnified.

I need information from my subordinates. I work in the day. The production people work at night. When I arrive in the morning, I must receive reports from my night foremen that are detailed and clear. Otherwise I cannot function nor can I respond to questions my superiors might have about the pressroom operation. I attend a daily meeting at 11 A.M. with other superintendents. If I am not adequately informed about nighttime activity and problems, I may not be able to participate intelligently at these sessions. I've been promoted internally here so I know that night workers typically go to sleep when their shift is over. Unless it's an absolute emergency I do not want to be phoning night employees for clarification until one or two in the afternoon. In an emergency I'd have to wake some folks up, but I want to be considerate. By not calling, I'm sending a message of sorts. I would be communicating a message beyond my questions if I were to regularly wake these people up in the middle of their nights.

Therefore, one of the key criteria for me in selecting my foremen is making sure I can count on them to communicate clearly and provide sufficiently detailed information. The other superintendents who attend the 11 A.M. meeting would say the same thing: They need information or they can't intelligently discuss the next day's paper at 11 A.M. Also I leave reports for the foremen when I depart. I have to trust that they will read what I've written and will understand how to do what needs to be done.

Sometimes the discussion at 11 A.M. is irrelevant to my work, but there is still a value to the sessions. It helps me "feel their pain" if you know what I mean. I can understand what is going on in other units. Sometimes we, or at least I, get so caught up in my own department's responsibilities and problems that I don't think about the other parts of the paper. Each unit has its own issues and it's good for us to become sensitive to each other's needs in order to work cooperatively. Some people engage in finger pointing when there's been a glitch, but for the most part we realize that we're in this together. As I said previously, the paper comes out every day, so every day we have to combine Editorial, Circulation, Advertising, and Printing concerns. We have had some real success at the *Herald* and I'd like to think it's due, in part, to interacting well—up, down, and across.

A Toolbox

1. Communication networks are the channels that provide "highways" for information travel.
2. Organizations must create, cultivate, and nourish these networks.
3. The following networks are necessary for effective organizational communication.
   - upward, downward, and horizontal networks
   - formal and informal networks
   - internal and external networks
4. Vigilance in terms of maintaining these networks is as essential as vigilance in terms of maintaining the quality of motor highways. Without navigable routes, messages cannot be communicated inter- or intradepartmentally. The result of poor networking can be organizational chaos and disaster.

1. What is the distinction between formal and informal networks?
2. Does Feynman's theory of organizational communication apply to any organization with which you are familiar?
3. Identify three problems with establishing genuine upward networks in an organization.
4. How does serial transmission affect the quality of messages that travel along downward networks?
5. Why would systems theorists consider horizontal networks essential?
6. Why would human relations theorists consider upward networks essential and informal networks inevitable?
7. Why would classical theorists consider downward networks essential?
8. Analyze the case that appears below. Please respond to the five-part question that follows the case.

Case 6.2 — Austin O'Brien and the Multiple Testing Sites

Austin O'Brien works in Wilmington, Delaware, at the central location for a company that has several facilities around the world. The company conducts tests on products and has at least one testing facility in Africa, Asia, Europe, Australia, Ireland, and South America. There are multiple sites in the United States. Each production facility has a plant manager who has tremendous autonomy in part due to the distant and localized nature of the individual operations, and in part because of the history and culture of the company. This autonomy has its advantages, but it also creates problems.

At present there is no assurance that new testing policies conceived at Central and, allegedly, communicated to the satellite facilities are being enforced by individual managers. One of the problems is that the policies created in Wilmington were derived with very little input from the satellite plant managers. Since the plant manager can, and has, operated the way she or he is accustomed, Central feels as if it has lost control. Central is very concerned about maintaining quality standards.

They cannot be certain that the way products should be tested are, in fact, the way products are being tested. Austin O'Brien's job is to make sure the channels of communication are such that

1. Information gets to the local plant managers.
2. Information gets from the local plant managers to the employees at the local plants.
3. Central receives communications indicating that policies are, in fact, being adhered to.
4. Customers have an opportunity to express satisfaction or dissatisfaction to both central and the local operations.
5. Employees at the local plants have access to Central to describe their reaction to the new policies.

How can Austin O'Brien accomplish these five goals?

ENDNOTES

[1] Quote attributed to Paul Strassmann in Richman, Tom, "Face to Face: Information Strategist Paul Strassman," *INC.*, March 1988, p. 40.

[2] Keith Davis's groundbreaking article was "Management Communication and the Grapevine," *Harvard Business Review*, September–October 1953, pp. 43–49.

[3] Hellweg, Susan, "Formal and Informal Communication Networks" in Byers, Peggy, *Organizational Communication: Theory and Behavior*, 1997: p. 43.

[4] Roy Rowan in "Where Did That Rumor Come From?" *Fortune*, August 13, 1979, p. 130.

[5] Op. cit., Hellweg, p. 51.

[6] Kreps, Gary, *Organizational Communication*, Longman, 1990: p. 208.

[7] Pace, R. Wayne and Don Faules, *Organizational Communication*, Prentice Hall, 1989, p. 116.

[8] Davis, Keith, "Management Communication and the Grapevine" *Harvard Business Review*, p. 43.

[9] Davis, Keith, *Human Behavior at Work*, New York, 1972: p. 263.

[10] Ibid., p. 271.

[11] Daniels, Tom and Barry Spiker, *Perspectives on Organizational Communication*, William C. Brown, 1997: p. 98.

[12] Beslin, Ralph, "Developing and Using Employee Feedback Mechanisms," Paper presented at IABC meetings, New Orleans, Louisiana, June 1998.

[13] Love, John, *McDonald's Behind the Arches*, Bantam, 1986, photo caption p. 149a. The franchisees were Herb Peterson (Egg McMuffin), Lou Groen (Filet o' Fish), and Jim Delligatti (Big Mac).

[14] With minor editing, this is a precise message received by a senior manager via an upward network system.

[15] Tompkins, Philip, *Organizational Communication Imperatives*, Roxbury Publishing Company, 1993: p. 58.

[16] Ibid.

[17]Richard Feynman as told to Ralph Leighton, *What Do You Care What Other People Think?* Norton, 1988; Richard Feynman as told to Ralph Leighton, *Surely You're Joking, Mr. Feynman.* Norton, 1985.

[18]Feynman, Richard, "An Outsider's Inside View of the Challenger Inquiry," *Physics Today,* February 1988, p. 33.

[19]Ibid., p. 34.

[20]Tompkins, p. 149.

[21]Op. cit., Feynman "An Outsider's Inside View. . .," p. 37.

[22]Adapted from Allen Kraut and Frank Freeman, *Upward Communication in American Industry,* NC. Center for Creative Leadership, 1992. The authors included these items on a list of networks that (a) were used as indicated by the literature or their experience with the network (b) were formal (c) could be used or not used by employees.

[23]Katz, Daniel and Robert Kahn, *The Social Psychology of Organizations,* New York, Wiley, 1978: p. 444.

[24]Op. cit., Tompkins, *Organizational Communication Imperatives,* p. 211.

[25]Ibid., p. 142.

[26]Leary, Warren, "Poor Management by NASA Is Blamed for Mars Failure," *The New York Times,* March 29, 2000, p. A-22.

[27]Ibid., p. A-1.

7

Communication Climate and Organizational Culture

Information and communication [in organizations] . . . are surface manifestations of complex configurations of deeply felt beliefs, values, and attitudes.[1]

—Andrew Brown and Ken Starkey in *The Journal of Management Studies*

Taken together climate and culture have everything to do with what it is like within an organization.[2]

—Julie Hay in *Transactional Analysis Journal*

The trouble with these guys is that after you've been with them for a couple of weeks you start to play like them.

—Baseball player Sid Gordon after having been traded
to the hapless 1951 Pittsburgh Pirates

© GETTY IMAGES/PHOTODISC

Case 7.1—*The Elan Corporation*

Background

n the summer of 2001, an economic recession was looming over the international manufacturing community. The Elan Corporation was not immune to the effects of the recession. Elan was faced with the prospects of downsizing and restructuring in order to cut costs and maintain its position as a globally competitive organization. Elan's communications regarding the restructuring affected (a) the credibility of management, (b) subsequent communication of task, maintenance, and human messages, (c) the quality of upward and horizontal communication networks within Elan; and even (d) employee willingness to exercise their communication skill sets during meetings. What had been an atmosphere characterized by shared values and open communication eroded into an atmosphere that was characterized by distrust, adversarial relationships, and poor organizational communication.

The VSP and QBS

The initial step in Elan's downsizing involved implementing a Voluntary Separation Program referred to as VSP. The program was announced in August 2001 and allowed employees to voluntarily leave the company in exchange for an attractive severance package. Management's (unannounced) goal was to eliminate 200 positions before December 3, 2001.

On October 20, 2001, nearly 2 months after the announcement of the VSP, the Elan Corporation announced that there would be a second downsizing plan. This one would not be voluntary. It was called the Quality Based Selection Program or QBS for short. The QBS program essentially required all employees to reapply for their own jobs or lower-level jobs. On the basis of the quality of their candidacies, the employees would either be retained or let go.

There was an important piece of information that was not communicated to employees when the QBS program was announced. *Employees were not informed that any QBS-related cuts would only take effect if, by December 3, the VSP program had not yielded the desired 200 resignations.* The employees assumed that the QBS cuts would be in addition to any downsizing that resulted from VSP.

It was the hope of management that the QBS announcement would serve as a stimulus for VSP participation. Each supervisor provided employees with information about the QBS in one-on-one face-to-face discussions. Each employee had to decide whether to participate in the QBS or opt for the VSP.

Management's hopes were realized. The QBS turned out to be a powerful means for encouraging employees to retire voluntarily before they might be required to leave involuntarily. Employees, apparently, did not relish the idea of being reevaluated for their current or subordinate positions. The QBS was so successful that on November 16, the Elan Corporation happily announced in a mass e-mailing that the QBS program would be put on "hold." Two hundred persons had already opted for the VSP.

However, many of those persons had opted for VSP because they had assumed that QBS was inevitable. Many of those who had not opted for VSP had already gone through the time-consuming and the emotionally wrenching activity of completing forms and applying for their own or subordinate jobs because of the QBS. Employees were angry that managers had not explained during their one-on-one sessions that the QBS would only be implemented if the VSP failed. Many managers claimed that they were not aware that QBS could be cancelled. Employees, by and large, found this defense not to be credible.

Ramifications

While the desired downsizing had been accomplished, the QBS and VSP programs had dramatic effects on the climate at Elan.

☐ *The credibility of upper management was questioned.*

☐ *The shared values such as mutual trust and respect that had been characteristic at Elan were no longer part of the fabric of the organization.*

☐ *Production activities were paralyzed from the time QBS was announced until the time QBS was put on hold. Afterwards, production activities did not resume to their prior VSP and QBS levels because of employee resentment.*

☐ *Most employees who had been with the company more than 10 years expressed feelings of abandonment, betrayal, and rejection even after the downsizing was completed and their jobs had been saved.*

☐ *Discussions between employees and supervisors led management to believe that QBS was actually a failure since the program had persuaded some of the better performers to opt for the VSP program.*

☐ *The absence of trust made subsequent communications between management and employees very strained and resulted in noncooperative and even adversarial relationships.*

☐ *Overall VSP and QBS resulted in a loss in respect for top management, poor morale, loss of productivity, and negative behaviors of employees.*

1. *Should Elan have communicated that the QBS program would only be implemented if the VSP program had failed?*
2. *Did the communications regarding the VSP and QBS create a poor working atmosphere, or would that atmosphere have been negative regardless of how these programs were communicated?*
3. *If you were the head of Elan, what three different steps would you have taken to reduce the effects of what happened to employee morale as a result of the VSP/QBS programs?*

4. Can the post-QBS climate at Elan affect

☐   Communication of task, maintenance, and human messages?
☐   The quality of upward and horizontal networks?
☐   The desire of employees to exercise their communication skill sets at meetings, during interpersonal exchanges, or when composing written documents?

5. How might the Elan organization recreate a positive communication climate in the wake of VSP and QBS?

ABSTRACT

The quality of communication in organizations depends on many factors. The communication climate may be the single most important one of these factors. Employee reading, writing, speaking, and listening skills are imperatives for effective organizational communication. However, will employees exercise the skills they have if they are led by tyrannical or noncredible supervisors? Horizontal networks are essential for interdepartmental interaction, but will employees use these networks if there is tension and distrust between departments? Ethical decisions are crucial for effective organizational communication. Will ethical factors be considered in a corporate culture that supports the credo: "Just close the sale; just get it done"?

Climate and organizational culture are related topics that affect communication in organizations. In this chapter we examine climate and culture in detail.

OBJECTIVES

When you have completed this chapter, you should be able to:

☐   Define and describe the phrase *organizational climate.*
☐   Identify the components of Redding's *ideal supportive climate.*
☐   Define and describe the phrase *organizational culture.*
☐   Explain the relationship between climate, culture, and organizational communication.
☐   Discuss the problems related to developing a supportive communication climate.
☐   Describe how persons can work toward improving the climate for communication in an organization.

ORGANIZATIONAL CLIMATE

In Chapter 1 you were introduced to W. Charles Redding, the late Purdue professor who was a pioneer in the field of organizational communication. In one of his books, *Communication Within the Organization,* Redding made the following comment about organizations, communication, and the organizational climate.

The "climate" of the organization is more crucial than are communication skills or techniques (taken by themselves) in creating an effective organization.[3]

Redding is, of course, correct. More important than individual employees' communication skills is the environment within which individual employees interact. If an organization employs 500 people and all of these employees have excellent communication skills—that is, they can speak, write, and listen well—it will matter little if the workplace has an unpleasant atmosphere that discourages interaction.

All but the charmed reader can recall jobs where a negative organizational climate damaged internal communication. Perhaps it was some ornery supervisor, belligerent co-worker, or defiant subordinate that contributed to the problem. Perhaps it was simply a system or culture that cultivated defensiveness. Whatever it was, your eloquence or willingness to listen meant very little. The defensive climate undermined your potential and the organization's potential.

Make no mistake about it. Do not delude yourself into thinking otherwise. The organizational climate is the single most important variable in determining the quality of organizational communication. Cultivating and/or maintaining a supportive climate is the essential initial step for any manager who is interested in organizational communication effectiveness. No expensive seminar on conference communication, no series of lectures on listening skills, and no external training consultant to improve presentations will be valuable unless the organization maintains a supportive climate.

What Is Organizational Climate?

Taguiri defines climate as the "relatively enduring quality of the internal environment of [the] organization that (a) is experienced by its members, (b) influences their [the members'] behavior, and (c) can be described in terms of the values of a particular set of characteristics (or attributes) of the environment."[4] Kreps writes that the climate "is the internal emotional tone of the organization based on how comfortable organizational members feel with one another and with the organization."[5]

Many authors use, appropriately, a weather metaphor when describing the organizational climate. They argue that "nasty," "cold" conditions retard organizational communication and "warm," "sunny," conditions are conducive to interaction.[6] The weather metaphor was used illustratively by Guion when he compared the organizational climate to the "wind chill index." Just as the wind chill index is a function of two objective conditions: temperature and wind velocity, the organizational climate is a function of two objective conditions: the actual conditions in the organization and the perceptions employees have of these conditions.[7]

In essence, the climate is the atmosphere in the organization that either encourages or discourages communication. A supportive climate is likely to encourage interaction and the flow of information. A defensive climate is likely to retard the flow of information.

Gibb identified dimensions of supportive and defensive climates. He characterized defensive climates as

- Evaluative (e.g., blaming, destructively criticizing)
- Manipulative
- Indifferent to personal needs of others
- Superior (condescending)

© GETTY IMAGES/PHOTODISC

A genuinely supportive climate can facilitate effective communication in organizations.

- Certain (Gibb used "certainty" in the sense of intransigence and dogmatism. He wrote, "Those who seem to know the answers, to require no additional data, and to regard themselves as teachers as opposed to co-workers put others on guard." The *certain* individual needs to be right and wants to win more than solve a problem correctly.)

Supportive climates were characterized as

- Nonjudgmental
- Spontaneous (in the sense of being devoid of deception and manipulation)
- Egalitarian (in the sense of considering others as equals and respecting others, thereby not being condescending.)
- Concerned and empathic
- Provisional (in the sense of not being dogmatic or *certain*)[8]

How would you describe the organizations to which you belong? Are they characterized by defensive or supportive climates?

The Ideal Supportive Climate

In an attempt to describe the conditions necessary for effective organizational communication, Redding constructed a list of elements that he deemed necessary for what he called "the ideal supportive climate."[9] These five elements are described as follows.

1. **Supportiveness.** Condescension, destructive criticism, and inconsideration of others are deleterious to the climate of an organization. Therefore, the ideal supportive climate is characterized by respect and constructive evaluation. We've previously discussed *human messages* and the theoretical foundations for relaying *human messages*. Redding's point is that human messages are essential for the ideal supportive climate. This does not mean that administrators should march around passing out lollipops while disingenuously stroking employees. It means that managers must acknowledge the human needs of employees and, without artifice, communicate messages that reflect this awareness.

2. **Credibility, Confidence, and Trust.** Employees need to have the confidence and trust in their superiors so that they may approach these managers in order to explain problems, concerns, or make suggestions. Credibility—as we will discuss in more detail later—is a significant feature of the supportive climate.

3. **Openness.** Openness in this context means both relaying information openly and being open to approach from employees.

4. **Participatory Decision Making.** Redding argued that when employees are able to meaningfully contribute to the decision-making process, the climate tends to be more supportive. This does not mean that management must relinquish decision-making powers. The idea is to, legitimately, include employees and, genuinely, consider their contributions. As we discussed in Chapter 6, employee involvement has several benefits related to organizational efficiency and organizational communication. One benefit is that such involvement tends to improve the organizational climate.

5. **Emphasis on High Performance Goals.** Some may believe that a relaxed environment is conducive to a supportive climate. Relaxed environments may work, but an organization must emphasize that the company exists in order to achieve and excel. Otherwise the climate will not be as supportive as it can be. Employees might initially be pleased if a manager were to say, "Look, I don't care what you do, as long as you don't make waves and I don't get in trouble." However, as suggested by the Hawthorne Studies and human relations theory, given the right conditions most people actually want to accomplish something meaningful with their work hours. Therefore, an attitude of "we will accept nothing but excellence" will resonate with workers assuming all other factors for a supportive climate are in place.

An easy acronym can be used to help remember the ingredients of Redding's *ideal supportive climate*. By taking the first letter of each of the elements, the word SCOPE is formed.

Supportivenees
Credibility
Openness
Participatory Decision Making
Emphasis on High Performance Goals

When you think of ideal supportive climates, it's important to remember how rare it is for organizations to be so characterized. Therefore, it is like a breath of fresh air when we work in, or observe, an organization that has such features. SCOPE provides the elements for a breath of fresh air.

Which would you prefer to hear?

Assume that it is your first day of work at a well-respected, very successful restaurant. Further assume that your manager takes you aside and gives you an "off the record" orienting speech before you begin serving your tables. Below are two versions of that talk. As a new employee at this restaurant, which would you prefer to hear?

1. "Look, this restaurant will make money no matter what. All I ask is that you get here on time, treat the customers with respect, get the meals out promptly, and clean up afterwards. When your shift is over you can disappear as far as I'm concerned. Bottom line: I don't want to hear about you. You don't want to hear from me. Got it?"

2. "Listen. We have been here for 50 years, and we have been here for 50 years because we make real sure that we are the best. Our food is the best, our kitchen staff is the best, and our waitstaff—where you come in—is the best. Every single person in this dining hall is striving to make this establishment the finest restaurant in the county if not the whole state. If you can be like all the other employees here, well welcome aboard. If you don't feel so motivated, then there are plenty of other restaurants that need waitstaff. Do you understand?"

Now that you have selected the better of the two choices, what message might you construct that you would prefer to *either* of the above options?

Additional Factors and Features

Pace and Faules elaborate on Redding's list in their summary of the literature. They conclude that six additional factors affect employee perceptions of the organizational climate:

1. The way employers attempt to motivate employees.
2. The quality of decision making (i.e., to what extent workers feel as if what they have to do is a function of good or bad decisions made by management).
3. The sense that human beings are perceived by the organization as important.
4. The quality of resources (e.g., computers, furniture, and furnishings).
5. The opportunities for upward communication.
6. The overall quality of organizational communication.[10]

PRACTITIONER'S PERSPECTIVE

Governor Michael Dukakis

Michael Dukakis served as governor of the state of Massachusetts from 1975–1979. He lost his reelection bid in 1978, but successfully regained the job by winning the 1982 gubernatorial race, and then, 4 years later, won reelection for a third term. In 1986, he was voted the most effective governor in the United States. In 1988, Governor Dukakis was the Democratic nominee for President of the United States. He has served as the Vice Chairman of the AMTRAK Reform Board, and is a professor at both Northeastern University and UCLA.

Communication is very important, both externally and internally. Obviously, there is a huge job that has to be done in an external sense. It's largely through the media that you give the public a sense of what you're doing. I'm not sure I took the external factor as seriously during my first term as governor as I should have, which is one of the reasons I got thrown out of the place. I certainly took it a lot more seriously during my second and third terms. I had seen what happened when you don't communicate effectively.

We have a new CEO at AMTRAK. His name is David Gunn, and he has an interesting technique when it comes to communicating internally. He rides the trains. He talks to the engineers and conductors, and asks questions. He doesn't come with an entourage. It's just him, talking to the employees. At AMTRAK, the buzz already is all over the company. "Geez," the employees are saying, "He's been on the trains." Gunn is a very good listener, which is an essential part of communication. Clinton was the best listener I ever knew. And it wasn't an act, he listened and he absorbed.

Now, what did I do as governor? Similarly, I tried to get out and talk to people. Of course, there were formal occasions when I would go out and visit agencies. Kind of say, "Hi, how are you? Nice to see ya; I'm the governor," this kind of thing. While I think that was helpful, it's not communication in any thoughtful two-way sense. You know the place has been scrubbed up for you, you know that people have been told to keep their mouths shut— that's just inevitable. I found riding the T [subway] to work and back was more effective than these planned visits. If you're at all open and invite communication, you'll have conversations on the train. In many cases, state employees would come up to me and talk. Another example: I would buy my groceries at the Stop and Shop. Kitty would say, "Why the hell does it take you an hour and a half to go shopping?" I'd tell her that people would come up to me to talk. And so, there's a lot to be said for sending the state limousine back to where it was leased, which is what I did, and doing the best you can to get out there. Now, I don't want to exaggerate the effectiveness of that only because you're talking about a state with 6,000,000 people and 65,000 employees, but I found it very important to have that kind of ongoing contact with state employees, with citizens, and to the extent that I could, try to get people to open up. Getting people to open up is difficult. I don't know how many meetings I've been to with people from the agencies where there'd be some polite questions and then the meeting would be over, right, but someone would stop by the door and say, "I didn't want to bring this up at the meeting, but. . ." which was another way of saying, "I can't level with you in that kind of atmosphere."

We had a Pride and Performance event. It was an awards ceremony held at the Park Plaza and it was a special night dedicated to honoring state employees who helped us reach our objectives toward state beautification. Three finalists from each of the several agencies that dealt with beautification attended the function. Somehow we got Sheraton to agree to a week or two in Florida and we got the airlines to provide seats on flights. Ten of the nominees would be identified as winners and receive a monetary award as well as the vacation. But all of the nominees were essentially winners who had been invited to this party because of their excellent contributions. This event was like the academy awards for these people. It was a great night and an opportunity for me to say "Thanks, you're doing a great job," and these folks—all of the nominees, not just the winners—could bask in the glow of being recognized for being outstanding public servants. Again, is this the kind of rich, informal, two-way communication that is best for folks who are public managers? No, it is not two way, but it was a way of saying that what you are doing is important to us, it's important for Massachusetts, and we appreciate what you've done.

When we started the Welfare to Work program in the 80s we had an extraordinary welfare commissioner who asked me to come down and be part of a meeting to be held with his welfare people on the Cape. The workers were given the time off. He was anxious to build a new kind of esprit within the department. Previously, the welfare employees were essentially in a thankless position where they were cops having to chase people down. Now, we wanted to emphasize that their principal responsibility was to help people become independent and self-sufficient. So, the commissioner asked me to come down. We gave out a whole series of awards. And it was amazing. This was the Welfare department? I felt like I was at a pep rally and these folks subsequently did a fabulous job for us. Now, you would have to talk to the employees to get a sense if they thought this was a dog and pony show or if they took it seriously, but my sense was that communicating this kind of appreciation and support was effective.

Bob Behn wrote a piece in the *Journal of Policy and Management* and talks about the value of rich, informal conversation. That's very important. Face-to-face communication is so important. There needs to be lots of rich, informal communication. That's one of the reasons that I'm not a huge fan of e-mail. I don't mean the exclusion of it. But people are always e-mailing each other; that's not rich, informal communication. What's important is person-to-person stuff. It's spending time with people.

Tom Glynn, who used to be the general manager of the MBTA and is now the COO of Partners Health Care, had brown bag lunches every Friday at noontime with eight or ten working folks at the T. Glynn is a terrifically talented public manager. He had a set routine. At about 11 o'clock on Friday, he would go over and meet with a supervisor. Then at noontime he would take his bag lunch and go over and meet with brown baggers without supervisors present. Very important—no supervisors were present. Glynn did this every Friday. Tom is not a "hail fellow well met" guy. He doesn't smile a lot, that sort of thing, but six months later I met with the head of the Carmens union—which is not an easy union. They represent most of the people at the T. And I asked how things are going. He told me, "This guy Glynn's terrific." I said, "Yeah, tell me about him." He said, "Well, he's talking to our people. These brown bag lunches. We never had anybody like this."

Pretty simple. [Boston Superintendent of Schools Thomas] Payzant has the teacher's union leadership in for coffee and doughnuts every Monday morning at 8 A.M. No set agendas. Just "what's happening, what do you hear?" Not too complicated. Not too difficult. Very important way to communicate. Now again, you've got to be a good listener. There's got to be some sense that this is not just some act, and that you will respond to what you hear if it makes sense to you. But brown bag lunches on Friday, coffee and doughnuts with union leadership, riding the trains. Very simple, but very effective communication techniques.

(continued)

I used to say to my people, "Thank folks, will you!" When was the last time you complained because someone said thank you to you too much? People don't say thank you enough. Just say thanks. Call them up; tell them, "You did a terrific job." Very important. Did I always do this? No. Did I get better at it? I think so.

We had an employee of the month program at the MBTA. One year, we thought we'd invite the twelve employees of the month and their families to Fenway Park for a day game with the Red Sox. At the time, the Red Sox had a very good pitcher named Greg Harris. He lived in Chestnut Hill and would take the Green line [a branch of the subway] to work. Work in his case was Fenway Park. So the twelve employees and their families all came down to the park at about noontime for a 1:30 game and they got to walk around on the field. Now, I've been on the field many times. We used to have a Democrat/Republican ball game there, but they stopped it because the Republicans didn't have enough legislators to field a team. Anyway, for the MBTA employees, being on the field at Fenway Park was an absolute thrill. Tony Peña talking to them. Dewey Evans around the batting cage. Because Harris rode the subway to work, we swore Harris into something we called the Green Line Hall of Fame. Just watching the employees and their families on the field was something. It didn't cost us anything, but it was a huge day in the lives of those employees. What was it? What did we communicate? Simple. It was, "Thanks, you're doing a great job."

ORGANIZATIONAL CULTURE

What Is Organizational Culture?

Organizational culture is an elusive concept. One reason for this is that the phrase has been defined in various, and sometimes incompatible, ways. However, there is a basic theme to most attempts at describing organizational culture. Below you will see a series of definitions that reflect this theme.

Organizational culture refers to:

- The basic values, assumptions, goals, and beliefs that guide the way the organization operates.[11]

- The set of shared, taken for granted implicit assumptions that a group holds and that determines how it perceives, thinks about, and reacts to its various environments.[12]

- The values, heroes, myths, and symbols that have been in the organization forever, the attitudes that say don't disagree with your boss, don't make waves, just do enough to get by, don't take chances.[13]

- A set of understandings or meanings shared by a group of people. The meanings are largely tacit among members, are clearly relevant to the particular group, and are distinctive to the group.[14]

Let's distill these definitions and make the concept of organizational culture more understandable and manageable.

We can say that, in essence, the culture of an organization is concerned with the belief and value system of that organization. This value system is passed along to the employees when they begin work and continue to be socialized at work. Employees learn the culture by becoming acquainted with organizational heroes, rites, rituals, and slogans, as they meet with company storytellers who spread the mythology of the organization. The mythology of the organization describes the attitudes, mores, goals, and credos that serve as foundational planks supporting how and why a company operates as it does.

Consider some of the examples below. They illustrate how storytellers explain organizational culture in terms of heroes, rites, rituals, and slogans.

- "Twenty years ago Milton Weiss worked eighteen hour days for twenty-nine days straight—Saturdays and Sundays included—in order to close a deal. Our stock rocketed after that. Now we have a name for working weekends on something major. We call it: 'A Milton.' Last year I only pulled one Milton, but in 1999–2000 with that Y2K stuff, forget about it. We were all pulling Miltons. In a way you don't want to do too many Miltons. But there was something special about the energy when we were all doing those Miltons together."

- "After your first mega sale you're taken to 'Alfie's' by the top brass. When you get taken to 'Alfie's' you know you're a big deal around here."

- "Once a month on Tuesday evenings we meet after hours for a 'good of the order' session. There's beer and sandwiches and we sit around and bring up anything that's bugging us. It's great. Clears the air. You know."

- "We are a 'play hard, work hard' environment. 'Second place is no place' around here. To close a sale here the message is simple: 'Anything Goes.' "

How would you describe your organization in terms of its

- Heroes?
- Rites?
- Rituals?
- Slogans?

Distinction Between Climate and Culture

As you have likely noticed there is a relationship between the concepts of corporate climate and culture. Denison, in an exhaustive article entitled, "What IS the Difference between Organizational Climate and Organizational Culture?" comments that some research that claims to be involved in examining organizational culture is indistinguishable from climate-related research.[15] He makes the case that climate and culture may, in fact, be the same phenomenon examined from different vantage points. However, the article does point out what readers by now may have deduced is the distinction between the two concepts.

In essence, the organizational culture contains the root value systems that create the organizational climate. Denison comments that culture relates to "underlying values and assumptions" whereas the climate reflects the "manifestations" of those underlying values and assumptions.[16] Therefore, the culture affects the climate. If a cultural slogan is "Don't test or question your boss" it is unlikely that "Participatory Decision Making" will be a managerial trademark. Since participatory decision making is a criterion for ideal supportive climates, the cultural credo that "the boss is always right" is likely to negatively affect climate conditions. If an organizational hero is a manager who "went to the mat" for his employees and whose word "you could take to the bank" then the climate would reflect that cultural value in that it would be characterized as supportive and credible. Using the weather metaphor that was introduced earlier in the chapter, one might think of the culture as the weather factors that, when taken collectively, generate the weather conditions, that is, the climate.

Relationship Between Climate, Culture, and Communication

We have already discussed Redding's perspective regarding the paramount significance of climate for organizational communication. We have looked at both Redding's and Gibb's list of elements that create supportive and defensive environments. Intuitively it makes sense that each of Redding's elements would facilitate effective organizational communication and that each of Gibb's defensive climate characteristics would retard any employee's desire to communicate.

A condescending superior, who dogmatically asserts "truths" without an inclination to listen to alternative notions, is unlikely to encourage the flow of information and is likely to retard that flow. The defensive climate would override any skill-related factors. What difference would it make if employees can write well if they decided not to write because any written communication would be destructively criticized?

Similarly, we can see how a culture marked by the maxim that "no idea here is a bad idea" would encourage suggestions from even the least articulate organizational member. A person with poor communication skills might be willing to crudely thatch together a message in an organizational culture that encourages ideas. An award-winning orator may be reluctant to say a word at a department meeting if the

---

ETHICAL PROBE

WE'RE ALL FAMILY

Assume that you are the head of a small family-run business. There are 60 people who work in your business and about two-thirds of the employees are not affiliated with the family. Assume that it is holiday time and you want to send out a message to all members of the organization wishing them a happy holiday season. Further, assume that there is a clear distinction in this company between those who are members of the family, and those who are not. This distinction will not disappear and assume that you really do not want the distinction to disappear.

Is there anything unethical about writing a message in your greeting card that reads:

Happy Holidays from the Emersons. At Emerson Appliances, we're All Family!

Dorothy and Willie Emerson

---

culture of the organization supported the notion "that here we say 'yes sir,' or we say nothing."

Writing specifically about trust and credibility—one of the five components of Redding's ideal supportive climate—Harshman and Harshman list several communication repercussions of poor organizational credibility:

- Employees stop listening to information.
- Employees won't believe messages even when they do listen.
- In the absence of credible information employees create interpretations of what is happening. This fuels the organizational grapevine.
- In the absence of timely credible information employees create worst-case scenarios.[17]

It's difficult to argue with the fundamental premise that climate and culture affect communication. The question is only this: How can you create a work environment that will facilitate effective organizational communication?

CREATING SUPPORTIVE CLIMATES

Creating the supportive climate is an extremely difficult task, even for the most personable and diligent administrator. It is certainly much easier to create Redding or Gibb-like lists than it is to create a supportive climate.

Supportive climates cannot be created the same way that a cake is baked or a building is constructed. A supportive climate cannot be "made" by mixing a dollop of "trust" with one-half pound of "participatory decision making." The human factors are too complex. If a manager tries to use a step-by-step cookbook approach and is careless and indifferent to the fragile nature of the human elements involved, the end result might be a creation that is toxic to the organizational system.

Cake dough is soft, malleable, and indifferent to manipulation. Employees are not. Any attempt to cultivate supportive climates must be founded on the implicit recognition that the elements needed for supportive climates are multifaceted, variable, and even capricious—to the extent that humans are multifaceted, variable, and sometimes capricious.

Supportive Climates and Granfalloons

"If you wish to study a granfalloon, just remove the skin of a toy balloon." So writes Kurt Vonnegut in his novel, *Cat's Cradle*.[18] A *granfalloon,* one of the many words Vonnegut has donated to the lexicon, is an entity with no substance; a body that appears to be meaningful, but after closer scrutiny is obviously meaningless.

One of the biggest problems with the attempt to create supportive climates is that the resulting constructions become—like granfalloons—nothing more than superficial and spurious entities. Root cultures and attendant organizational climates that are granfalloon composites not only aren't substantive, but like the punctured balloon can make quite a pop when they are exposed.

Often organizations claim to foster supportive environments, but the attempts to manufacture them are unsuccessful. Hare and Wyatt report that a majority of managers continue to practice autocratic, dictatorial behaviors in a world that talks teamwork.[19] No one wants to be part of a "family" that is really a bogus contrivance to

Focus on Applications

Cultivating supportive climates

Earlier in the chapter we discussed the factors that can help create a supportive climate in an organization. Below you will find a list of different types of organizations. For each organization identify those three factors that are most essential for the cultivation and maintenance of a supportive climate.

- ☐ Athletic teams
- ☐ Restaurants
- ☐ Wall Street financial institutions
- ☐ Classes at universities
- ☐ Department stores
- ☐ Municipal offices
- ☐ Hospitals
- ☐ Start-up bio tech companies
- ☐ Cultural institutions (e.g., museums, theaters)

motivate staff to work harder. No one wants to work together to create a "team" when that notion was fabricated as a ruse to dupe employees to sweat harder and longer to improve the lots of those who designed the team.

In Peters and Waterman's best selling book, *In Search of Excellence,* the authors list 10 trademarks of successful cultures. Two of these trademarks are identified as (1) autonomy and entrepreneurship and (2) productivity through people.[20]

The former of these refers to granting employees independence so that they will take risks, be innovative, and excel. The latter suggests that an organization is productive when it respects employees in terms of their potential and personal needs. This second trademark also refers to the perspective that employees are the fundamental plank in any organizational enterprise.

These cultural trademarks are, undeniably, characteristic of organizational excellence. Yet if an organization states that it supports autonomy, and asserts that it respects associates, it is making the type of claims that require "walking a walk" that is obstacle strewn—particularly when management glibly and myopically "talk the talk."[21]

Let's consider a number of factors that affect the quality of the organizational climate.

- Organizational credibility
- Leadership
- Motivated personnel
- A Theory Y orientation

Organizational Credibility

In large part organizational culture and climate fails or thrives on the basis of one of Redding's ideal criteria components: credibility.

Management consultant and communication expert Roger D'Aprix conducted a study at a company where management had positioned huge billboards on the outside of the plant building. The billboards exhorted employees to strive for quality. When D'Aprix asked employees about the impact of the message, one burly guy looked at him and said with disgust, "Look, there are two signs you can believe around here. One says, 'wet paint' the other says 'pardon our appearance.' The rest is baloney.' "[22]

Organizational credibility is essential for the creation of supportive climates. It nourishes such climates. The absence of such credibility has a corrosive effect. Lardner comments that "what ruined Enron wasn't just accounting. It was a culture that valued appealing lies over inconvenient truths."[23]

Under the heading of "No-No's" in *Up the Organization* Robert Townsend makes the following suggestion regarding managerial credibility:

Except in poker, bridge, and similar play-period activities, do not con anybody.

Not your wife,

not your children,

not your employees,

not your customers,

not your stockholders,

not your boss,

not your associates,

not your suppliers,

not your regulatory authorities,

not even your competitors.

Don't con yourself either.[24]

Example

A number of years ago I conducted a multiweek seminar in Western New York on improving presentation skills. Early in the seminar, a participant (Mitchell) gave a persuasive talk urging the other attendees to vacation in North Conway, New Hampshire and to avoid the more popular Florida jaunts.

The presentation was brilliant. He began by quoting others who had visited North Conway using testimonials to enhance the attraction of a vacation at the New Hampshire retreat.

After referring to the testimonials, Mitchell displayed a map of the United States and illustrated in clear terms the difference in time and tolls—the toll on one's car and the toll on one's body—how much easier it would be to vacation in North Conway. Finally, he produced a chart that indicated the costs for lodging and food in Florida as opposed to the relatively inexpensive costs in North

Conway. Mr. Mitchell concluded emphatically that a trip to North Conway was, all things considered, an intelligent vacation choice.

As Mitchell sat down, I remarked that the presentation was excellent and asked him when he had last been to North Conway.

"Ahhch," he shrugged. "I don't go there. Too many bugs."

At the time, the other seminar participants laughed heartily at this retort. Mitchell himself smiled at how he had amused the others. However, Mitchell was less than amused when he made a subsequent presentation. This talk was about a serious topic, yet Mitchell was unable to engage the audience. As far as the audience was concerned, he was "Too Many Bugs Mitch" and was not to be taken seriously.

Managers must resist taking misleading approaches to organizational problems. After employees discover that management does not "go to North Conway" after all, they will be reluctant to pay serious attention to management's claims. Simply, the climate and the overall organizational communication effort will be undermined if the organization's credibility is questionable.

Bartolome makes several suggestions regarding establishing credibility and trust. These too are more easily listed than accomplished, but they do suggest a path to follow.

- Make communication two way. Establish and utilize upward and downward communication networks.
- Respect employees implicitly by delegating authority.
- Relay appropriate human messages. That is, fairly attribute blame and give credit when credit is due.
- Be predictable, that is, react consistently to situations.[25]

In essence, the best and only advice to those who wish to earn a reputation for credibility is simple: Be credible. As Mark Twain once remarked, "When in doubt, tell the truth. You'll amaze some and astonish the rest."

Leadership

In large part, Phillip Tompkins's book, *Organizational Communication Imperatives,* is a comparison of leadership styles. Tompkins juxtaposes the leadership style of the aforementioned Dr. Wernher von Braun, who led NASA's Marshall Space Flight Center in the 1960s, with that of Dr. William Lucas, who headed the center in the 1980s. Lucas was at the helm when the Challenger exploded on January 28, 1986.

Tompkins underscores the point that the leadership styles of the men significantly affected the internal communication at the center. Whereas von Braun was encouraging, supportive, and engaging, Lucas was aloof and critical. Tompkins interviewed several of Lucas's subordinates. Below are some revealing descriptions of their leader:

"Lucas was a dead fish. Cold, vindictive, he would embarrass people publicly."

"I feel bad about saying this, but people were afraid to bring bad news to Dr. Lucas for fear that they would be treated harshly."

"I thought the world of Dr. Lucas even though he was so rigid and formal. [However] people were afraid to raise problems with him. We started canning and preprogramming what went up to Dr. Lucas."

"Dr. Lucas's group expected us to be conversant about every technical detail. They made us apprehensive—reluctant to volunteer information."

"Communication with Lucas was more constrained than with von Braun, not as open, but you could get through if you wanted to. My opinion is that if somebody was forceful he could have been heard."

"Lucas wanted information filtered. His communicative style was intimidation."[26]

It's obvious that a leadership style like Lucas's would create a defensive climate and retard the flow of information in an organization. *In similar ways, in every unit in every organization, the leaders are in a position to support or retard the flow of information.* The individual departmental climates that affect communication *within* each unit will also influence interaction *between* departments, and consequently will affect the overall quality of communication in an organization.

A good way to illustrate how leadership affects the climate, and how the climate affects communication, is by discussing the MSFC communication tool known as *Monday Notes.*

Monday Notes was developed under von Braun to allow each unit at the center an opportunity to become familiar with other units' work. The Notes also served to keep von Braun aware of department activities.

Each Monday, departments would produce a one-page report related to their weekly business. The departments would send these reports to von Braun. Von Braun would read each submission and write feedback in the margins "asking questions, making suggestions, and dishing out praise."[27] Then, all of the week's Monday Notes would be collated and distributed to each manager.

The Monday Notes system created upward, horizontal, and downward networks for the MSFC. Monday Notes was so successful that it spawned a related tool called *Friday Notes.* Friday Notes were reports generated on Friday by managerial subordinates. With their subordinates' Friday Notes in hand, the managers were able to do a better job constructing the following week's Monday Notes. Thus, with Friday Notes, another level of upward networks was established.

Had the climate under von Braun not been supportive, the Monday Notes would likely have been either valueless or not as valuable as they were. If departments had begun to wonder if the Notes would be critically evaluated, used as comparative indicators of one group's success as opposed to another's, or instruments that would justify financial rewards or demerits, the Notes would have lost their credibility and their value. In fact, Friday Notes gradually faded out of existence after the von Braun era. While Monday Notes survived (the name was changed to Weekly Notes), they became more sterile and less vital.

What made Monday Notes a vital communication tool had little to do with the writing skills of the employees. What made Monday Notes a success was the climate at the Marshall Space Flight Center. That climate was, in large part, a function of the kind of person who headed the operation.

As it relates to the effects of leadership on organizational communication, consider the box "Turn the Beat Around" that follows. Can you identify organizational leaders whom you've known who've had a significant positive or negative effect on internal communication because of their leadership styles?

Turn the Beat Around: Leadership, Climate, and Communication

"Mr. Seviroli, how was the percussion?"

The issues surrounding this question are at the heart of quality communication in organizations. The inquiry was made by Stephen Hill, a sixth-grade ne'er do well who banged the drums (indiscriminately it sometimes seemed to me) directly behind my seat as second trumpeter for Mr. Joseph Seviroli's Fern Place Elementary School band.

I was reminded of Hill's query recently when a colleague told me about a local organization that was going to test the quality of its internal communication. When I asked how they would undertake this task, my friend said that the company intended to collect all their "communications" and examine the effectiveness of each. This meant that the organization would examine their newspapers, bulletin boards, e-mail systems, and so on, and then draw a conclusion about their overall communication quality. This company's test results *will not* be valid. They may discover some valuable information, but they will not find out about essential dimensions of their organization's communication.

Communication Quality and Human Needs

A key element in quality organizational communication relates to managerial sensitivity and effective superior–subordinate interaction. This comment may seem as if it's the stuff of airy philosophy, but there is nothing impractical about it. *If you want to assess your organization's communication quality, you'll need to examine the quality of the humans who communicate in the organization.* Moreover, you'll need to assess your leaders' willingness (and ability) to meet the human needs of their subordinates, particularly when communications regarding these needs require perspicacity and diplomacy.

These communications are every bit as important to the overall communication quality of the organization as video tapes, house organs, and e-mail capabilities. In fact, they may be more significant. Interpersonal interaction that is gratuitously brusque, condescending, or otherwise insensitive can affect the entire climate of an organization—indirectly, if not directly—undermining communication and overall quality. And this brings me to Joseph Seviroli's Fern Place band, Stephen Hill, and Mr. Hill's inquiry.

Controlled Authority

Joseph Seviroli was the leader of the Fern Place band and the instrument teacher for the elementary school. He taught grade school children how to play and then conducted the collective musicians. Seviroli was a kind and patient man. I clearly remember my first trumpet lesson with him. On that day, Seviroli sat with me and two other fledgling trumpeters in the tiny lesson room—a space that certainly had been a storage closet at some time in the past. The goal of this initial session was simply to get us to produce a sound from the end of the horn.

The others quickly blurted out something, were dismissed, and told to return to the regular classroom. However, nothing came out of my trumpet. I couldn't get it. I was blowing ferociously trying to make a peep and Seviroli kept sitting there telling me not to panic. Suddenly I connected with a cacophonous blast that nearly rocketed the poor man into the wall. Without so much as a blinking of an eye he told me that I'd done very well and I marched back to my classroom feeling like I'd accomplished something, and eventually I became a member of the band.

Seviroli was no mollusk. For some reason the entire band, particularly the percussion section, seemed to be populated by wise guys, classmates who like the aforementioned Hill, when not banging the drums might otherwise be unleashing their energy in societally counterproductive ways. Yet Seviroli kept us in check. He seemed to have the right combination of control and support. We had become, the percussionists and others, truly a band of young kids following the lead of our respected director. The payoffs were internal, more than anything else.

For weeks, if not months, the band was preparing for the big musical spectacular that annually was the event of events for the school. We were to accompany the Fern Place thespians in some original musical. While Seviroli led the band, a Mr. Mushnick directed the stage actors. Mushnick was no Seviroli. He may have been as musically talented, but the man was a screamer. Unlike Seviroli, Mushnick could lose control easily and go into tirades that were remarkable and, apparently, memorable. While bellowing admonishments, his face would contort as if he were holding his breath for some contest. After he began one such outburst, Stephen Hill leaned over to me and whispered, "Hey, watch this one now. Watch the veins pop out of his head."

So it was Seviroli and Mushnick leading our troops with different styles. Seviroli with strong controlled authority led the band below and Mushnick, without the same control—but with more volume—led the actors above us.

Got to Have Percussion

Nerves became frayed as the day of the event approached. Each rehearsal had one form of crisis or another and Mushnick, under what must have been considerable pressure real or imagined, was spewing volcanically at least once an hour. One particular scene in the show had become a recurring problem. In it, a group of child actors emerged from audience level while singing to our music. They were to access the stage by climbing a short set of stairs that were near the percussion section of the band. We musicians were supposed to keep playing until the actors were all in place at their spots on the stage. Almost every time we rehearsed this scene something would go wrong. The actors wouldn't find their spots; the band would stop playing too soon; some of the kids would stop singing while they climbed the stairs—something would go wrong.

The day before opening night, during dress rehearsal, this scene from the Styx took a dive for the worse. It became clear that with costumes and various props the actors would have a difficult time negotiating the walk around the percussion section to gain access to the stage. Mushnick became absolutely enraged by what must have seemed like a conspiracy and burst into a panicked screeching during which he shouted that there were too many drummers and that we simply couldn't have that many. From his perch on the stage he pointed down to Hill who was the last drummer in the line and told him that he had to go.

This, to me, was unthinkable. I couldn't imagine how I would have felt if after all this time I would have been booted from the band. I turned around and saw that most of the members were stunned. Big, tough Stephen Hill was crying eleven-year-old tears. Seviroli waved to Hill as if to say not to worry. He hoisted himself on the stage and put his arm around Mushnick. Within minutes the matter seemed to be resolved. Seviroli moved the drums around a bit, and Stephen Hill could stay.

We went through the scene, and it worked just fine. We belted out the music, and the thespians accessed the stage. And then, during the temporary break that followed, Stephen Hill, this truculent young tough, who went on to a career of petty theft and various scrapes with the law, asked both plaintively and genuinely,

(continued)

"Mr. Seviroli. How was the percussion?"

Seviroli made the okay sign. I turned around and saw Hill positively beaming.

If an organization wants to test the effectiveness of its internal communication, it needs to begin by looking at personnel and the organizational climate and culture that is a function of its personnel. This, more than the internal newsletter, will determine the communication efficiency and quality.

We all need to do something meaningful in the band we call our work. And we need to have that work meaningfully acknowledged. As Vickie Sue Robinson crooned, "Turn the beat around."

"Got to have percussion."

Motivated Personnel

Redding refers to emphasizing "high performance goals" in his ideal supportive climate. Gibb, in "Defensive Communication," refers to problems inherent in motivation through manipulation. Gibb writes that people react negatively to "what are perceived as gimmicks or tricks to fool or 'involve' people."[28] Clearly, a motivated workforce is essential for a supportive climate. A work team laden with dissension is likely not to be motivated to excel, nor participate meaningfully in decision making, nor be concerned with information that is disseminated in the organization. How does an organization develop a motivated workforce?

Having the Horses. A high school football coach was asked once to assess his team's chances for the upcoming season. The coach paused, sighed, and then said ingenuously. "We don't have the horses."

Managers need the horses also—not only to produce at maximum efficiency, but also as a seed element of the supportive climate. The *horses* in organizations refer to a motivated population of workers, not just capable employees, but workers who will perform to their capacity.

Recognizing Responsibilities and Purpose for Work. In order to motivate employees, workers must see and understand why it is important for them to do what they do. Often top management feels that goals are clearly relayed when, in fact, they have not been so communicated. D'Aprix states,

> When you talk to senior management they believe that objectives and issues of the business are fairly well understood. They certainly can recite them with little hesitation. Yet as you interview people further down in the organization you find that there is less and less agreement and more and more confusion. And yet, how can people manage their own jobs if they don't understand the company priorities that should guide their work?[29]

In order to motivate employees, employees should have an opportunity to see how what they do fits in with organizational objectives.

Screen Effectively. Groucho Marx once said, "I never forget a face, but in your case I'll make an exception." In order to have motivated personnel, managers need to effectively screen incoming employees and make intelligent exceptions. This means screening employees not only in terms of what they can do but how they will interact with others. If managers make the intelligent assumption that communication is vital, just as the actual physical constructing of a product is vital, then it is clear that an employee who is not willing or capable of interacting effectively with others is not a good person to let through the screen.

Find Strengths and Assign Responsibilities on the Basis of Strengths. Almost every person who gets through the screen has certain attributes that are areas of particular strength. A good policy is to assess what those attributes are and assign responsibilities on the basis of those strengths.

Delegate Responsibility. Managers who try to do everything will fail and become frustrated. Also, they will erode the organizational climate. Tacitly, they are communicating that they do not have confidence in the employees to do things for themselves. While there might be times when employees give managers good reason to question competence, as a general rule, managers must delegate responsibility to facilitate the creation of a supportive climate.

Prepare for Nonmotivated Employees. Despite all precautions employees who cannot or will not be motivated will get through the screen. Managers should prepare for this eventuality and establish a fair system for purging them from the organization. Weak employees beget other weak employees. If your company has no way to eliminate undeserving, underachieving employees, the trademark of "emphasis on high performance goals" is implicitly undermined.

A Theory Y Orientation

We discussed McGregor's Theory Y in Chapter 2 of the text. Supportive cultures and climates are based, inherently, on a Theory Y orientation.

Recognizing that employees are human—with all the needs, desires, fallibilities, and energy of people—is at the core of supportive climates. When employees are managed as if they are chairs or inanimate cogs in a system, problems will inevitably arise. The classical theory notwithstanding, people can be made to enjoy work.

Noel Coward wrote, "Work is much more fun than fun." It can be. American author Sydney Harris commented, "Few men [sic] ever drop dead from overwork, but many quietly curl up and die because of undersatisfaction." But perhaps psychiatrist Theodor Reik was most to the point when he said, "Work and love—these are the basics. Without them there is neurosis."

Managers who can genuinely tap employees' human needs and desires to do something fulfilling and rewarding with their lives will have taken a giant step toward creating the supportive climate that facilitates effective organizational communication.

One absolutely needs "the horses" to have a supportive climate, and those horses must be able to not only "make the widget," but they also must be, if not personable, palatable. It's difficult to ensure that an organization or even a department will be so populated. People come to work with assorted problems from their life experiences. It would be fine if everyone led idyllic existences and had peaceful childhoods, but few of us do. All of us come to the workplace with so many bags that it is difficult to create a supportive climate because the climate is simply burdened by the collective weight.

Supervisory personnel can further complicate the problem of creating supportive climates. Managers have both power and pressures. The power, for some, serves as an intoxicant. The pressures, for some, increase stress and decrease diplomacy. Individuals who become infused with an inflated sense of self-worth and who need the power of authority to allow them to function, can severely damage any efforts to create supportive climates in organizations. Individuals who are unable to deal with the stresses of supervision are likely to react to problems with poor communication skill, inevitably infecting the organizational climate. Managers cannot attempt to win "popularity contests," yet they must maintain good relations with their subordinates. These requirements are essentially in conflict, and therefore managers are forced to stay balanced on a narrow line.

However, despite these complicating realities, all organizational men and women can take strides toward improving the climate. The bottom line is simply this: The heart of the organization (and the climate) is a function of the character and interactions of the employees who work in the organization. Walt Kelly's cartoon character Pogo once said, "We have met the enemy and it is us." Maybe so. In that case, turn the beat around.

PRACTITIONER'S PERSPECTIVE

Pamela Olton, Lab Manager

The Haight Ashbury Free Medical Clinic (HAFMC) was created to meet the health care needs of thousands of youth during the 1967 so-called Summer of Love. Now the clinic has grown into one of San Francisco's largest multiservice agencies. Pamela Olton has worked at HAFMC since 1975. For more than 20 years she has staffed laboratory volunteers and acupuncture providers for the clinic.

We are a nonprofit with a particularly effective style of consensus-based decision making. Every week on Fridays we pay people half a day to meet and talk and get things off their chests. At times it feels totally self-indulgent, but it works. As unusual as it may be, the team usually stands together. When I began working here I saw a list of clinic objectives regarding teamwork and how we were going to create a foundation for collective involvement. I thought it was a bunch of dated hippy nonsense. But the fact is that the people worked to make it a reality. This is in sharp contrast to my experiences in other organizations. I worked as a Research Scientist in an environment where everyone was competitive. I worked in hospitals where there were warring factions and if you took the side of one unit, others would not talk with you and, moreover, you might lose your job because of your alliances. I've worked in other nonprofits where the power structure is so hierarchical that trying to get access to the leader was like waiting in the courtyard in the hopes that one of the czar's toadies might come to get you so that you could have a few moments with the almighty. It really is different here at the clinic. We try to do things that foster communication and not stifle it.

The meetings on Friday mornings have been successful. We close the clinic for that half-day. Every other week we bring in someone for professional development. We had someone come in to talk about suicide prevention recently, for example. On the weeks when we don't have professional development we have discussions about how we can make the clinic a better place. Some Fridays we use the time simply to vent, but the value transcends the catharsis. We identify problems that we're able to address because we hear of them at these sessions.

We decided to take proactive steps to ensure that the clinic could meet the objectives of a team-based operation. So, we established a management team comprised of the Administrative Director, Medical Director, Clinic Operation Manager, Psycho-Social Case Manager, Manager of Grants & Contracts, and a rotating representative from Technical Support. I've served in the Technical Support position. We vote on decisions that affect the clinic. It may sound strange to people who are not in such supportive environments—and it might even have seemed strange to me had I not been here for so long—but this participatory decision making works. I believe it could work regardless of the organizational enterprise, but the key players would have to be committed to making it successful. If you throw up your arms and say that a system of participation is not feasible, then it will not be. There are times when administrators have to make decisions, which not everyone agrees with. That comes with the territory of any organization regardless of how democratic it may be. However, I think that since there are other times when employees can have a legitimate say in what occurs, the quality of the work environment is enhanced. People are more expressive here than they otherwise would be.

We do something else at the clinic that works to improve the environment and quality of communication. In general, people are happier when they are doing something that they are good at. If you encourage employees to discover their strengths and work in areas that are related to their strengths you will have a more exciting and productive work atmosphere. We do that here. We help employees identify their particular occupational niche. Then we work with the employees to actually redraft their job descriptions so that they can be doing what they excel at doing. When we identify an employee who really fits in the team because of some outstanding qualities or talents, and they really feel committed to our mission, then we supplement their training to boost weaknesses and eventually shift around duties to frame the things they are most likely to succeed at. Then we look at what other things need to be done that would be best addressed by someone else's evolving job. By encouraging people and coaching people in this way, we bring new frontiers of excellence to our clinic. This creates a vibrant atmosphere and fosters healthy discussions related to how we can meet our mission.

I'm very lucky to be doing what I do where I do it. The people at the clinic love it. Our mission is to provide "quality health care to those in need." We are committed to that goal, and we are committed to communicating effectively in order to realize it.

SUMMARY

A Toolbox

1. The climate in an organization may be the most significant factor affecting organizational communication.
2. The organization's culture can determine, or at least affect, the nature of the climate.
3. It is far more difficult to prescribe the ingredients for a supportive climate than it is to create the climate. Similarly, it is easy to identify desirable cultural traits of an organization and far more difficult to embed those traits in an organization.
4. Redding identifies five characteristics of an ideal supportive climate. They are
   - Supportiveness
   - Credibility
   - Participatory decision making
   - Openness
   - An emphasis on excellence
5. Organizations are likely to cultivate and nourish the ideal supportive climate with quality leadership, a motivated workforce, and a Theory Y managerial perspective.

DISCUSSION QUESTIONS

1. What is the distinction between *organizational climate* and *organizational culture*?
2. How can a Theory X orientation increase the chances of an organization having a defensive climate?
3. What is the relationship between climate and organizational communication?
4. How can leadership affect organizational communication?
5. How can the climate of an organization affect the credibility of human messages?
6. How would you describe the culture of any of the organizations in your life in terms of its
   a. Mottoes
   b. Values
   c. Heroes
   d. Rituals
7. Please read the following case and respond to the questions at its end.

CASE FOR ANALYSIS

Case 7.2—Jamie at the Wayfarer

Background. Jamie Levesque worked at the front desk of Longfellow's Wayfarer Inn for 1 year. At the time of Levesque's service, many of the Wayfarer's over 100 employees had been working at the inn for more than a decade. The 130-acre inn has 10 rooms for lodging as well as a chapel and restaurant. There's also a gristmill on the premises. Because of its historic status, the inn is a nonprofit organization.

After her first 6 months of employment, Levesque heard through the grapevine that Mr. Osias, the Innkeeper, was planning to retire. The rumor was not taken seriously by most of the Wayfarer's employees. Osias had contemplated retirement on several occasions in the past and had always decided to stay on at the inn. However, this time Osias did follow through and retire.

Before and After Osias. Mr. Julius Osias had inspired a strong loyalty toward the inn among his employees. He worked hard to ensure a family environment and offered many perks to employees that had endeared him to the staff. Some examples of these perks were:

- The free daily lunch and dinner, eaten with Mr. Osias, provided to all employees.
- The opportunity to always hire a relative in need of employment.
- The annual certificate given to every employee entitling him or her to a free dinner, as a patron, in the restaurant.

Mr. Osias was highly regarded by both the employees *and* the patrons. He was always visible, 12 hours a day, 6 days a week either helping the employees during busy times or chatting with the customers. Osias had taken charge of the failing inn during the mid-1950s and re-established its classic reputation solely by word-of-mouth advertising. According to Levesque, Osias's leadership created an environment that made employees desire to maintain the excellent reputation the inn enjoyed.

Osias operated more like an innkeeper than a businessperson. His motto was "if it isn't broke don't fix it." This would apply to the inn operation as well as to equipment. He would rather spend his time repairing the broken tractor in the field or the dishwasher than to replace it with new technology developed for the twenty-first century.

This is how Levesque characterized communication channels at the inn under Osias.

Formal Channels:
- None.

Informal Channels:
- Impromptu meetings held in the employee break room for those eating lunch or dinner prior to their shift.
- Grapevine.

The New Innkeeper. After Osias retired, Brendan Gagnon replaced him as the new innkeeper. Brendan was 38 years younger than Osias and full of energy and new ideas. He had big plans for implementing the inn's first computer system. He also intended to increase the restaurant sales volume through both an advertising program and a reduction in meal prices. Mr. Gagnon ran the inn as a business. He worked from 9 A.M. to 5 P.M. and spent the majority of time in his office planning the inn's future.

Gagnon was not well received by most employees. Two weeks after his arrival, all employees received a memo with their paychecks informing them of a scheduled morning meeting. At the meeting, Gagnon introduced himself and informed people that the "fun and games"—as he put it—were over. His first two decisions were to lay off all of the part-time employees and to discontinue the employees' free lunch and dinners. In addition, he expressed the importance of speaking with one's immediate supervisor if there was a problem. Mr. Gagnon wanted to communicate only with the supervisors.

This is how Levesque characterized communication channels under Gagnon.

Formal Channels:

- Scheduled meetings by the innkeeper for all employees during nonoperating hours.
- Other specified channels described to employees in an encyclopedic first-time-ever employee handbook.

Informal Channel:

- Wild angry grapevine.

Reactions from the Employees The employees were devastated and angry regarding their friends' layoffs. They also felt that the full-timers should be compensated monetarily for lost benefits. Many employees expressed their anger by spending much of their spare time breaking the equipment or stealing food from the kitchen. Most did not volunteer to help with extra work as they had in the past.

The employees were upset about the change in the formal communication channels. In the old inn, all of the employees were of equal status. Those who held the supervisory positions had almost no power. Therefore, in the new inn, it was difficult for the employees to accept the supervisors' power.

The grapevine was in a hyperactive state. The rumors being spread suggested more layoffs. The suggested layoffs were directed toward those positions that would require re-training to use the new equipment.

"Gagnon's coming was like a hurricane," said Levesque. "There was a lot of sudden damage and then the climate at the Wayfarer was just different. People started grousing about Brendan and even became ornery with one another. Some of us even witnessed employees take it out on the customers. I left after a while."

- Can the atmosphere in an organization affect the way the people in the organization communicate?
- Is leadership a factor in determining how people communicate with one another?
- Will Gagnon's approach be more conducive to effective communication than Osias's had been, once the staff gets used to Gagnon?
- Levesque was one of the angry employees. Did she have a right to be so angry?

ENDNOTES

[1]Brown, Andrew and Ken Starkey, "Effects of Organizational Culture on Communication and Information," *Journal of Management Studies*, November 1994, vol. 31, no. 6, p. 808.

[2]Hay, Julie, "Organizational Transactional Analysis: Some Opinions and Ideas," *Transactional Analysis Journal*, July 2000, vol. 30, no. 3, p. 230.

[3]Redding, W. Charles, *Communication Within the Organization*, New York, Industrial Communication Council, 1972: p. 111.

⁴Taguiri, R., "The Concepts of Organizational Climate," in R. Taguiri and G. H. Litwin (editors), *Organizational Climate: Exploration of a Concept,* Boston, Harvard University Press, 1968, p. 27.

⁵Kreps, Gary, *Organizational Communication,* Longman, 1990, p. 193.

⁶Kreps, for example, uses this metaphor in the above citation, as does Tompkins in "The Functions of Human Communication in Organization," in *Handbook of Rhetorical and Communication Theory,* edited by C. C. Arnold and J. W. Bowers, Allyn and Bacon, 1984: pp. 659–719.

⁷Guion, R., "A Note on Organizational Climate," *Organizational Behavior and Human Performance,* vol. 9, 1973, pp. 120–125.

⁸Gibb, Jack, "Defensive Communication," in John Stewart (editor) *Bridges Not Walls,* Seventh Edition. McGraw Hill, 1999: p. 444 (originally in *Journal of Communication,* vol. 11, 1961: pp. 141–148).

⁹This list of components is found in op. cit. Redding, *Communication Within the Organization.*

¹⁰Pace, R. Wayne and Don Faules, *Organizational Communication,* Prentice Hall, 1990: pp. 121–122.

¹¹"Culturing Change," *The Economist,* July 7, 1990, p. 65.

¹²Schein, E. H., "Culture, The Missing Factor in Organizational Studies," *Administrative Science Quarterly,* June 1996, p. 236.

¹³Dumaine, Brian, "Creating a New Company Culture," *Fortune,* January 15, 1990, p. 127.

¹⁴Reis Louis, Meryl, "An Investigator's Guide to Workplace Culture," in Peter Jr. Frost et al., editors, *Organizational Culture,* Sage, 1985: p. 74.

¹⁵Denison, Daniel, "What IS the Difference Between Organizational Culture and Organizational Climate? A Native's Point of View on a Decade of Paradigm Wars," *Academy of Management Review,* July 1996, pp. 619–654.

¹⁶Ibid., p. 625.

¹⁷Harshman, Ellen and Carl Harshman, "Communication With Employees: Building on an Ethical Foundation," *Journal of Business Ethics,* March 1, 1999, p. 3.

¹⁸Vonnegut, Kurt, *Cat's Cradle,* Delacorte Press, 1963. Reference to granfalloon is on p. 82.

¹⁹Cole, Larry, and Michael Cole, "Why Is the Teamwork Buzz Word Not Working?" *Communication World,* February/March 1999, p. 29 referring to Hare, Chauncey and Judith Wyatt, *Work Abuse: How to Recognize and Survive It,* Schenkman Books, 1997.

²⁰Thomas Peters and Robert Waterman, *In Search of Excellence,* Harper and Row, NY, 1982, p. 14.

²¹Schein, E. H., "The Role of the Founder in Creating Organizational Culture," *Organizational Dynamics,* Summer 1983, p. 22. Schein lists 10 ways that culture is embedded in organizations. "Formal statements of organizational philosophy" is one such way and "deliberate role modeling and teaching" is another. However, he complements these two "talking the talk" elements with others that reflect "walking the walk" (e.g., "what leaders pay attention to, measure, and control"; "leader reactions to critical incidents and organizational crises"). The point is that simply *articulating policy,* or *training,* in and of themselves cannot embed a culture. Management needs to demonstrate a willingness to behave in ways that reflect what they articulate and teach.

²²D'Aprix, Roger (as interviewed by David Hoffmann) in *Communications and Management: A Strategy for Success,* Towers, Perrin, Forster, and Crosby publication series, January/February, 1985, p. 1.

²³Lardner, James, "Why Should Anyone Believe You?" *Business 2.0,* March 2002, p. 41.

[24]Townsend, Robert, *Up the Organization,* Knopf, 1975: p. 125.

[25]Bartolome, Fernando, "Nobody Trusts the Boss, Now What?" *Harvard Business Review on Effective Communication 1999:* p. 80.

[26]Tompkins, Phillip, *Organizational Communication Imperatives,* Roxbury Press, 1993: pp. 164–165.

[27]Ibid., Tompkins, p. 63.

[28]Gibb, Jack, "Defensive Communication," in John Stewart, *Bridges Not Walls,* Seventh Edition. 1999, p. 446.

[29]Op. cit., D'Aprix, p. 2.

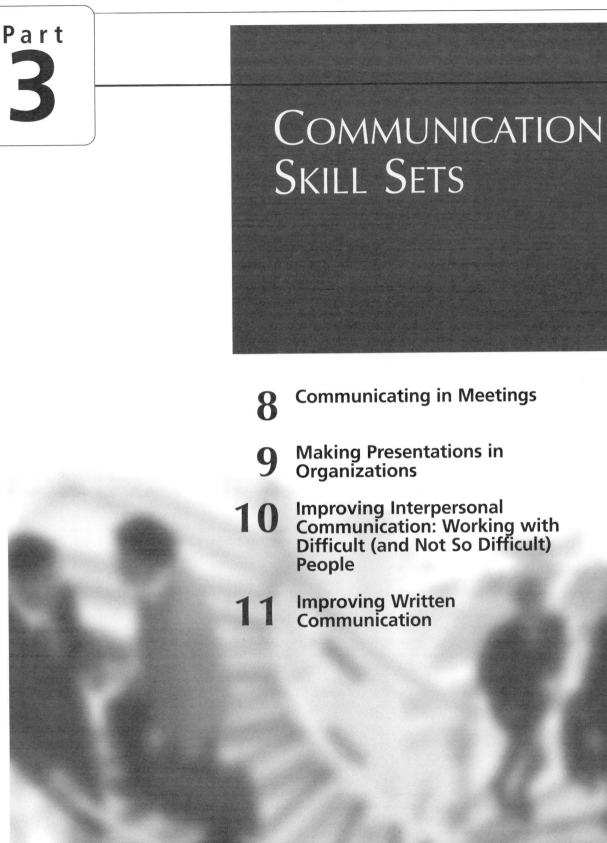

Part

3

COMMUNICATION SKILL SETS

© PHOTODISC

8

Communicating in Meetings

I have witnessed so many staff meetings, so many conferences, and so many extended task forces, where intelligent and industrious people were getting into deeper and deeper confusion—getting more and more frustrated with each other—primarily because no one had thought to get an agreement on exactly what they were trying to do.

—David Emery, *The Compleat Manager*[1]

After a lifetime, I can't remember one meeting that ended happily.

—Isadore Barash, "A New Economic Indicator"[2]

If you had to identify, in one word, the reason why the human race has not achieved, and never will achieve, its full potential, that word would be "meetings."

—Dave Barry, "Twenty-five Things I Have Learned in Fifty Years"[3]

© GETTY IMAGES/PHOTODISC

Case 8.1—*Gerald Sweeney and the Regular Wednesday Meetings*

Gerald Sweeney was a senior managing director who supervised several subordinate managers. One of Sweeney's obligations involved attending regular Wednesday meetings of all like managing directors. Subsequently, he was responsible for relaying information from these meetings to his subordinates at his own staff sessions.

Sweeney frequently complained to his staff about the Wednesday sessions. Among his complaints were that the meetings started late and they took up time that could otherwise be more usefully served. One regular item on the agenda was for each managing director to brief the others about what was "up" in their area. Sweeney felt that this was the biggest time waster.

"Nobody really cares what is happening over in another department. Everyone pretends to care. They nod their heads, say the strategic 'mmm' and 'ah ha' and 'interesting' but nobody really listens. Ask someone to reiterate what's been said during one of the sessions and they'd be silent or blabber nonsense. Some of these directors think they're on stage and make a big production about what their department is doing and how efficient they are. Number one, I don't believe what they are saying, and number two, worse, I don't care if they're telling the truth or not. They're posturing or have hidden agendas. The guy from the budget office brings slides and graphs and you really need an extra cup of coffee to stay awake."

Another problem identified by Sweeney was that sometimes managing directors don't attend, or send ambassadors to the meetings in their stead. At the beginning of the session the chair might announce that one director or more had e-mailed, claiming that something had come up and that he or she was either not going to be there or was sending another to represent the department. When this occurred some of the following session was spent familiarizing last week's absentees. The ambassadors, apparently, hadn't relayed information to the managing directors. There were minutes for each session, but they were distributed on the following Tuesday, a day prior to the Wednesday gathering. Attendees would bring these minutes to the meeting and would scan them during the early moments or while directors were chatting informally waiting for the session to begin.

Sweeney felt that any information that was relayed at the meetings could just as easily be communicated via e-mail or print. For this reason, because he saw the time as a period that could be more usefully spent, and because others were doing it as well, Gerald Sweeney began to attend these sessions only sporadically, e-mailing in his regrets now and again.

When presiding over his own staff, Sweeney had a clear agenda, followed it, allowed for little in the way of digressions, and made sure the session ended on time.

However, on one occasion he did not relay to his subordinates some information that had been disseminated at a Wednesday meeting that he'd missed. This was vital information about a new procedure. Because he hadn't attended the session nor read the minutes, he could not and did not relay the message about the new policy to his subordinates. Subsequently, the subordinates were reprimanded by top management for not following the policy. They had to spend an extraordinary amount of time redoing the tasks. Somehow, Sweeney's reputation remained untarnished. His subordinates did not have easy access to top management nor did anyone want to criticize the boss perhaps for fear of reprisals. Sweeney, himself, did not want to communicate a message to his superiors indicating that he had been responsible for the errors. "It would hurt our department in the long run," he claimed.

Gerald Sweeney apologized to his staff, but they were not easily soothed. "Look, I'm sorry," he said. "But I couldn't stand going to those meetings."

☐   *Should Sweeney have attended the meetings?*

☐   *What, if anything, could Sweeney have done to change the way those meetings were run?*

☐   *Did Sweeney have an ethical responsibility to notify top management and explain that it was he who was responsible for the incorrectly completed tasks?*

ABSTRACT

In a recent survey 27 percent of identified organizational communication problems included some reference to frustration and tension during meetings.[4] Meetings have been referred to as cul de sacs where ideas are lured and quietly strangled. Nevertheless meetings are necessary contexts for organizational communication. They are important for information dissemination, can serve as problem-solving venues, and can provide opportunities for social interaction and department cohesion. This chapter examines the problems related to communication in meetings and identifies interventions that can be used for improvement.

OBJECTIVES

When you have completed this chapter, you should be able to:

☐   **Identify common conflicts that surface during meetings.**
☐   **Describe counterproductive tendencies of participants and groups.**
☐   **List and explain interventions (techniques) that can be used to reduce conflict and improve meeting interaction.**
☐   **Identify and describe types of meeting leaders.**
☐   **Explain what is meant by same site electronic meetings.**

THE PHENOMENON OF MEETINGS

Meetings, Bloody Meetings

People often have negative attitudes about meetings. Humorist John Cleese used the title, *Meetings, Bloody Meetings,* for his educational (but humorous) videotape on the subject.[5] DeWine writes that meetings are "usually thought of as time wasters."[6] A *Newsweek* commentary includes this commonly held sentiment: "Meetings. . .have become our national pastime, yet one is hard pressed to see any advantage to them."[7]

Meeting pessimism and frustration is also reflected in the following remarks made by business persons:

- I become annoyed during our regular—allegedly important—problem-solving meetings when participants leave the room when they receive so-called urgent calls on their cell phones to which they "must" respond. If we need to meet, we should meet and take care of other business afterwards.

- I am in a group with 13 others. About seven of these persons come in 5–10 minutes after the scheduled time of our meeting, and we don't begin until all persons are present. The next 10 minutes are spent discussing the weather and social news. Therefore, we begin the session wasting 20 valuable minutes of my time. And this, of course, doesn't count the time we waste once we get started.

- Our regional director schedules monthly meetings of the sales force. Regularly, the scheduled meeting time is changed at short notice causing resentment from those of us who had planned our appointments around the scheduled meetings. In addition, the agenda for the meeting is disregarded within moments of the start. The meetings run 3 to 4 1/2 hours and right through the lunch period.

- Tuesday mornings we have a weekly staff meeting. Staff members have grown to dread Tuesday mornings and feel that the meetings are nothing more than perfunctory.

- Our head manager calls regular staff meetings and spends valuable time discussing her personal life and passing around pictures of her children.[8]

Values of Meetings

Despite the common tensions, there are legitimate reasons for organizations to use meetings as a venue for organizational communication. DeWine lists four such reasons:

- To announce organizational changes and keep employees up to date.
- To produce solutions and to increase the number of different solutions to organizational problems.
- To gain "buy in" or acceptance of a decision through participation.
- To "cultivate members as individuals" and create group cohesion.[9]

How can organizations obtain the potential benefits from meetings and not unintentionally encourage employees to mutter, "Meetings, bloody meetings"? An initial step is to analyze why communication problems in groups tend to surface.

Primary and Secondary Tension

Berko, Wolvin, and Wolvin define primary group tension as the "normal jitters and feelings of uneasiness experienced when groups first congregate." Secondary tension is defined as "the stress and strain that occurs in a group later in its development."[10] Essentially, primary tension refers to the anxiety that occurs before a meeting begins, and secondary tension refers to the conflict that occurs once the session or sessions are underway.

Primary Tension

There are a number of reasons why people and groups could feel tense even before a meeting begins. Participants may experience primary tension because

- They have high "communication apprehension." A participant may be very nervous about communicating in general. Such participants may feel as if they will be compelled to speak during the session and feel uncomfortable about their abilities to do so effectively.
- They are unaware of the topic for the meeting and are anxious because they imagine potential topics that would make them uncomfortable.
- They *are aware* of the topic but the topic itself creates anxiety. A department, for example, may be meeting to discuss criteria for individual evaluation and people may be nervous about how their job performance will be rated.
- They are concerned that the meeting will result in an increased workload or an assignment outside of their participants' range of abilities.
- They are unprepared to participate.
- Their experience in groups, or with this particular group, has been negative.
- Their experience with an individual or individuals within the group has been negative. Similarly, they may not have a positive working relationship with the person who is chairing the session.
- They have other projects that are more urgent and don't have time for the meeting.
- There are personal issues that are pressing which make concentrated group work difficult.

Any one of these or any combination could result in primary tension and make it difficult for work in groups to be successful from the beginning. How many of these have affected your attitudes prior to attending a meeting?

Secondary Tension

Once the meeting begins, secondary tensions or conflicts are likely to surface. These can be categorized into four areas: procedural, equity, affective, and substantive.

Procedural. These tensions stem from feelings that the *process* of interacting in the group is unproductive. Members of the group may feel that the agenda is weak or are dispirited because the leader is not adhering to the agenda. There may be no agenda at all which could cause procedural anxiety. Individuals who experience this type of conflict feel that if the session were to be conducted differently it would be more effective and productive.

Equity. Equity tensions occur when there is a perception of inequality. Participants in the group feel as if something is not fair. Typically, equity tensions fall into two subcategories. The first occurs when members feel as if they are assuming a disproportionate share of the responsibilities. In this instance, it may seem as if other participants are slackers or *social loafers*—a term used in the literature of group interaction to describe those who are derelict and allow, if not compel, other group members to do their work.[11] If participants sense that they must carry the weight of noncontributing members, tension may surface because of the inequity.

A second type of equity tension occurs when participants want to be involved in the group but are ignored by more powerful or controlling members. In this situation potential contributors feel bruised because what they say is not taken seriously. Members begin to wonder, "Why am I here?"

Affective. Affective tension surfaces when people in the group begin to dislike one another. Perhaps this could be the result of residual procedural, equity, or even primary tensions, but when this surfaces group interaction becomes very difficult. Participants will find it difficult to "hear" what adversaries are saying let alone consider the wisdom of any suggestions. The personality tensions may make individuals contrary and the discussions gratuitously argumentative. A perceived foe may suggest a plan that is well grounded in logic, but the rival is unable to see through the personal tension to legitimately evaluate the proposal.

Substantive. A positive type of tension is called *substantive conflict*. This refers to conflict that surfaces because of legitimate disagreements regarding the subject being discussed. Most people typically think of conflict as something negative, but this is not necessarily the case. Kreps identifies three beneficial aspects of conflict. It can

- Promote creativity and therefore facilitate problem solving.
- Promote the sharing of different ideas and therefore increase the amount of relevant information available.
- Serve to test the strength of opposing ideas.[12]

For example, let's assume your organization is considering building an indoor parking facility for employees. Further let's assume that a committee has been formed to discuss where the facility should be built. If one member of the committee suggests a lot on the west side of your property, another may disagree, point out the drawbacks of such a location, and offer another venue for parking. There's conflict between these two positions. But the conflict may well yield a better solution for the organization.

In short, substantive conflict is what you desire when you meet as a group. Leaders and all participants should actively try to create disagreement even when there seems to be total agreement on a particular subject. In the section of this chapter that deals with interventions we will discuss methods of generating substantive conflict.

What are your group attitudes and tendencies?

Do the statements below describe your attitudes or your behavior in groups? Please write a number 1–5 next to each item.

1. *The statement describes me very accurately*
2. *This statement is somewhat accurate.*
3. *The statement neither describes me well, nor describes me poorly*
4. *This statement is mostly inaccurate.*
5. *This statement does not describe me at all.*

_____ A. I'd prefer to work independently and not in groups.

_____ B. I don't mind confronting people when they're wrong.

_____ C. I'm a high communication apprehensive in meeting situations.

_____ D. When two people are arguing in a group meeting it bothers me.

_____ E. I like doing things in a structured way.

_____ F. When I'm in a problem-solving meeting my objective is to get things done, period.

_____ G. I make friends easily in groups.

_____ H. It doesn't bother me when people come in late to meetings.

_____ I. I'm often a pseudo listener in meetings. That is, I tend to pretend to listen.

_____ J. I think it's essential to respect the values and communication norms of people from other countries and cultures. This rarely happens.

_____ K. I'm reluctant to speak in groups because I think people won't understand me.

_____ L. I can't understand why some people won't compromise.

_____ M. I have sympathy for some people who "loaf" during meetings because I do that myself sometimes.

_____ N. I can't respect people who won't come to a meeting prepared.

_____ O. I enjoy being a leader in a group.

_____ P. I have a difficult time with people in authority, for example, people who are chairing meetings.

_____ Q. When someone else is the leader of a meeting I find myself thinking about how I might do things differently.

_____ R. Minorities and women seem to get "dissed" during meetings. No one seems to pay attention to minorities and women or respect their ideas.

_____ S. When a leader doesn't follow an agenda I get nervous.

_____ T. For me primary conflict is great when I spot someone in a group who has a huge ego.

_____ U. Side talking during meetings is not such a bad thing. I think people in general should relax and not be so uptight.

_____ V. I don't think it is appropriate for people to use profanity in a business meeting—even if we all know each other.

_____ W. I have difficulty making eye contact with people when I speak about sensitive issues.

_____ X. I'm reluctant to speak in meetings because I think people won't like what I say and therefore won't like me.

(continued)

_____ Y. When a subject is very sensitive to me I just clam up.

_____ Z. I don't think there's ever a reason to raise your voice and shout during a meeting.

Do your attitudes and tendencies help make groups effective? How would you want those with whom you interact in groups to respond to these questions?

COUNTERPRODUCTIVE GROUP TENDENCIES

In the musical *Annie Get Your Gun* Ethel Merman as Annie Oakley sang a song about how, despite her uneducated ways, she and others of her family knew how to behave by "doing a what [sic] comes naturally." While this may have worked for Annie and her brood, the fact is that "doing a what comes naturally" causes problems for groups. Default tendencies of groups and group members are counterproductive and create tensions. Below are some of these counterproductive group behaviors.

Conformity: Groupthink, the Asch Effect, and Goal Lining

Groupthink, the Asch Effect, and goal lining all refer to threats to group success. An assumption when convening in groups is that "two heads are better than one."[13] However, if two or more "heads" *actually act as one* then the value of collective communication is diminished. When this occurs meeting sessions will *not* do what they purport to do: provide an arena for sharing multiple perspectives that can result in high quality solutions.

Groupthink. Irving Janis popularized the word *groupthink* in a book about political decision making and a *Psychology Today* article.[14] Some authors have written that Janis actually coined the term, but the word was first used in 1952.[15] However, largely because of Janis, *groupthink* as a word has crept into the lexicon and has a home in a standard desk dictionary nestled securely between *group therapy* and *grouse*.[16]

Groupthink refers to the tendency for groups to make decisions without considering alternatives. Janis described it as

> . . .*a mode of thinking that people engage in when they are deeply involved in a cohesive in-group, when members' striving for unanimity override their motivation to realistically appraise alternative courses of action.*[17]

Essentially, when groupthink occurs, one member puts forth an idea and others readily agree without considering the advantages and disadvantages of the proposition. The group might do this because the suggested idea was presented by a powerful member, or because individuals don't want to "rock the boat," or because the members have no great individual stake in the decision. The 1961 decision of the Kennedy administration to invade the Bay of Pigs is typically cited as an example of groupthink.[18] Had there not been such a collective agreement it would seem to be impossible that all members participating in the deliberation would have agreed to an undertaking so unlikely to succeed. As recently as October 2001, the U.S. congress passed a controversial terrorism bill in the aftermath of the September 11 tragedy. Some people consider this quick collective response to be representative of groupthink.

Fear, inertia, or the desire to produce or conform reduces the potential for a group to be a dynamic unit where people think as individuals and pool their ideas. When groupthink occurs there are few individual thoughts, just "group think." Because of groupthink, meetings sometimes result in unimaginative short-sighted solutions to organizational problems. In addition, participants can become frustrated since they might wonder why their presence was necessary at a meeting characterized by groupthink. Why should one spend valuable time at a meeting if the predisposition of the group is simply to support the positions articulated by a powerful member?

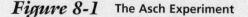

Figure 8-1   **The Asch Experiment**

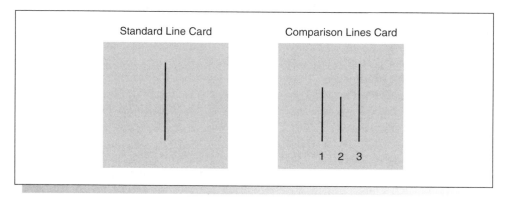

The Asch Effect. Solomon Asch designed an experiment to gauge how willing individuals would be to conform to clearly incorrect conclusions. The Asch Effect is the derivative of the experiment and explains a good deal about conformity and how it can affect groups.

Asch's experiment involved graduate students who were asked to compare 12 pairs of cards. Each pair consisted of what was called a "standard line" card and a "comparison line" card. On the standard line card was a single line. On the comparison line card there were three lines of varying lengths (see Figure 8-1).

The procedure for each study was the same.

- Seven to nine graduate students were brought into a room.
- The students would view the first of the 12 pairs of standard line cards and comparison line cards.
- The first student would then state aloud which line from the comparison line card was the same length as the line on the standard line card.
- Then the remaining students would, one by one, announce which line from the comparison line card was the same length as the standard line card.
- When all 9 had announced the selection for the first pair, the students would view the second pair and follow the same procedure.
- The study would continue until each of the 12 pairs had been viewed, and each of the subjects had orally declared his or her votes.

The correct answer in each case was obvious. For each of the 12 pairs of cards only one line on the comparison card could possibly be construed as the correct match.

However, among the seven to nine students involved in the experiment *only one* student was an actual subject. The others were conspirators helping to conduct the experiment. For each of the 12 comparisons, the helpers declared aloud that *another* line—**clearly not the correct one**—was indeed the one that matched the length of the line on the standard line card. After each of the conspirators would state that the *incorrect* line was the match, the lone actual subject (who was always the last to declare his or her vote) was put in the position of conforming, or disagreeing and identifying the correct and obvious answer.

Four out of five of the (real) subjects yielded to the pressures at least one time out of the twelve. Nearly three out of the five subjects yielded to the pressure at least two times out of twelve. As Goldhaber points out, what may be the most stunning feature of this study is that these groups were not cohesive groups, nor any kind of standing committee.[19] What might have been the tendency to conform had these persons been part of a cohesive group? Asch's study has been replicated in countries and cultures beyond North America. Bond and Smith report Asch studies with similar results conducted in Portugal, Kuwait, Brazil, France, Zimbabwe, Fiji, and Ghana.[20]

If people are willing to succumb to peer pressure when to do so is to agree to an absurd conclusion, how likely are people to succumb to such pressure when the idea, however inappropriate, is not entirely beyond reason?

Goal Lining. Goal lining, while slightly different from groupthink and the Asch Effect, also results in an absence of valuable substantive conflict. When goal lining occurs participants see reaching the goal as the lone criterion determining quality meeting interaction. If a group is meeting to come up with a list of the advantages and disadvantages of building a health facility for employees, then the objective of the meeting is seen by goal liners as that and that alone.

At first, one might wonder what is wrong with that. Why should the group be concerned with anything other than the goal? The problem with goal lining is that it tends to encourage participants to seek a conclusion without necessarily seeking a *group* conclusion. In the rush to cross the goal line, the group loses the potential value of discussion, creativity, and interaction.

Focus on Applications

Does your organization or class have a tendency to conform?

In order to assess the effects of conformity on meetings, consider conducting this exercise with an organization with which you are affiliated.

Explain to your organization (fraternity, club, class members) that you're doing an exercise to strengthen the quality of future club or organizational meetings. Randomly, break up your organization into subgroups of equal numbers. Ask each subgroup to rank the following in terms of the value of the terms/phrases for meeting success.

_____ Communication skills of individual members
_____ Commitment to goals of group
_____ Leadership
_____ Individual Preparation and Responsibility
_____ Site/Setting for meeting
_____ Creating and adhering to group agenda

(continued)

For example, if *Leadership* is considered by the subgroup to be the most significant factor for meeting success, then the subgroup should rank it as 1. If *Site/Setting for Meeting* is considered the second most significant then the subgroup should rank it as 2, and so on.

What do you predict will occur in the subgroups? Will there be goal lining just to get the exercise done? Will the Asch Effect be obvious? That is, will people conform regardless of the wisdom of ideas presented? Will groupthink prevail? That is, will the group agree quickly to one idea in order to "not rock the boat" or satisfy influential others?

Ethnocentrism: Cultural Elitism

Rhum describes ethnocentrism as "the belief that one's own culture is superior to others, which is often accompanied by a tendency to make invidious comparisons."[21] Varner and Beamer argue that there is a tendency for persons to perceive their own culture as superior and the values of others as primitive or backward.[22] (*Note:* Issues of ethnocentrism and intercultural communication will be discussed in greater detail in Chapter 12, Intercultural Communication and the Organization).

In an increasingly diverse workplace ethnocentricity can create *affective* tension in groups which will militate against successful communication. Ethnocentrism is also likely to create *equity* tensions as members of minority cultures may feel as if their opinions are discounted. Beebe, Beebe, and Ivy comment that "ethnocentrism and cultural snobbery is one of the quickest ways to create a barrier that inhibits rather than enhances communication."[23]

In your experience working in groups, has ethnocentricity been a factor? Do women and minorities tend to get the same "floor time" as other participants?

Inadequate Agendas and Hidden Agendas

Mosvick and Nelson asked 1,600 managers what went wrong with meetings. Of the top six items cited as obstacles, five related to either a poor agenda, no agenda, or not following an agenda.[24] An agenda is a list of topics to be addressed at a meeting session. Problems relating to agendas occur if (1) agendas are created to provide an illusion of structure and order as opposed to being designed to actually facilitate structure and order or (2) they're ignored. Some of the examples in the beginning of this chapter reflect *procedural* conflict that developed because agendas were illusory or disregarded.

Think of an agenda as a road map—as if it is the print out from a mapquest.com search you did on-line. If groups want to get from a starting point to a destination they need to follow the directions. Otherwise they will spend hours traveling but will be terribly frustrated after the journey because while they spent time "motoring" they didn't get where they wanted to go. Of course, it is likely that they wouldn't get where they wanted to go since they hadn't pursued a course that would get them there. An agenda is a road map that needs to be followed to allow groups to reach their meeting objectives.

Hidden agendas refer to personal and/or political meeting objectives that are hidden from the group. Let's assume that a department meets to discuss budget cutbacks. The alleged goal of the department is to determine what resources, programs, or personnel can and should be cut. The hidden agendas for each member are likely to be different from the alleged goal. Each member may want to preserve resources that they require and may fight for their individual needs as opposed to the group objectives.

© 2002 THE NEW YORKER COLLECTION FROM CARTOONBANK.COM. ALL RIGHTS RESERVED.

"On the one hand, eliminating the middleman would result in lower costs, increased sales, and greater consumer satisfaction; on the other hand, we're the middleman."

Employees often bring hidden agendas to meetings. These hidden agendas can reduce the effectiveness of group decision making.

THE ETHICS OF HIDDEN AGENDAS

ETHICAL PROBE

1. Assume that the following were the actual objectives for individual meetings. Can you list the likely hidden agendas that participants may bring to the session?
   a. To decide on whether to use print or the intranet for procedural manuals.
   b. To discuss the merits of flex time for middle managers.
   c. To examine criteria for annual bonus amounts.
2. Would there be anything unethical about pursuing any of the hidden agendas you have identified?

Consider another example. Assume you want a friend hired in your organization. Further let's assume that you are on the hiring committee and the committee decides that prior to interviewing anyone, they will identify those qualities necessary for any successful candidate.

If you were to attempt to engineer the discussion so that the "successful candidate qualifications" happened to coincide with your friend's credentials, you would be pursuing a hidden agenda. As is obvious these hidden agendas can undermine the success of the group interaction. They can also create *affective* conflict that may carry over to subsequent discussions on entirely other matters.

Competition Versus Cooperation

A spirit of cooperation, as opposed to a spirit of competition, facilitates effective communication in groups. What often happens in groups, however, is that participants tend to become ego-involved and competitive. Differences of opinion are good for groups, but fighting for your opinion *simply because it is yours* can create affective conflict.

As discussions develop in meetings individuals may become more and more attached to their stated perspectives on an issue and be reluctant to consider opposing points of view. A discussant's position on an issue may become intertwined with that person's ego. Julie's *position* on the new hire may become *Julie's* position. If you disagree with the position it may seem to Julie as a personal attack. What can occur is that participants cease discussing the merits of an issue and simply want to win. Very highly ego-involved individuals are a bane in groups since the meeting may not develop beyond these persons' need to be victorious. Cooperation versus competition is a key to success in groups, yet cooperation should not be construed with conformity or "going along to get along." Cooperative participants seek substantive conflict. They don't, however, consider the meeting a battleground where the successful members are the ones whose ideas are adopted by the group.

Tolerating High-Level Term Abstraction

Words have different levels of abstraction. A term with a high level of abstraction is more vague than a word with a low level of abstraction. For example, words like *benefits, success,* and *love* have relatively high levels of abstraction when compared to words like *cat, telephone,* and *stapler.* A group could be discussing the steps needed for a *successful* year and members of the group could be defining *success* differently. Some people might think success means that individuals would get large pay raises. Others might think that the organization would add staff; still others might think that at year's end all employees would be *spiritually* enriched. Without clarifying the precise nature of the terms being discussed, meetings can be frustrating simply because individuals are not speaking about the same thing.

Consider this second illustration. Assume you were on a school committee and were being asked to decide which of the following subjects should be required of high school students.

- Health
- Religion
- Citizen responsibility
- Art appreciation
- Personal economics
- Sexual education
- Cultural diversity

Further assume that your group knew that only some topics could be taught, and you had to rank the items in terms of "value for an educated student in a great society." Would you think that "high-level term abstraction" would affect your discussions?

INTERVENTIONS

An intervention is a tool or technique used to alter behavior that would likely not be altered had there been no intervention. As it relates to meetings, interventions are techniques that can be used to make these communication contexts less problematic and more successful. They are tools that can be used to alleviate primary or negative secondary tensions. Some interventions can help create positive substantive conflict and reduce the harmful effects of ethnocentricity, conformity, high-level abstraction, and even—in some cases—ego involvement.

Can meetings work? What makes them effective?

Below you will see a series of statements.

☐ Indicate how you feel about each statement by using the following scale.

1. strongly agree
2. agree
3. neither agree nor disagree
4. disagree
5. strongly disagree

☐ Then, for each statement, explain why you feel as you do providing an example from your experience to support your position.

_____ A. Business meetings must have an agenda.

_____ B. The key factor for successful meetings is responsible participants.

_____ C. Meetings are a necessary time for social cohesion. They can help to create a team attitude.

_____ D. The expression "two heads are better than one" makes sense as it applies to business sessions. You usually get a better result when you solve problems with others in a business meeting.

_____ E. Leaders in groups should run the session but essentially stay out of the way. Otherwise meetings become little more than presentations.

_____ F. Personality conflict can reduce meetings to battle grounds with people taking entrenched positions regardless of their true attitudes on a subject.

_____ G. Brainstorming typically provides more drizzle than rain.

_____ H. Information disseminated during meetings could as easily be communicated via e-mail or print.

_____ I. A challenge for leadership is making sure each person in a group has a genuine chance to participate. Most of the time this doesn't happen.

_____ J. Discussing ideas in meetings never works, because people are too "sold" on their own suggestions to be objective when listening to criticisms, even when the criticisms are constructive.

Types of Interventions

Buzz Groups. Assume that you are working in a large group and it seems as if only some people are participating. You might want to employ the intervention technique called *buzz groups* to increase participation and decrease the potential for problems related to *equity* conflict. With buzz groups, larger groups are divided into smaller ones. A group of 12 persons discussing the merits of a particular plan would be broken into six groups of two. See Figure 8-2.

Each group of two would discuss the same issue. After a period of time the six buzz groups of two would reconvene as a group of 12. Each buzz group would express to the group of the whole what they had discussed within their particular dyad.

Figure 8-2 Buzz Groups

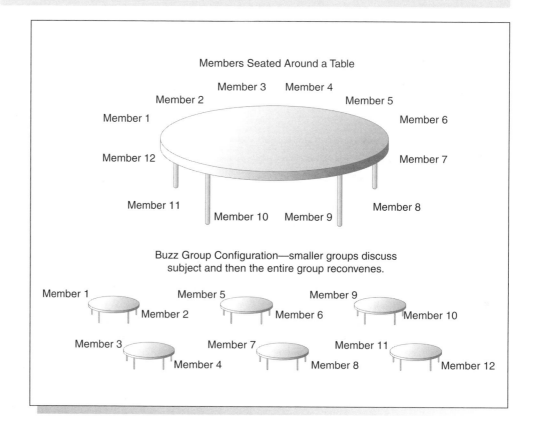

Members Seated Around a Table

Buzz Group Configuration—smaller groups discuss
subject and then the entire group reconvenes.

The main value associated with buzz groups is that it requires the participation of all and therefore tends to reduce equity tensions. A social loafer will have no place to hide in a buzz group and a high communication apprehensive is likely to feel more comfortable speaking to just one other as opposed to speaking to a larger group.

Brainstorming and Brainwriting. *Brainstorming* is a commonly used term that is misused much of the time. It has a precise meaning as a meeting intervention and can be used to generate desirable substantive conflict. The following is **not** an example of brainstorming.

> A pan-Hellenic campus group gets together to discuss establishing a code of ethics for campus fraternities and sororities. The group leader suggests that they brainstorm on the issue. One participant offers that it's probably a good idea to have a code of ethics because this way people will know what is morally appropriate and abide by the code. Another member responds and comments that the previous speaker is incorrect because people will not adhere to any code of ethics. A third person remarks that maybe a code of ethics will be recognized and adhered to because, after all, other pan-Hellenic codes are followed.

While this type of conversation might result in a valuable discussion, it is not an illustration of brainstorming even though most people tend to think of brainstorming this way. Brainstorming is not an "advantages and disadvantages" discussion.

Brainstorming is an idea-generating intervention that involves the identification and recording of any and all ideas germane to the topic being discussed. A key and essential feature of brainstorming is that at no point during the intervention is anyone permitted to criticize a "brainstormed" idea that another has offered. Indeed some people have argued that even outlandish ideas are welcome, because these ideas might be springboards for perhaps less bizarre but more creative ideas than others would consider and offer.[25] Below is how a brainstorming session might work using the illustration of the pan-Hellenic meeting.

The leader of the group would ask to hear the advantages of implementing a code of ethics. Group members would then identify, even shout out, any advantages they think to be appropriate. A member of the group would record, perhaps on a chalk board or on a flip chart, any comments made. A code of ethics would:

Increase the visibility of the Greeks

Increase the perception of the Greeks

Help the Greeks get funding

Reduce drugs on campus

Make my father happy

Encourage my mother to send me money

Improve race relations

Make it easy to recruit students

Result in the university supporting Greek activities

Cut down on profanity

Decrease communicable diseases.

Even comments like "Encourage my mother to send me money" are not to be derided. True brainstorming encourages any and all notions.

Subsequently, the ideas are discussed and evaluated. Brilhart and Galanes suggest that the group take a break after creating the brainstormed list before evaluation. Further, the authors comment that it might be wise to wait for a separate session for the evaluative discussion or have another group of persons examine the brainstormed ideas.[26]

A variation of traditional brainstorming is *polling brainstorming*. In polling brainstorming, the leader "polls" group members. Using the pan-Hellenic scenario, each participant in turn would be asked to identify an advantage of establishing a code of ethics. When their turn came, the members would offer an advantage until such time as all individuals had exhausted all ideas.

The advantage of polling brainstorming is that it encourages the participation of social loafers and high communication apprehensives. High communication apprehensives particularly may have valuable suggestions but may be unwilling to speak in a brainstorming session unless compelled to do so. A related advantage is that polling brainstorming makes it difficult for a dominating personality to overwhelm the session.

The polling approach can result, however, in a loss of spontaneity. Participants may just focus on having something to say when their turn comes and the session may not lather in the way it otherwise could. A way to deal with this disadvantage is to use the alternative of *brainwriting*. With brainwriting all individuals write down ideas and then subsequently draw from their individual list during a brainstorming session. Brainwriting does not fully address the concerns of not being able to piggy back off of other person's ideas. However, with brainwriting a participant is not restricted to the prewritten list so she or he could react to another's idea.

Nominal Group Techniques. Nominal group technique (NGT), developed by Delbecq and Van de Ven, attempts to avoid affective and procedural tensions.[27] This elaboration of brainwriting involves very little group interaction. The word nominal means, "in name only," and this technique is, in fact, a *group* approach in name only.

In NGT participants are asked to write down their solutions to a particular problem as they would in brainwriting. Persons, in a polling format, then express their ideas for solving the problem. Subsequently, all of these ideas are written on a board or flip chart. The leader proceeds to review each item so that the authors can clarify what is meant by each suggestion. At this point in the process there is no defense or criticism of any of the presented ideas.

After the clarifications are made, each participant is asked to vote on the ideas that are most preferable. On a sheet of paper the participants rank the top five solutions that have been advanced. The leaders collect the papers with the rankings and tally up the votes. The ideas that receive the most votes are then discussed and evaluated.

Since there is relatively little discussion, this is considered a nominal group technique—a group in name only. NGT is designed to decrease the negative effects of affective conflict.

An intervention that involves division of labor is a more common type of nominal group technique. This approach is used so frequently in task-related groups that it is unlikely that you have not employed this technique when working on group projects at your college.

When given a task, some groups will divide the task into subsections equal to the number of people in the group. A group of five assigned to describe the American presidency since Truman might decide to count the number of presidents since Truman, divide by five, and then assign each person two "presidencies" to research and describe. Subsequently each member of the group returns with 20 percent of the assignment and the group patches together the individual pieces.

The advantages of this approach are it

- Saves time
- Allows individuals to go into greater depth on their individual subjects
- Avoids affective tensions that might surface otherwise
- Avoids equity conflict if the separation of responsibilities is indeed equitable

The disadvantages are important to note as well. Dividing responsibilities

- Reduces positive substantive conflict
- Can create affective and equity conflicts if individuals do not or (legitimately or otherwise) can not do their work efficiently
- Can result in a disjointed product as different sections may not seamlessly fit together.

This approach of dividing tasks in problem-solving groups is very risky. It can be used to avoid affective and equity tensions, but if participants are not responsibly willing to complete their share *and* work to seamlessly join individual sections, the solution to the problem may be incomplete and disjointed. The technique also circumvents and subverts the ostensible goal of problem-solving meetings, that is, to gain collective insights that would be lost if work was done individually. Highly responsible group members can overcome some of these risks by being diligent to their own responsibilities, participating in the evaluation of other contributions as well as they are able, and working to seamlessly connect the various sections into a sensible whole.

Problem Census. In order to avoid problems related to high-level term abstraction or procedural conflict, groups may wish to use *problem census*. In this technique members are polled initially regarding their individual perspective and perceptions of the problem. This intervention is valuable because before you begin to discuss a topic the group can become relatively certain that participants are on the same page regarding the nature and dimensions of the topic.

Let's assume your group has been given the following charge: "Assess the value and wisdom of implementing a companywide training program for dealing with multicultural sensitivity and diversity." Prior to discussing ideas for the program, you might want to conduct a problem census. This polling process could reveal that individuals attending the workshop have a different sense of the meaning of

- Multicultural
- Sensitivity
- Training
- Program
- Diversity

You may discover that when thinking of *value and wisdom* of such a program some members would be concerned with

- Financial costs
- Long-term financial benefits
- Interpersonal social benefits
- Community service benefits
- Public relations value

You may discover that some people will consider the best way *to assess* the value and wisdom is by

- Looking at how other organizations have done it
- Reviewing prior attempts
- Examining the ethnic diversity of the organization
- Polling other members of the organizational community

By using problem census you may derive, before you actually begin, a better sense of the task at hand and a clearer method of how your group intends to proceed to meet the group goals.

Risk Technique. To avoid issues that surface relating to the Asch Effect or groupthink, meeting members might consider using *risk technique*. This approach requires each participant to play the role of "devil's advocate."

Devil's advocacy is a phrase used to mean arguing for a perspective that is contrary to whatever position has been advanced. For example, if your department meets and proposes making Fridays "casual dress days" you may want the department members to play the devil's advocate to that proposition. To play the devil's advocate, members would take the stance that casual dress days were *inappropriate* and argue, regardless of their actual perspective on the matter, that Fridays should *not* be casual days. The value of devil's advocacy is that it forces groups to examine a proposal in depth by exploring opposite perspectives.

Risk technique works as a polling technique. After a group has decided on a solution each member of the group plays the devil's advocate and identifies a risk associated with implementing that solution. These lists of risks are recorded. Subsequently the group reviews the list of risks and reevaluates the proposal. Most of the time the reevaluation does not result in the elimination of the proposal, but with the fine tuning of the resolution so that it addresses the concerns suggested by the risks.

For example, assume your group has decided to implement a new logo for your organization. When using risk technique you would ask each member of the group— *that had already decided to employ this new logo*—to play devil's advocate and identify problems with the utilization. For example, Donna might say that it would be too confusing to some customers to change the logo. Jermaine might suggest that it would be costly to implement. Rita may argue that the new logo will be too similar to a competitor's.

On the basis of these risks your group may fine tune your proposal, adopting a revised version that accommodates these risks. It is possible that you might decide to retain what your group had originally identified, despite the risks, because the value of that proposal exceeds the problems that were identified by the risks. In either case the risk technique has strengthened the quality of your group activity and solution.

It can be difficult for people to assume the role of devil's advocate particularly if moments earlier they presented the logic behind and supported the plan that's being considered. Yet, in order for risk technique to work, each person, regardless of how involved she or he may have been in the composition of the plan, must play the devil's advocate and assume a posture of someone who identifies proposed flaws. That way, the potential for groupthink and Asch Effect conformity is reduced.

General Procedural Model. An intervention that combines many of the techniques described previously is called general procedural model (GPM).[28] GPM is an effective approach for problem-solving meetings and an excellent technique for those groups who are experiencing procedural conflict and perhaps, consequently, affective and equity conflict. It is a five stage model.

1. **Identify the problem.** In this stage the group clarifies the objective for the meeting or the particular topic being discussed within the meeting. It is a good idea in this stage to use problem census.

2. **Brainstorm.** In this stage the group uses brainstorming as it was designed to be used, that is, without any evaluative component. Individuals brainstorm regarding solutions to the problem or dimensions of the problem. A group representative records the brainstormed ideas.

3. **Evaluation.** In this stage of GPM group members assess the merit of the brainstormed ideas. With large groups it is a good idea to consider buzz groups for step 3 of GPM.

4. **Selection of best idea.** At this point, the group attempts to come up with a consensus of the best solution, or more likely, the best combination of solutions to the group issue. At the conclusion of this stage you should consider using risk technique to evaluate the merit of the proposal. After using risk technique, fine

tune your solution so that it reflects the concerns identified during the risk technique intervention.

5. **Put the solution into effect.** Your group may need to generate a report, make a presentation, send a memorandum, contact officials, and/or even call another meeting to articulate the solution you've created. At this point in the process you decide how and when you shall put your solution into effect.

MAKING INTERVENTIONS WORK

Group Members as Participant-Observers

Any intervention technique is as good as the people who attempt to use the technique. Individuals need to be willing to employ interventions and not default to tendencies that are counterproductive. This is easier said than done. When I witness groups attempt to use, for example, brainstorming—regardless of the level or intelligence of the participants—it takes considerable effort for the members to avoid evaluating ideas as the brainstormed suggestions are made. When this occurs steps 2 and 3 of the general procedural model are combined rendering each step less valuable than it might otherwise be.

In order for interventions to work members need to become participant-observers. A participant-observer is someone *in* a group who concurrently participates and observes the process of participation.[29] A participant-observer, for example, comments on items on the agenda and also ensures that the agenda is followed.

This is work. Most people aren't accustomed to being participant-observers. Some individuals may be conscientiously active contributors, but few typically will concurrently evaluate the interaction process. However, in order for groups to function effectively members have to be vigilant. Interventions can work, but participants need to be committed to working at the interventions for them to be successful. *Intelligence, knowledge, even communication skill* does not guarantee effective group interaction. Members have to be both responsible participants and responsible observers of the process.

Leadership

Leadership Responsibilities. An important dimension for effective meetings is group leadership. Leaders in groups have a number of specific responsibilities. They should:

- **Plan for the meeting.** Decide if a meeting is necessary. Define the meeting objectives. Solicit agenda topics, prepare, and distribute an agenda.

- **Get the meeting started.** Group participants often assemble slowly. Discussants will engage in pastimes until some member calls the meeting to order. The duration of the preliminary chit chat sometimes exceeds the appropriate few minutes for such orientation. A leader has the responsibility to ensure that not too much time is wasted at the beginning of a session.

- **Keep the discussion on track.** Meetings are notorious for lengthy digressions. Discussion that might begin with an analysis of departmental purchasing can result in commiserating about the cost of Amanda's home basement refinishing and the difficulties of finding a responsible contractor. A leader has the responsibility to keep the discussion on topic. Meetings typically have time limits and lengthy digressions result in jamming the last few items on the agenda into an inappropriate time space.

- **Summarize periodically.** Because of different input and tangential commenting, it is wise to periodically summarize what has been brought out. After discussing one area on an agenda, a summary statement by the leader can provide closure for that area and allow the group to seamlessly segue to the next topic of the session.

- **Solicit comments from taciturn members.** Effective meetings require input from all participants. Often quiet members need prodding to voice their opinions. Quiet, here, is not synonymous with irresponsible. Taciturn members may be simply quiet and require encouragement. Leaders, to the extent that they can, should ensure that reserved participants do contribute to the discussion.

- **Curtail verbose members.** The other side of the problem is related to the loquacious discussant. Some people do not realize that they are monopolizing conversation. Others are aware and have no qualms with such inconsiderate behavior. A leader has the uncomfortable task of intervening when a group member is hogging time to allow for others' comments, and to facilitate progress toward the completion of the meeting's agenda.

- **Employ interventions.** A leader should consider and utilize approaches that can reduce negative group tensions.

- **Conclude the meeting.** Just as the leader has the responsibility to start the meeting, it is the leader's responsibility to end the session. At that time, the leader should summarize the progress of the session, indicate what remains to be done, and announce, if the information is available, when the next meeting will take place.

- **Plan for the next session.** Between meetings the leader has the job of planning for the next session. This includes sending out the minutes of the preceding session to committee members; taking care of the logistics for the next meeting (e.g., reserving meeting rooms and ensuring that the meeting time is appropriate for all parties and any guests who are to be invited to the next meeting); and soliciting additional agenda topics for the next session.

Being a leader is not an easy job. It's a complex task that requires tact and communication skill. As American author Caskie Stennett once wrote about diplomats, a leader has to be "a person who can tell you to 'go to hell' in such a way that you actually look forward to taking the trip."

Leadership Styles. There are three basic leadership styles. **Authoritarian** or **autocratic** leaders are, as the label suggests, dictatorial and nondemocratic. **Laissez-faire** leaders are the opposite of authoritarians. They believe that the best way to lead a group is by keeping your "hands-off." A laissez-faire leader believes that a group can run itself and, therefore, to guide it is to wield power that is not only unnecessary but counterproductive. A **democratic** leader is different from either a laissez-faire or an authoritarian leader. The democratic leader seeks the input and advice from group members. She or he may make the eventual decisions regarding directions for the group, but those decisions are not made without considering the concerns of other members of the group.

- An authoritarian leader would determine a meeting agenda.
- A laissez-faire leader would assume that if meeting members needed an agenda the group would decide to create one.

- A democratic leader would ask for input on what should be in the agenda and when a meeting might be. Then she or he would construct the agenda.

There are a few other related labels that are used to describe leadership types in groups. A **de facto** leader is someone who, essentially, is the leader despite the fact that there is a **designated** or **nominal** other leader. Someone may have been designated as the leader but acts as a leader in name only. When that is the case someone else may begin to assume the natural leadership responsibilities. That person is, in reality or de facto, the leader. Occasionally an autocratic leader may incur the wrath of a group such that another member becomes the de facto leader. In these instances the de facto leader emerges because the other group members are not attending to the directives of the designated autocratic leader.

Leadership is important for most groups. If it were not, then there would be no such phenomenon as a de facto leader. The democratic leadership style is likely to be most effective in organizational contexts. There could be some very low energy groups for which an authoritarian group leader might be necessary and some very highly responsible groups for whom anything other than a laissez-faire leader would be counterproductive.

ELECTRONIC MEETINGS

As we discussed in Chapter 5, technology has had an effect on much of organizational communication. In the late 1980s researchers at the University of Arizona devised a way to utilize technology for same-site meetings.[30] This technology would be employed to avoid problems related to affective conflict and equity conflict. Also these same-site electronic meetings were designed to increase the chances for positive substantive conflict.

Same-site electronic meetings are held in horse shoe shaped rooms. Participants at the meetings have personal computers at their desks and a facilitator stands at the

Example of an electronic meeting room configuration.

COURTESY OF DANIEL MITTLEMAN, DEPAUL UNIVERSITY CTI.

boot of the horseshoe, leading the session. Instead of members conversing on the subject of the meeting, the facilitator will pose a question to participants and then members would type in their responses on their computers. The comments of all members would appear anonymously on a screen behind the facilitator. On the basis of the response, the facilitator would pose another question. Again, instead of conversing, the participants would type in their reactions. When the meeting ended participants could immediately receive a written summary of the meeting.

Several of the purported advantages of electronic meetings relate to the anonymity of the process. The assumption is that anonymity will result in greater substantive conflict and less equity conflict. Group members would not be shy about offering ideas. They could not be identified and therefore would not be afraid that they might be attacked because of their ideas or because of pre-existing personality tensions.

In addition, supporters of electronic meetings claim that their system allows for "simultaneous entry." This means that, unlike conventional face-to-face meetings, participants do not need to wait for their turn to offer an idea but can type whenever they get a notion and their idea will get "heard."

Further, proponents believe that because of the structured nature of the session and the format, there is less chance of procedural conflict and digression, and greater chances that the group will adhere to the time limits and be productive. At the end of the session a printed copy of the minutes—an immediate record of the session—is available.

Detractors of electronic meetings argue that the process is dehumanizing. One respondent to a proposal for electronic meetings commented that if "we can't talk face to face about this stuff, forget about it." Like other electronic/print methods for communication electronic meetings lack the nonverbal components that complement orally communicated information. Also, detractors claim that the advantage of anonymity is a non factor since people can be identified by the nature of their writing style or because of pet phrases they tend to use.

There is yet another reason why anonymity can actually prove to be a negative. If motivation is a function of recognition as was proven with the Hawthorne Studies, not getting credit for good ideas might reduce the desire for some people to make proposals. Some may fear that their ideas could be easily "stolen" by others.

There is also a cost factor related to these same-site meetings which can be prohibitive. This is reflected by the fact that users are typically financially secure operations. Therefore, electronic meetings may well be an unrealistic idea for some companies. Finally in terms of problems, there are still persons who are uncomfortable with technology and their input would be limited with electronic meetings.

The emergence of electronic meetings reflects both the desire for organizations to reduce tensions in the meeting context and the apparently natural tendency to use technology when it is available.

Lois Kelly, Founder and Principal: Meaning Maker

Lois Kelly launched the marketing consulting firm Meaning Maker in 1997. Prior to Meaning Maker, Kelly co-founded Thunder House, a pioneering Internet marketing agency that was subsequently acquired by advertising giant McCann-Erickson. She was also senior vice president of Weber Group, one of the largest public relations firms in the world, and president of Potter Hazelhurst Public Relations. Early in her career she was a CEO speechwriter for Fortune 100 companies and a communications specialist for AT&T. She has ghost written more than 75 speeches and articles for CEOs.

Meetings have become "let me show you my PowerPoint presentation." The best thing that can happen in corporate America is that there is a ban on PowerPoint. To me a meeting is a place where there is interaction and something gets decided and learned. I have sat through so many meetings where people just go through their slides. I have also attended too many sessions where dominant personalities control the meeting in a counterproductive way.

When we communicate we have a responsibility to help people understand, not just send out information. When a meeting becomes a session where participants simply want to hear themselves talk, or present their graphics, without regard to what is being understood, then the meeting—which might have otherwise had some value—becomes a colossal waste of time. Similarly, e-mail is a wonderful tool but it highlights problems people have communicating. People just spew information without regard to its quality. People have, excuse me, but e-mail diarrhea. Often what is disseminated electronically in organizations has little value to the receivers. Also, we have become so dependent on communication technology that we become powerless when we are without it. I was in San Francisco with a client, when there was a blackout, and the client could not plug in the computer. The poor man was sweating bullets. Without his computer he was powerless. I had to give the presentation for him. He couldn't deliver the talk without the crutch of the so-called Visual Aid.

On Meaning Maker's web page I describe the company as one that helps organizations develop communication strategies that "cut through the clutter" and deliver what I call the "aha" factor. We want our receivers to say "aha" when they receive our messages. We want there to be meaning. And we want to be honest in doing so. Lying is right up there with stealing, and I'm referring to either implicitly or explicitly communicated falsehoods. *Transformational* and *Revolutionary* are two terms I have heard too often to describe products which are neither. When I tell clients that deceptive communication is inappropriate, I am told—occasionally—that "I don't get it" that I don't get the fact that deception is okay in contemporary society. Believe me, I get it. Deceptive communicators do not. Ethical communication is critical for CEOs.

The three things that I emphasize about communication is context, relevance, and emotion. Communicators must frame the message for their audiences, explain the relevance of the communication and be passionate. Emotion is the superhighway to meaning. When you hear someone talk at a meeting, or anywhere actually, when that person is passionate, sad, angry, it gets through. In corporate communication much has been sterilized to be corporatespeak and we tend not to get the passion and we tune out because we as receivers miss that passion.

A Toolbox

1. Meetings are both problematic and necessary for effective organizational communication.
2. Successful communication in groups requires
   - Awareness of common conflicts that affect all groups.
   - Identification of conflicts and counter-productive tendencies that are typical of your group.
   - A willingness to work in order to overcome these problems.
3. Intervention techniques can be used to
   - Increase participation
   - Reduce personality tension
   - Increase the quality and quantity of ideas
   - Reduce tensions associated with meeting procedure
4. Some intervention techniques include
   - Buzz groups: to increase participation
   - Risk technique: to reduce "groupthink"
   - General procedural model: to decrease procedural conflict
   - Brainstorming/brainwriting: to increase creativity

1. What are the sources of primary tensions?
2. Why do secondary tensions surface in the organizations to which you belong?
3. Why do you find the results of the Asch studies surprising or not surprising?
4. Is it inevitable that groups will be burdened by social loafers? Explain.
5. Of the intervention techniques discussed in this chapter which are likely to
   a. Involve communication apprehensives
   b. Avoid procedural tension
   c. Reduce equity tensions
   d. Increase substantive conflict
6. What are the benefits and drawbacks of problem-solving techniques that involve division of labor?
7. Describe the type of leader that you find to be the most effective.
8. Please read the following case and respond to the questions that follow.

Case 8.2—Efficient Employees and Inefficient Meetings

Background. Richard Hilton works in a department with 14 intelligent, creative, and diligent others. Hilton is the designated team leader, but the department culture is such that everyone is strongly encouraged to actively take responsibility for projects and problems. In most instances, the employees do not require or desire any authority figure. Hilton maintains that, in nearly every activity, the employees in his department work cooperatively and supportively. However, this tendency to work well together is not characteristic of behavior during meetings.

Problem Description. In Hilton's department, there are no regular weekly or biweekly meetings. A meeting is called only when someone feels as if the team needs to discuss a particular matter. The meeting host—the person who called for the meeting—becomes the de facto chair for the session.

The host will not begin a meeting session until at least seven of the team members arrive in the conference room. Since many individuals arrive late, the meetings tend to begin 5 to 10 minutes after the designated starting time. The next 10 minutes of each meeting is spent discussing mundane topics such as weekend activities or the weather. As a result of waiting 5 to 10 minutes for the seven members to arrive, and then spending 10 minutes speaking about social matters, Hilton reports that the department actually begins discussing business issues 15 to 20 minutes later than scheduled. The meetings are (eventually) attended by all 14 members of the department.

When the session formally starts, the host orally outlines the reasons for the meeting. These prefatory comments constitute the meeting agenda. The group then aimlessly discusses the issues raised in the prefatory remarks. The conversation rapidly disintegrates. Several sidebar conversations develop. Typically those who are unaffected by the meeting topics begin to discuss matters that are not even tangential to the purported goals of the session. Participants frequently talk over and interrupt each other. Points of view on matters of no consequence are disputed, sometimes heatedly, which occasionally results in offended members remaining silent for the remainder of the session. The meeting host frequently loses control and the group strays further and further from the alleged goals of the session.

As the meeting comes to a close, Hilton's group finds itself in one of the following scenarios:

- No agreement was reached and another meeting is deemed necessary.
- Additional items were identified and assigned to people for follow-up.
- Action items were identified but not assigned to people.
- Some agreement was reached but the group would not be able to articulate what they had agreed to.

Each of these scenarios is unattractive:

- Another meeting is considered a waste of time for all involved.
- From past practice, additional items assigned to people get little to no further attention and tend to drop by the wayside as other items become more crucial.
- By not assigning items to people, the department guarantees that nothing further will be done on the issue.
- The value of coming to agreement becomes relatively inconsequential if there is no collective understanding of the agreement.

In sum, this highly intelligent group communicates very poorly during meetings. While the group would not tolerate a lack of productivity or inefficiency outside of the meeting contexts, no person appears to be willing to, or know how to, restructure the meeting for efficiency.

1. What recommendations do you have for Richard Hilton?
2. How would you recommend that Hilton communicate your recommendations to the team members? In a meeting? By memorandum?
3. Would you limit the numbers of people who attend future meeting sessions?
4. Would electronic meetings work with this group?
5. Is it inevitable that this group will have problems with meetings?

ENDNOTES

[1] Emery, David, *The Compleat Manager*, McGraw Hill, 1970, pp. 27–28.

[2] Barash, Isadore, "A New Economic Indicator," *Newsweek*, September 9, 1985, pp. 11–12.

[3] Barry, Dave, "Twenty-Five Things I Have Learned in Fifty Years," in *Dave Barry Turns 50*, Crown, 1998, p. 183.

[4] Four times a year I conduct a study that involves asking evening MBA students who concurrently are full-time employees to describe communication breakdowns they've experienced on the job. In one three-quarter period 27 percent of the problems were meeting related. In one particular quarter 55 percent of the problems dealt with communication in meetings. A discussion of meetings based on this study is found in my article, "Meetings: Why We Need Them, Why We Hate Them. How to Fix Them," *Journal of Employee Communication Management*, May/June 2001, pp. 23–29.

[5] Antony, Jay and John Cleese, *Meetings, Bloody Meetings*, directed by Peter Robinson, Video Arts Limited, Chicago, 1993.

[6] In Sue DeWine's *The Consultant's Craft: Improving Organizational Communication*, the author actually **entitles** her chapter on meetings: "Why Are Meetings So Boring and Unproductive?" Bedford/St. Martin's, 2001 p. 206.

[7] Op. cit., Barash, p. 12.

[8] Zaremba, Alan, "Meetings: Why We Need Them, Why We Hate Them. How to Fix Them," *Journal of Employee Communication Management*, May/June 2001, p. 25.

[9] DeWine, Sue, *The Consultant's Craft: Improving Organizational Communication*, Bedford/St. Martins, 2001, pp. 208–211.

[10] Berko, Roy, Andrew Wolvin, and Darlyn Wolvin, *Communicating: A Social and Career Focus*, seventh edition, Houghton Mifflin, pp. 427, 429.

[11] *Social Loafing* as a term was first used in an article by B. K. Latane and S. Harkins entitled, "Many Hands Make Light the Work: The Causes and Consequences of Social Loafing," *Journal of Personality and Social Psychology*, vol. 37, 1979, pp. 822–832. Also see Beatrice Schultz, "Improving Group Communication Performance: An Overview of Diagnosis and Intervention," in *The Handbook of Group Communication Theory and Research*, Lawrence R. Frey editor, Sage, 1999, pp. 388–389.

[12] Kreps, Gary, *Organizational Communication second edition*, Longman, 1990, pp. 191–192.

[13] The technical term for this phenomenon is "nonsummativity." This means that the result of a group interaction will be unequal to the sum of its parts. The hope is that the interaction of all persons will result in a discussion that is positively nonsummative. However, because of the primary and secondary tensions discussed in this section, it is not impos-

sible that the result could be *negatively* nonsummative. In this case "two heads" are actually "worse than one."

[14]Janis, Irving L., *Victims of Groupthink: A Psychological Study of Foreign Policy Decisions and Fiascoes.* Houghton Mifflin, 1972. Subsequently revised and entitled as *Groupthink: Psychological Studies of Policy Decisions and Fiascoes,* Houghton Mifflin 1982. The *Psychology Today* article was entitled simply "Groupthink," November 1971, vol. 5, no. 6, pp. 43–46, 74–76.

[15]Date of origin of "groupthink" varies depending on the dictionary one uses. *The Third Barnhart Dictionary of New English* published in 1990 lists the date of origin as 1959. *The Random House Unabridged,* Second Edition published in 1987 lists the origin between 1950–55. It is the *Merriam Webster Collegiate* Tenth Edition 1993 that lists the origin as 1952. Brilhart and Galanes use the expression "coined the term" on page 269 of *Effective Group Discussion.* They are essentially correct in that the meaning prior to Janis's publications referred to the thoughts that came out of group work as opposed to the counterproductive qualities of what is contemporarily considered as groupthink.

[16]*Merriam Webster's Collegiate Dictionary,* Tenth Edition, 1993, p. 515. Interestingly the 1964 *American College Dictionary* that omits "groupthink" also omits "group therapy."

[17]Janis, Irving L., *Groupthink: Psychological Studies of Policy Decisions and Fiascoes,* Houghton Mifflin, 1982, p. 9.

[18]For example, Janis, Irving, *Crucial Decisions: Leadership in Policymaking and Crisis Management,* Free Press, 1989, p. 57.

[19]Goldhaber, Gerald, *Organizational Communication,* Sixth Edition, *Wm C. Brown/Benchmark,* 1993, p. 249.

[20]Bond, Rod and Peter Smith, "Culture and Conformity: A Meta Analysis of Studies Using Asch's (1952b, 1956) Line Judgment Task," *Psychological Bulletin,* January 1996, p. 112.

[21]Rhum, Michael, in *The Dictionary of Anthropology,* Thomas Barfield editor, Blackwell, 1997, p. 155.

[22]Varner, Iris and Linda Beamer, *Intercultural Communication in the Global Workplace,* Second Edition, McGraw-Hill Irwin, 2001, p. 16.

[23]Steven Beebe, Susan Beebe, and Diana Ivy, *Communication Principles for a Lifetime,* Allyn and Bacon 2001, p. 161.

[24]Mosvick, Roger and Robert Nelson, *We've Got to Start Meeting Like This,* Park Avenue, 1996, p. 31. The sixth item, ranked number two on the list, was "Inconclusive: No results, decisions, assignments or follow up."

[25]Sunwolf and David Seibold, "The Impact of Formal Procedures on Group Processes: Members and Task Outcomes," in *The Handbook of Group Communication Theory and Research,* Lawrence R. Frey editor, p. 400.

[26]Brilhart, John and Gloria Galanes, *Effective Group Discussion,* Ninth Edition, McGraw Hill, p. 302.

[27]Delbecq, Andre, Andrew H. Van de Ven, and David H. Gustafson, *Group Techniques for Program Planning: A Guide to Nominal Group And Delphi Processes,* Scott Foresman, 1975 pp. 7–10.

[28]Brilhart, John and Gloria Galanes, *Effective Group Discussion,* Seventh Edition, p. 238.

[29]Op. cit., Brilhart and Galanes, *Effective Group Discussion,* Ninth Edition, p. 16.

[30]Nunamaker, Dennis, Valicich, Vogel, and George, "Electronic Meeting Systems to Support Group Work," *Communications of the ACM,* vol. 34, no. 7, July 1991.

9

Making Presentations in Organizations

Why doesn't the fellow who says, "I'm no speechmaker" let it go at that, instead of giving a demonstration?

—Kin Hubbard

The breastplate and the sword are not a stronger defense on the battlefield, than eloquence is to a person amid the perils of prosecution.

—Tacitus

"We can't hear you, George."
"Well, I can hear you."

—President George W. Bush using a bullhorn in response to a New York Fire Department worker at Ground Zero September 14, 2001.

© CORBIS

Case 9.1—*The Gamble and Kelliher Study*

P aul Gamble and Clare Kelliher published an article in 1999 related to the quality and value of organizational briefings.[1] The researchers studied short presentations that were delivered by managers to employees at the start of a business day in a retail outlet. During these briefings the managers intended to "disseminate information to staff, affect motivational stance, engender a commitment to sales targets, and build a sense of common goals."[2] The sessions were indeed brief—between 5 to 9 minutes in length. The researchers distributed questionnaires to the employees who had been briefed, and subsequently evaluated the completed questionnaires. The goal of the study was to assess the effectiveness of the briefing sessions.

The results of the study indicated that there was almost no correlation between what the employees contended had been the subjects of the briefings and what the managers contended were the messages that had been relayed!

In an abstract to their article the authors wrote that had the managers been aware of the results they would likely have remarked, "I might as well have been talking to myself."[3]

It would seem as if while the presentations were being made, and the managers were under the illusion that the employees were absorbing information, very few employees were paying attention *or* employees were paying attention but could not comprehend what was being uttered by the managers. Remarkably, the results of Gamble and Kelliher's study are similar to a previously conducted one.[4]

Another interesting aspect of the study is that while the briefings were considered important components of managerial activity, only one of the nine managers involved in the study had had any form of presentation skills training. Moreover, formal managerial evaluations did not include an assessment of managers' speaking capabilities.[5]

Apparently it was assumed that (1) All managers could deliver these presentations well and therefore training was unnecessary. (2) Even though briefings were considered—in the words of their Head of Management Development—"so integral to the role of management,"[6] there was no need for formal evaluations to include an assessment of speaking abilities.

☐ *Do the results of the Gamble/Kelliher study surprise you?*

☐ *In your experience have you found business presentations (of any length) relatively easy to understand?*

☐ *What are the "communication noises" that can account for the results of this study?*

☐ *Do you find it surprising that the organization simply assumed that managers would be able to deliver these presentations well?*

☐ *Do you find it surprising that managerial evaluations did not include an assessment of speaking abilities?*

ABSTRACT

It has been said that one of Abraham Lincoln's greatest assets was "his ability to express his convictions so clearly and with such force that millions of his countrymen made them their own."[7] Organizational leaders also have to express convictions clearly and forcefully. What separates great leaders from average ones is not necessarily their innovative ideas, but their capacities to articulate these ideas in presentational contexts.

Not only senior corporate leaders, but all managers and many employees must deliver presentations at one time or another. Organizational communicators can make successful careers out of excellent presentation skills or can be ruined because of their fears of speaking in front of an audience. Surveys repeatedly indicate that people have tremendous anxiety about making presentations.[8]

This chapter deals with effective business presentations and how individuals can improve their capabilities and comfort levels in this area.

OBJECTIVES

When you have completed this chapter, you should be able to:

☐ **Identify four styles of speaking and their advantages and disadvantages.**
☐ **Describe the structural requirements of a presentation.**
☐ **List factors to consider when using visual support.**
☐ **Explain the steps to preparing for a question and answer session.**
☐ **Describe what is meant by *communication apprehension* and employ techniques for reducing presentation anxiety.**

THE POWER OF QUALITY PRESENTATIONS

In July 1987 Lieutenant Colonel Oliver North wowed the American public, and within the course of one short week went from potential villain to national hero. Crowds shouted hosannas for North, chanting "OL-LEE, OL-LEE" the same way that boxing enthusiasts used to cheer for former heavyweight champion Muhammad Ali. People sent North thousands of telegrams wishing him support, and the Lieutenant Colonel found himself on the cover of almost every major news magazine in the country.

The primary reason for North's instant success was nothing other than North's excellent communication skills. Oliver North was a brilliant speaker. He was eloquent. He was forceful vocally. He was expressive with gesturing and eye contact. He wowed the television viewing public because of his ability to speak publicly in a way few others can.

Our history is marked by leaders who had, as an unusual skill, an ability to speak well. Ronald Reagan, aptly dubbed the great communicator, had an innate ability to speak in front of crowds. This ability played no small part in his so-called Teflon presidency.

New York mayor Rudolph Giuliani has become a national figure because of how effectively he has spoken to his bruised constituency after the September 11 attacks. President Bush, similarly, earned extraordinarily high approval ratings after his various addresses to the nation in the wake of the tragedy. The profile of British Prime Minister Tony Blair has also become more positive as a result of several presentations he has made since September 2001.

In the 1960s John Kennedy and Martin Luther King were successful leaders in that era's social revolution. Both Kennedy and King were vibrant speakers whose rhetorical abilities were essential assets as they led the nation through tense historical periods.

On the downside of this phenomenon there is the specter of the eloquent Adolf Hitler mobilizing the masses in Germany to participate in atrocities so incredible that even the incontrovertible evidence leaves honorable people incredulous. The power of public speaking is, simply, one of the strongest weapons humans have.

Organizational communicators can make careers out of excellent presentation skills or can be ruined because of their fears of speaking in front of people. Managers may not need to possess the presentation skills of a Reagan, King, or Giuliani, but they do need to know how to engage their organizational audiences. All organizational communicators should understand the basic principles that govern how to prepare for and deliver quality presentations.

PRESENTATION STYLES

All presentations can be grouped into one of four categories. Speeches are either impromptu, extemporaneous, manuscript, or memorized presentations.

Impromptu presentations are "off-the-cuff" presentations that are delivered without any preparation. Responses to questions, when the inquiry was not anticipated, also fall into the category of impromptu speeches.

Extemporaneous presentations are those that are delivered from notes. The notes can be as detailed as a formal outline presented on PowerPoint slides, or as brief as a few words listed on a 3-by-5 index card. Many, if not most, business presentations are extemporaneous. Even when speakers are following an outline that is memorized (note that the outline is memorized, not each word in the presentation) the presentation is said to be extemporaneous. In extemporaneous talks, speakers use the outline to spark recollections of the message to be conveyed, but must, while in front of the audience, select the correct word to match the ideas.

Manuscript presentations are delivered, *not read,* from a prepared text. Manuscript presentations are delivered, word for word, from that prepared text.

Memorized presentations are simply manuscript speeches that have been committed to memory. A presentation is only classified as a memorized talk if the delivery is a word-for-word memorization.

The goal for any source is to reach the receiver with the intended message. Public presentation contexts are no different in terms of communication objectives. However, in presentations, as opposed to other types of communication—interpersonal or group, for example—the speaker has a distinct and important advantage. In presentation contexts, the source typically has time to consider the best possible method for communicating the message. The speaker can analyze the nature of the audience, the nature of the situation, and the physical characteristics of the setting for the talk. In short, the speaker can and should prepare comprehensively in order to maximize the chances for effective receipt of information. One preparatory step involves selecting the best of the four styles for the particular audience and speaking event. Below is a discussion of the advantages and disadvantages of each style.

Impromptu Formats

There are very few advantages to using impromptu formats when making presentations. When speakers use this style they are essentially surrendering the advantage that public communication contexts afford. Typically, when we make presentations we have the opportunity to think about what we will say before the communication event. Since, by definition, an impromptu talk is one given without any prior preparation, when one elects to speak using the impromptu style she or he forfeits an advantage.

The simple reason that explains why we hear so many impromptu speeches—despite the dubious wisdom of the choice—is because many people prefer not to invest the energy necessary to prepare for other presentation formats. Speakers either assume that they don't need to prepare, or are lazy and decide to "wing it." Some persons who are extraordinarily knowledgeable about a subject assume that their knowledge alone will enable them to speak without preparation. One can be a professional expert in an area and still speak about the area unprofessionally.

> Knowing what you're talking about is important, of course, but it should not give a speaker the illusion that he or she need not prepare for a presentation.

It is good for speakers to *be able* to make impromptu talks. There are times when people simply have to deliver presentations in this way. If at a large meeting, for example, the coordinator suddenly calls on a participant and says, "Why don't you come on up here and tell us what you've been doing over these past few months." The participant's ensuing description of activities will be an impromptu presentation.

Additionally, if at the end of an extemporaneous or manuscript speech, the speaker solicits questions from the audience, the answers to these questions will be impromptu speeches. (Such responses would not be impromptu speeches if the speaker had anticipated the questions and had prepared responses for the anticipated queries).

In sum, while it is good to be able to speak without preparation it is unwise to use an impromptu style when you have an alternative. While some speakers might be able to impress audiences with their verbal dexterity when employing this format, most speakers are more likely to negatively impress audiences.

ETHICAL PROBE

DELIVERING IMPROMPTU TALKS

Assume you are a person who has achieved considerable fame because of business decisions that have made you and stockholders wealthy. Assume further that you have been asked to speak to business students at a university to discuss the nature of your success. Finally, assume that you are being paid a large sum to speak to the students.

- ☐ Is there anything unethical about delivering an impromptu speech?
- ☐ Would there be anything unethical about delivering an impromptu speech if you were speaking without payment?

Memorized Formats

Memorized formats are also problematic and are strongly discouraged. Unless one is an actor or actress, memorized talks pose many more disadvantages than advantages. Remember, a memorized presentation is a manuscript presentation committed to memory. Actors and actresses spend months trying to get their speeches "right." Most managers do not have months to get their manuscripts right. Trying to memorize the manuscripts in their entirety, and subsequently delivering the speeches in this memorized mode, can be disastrous.

> A seminar participant, Kelly, once began a presentation by standing behind the lectern and staring seriously out at the audience. Kelly then slowly moved around the podium and stood in front of the speaker's table. He pointed out at his audience and declared, "Remember this!"
>
> Kelly's stern face then turned ashen, and his imperiously pointed finger became limp, as he had completely forgotten the line in his speech that followed "remember this."
>
> It is one thing to forget a line, but it is far more humiliating to do so immediately after saying, "Remember this."

When words are forgotten in a memorized presentation, the speaker is typically without resources. People memorize speeches in a word sequence. That is, people—unless they are willing to put the time into the memorizations that professional performers expend—tend to memorize the sequencing of the statement with less than the appropriate regard for the meanings behind the words. Therefore, if the place is lost, so are the speakers, because in terms of content, there are few clues as to where they are in the presentation.

A memorized speech can be effective if a speaker delivers the same exact talk over and over again to different audiences. Some organizations give their spokespersons scripts that they must deliver to several audiences. It is inevitable that one would eventually memorize a script that is delivered on multiple occasions. Also, because of the many opportunities to present the same message, the speaker will become intimate with the content in the same way that performers become familiar with their speeches. As a rule, however, people who give presentations infrequently should not memorize the talks. Too many factors are likely to negatively affect the process.

Extemporaneous and Manuscript Formats

Both manuscript and extemporaneous styles can be effective in business environments. Let's examine the comparative value of both approaches.

COMPARING MANUSCRIPT AND EXTEMPORANEOUS FORMATS

Advantages of Extemporaneous Approaches	Advantages of Manuscript Approaches
Flexibility and mobility	Total preparation
Informality and interactivity	Precision with word choice
Allows for audience adaptation and feedback induced responses	Easier to time
Potential for fluid utilization of visual support	Can be delivered by non experts
Relatively easy to maintain eye contact	Avoids digressions and omissions
Reduces chances of monotonous reading	Avoids use of speech fillers
Less time required for construction	Can be available for distribution concurrently

Benefits of Using the Extemporaneous Approach

Flexibility, Informality, and Interactivity. Extemporaneous presentations have several advantages over the manuscript format. In general, the extemporaneous approach affords much more flexibility. Extemporaneous speakers have the option of moving away from the lectern and can move toward or away from sections of the audience as appropriate. For this reason and others, extemporaneous talks tend to create a more informal atmosphere than do manuscript presentations and there are times when such informality is beneficial.

Manuscript talks also tend to be linear in that the orally communicated message is consistently sent one way from presenter to audience. In an extemporaneous format there can be multiple and easy opportunities for audience members to react, comment, and participate in the presentations. In certain presentation contexts, this interactivity is essential. Trainers, and most salespeople, for example, could not give manuscript talks and still maintain the interactive environment necessary for effective teaching, learning, and selling.

Eye Contact. Another benefit of extemporaneous speaking pertains to the potential and capacity for more eye contact. Let's take a moment to examine this issue of eye contact as it pertains to presentations and speaking styles.

Poor eye contact during talks can occur regardless of presentation style. Manuscript speakers sometimes read their entire message, rarely looking at the audience. Extemporaneous speakers who are apprehensive may be unwilling to look into the eyes of the receivers and will find some inanimate object on which to focus their attention. I have witnessed extemporaneous business talks delivered to PowerPoint projections, windows, air conditioners, handouts, shoes, ceilings, and finger nails.

The purpose of eye contact is to establish rapport with the audience, and it is essential to have sustained eye contact often enough to obtain such rapport. Many beginning speakers attempt to finesse this requirement by snapping their heads up periodically, as if to meet a certain quota of "eye contacts" for the presentation. There is little value in jerking your face up intermittently during a presentation. The value of eye contact is derived from creating a meaningful bond.

The reason people have difficulty with eye contact is basic. Apprehensive or untrained speakers fear the reaction that their words are having on the audience. By not looking at the audience, they avoid the possibility that they will notice an uninterested consumer of the message, or worse, a receiver whose facial expressions indicate disapproval. As mentioned in Chapter 3, nonverbal messages such as facial expressions are difficult to accurately decode, but they are decoded regardless. Apprehensive speakers are often afraid of the nonverbal messages that they may receive and, therefore, avoid looking at the audience. The cure for this malady is twofold: a simple determination to improve eye contact coupled with experience in public speaking. Focusing on some spot on the wall, or cluster of faces, may work at times, but it may well look like the speaker is only looking at a spot on the wall or into clusters of faces.

Extemporaneous speaking—all other factors being equal—increases the chances for effective eye contact. That is, assuming the same level of anxiety, the same types of audiences, and the same message content, an extemporaneous speech will afford a speaker a greater chance of establishing sustained and frequent eye contact than will a manuscript presentation. The manuscript speaker must look down to read portions of the message; the extemporaneous speaker is not so attached to a document.

Adaptation and Feedback Induced Response. Extemporaneous presentations allow speakers to adapt to audiences. *Feedback induced response* is a phrase that was introduced in Chapter 3. As you may recall, it refers to a source's adaptation to receiver response. When any communicator in any communication context speaks to a receiver, the communicator (source) is likely to glean feedback in the form of nonverbal messages from the receiver. On the basis of this feedback the source may alter a forthcoming message.

In public speaking situations a good speaker attempts to accurately read the audience and assess how the presentation is going. In extemporaneous presentations, the speaker has the flexibility to alter both the content and the delivery of the message on the basis of this feedback. This is a very real advantage for the comfortable speaker. The apprehensive speaker is likely not to be calm enough to take advantage of it. However, the ability to cut material, use an anecdote for illustration, or alter in any way the prepared presentation to meet the needs of the audience is advantageous and improves the chances for effective communication.

Benefits of Using the Manuscript Approach

Despite the advantages of extemporaneous speaking, some people will deliver nothing but manuscript presentations. Melvin Grayson, the former Vice President for Corporate Affairs for Nabisco, is one such person. Grayson comments:

> I have a horror of extemporaneous speeches, whether I'm speaker or "speakee." I don't like to listen to them, because they're invariably dull and studded with platitudes, not to mention "ers" and "ahs." . . . I don't like to give [extemporaneous] speeches because of the fear that while groping for the right phrase, I may deliver the wrong phrase—some remark that will come back to haunt me. . . . As corporate communicators, we sometimes forget—whether we're communicating orally or on paper—the immense significance of each word we use. Yet those words are our weapons: our only weapons. . . . The right words strung together in the right way are what separate a good speech—an effective speech—from one that's a waste of everyone's time. Or worse.[9]

Although there are times when extemporaneous speeches are the only appropriate choice, Mr. Grayson is correct about much of what he says. The advantages of manuscript speaking are significant and important to consider.

Preparation. The primary advantage is that this format allows the presenter the opportunity to prepare as comprehensively as possible for the presentation. When a presentation is written out word for word, the conscientious speaker works on the language of the speech well before the talk. Extemporaneous formats do not afford such luxury, since the speakers must find the appropriate words while speaking.

In addition, in terms of pre-talk planning, the preparation for the manuscript speech can include vocal and other nonverbal preparation. A speaker can decide what words need emphasis; which sentences require a rapid delivery, which sections should be delivered in soft tones; and what moments would be most appropriate for pauses, eye contact, and gesturing.

Although a hazard in manuscript speaking is the potential for the speech to be read and not delivered, there is no reason why manuscript speeches cannot be delivered forcefully with all the vocal variations that make a speech successful. Also, by their very nature, manuscript presentations are devoid of pervasive interjections. Whereas extemporaneous speakers might infuse multiple "ers," "ahs," and "ums" in their talks and not even be aware of it, manuscript speakers will not include these speech fillers, since speakers will not write "er," "ah," and "um" in the manuscript. There may be a tendency for a few interjections at the tail end of some sentences, but for the most part the format eliminates the concern for interjections.

Timing Concerns. Timing problems can undermine the otherwise positive aspects of a business talk. When one uses a manuscript format these time-related difficulties are less likely to surface.

Audience members prepare themselves for presentations of certain lengths. If a speaker goes beyond the expected time limit for the talk, audience members tend to become restless, and in general, lose their concentration. Similarly, if speakers speak for less than the time length expected, the audience will be unprepared for what will appear to be an abrupt conclusion.

When you attend your classes and expect a session to last for 60 minutes you are likely to become an inattentive listener if the session were to extend to 65 minutes, even if you had no particular place to go to at the end of your session. However, if you were expecting the class to last 90 minutes, you would likely experience the restless sensation at the 95th minute, and not after the first hour. Typically, audience members set their cerebral alarm clocks for a period of time. Speakers, therefore, need to be sensitive to the audience expectations or risk losing the focus and attention of audience members.

Timing a manuscript talk is relatively easy. Since the words that will be spoken will be the same during practice and delivery, a manuscript speaker can determine the length of a talk prior to the actual presentation. One can call a theater and ask ahead of time how long a play will run. Since the actors and actresses use the same lines night after night, the box office agent can inform a customer that a show runs approximately 95 minutes counting intermission. There might be some variation due to audience reaction, but essentially, since the text is the same, the length of the production is predictable. Similarly, a manuscript speaker can determine in advance how long the talk will be and therefore meet the expectations or directives of the client and audience.

In extemporaneous formats one follows an outline and might find that more or less time than expected is needed to convey a certain idea. In addition, extemporaneous speaking can lead to digressions, with the result that a speaker might be forced to leave out certain sections as time runs short. Extemporaneous speakers might also, inadvertently, omit sections that they had planned to include. In manuscript talks, prepared speakers are less likely to skip important sections or be forced because of time constraints to rush conclusions.

Word Choice. Lastly, there are certain times when one must, because of the magnitude of the moment, deliver a manuscript speech. International figures often give manuscript talks, because they are speaking on the world stage. The international audience may be hanging on every word that is uttered. The press is ready to jump on any faux pas and, therefore, it is essential to get it exactly right or suffer the consequences. During the Carter presidency, President Carter delivered a speech in Poland during which he remarked that he had come to learn about Polish *desires* for the future. The talk was a manuscript presentation but was being translated simultaneously for the Polish people by an American interpreter. The interpreter, when translating the word *desire*, selected a Polish verb that meant *sexual desire*. Carter's statement, therefore, sounded as if he had traveled to Poland to discover their "lusts," as if the Poles had a distinctive Eastern brand of fantasies and he was curious. Journalists had a party with this error.[10]

On October 22, 1962, during President Kennedy's stirring Cuban Missile Crisis speech, the president used the word *quarantine* to describe the decision to blockade Cuba. Notably, he did not select the word *blockade*. Kennedy had been advised to use quarantine because "the word 'blockade' carried ugly, warlike, overtones" and the country wanted to do nothing that might exacerbate an already volatile situation.[11]

In the mid-1990s I attended an annual stockholder meeting of the beleaguered Copley Pharmaceutical company. Copley Pharmaceutical had been a strong generic drug company that had fallen on difficult times. Whistleblowers at Copley had claimed that shoddy production had been the cause of consumer illness. As a result of the charge and subsequent litigation, Copley's stock plummeted. The stockholders meeting I attended was completely scripted. Every word uttered by the Copley representatives was read verbatim from a text prepared in advance.

Addresses to stockholders are often manuscript talks because of the desire to be precise with word choice. In a case like Copley's when concerned stockholders attended the session, and journalists covered the meeting with an awareness of the company's recent travails, it became even more important for the messages delivered to be precise. An extemporaneous format under these circumstances would simply have been too risky.

Summary: Making the Choice

In order to select an appropriate presentation style, the following is recommended:

- Unless there is no alternative, do not give impromptu speeches.
- Similarly, memorized speeches are a problem and, as often as not, can result in disaster unless a speaker is intimately familiar with the content.
- When deciding between extemporaneous and manuscript formats remember
  - ☐ There are certain audiences and contexts that prohibit the use of one or the other of these options. A training session, for example, requires interaction and therefore precludes manuscript approaches. A formal political address, for example, requires precision and therefore precludes extemporaneous approaches. In certain situations, then, there is no real option.
  - ☐ In the case where such an option does exist beginning speakers who are willing to put in the necessary preparation time for constructing the message and practicing delivery should try the manuscript format because it allows for total control of the message and tends to reduce presentation anxiety. Experienced speakers, in those contexts that permit it, should try the extemporaneous approach because of the flexibility afforded in these presentations.

Perspectives on speaking in organizational contexts

Indicate your reaction to the following statements by using the following scale.

1. I strongly agree with the statement
2. I agree to some extent
3. I'm ambivalent on the issue
4. I disagree to some extent
5. I strongly disagree

Explain why you feel the way you do for each item.

_____ A. Skill in formal speech settings should be a criterion that makes or breaks a job candidate.

_____ B. Audience analysis trumps skill sets in terms of importance for business speaking success.

_____ C. When speakers utter interjections such as *er, um, you know,* it reduces their credibility as an expert regardless of presentation content.

_____ D. Given the global marketplace company spokespersons MUST be bilingual.

_____ E. There is nothing unethical about issuing inaccurate statements to the media if the truth will hurt your company.

_____ F. In sales, speakers are not bound by honesty.

STRUCTURING CONTENT

Every business presentation ought to be structured to include an introduction, body, and conclusion. In addition, many presentations include a question and answer session following the speech.

Introduction

The introduction to a presentation is a crucial part of the talk. It can be a determining factor in the success of the presentation, as it will affect the extent to which the receivers attend to the message. Introductions should contain a

- Statement of purpose
- Persuasive hook
- Verbal and/or nonverbal message pertaining to speaker *ethos*

Statement of Purpose. In the beginning of the talk, although not necessarily the very first words that a speaker utters, a presenter is obliged to make some statement indicating the objectives of the presentation. This is particularly important in business contexts. The specific intent of the speaker ought to be clear from the outset.

© GETTY IMAGES/PHOTODISC

The introduction to a presentation is crucial for the success of the talk.

In essence, the presenter establishes a contract with the audience in the introduction and pledges to meet certain goals. At the end of the presentation, the receivers can evaluate the message on the basis of the articulated goals. In briefing sessions like those described by Gamble and Kelliher in Case 9.1, the objectives can be simply enumerated in the beginning of the talk. For example,

> Before we begin the shift today I want to (a) highlight the week's production expectations; (b) discuss the new safety protocols; and (c) explain the incentive program that was described in the mass e-mailing you each received.

Persuasive Hook. In addition to the statement of purpose, the speaker needs to engage the audience at the outset. In some way, the audience needs to be convinced to listen to the presentation. This factor is especially important when the collective receivers did not voluntarily choose to attend the presentation, or when receivers will be listening to a number of speakers during a session.

Audiences can be difficult to reach. The speaker has the advantage in public speaking contexts of being able to prepare for the audience, but the speaker in this context also has the disadvantage of having to reach a large number of receivers, all with disparate interests, attitudes, and backgrounds.

In addition, people are, as a rule, notoriously poor listeners and many are more adept at feigning attention than actually being attentive.[12] Audience members can contemplate various unrelated activities while appearing to listen to a presentation about company safety procedures. Receivers are even skilled at nonverbally indicating attention while not missing a beat with their cerebral meanderings. Audience members who are not being attentive can nevertheless nod sagely when it seems appropriate to do so.

Speakers need to convince audience members that it is worth their while to pay attention. There are a number of ways to engage your receivers in the introduction to a talk.

- *Explain what is in it for the audience to pay attention.* This is a powerful way to get the audience's attention. People want to know why they should listen. If a speaker can establish that there is a benefit to paying attention (and then follow through with the promise), the speaker can reduce the likelihood of daydreaming.

- *Use a startling and relevant statistic.* If a manager is speaking to employees about safety information, it may well be engaging to cite a statistic indicating how many people are injured because they do not understand basic rules.

- *Refer to a related anecdote.* Some topics can be introduced by relaying a story that is related to the subject of the presentation. An analysis of a weak sales quarter might be preceded by a story about a prior similar period that, in the final analysis, was the vestibule to successive strong sales periods.

- *Ask questions of the audience.* This tactic can work but can be hazardous. If you prepare remarks to be made subsequently on the basis of predicted answers, you need to be ready for audience responses that are inconsistent with what you've anticipated.

Recently, a seminar participant, Lane, began a manuscript presentation about money market funds by asking 25 business people this question: "How many of you would like to make more money?" To this simple query only two people raised their hands. One of them did so as if his arm was encased in cement. Lane became concerned as the next line in the prepared text was supposed to be,

"Well, since all of you are interested in making money, may I suggest an excellent new money market fund that is guaranteed to increase your personal treasury?"

Because of the lack of response to the question, the second line did not follow, so Lane found herself stammering as she clumsily offered,

"Er, perhaps some day you will want to make money, and uh, then, I have this good idea."

Lane's rhythm was ruined. She muddled through the presentation and when she finished, she was embarrassed, and even a bit angry.

"Who doesn't want to make money?" she muttered in exasperation as she took her seat.

Everybody wants to make money, but not all people will respond to speakers' questions in the expected manner. If a speaker were to ask 25 people if they were breathing at the beginning of the speech, the speaker would be lucky if 13 people would raise their hands.

- *Use humor.* A joke or anecdote can "break the ice" in some contexts and engage your receivers. However, the use of humor in introductions is not without its risks.

For some audiences and some topics, humor is, categorically, not a good idea. There are audiences who consider business presentations very formal events. To inject a joke in an attempt to gain attention may result in getting the wrong kind of attention. Even when humor is not inappropriate it is a risky strategy for the novice speaker. Humor intended to engage an audience must be in good taste and also, very importantly, must be funny. An apprehensive speaker does not want to begin a talk with humor that she or he expects will result in belly laughs and then witness only silence as a reaction.

Ethos Factor. Ethos refers to the status that is attributed to a speaker by receivers. It is a crucial communication factor and especially affects success in presentation settings. Audience members are more likely to listen to, and be influenced by, speakers with high ethos.[13]

There are three types of ethos: initial, intermediate, and terminal ethos.

- **Initial ethos** refers to that status attributed to a speaker before a word is uttered by the speaker. Initial ethos is a function of appearance and reputation.

- **Intermediate ethos** is the attributed status that fluctuates during the course of a presentation. It is the presenter's personal Dow Jones average that will go up or down depending on a number of factors. Intermediate ethos is affected by

  □ *Content of the message.* If a speaker makes a comment that is factually inaccurate then intermediate ethos is likely to decrease. Similarly, if the content makes sense or if word choice is particularly appropriate then intermediate ethos is likely to increase.

  □ *Quality of delivery.* A speaker who uses rate, emphasis, and pausation to advantage is likely to increase intermediate ethos.

  □ *Ability of the speaker to establish rapport with the audience.* Regardless of content or delivery, if a speaker does not spend time analyzing the audience, then she or he will get into difficulty. If a group is sensitive to comments about organized labor, for example, it is wise to be aware of those attitudes and not, gratuitously, criticize unions and their representatives.

    Speakers need to analyze the audience in terms of its demographics and psychographics in order to plan the presentation. We have emphasized throughout this book the essential nature of knowing your receivers, regardless of communication context. In presentation settings, being ignorant of your audience can have severe repercussions.

    Study your audience to discover their backgrounds, attitudes, interests, knowledge base, vocabulary level, and particular perspectives on the presentation topic. This analysis will not only help you tailor your message to your audience, but also—as it relates to this section—help you elevate your intermediate ethos.

- The final type of ethos is **terminal ethos.** This refers to the ethos a speaker is attributed at the conclusion of the talk. Terminal ethos is especially important to anyone who suspects that there might be a return engagement with a particular audience or members from that audience. Terminal ethos directly affects the speaker's initial ethos in subsequent presentations.

As it relates to ethos and the introduction, presenters should do what they can—in terms of delivery and message content—to enhance the likelihood of being attributed high ethos. Appropriate dress, content accuracy, quality delivery, attractive visuals, and understanding your audience are all factors that affect your ethos and contribute to an introduction that will engage rather than disengage your audience.

In sum, the introduction to a business talk needs to engage the audience, specify the presentation objectives, and assist the speaker by increasing the likelihood that the audience will consider the speaker a credible and valuable source.

Focus on Applications

Creating effective presentation introductions

Assume that you are

1. A manager trying to convince your subordinates to join you in giving blood during the company blood drive.
2. A salesperson explaining the advantages of purchasing particular computer software to a group of potential customers.
3. An employee describing the benefits of unionization to other employees.

In each case, how might you introduce a brief—4-to-5-minute—talk you would deliver to achieve your communication goals? Attempt with each response to include the three components of quality introductions.

Body of the Presentation

In the body of a business presentation, speakers simply do what they have set out to do. In the introduction to a presentation the speaker has articulated what subject or material she or he intends to cover. In the body of the talk the speaker should fulfill the promise. An old "saw" of speaking suggests that when you deliver a talk, "*You tell 'em what you're going to tell 'em, you tell 'em, and then you tell 'em what you just told 'em.*" In the body of the speech, the speaker should simply *tell 'em what you said you'd tell 'em.*

There are a number of methods one can employ to structure the body of a talk. Below is a description of several methods. In each case, for the purposes of illustration, we will assume that the speaker is delivering a talk about her or his university.

Type of Pattern	Description	Example of Outline Using University Talk as Example
Topical	An easy and effective way to organize presentation content. The approach involves dividing the talk into subtopics and addressing each topic in turn.	— academic departments — residential life — extracurricular activities — career opportunities for students.

Topical. The topical approach is an easy and effective way to organize presentation content. This approach involves dividing the talk into subtopics and addressing each subtopic in turn.

An informational presentation about your university using this format might divide the content into topics pertaining to

- Academic departments
- Residential life
- Extracurricular activities
- Career opportunities for students.

Chronological. If your talk involves discussing the evolution of an organization or product, then this approach will be effective. The speaker, simply, structures the presentation in chronological order. Using the topical approach, the talk about the university would begin at the school's origin and discuss key events in the historical development of the institution.

Type of Pattern	Description	Key Events
Chronological	The School was founded in 1898	1908—Establishment of College of Liberal Arts 1928—Construction of West Campus 1948—Post-war student enrollments double university population 1969—Student riots. Destruction of the West Campus 1990—University becomes one of the top 10 research institutions in the world 1998—Institution builds new Media/Print Mega Library

Advantages and Disadvantages. As the label suggests this approach identifies the positive and negative features of your topic. Your presentation would discuss the plusses and minuses related to attending and/or working at your university.

Advantages of Attending	Disadvantages of Attending
Cooperative education	High tuition rates
Mega Media/Print Library	Demanding workload
Bucolic location	Few cultural outlets beyond university
Excellent cocurricular activities	Spartan dormitories

Various organizational patterns may be effective for any one presentation topic. When considering the body of the talk, remember that your goal in this section of the presentation is to discuss the topics you indicated would be addressed during the introduction. Select an organizational pattern that will be most effective, given your audience and speaking objectives. Consider using the topical approach as your default organizational pattern. In business talks, topical approaches are nearly always appropriate. For your presentation objectives, another pattern may be more effective, but when in doubt, use the topical approach.

Visual Support

Visual support is important for any presentation, particularly business talks. Visual complements can help to maintain attention, explain information, and elevate speaker ethos.

Hattersley and McJannet make the following recommendations for *preparing* visuals. They suggest:

- Keep the graphics simple
- Don't hide behind your graphics

- Use the minimum number of graphics necessary
- Don't use visual support that you cannot manage well.[14]

The purpose of using visual aids is to facilitate the accurate receipt of information. A visual aid should indeed be an aid. A visual aid should not be the presentation in its entirety, it should not detract from the oral delivery, and it should add to your ethos.

If you are uncomfortable speaking in front of audiences, using the Power Point program extensively in an attempt to deflect attention from yourself may seem wise, but could backfire and make people wonder why they need to listen to a speaker. If everything you intend to express is written on the graphics, and all you are doing is reading a message aloud that audience members can read to themselves, there doesn't appear to be much value in the oral component of the presentation.

Sorenson, DeBord, and Ramirez make suggestions regarding how to use graphics *during delivery:*

- Reveal the aid only when it is used in the presentation.
- Face the audience when using the visual.
- Avoid passing visuals around a room.
- Practice with the visuals prior to delivery. Examine the room before delivery to ensure that the room is properly equipped to allow for your graphic display.
- If you use a marker or pointer, put the marker down once you have finished using it.[15]

If you were to engage in any of the common behaviors listed below, your visual would *not* be a complementary aid and would *undermine* the quality of your presentation:

- Speak to the screen instead of your audience.
- Say "as you can see" when putting up a slide that none can see because of tiny print or room configuration.
- Wield a pointer to the point of distraction.
- Fumble with nonfunctional equipment. Predictable logistical or technological problems cripple your talk. For example, you discover that you need an extension cord, or equipment that could have been tested beforehand proves to be damaged.
- Circulate intriguing photographs that implicitly, if not explicitly, encourage listeners to disengage from your orally communicated messages so that they can focus on the photos.

Presentation Conclusion

The conclusion to the talk is crucial. At the end of a presentation speakers should provide a sense of closure for the audience. Too many talks end with speakers scanning notes and then lifting up, in order to say, "Well, that's about it. Can I take any questions?"

"That's about it" does not make for a strong conclusion. Such remarks are likely to damage the speakers' terminal ethos, and they do not provide for the kind of closure that is necessary.

In addition to the "that's about it" method, speakers sometimes conclude presentations by dropping their voices to an inaudible level while rushing from the lectern as if they are late for a train. Physically, visually, vocally, and verbally a presentation should have a strong conclusion.

Below are four approaches that can be used to effectively conclude presentations. Combinations of these approaches can work as well.

Summary. A summary of the main points of a business presentation is essential. It is a good idea to complement this recap with visual support.

Challenge. The challenge method can be effective for certain types of presentations. For example, "I urge you to consider investing in this fund with your 401 allocations. You owe it to the future of yourself and your family."

Probing Question. In this case the speaker ends the presentation by leaving the audience with a question to ponder. The question summarizes the theme of the presentation. For example, "And so I ask you, do you really want to waste your assets as they atrophy in underperforming certificates of deposit, or do you want to invest in a fund that has a historical double digit growth rate?"

Quotation. A quotation that captures the essence of the message can be another effective way of concluding the presentation. For example "As investment guru Peter Lynch has said, 'If I were recommending funds to a friend or family member, this product is one that I would include first and foremost.' "

In the words of Brendan Francis, "A quotation in a speech, article, or book is like a rifle in the hands of an infantryman. It speaks with authority."[16]

QUESTION AND ANSWER SESSIONS

. . . we [President Reagan's Press team] would anticipate questions and answers on the subjects that . . . might come up. Then we would put together a briefing book by the Friday before a press conference for the President to take along to camp David and study over the weekend. It would have several dozen domestic and foreign topics, with questions and answers on each topic. . . . In press conferences, out of thirty questions and follow-ups we might fail to anticipate one.[17]

Larry Speakes, President Reagan's Press Spokesperson.

At the conclusion of presentations, speakers often ask for questions. This is an important time because if there is a question and answer session, the presentation is not really over until the questions have been answered. The formal part of the talk may be over, but the effort has not ended, nor has the book been closed on your message (or ethos) until the last question has been answered. Therefore, it is important to deal carefully with questions.

Despite the fact that the questioning period is an important part of the presentation, it is remarkable how poorly many speakers—otherwise good and bad—handle these sessions. Many times I have heard speakers, who had performed quite well during the formal presentation, butcher their efforts by handling questions with all the aplomb and wisdom of a bumbling fool. In June 2001, a representative of a major international corporation delivered an address at an International Association of Business Communicators meeting. The speaker, a member of the company's corporate communication team, violated nearly every tenet of managing and delivering answers during the question and answer session—after having done an adequate job of making the formal presentation. The speaker apparently had not recognized the importance of the question session and simply had not prepared for it.

Planning for the Questioning Session

Speakers can do a number of things to prepare for question sessions:

- Anticipate potential questions
- Formulate and practice mini-extemporaneous responses
- Comprehensively research the subject
- Prepare for ego-involved responses

Anticipate Potential Questions. The wisest preliminary planning is to anticipate the questions that might be posed during the question session. A good strategy is to examine the speech and identify a number of items that are potential areas for questioning. For each item, write out the various questions relating to that item that might be posed by members of the audience.

Of course, only seers can predict with certainty all of the questions that might surface. However, a careful analysis will yield a number of questions that might surface. As previously indicated, President Reagan's team was able to predict a high percentage of the questions that were asked during his press conferences.

Formulate and Practice Mini-Extemporaneous Responses. A good strategy is to consider not only the potential questions, but appropriate responses to those questions. Those prepared responses likely would be in an extemporaneous outline format. Next, practice the prepared responses in the same way you would practice your oral presentation.

Comprehensively Research the Subject. Since it is impossible to completely predict all questions, speakers should become as expert as possible regarding the content of the presentation. I have witnessed a number of disastrous situations in which speaker reputations were destroyed because they could not respond to basic questions. In these cases the formal presentation indicated that the speakers were indeed expert or at least knowledgeable on the subject. However, their inability to answer fundamental questions revealed that they were familiar only with a prepared presentation text, and not the substance of the subject. The credibility attached to not only the speakers, but to the material the speakers had presented, was severely affected.

Prepare for Ego-Involved Responses. Speakers tend to become "ego involved" in question and answer sessions. That is, there are speakers who take each question as a challenge to their authority and respond as if they are being challenged. Certainly, there are times when audience members will be argumentative with their queries. For some speakers, however, all queries are perceived as attacks. Presenters must know themselves and resolve not to let their egos interfere with the process of responding to questions.

This is difficult for some people. For those who simply cannot see that questions are not always credibility challenges, there is little that can be suggested in the way of remedy. For those less defensive, the suggestion is to be aware of the potential for counterproductive, ego-involved reactions to questions.

Delivering Responses to Questions

Step 1: Repeat the Question. Not always, but more often than not, a speaker must repeat the essence of the question. Below are some reasons why it is typically necessary to do this.

Simple audibility problems Sometimes a question is asked in such a soft voice that no one but the people surrounding the questioner can hear the inquiry. The ensuing response is, therefore, meaningless to most of the audience. Some audience members may attempt to ask their neighbors about the nature of the question. Some, however, may be content to be excluded. If a speaker is including a question and answer session in the presentation, then allegedly there is a desire to have the entire audience participate in the discussion. All too often question and answer sessions digress to private dialogues between inquirer and respondent. By allowing all to hear the question, the response should become a presentation to all who are in the room. The query, "Can you all hear that?" is almost valueless. Not everyone who did not hear the original question will respond honestly to "Can you all hear that?"

Repeating the question "buys" time For example, let's assume that you are asked the following question after your talk about management in the twenty-first century.

> *Question: On the basis of your presentation I am led to believe that you support participatory decision making in management. Have you read Theory Z? If so, what is your reaction to that book?*

Perhaps it has been quite some time since you've read *Theory Z*. Perhaps you never heard of *Theory Z*. Perhaps you've heard of *Theory Z* but can't recall the correlation to participatory decision. By repeating the question, you allow yourself some time to formulate as intelligent a response as possible given the nature of the query. You might, therefore, answer in the following way.

> *Answer:* The question is, "Given my perspective, do I agree with the positions expressed in the book *Theory Z*?" While I have read much about management styles, I confess to not having read the book *Theory Z* completely. However, I am somewhat familiar with the author's orientation. My understanding is that much of Theory Z revolves around utilization of Quality Circles. Therefore, from my admitted limited understanding, I would tend to support Ouchi since quality circles and participatory decision making go hand in hand.

Repeating the question allows the speaker to make sense out of an unwieldy question Sometimes audience participants can ask questions that are poorly constructed. A good speaker will not ridicule the questioner even though the question may be cumbersome. A good speaker will simply "find" the question and repeat it so that the audience will understand the focus of the response. For example,

> *Question:* I think I have a handle on what you're saying, because it seems to me that when I was with Kodak there was a similar type of situation. However, given the nature of today's employee can we still, during this particular time frame and I recognize that this is no longer the 'Me Decade' but another decade and I also recognize the legacy of the Clinton-Lewinsky impeachment, the Bush-Gore fiasco, and even the Enron scandals for that matter, on this stuff—but can we continue to do the same thing now, given all that's transpired, historically-wise and politically-wise, you know?
>
> *Repetition:* The question was, "Given the changes that have taken place over the last decades, can we still effectively use my suggestions for management?"

By repeating the question in this way, the speaker provided a semblance of respect for the question and created a framework for an intelligent response.

Repeating the question allows the speaker to change it subtly Assume a question is asked that the speaker does not want to answer. By changing the question slightly in repetition, the speaker can create a hook onto which the response can be focused.

This is not easy to do. Persistent questioners might recognize the dodge and may ask a follow-up question. Also there are ethical issues related to altering the question for speaker convenience. I do not advocate altering the question to avoid answering particular inquiries. However, avoiding difficult questions is a reason why some speakers might want to repeat a question, particularly when the presenter is dealing with a hostile audience. For example.

Question: Given your position in support of corporate training aren't you essentially encouraging early retirement for people like me and saying, "Forget about the old timers. Let's push them out with a group of low-cost and low-quality kids who we'll claim to train?"

Answer: The questioner asks me to comment about my position regarding training and how it will affect veteran employees. My posture on training is basic. We must train employees to be better equipped to handle our new technology. This refers to veterans as well as others.

Step 2: After Repeating the Question, Direct the Answer to Everyone. The speaker should direct the response to the entire audience. In this way the speaker significantly reduces the chances of the response taking the form of a dialogue. In fact, the repetition of the question itself should be directed to the entire audience. Occasionally during the response, and at its conclusion, the speaker should make eye contact with the questioner. However, the speaker should otherwise have the same eye contact with the audience during question and answers as during the formal presentation.

As a rule, one follow-up question should be allowed. (*Follow-up questions* here do not refer to related queries from other audience participants.) After one, however, your presentation is likely to digress into an interpersonal conversation. You might invite tenacious questioners to see you at the conclusion of the meeting if they would like to continue the discussion.

Step 3: Maintain a Professional Tone. Do Not Debate or Deride. As suggested previously, questioners can ask foolish questions and there are times when a biting retort would be most desirable. Often, questioners do not ask questions at all, but rather use the "floor" as an opportunity to espouse unrelated philosophies. It is tempting to confront these speakers on this behavior. In addition, there are instances when questioners make statements—not to posture; the statements are to the point—but their remarks are still not questions, only statements. At these moments, it is enticing to react with a short, "Well, what's the question? Do you have a question, please?"

To these enticements, restraint is urged. There is nothing to be gained by disparaging questioners. While speakers might get a laugh out of sympathetic audience members, it is not worth the short-term value of such sympathy. Instead, take the high road and do not let your ego interfere.

Step 4: Conclude the Question and Answer Session. There ought to be a designated time for questions and answers. Even the most careful speaker will be unable to hold audience attention for too long during question and answer sessions. Therefore, after a number of questions have been addressed, the speaker should indicate that one or two more will be taken, and then attempt to end the session after addressing a question comfortably. After taking the last question, the speaker should summarize the presentation very briefly, and thank the listeners for their attention.

In sum, prior to the presentation:

- Anticipate possible questions
- Prepare responses to anticipated questions

- Research exhaustively
- Prepare for the possibility of defensive retorts.

When responding to questions:

- Repeat the essence of the questions
- Address responses to entire audience
- Resist temptations to debate
- Conclude in a timely fashion.

PRESENTATION ANXIETY

One of the more difficult obstacles for beginning speakers relates to their sheer terror of giving a presentation. Some people claim to fear speaking more than death. The title of a *Saturday Evening Post* article, "Public Speaking and Other Coronary Threats," reflects the attitudes of so many who are apprehensive when speaking publicly.[18] Speaking anxiety is a remarkable phenomenon. Consider the case of Sandra Winston:

Sandra Winston enrolled in a speaking skills workshop. She told me before the first session that she had never spoken in front of a group before and was "deathly afraid" of doing so. Nevertheless, she wanted to take the course in order to conquer her fears. On the first day of presentations, Winston rushed to the lectern determined to be the first speaker so, she told me later, she could get it out and get it over with. Her talk began quite well. Shortly after it began, a rude latecomer crashed through the door making a racket like one would hear in a factory. The tardy man glanced around the room looking for a chair, spotted one on the far side of the room, and marched directly in front of the speaker swinging his coat as he walked past her. In fact, while hustling by Ms. Winston, he swiped the lectern with his jacket. I was happily surprised to note that the speaker was able to maintain her composure throughout this rudeness. She continued to speak effectively as the tardy man made even more noise while settling into his seat.

At the end of the session, I commented that late seminar participants should wait until each speaker is finished before entering the seminar room. I mentioned that Winston had done a remarkable job of maintaining her poise despite the noise.

I asked Sandra Winston to stay after class and repeated that I had been impressed with her poise given the rude latecomer.

"How did you keep going?" I inquired.

"I didn't even see him," she immediately replied.

Speech anxiety is normal. It is important to remember that audience members typically do not see speakers as the apprehensive person they may be.[19] That is, often when you are certain that people are aware of your fear, audience members are looking at you thinking that they wished they possessed your poise. It is natural for speakers to feel anxious when they:

- Are the center of attention.
- Consider themselves to be different from other members of the audience.
- Have had difficult experiences making presentations previously.
- Have had very few prior public speaking opportunities.[20]

McCroskey uses the term *communication apprehension* to refer to oral communication anxiety. McCroskey defines communication apprehension as "an individual's level of fear or anxiety associated with either real or anticipated communication with another person or persons."[21]

There are four categories of communication apprehension:

- *Traitlike.* Oral Communication anxiety that is consistent across contexts. For example, a high traitlike communication apprehensive feels anxious in meetings during interpersonal communication and also when giving presentations.
- *Context.* Apprehension that is experienced in one context as opposed to another. For example, a person may have no problem speaking interpersonally or in groups, but does experience tension when speaking in public address settings.
- *Audience.* Anxiety that surfaces depending on who will be listening to you speak. A person may become anxious when speaking to peers, but not when speaking to subordinates.
- *Situation.* Apprehension that is a function of a particular event. For example, if you are anxious when speaking in front of a group who will, on the basis of your oration, determine if you can keep your job, you are experiencing situational apprehension.

How would you categorize your level of communication apprehension? Do you ever experience any of the forms of communication apprehension that are described above? Adler and Rodman make four basic suggestions for dealing with speaking anxiety.

- Take a positive attitude
- Focus on the receivers as opposed to yourself
- Be prepared
- Be rational—that is, understand that some of your anxieties are irrational.[22]

Some authors suggest visualization techniques—"walking through" the speech cerebrally and imagining a positive result.[23] Other ideas include relaxation techniques such as breathing exercises, physical stretching, and pre speech silent concentration.[24]

One could distill most recommendations regarding how to deal with presentation anxiety into the following categories:

Using Your Nervous Energy. Realize that anxiety is normal and try to use that energy. Like an actor who is energized, yet nervous, for opening night, the speaker can use the nervous energy to enhance the quality of performance.

Preparation and knowledge. Become knowledgeable about your subject, your audience, your equipment, and your space. Prepare your message so that you are as comfortable as you can be with the content. That is, be sure that what you intend to say is consistent with what you believe and want to communicate.

Making the presentation context less uncommon. Put yourself in situations where you must deliver presentations. The more normal public speaking is as an activity, the less apprehensive you will be in speaking settings. Organizations like Toastmasters can provide multiple practice speaking opportunities. As you become more familiar with the nuances of the presentation setting, the anxiety level is likely to dissipate.

In the 1800s, Scottish essayist Thomas Carlyle remarked, "Can there be a more horrible object in existence than an eloquent man not speaking the truth?"

When we think of Adolf Hitler, Carlyle's comment is especially true. While demagogues like Hitler have a more significant impact than the typical corporate manager, it is also chilling to think of managerial careers that have been thwarted because of poor speaking skills. There are many individuals who never "made it" because they could not or would not learn how to speak effectively.

PRACTITIONER'S PERSPECTIVE

Gail Hunter, Vice President in Events and Attractions, National Basketball Association

Gail Hunter has both an MBA and a law degree. Before working for the NBA she held positions with Major League Baseball, the NCAA, the Seattle Mariners, and the Seattle law firm of Scheweppe, Krug & Tausend.

My group produces grassroots marketing events for the NBA. We execute programs that have been either created by the NBA solely or developed in conjunction with our league-marketing partners. For example, Gatorade might want to work with us. They'll suggest an idea based on their marketing strategies and overall marketing goals, and we work with them and try to develop a joint program. Or we conceive of a program and then seek out a marketing partner to determine if our objectives are similar. The current Rhythm 'n Rims tour, the NBA All Star Jam Session, and the WNBA Summer Jam are examples of our programs.

Communication is vital for what we do. We have to present ideas, listen to suggestions, respond to reactions, and persuade internal audiences that proposals have merit. For example, I (or someone from our staff) will need to make a presentation to sell a concept to other divisions. Communicating well during these presentations is essential. If we can't effectively describe the project, it may never get off the ground. We need people from these internal audiences to help us produce and launch the program so we have to persuade them that we have an idea that's worth their buy-in.

I believe that a good speaker frames the talk for the audience, and becomes aware of the audience's needs and concerns well before the talk begins. It's not very prudent to arrogantly explain the advantages of a concept as if to say, "You would have to be crazy not to want to work with us on this project." One has to listen to the audience. If a potential partner tells you that they're not attracted to some facet of your plan and that they'd like to see a revision, you don't come back the following week hammering home the advantages of precisely that facet that the audience has already rejected. You're essentially being disrespectful if you do that, and one is not very successful in business contexts by dismissing the concepts that are important to your potential business partners.

It's also important that a speaker demonstrate that she or he really believes in the concept. I don't want people in my group delivering a talk on an idea if they are not sold on the idea. It's important to convey some passion and that cannot be easily manufactured, if it can be manufactured at all. We're fortunate. We, most of us, like what we do here. I mean this is fun. This is basketball. Programs like the WNBA Summer Jam are enjoyable for us as well as for the kids who participate. It's not that difficult to become passionate about we do.

More importantly, our staff must know about all aspects and components of our product to effectively communicate with partners and co-workers. Each project is filled with multiple levels of execution, many of which are specialized and not applicable to all audiences, but critical to the overall program.

SUMMARY

A Toolbox

1. Presenters can select any one of four speaking styles.

   - Extemporaneous and manuscript approaches are the best of the four choices.

   - Some contexts require certain styles.

   - When an option is available select the style that is more appropriate for your audience and your speaking abilities.

2. Structure talks with a clear introduction, body, and conclusion.

   - The introduction should engage the receivers, articulate the presentation objectives, and establish yourself as a credible source.

   - The body should fulfill the objectives articulated in the introduction.

   - The conclusion of a business presentation must summarize the key components of the talk.

3. Prepare for question and answer sessions.

   - Anticipate possible questions.

   - Create responses to the anticipated questions.

   - Practice delivery of these responses.

   - Deliver responses recognizing that the questioner is not the lone receiver. All audience members are receivers.

4. Presentation anxiety is normal particularly for persons who rarely deliver public addresses. There are a number of things speakers can do to reduce the effects of speaking apprehension.

DISCUSSION QUESTIONS

1. What style of speaking is most appropriate for the kind of business presentations you are likely to deliver?

2. When you listen to talks do you typically prefer listening to extemporaneous, manuscript, impromptu, or memorized talks?

3. Who is the most effective business speaker that you personally know? What makes her or him so effective?

4. When you listen to presentations, what most influences the speakers' intermediate ethos?

5. What structural approach do you typically use when you have to make presentations?

6. As an audience member what three behaviors do you find most effective when speakers are responding to questions?

7. As an audience member what three behaviors do you find most effective when speakers are using visuals?

8. Please read the case that follows and respond to the questions at the end of the case.

Case 9.2—Regina Ostrowsky and the "Nonbank" Manager

Background. Regina Ostrowsky is a manager at a "nonbank" bank located in downtown Chicago. The bank is classified as a "nonbank" because of a government restriction prohibiting the bank from engaging in any traditional commercial products (e.g., commercial loans and credit cards).

The "nonbank" bank employs nearly 600 people, 30 of whom work in the trust administration division where Regina is employed. The trust administration division is under the management of Adele Dackmun who has five direct reports. Regina Ostrowsky is one of those reports. Each of the employees like Ostrowsky has between three to six reports.

The Problem. Ostrowsky and her peers, as well as Ostrowsky's reports and her peers' reports, are required to attend a meeting every third Tuesday of the month. At this session Adele Dackmun delivers a presentation on the state of affairs in the trust administration division. Ostrowsky believes that these presentations are unbearable. While Regina claims that Dackmun is, in fact, brilliant and has "a good heart," the orations on these Tuesdays have earned Dackmun the unenviable label of " 'nonmanager' manager of the 'nonbank' bank." Alternately, she has been nicknamed, "Speechless." Regina occasionally hears her subordinates mumble comments parodying the Mastercard commercial. "An hour with Dackmun: Speechless."

Ostrowsky claims that Dackmun once uttered 172 "ums" during a 25-minute presentation, excluding any such speech-fillers used during the question and answer session that followed. In addition, Ostrowsky lists other problems with the Tuesday presentations:

- Nearly the entire presentation, except for digressions, is on PowerPoint slides. Why bother having to listen to a talk if all the information is on the slides? Dackmun also has a tendency to speak to the slides.

- The digressions are interminable. It is during these digressions when the speech-filler "um" is so pervasive.

- Dackmun will say, "Is that clear?" but then resumes too quickly for a respondent to comment.

- Dackmun begins speaking as she comes through the door—usually 5 minutes late—and it takes some time to understand what she is talking about and where she is going with her message.

1. How typical is Adele Dackmun?
2. If you were Regina Ostrowsky how would you tell your superior about the problems with her presentations? Would you tell her?
3. If you were Ostrowsky would you discourage your subordinates from referring to Dackmun as the " 'nonmanager' manager"?
4. Is the problem really Ostrowsky's and the other members of the trust department? That is, should they just "get through" the interjections and other distractions and focus on the message that Dackmun is relaying?
5. If you had an opportunity to sit down and talk with Dackmun, what three recommendations would you make that she could use to improve her speaking abilities?

ENDNOTES

[1]Gamble, Paul and Clare Kelliher, "Imparting Information and Influencing Behavior: An Examination of Staff Briefing Sessions," *Journal of Business Communication,* vol. 36, July 1999, pp. 261–277.

[2]Ibid., p. 270.

[3]Ibid., p. 261.

[4]The referred to similar article is entitled "Evaluating the Impact of a Communications Exercise in an Industrial Works." It was published in the *Industrial Relations Journal,* vol. 11, May/June 1980, pp. 37–48. The authors of the referred to piece are Alistair Ostell, Iaian MacFarlane, and Alexander Jackson.

[5]Op. cit., Gamble and Kelliher, p. 268.

[6]Ibid., p. 270.

[7]Angle, Paul, *World Book Encyclopedia* entry, vol. 12, 1984, p. 275.

[8]Ayres, Joe and Tim Hopf, *Coping with Speech Anxiety,* Ablex Publishing Company, 1993, p. 3.

[9]Grayson, Melvin, "The Last Best Hope: Words," *Vital Speeches of the Day,* July 15, 1981, vol. 47, p. 585.

[10]"Lost in Translation," *Newsweek,* January 9, 1978, p. 20. The translater, Steven Seymour, was subsequently fired. In addition to the *desire, sexual desire* error, when the President stated that he had *left the United States* to begin the trip, Seymour used a verb for *left* that meant "abandon" so it sounded as if Carter was abandoning the United States.

[11]*The Cuban Missile Crisis, 1962. A National Archive Documents Reader.* Edited by Laurence Chang and Peter Kornbluh, The New Press, 1992, p. 365. Also, Elie Abel, *The Missile Crisis,* Lippincott, 1968, p. 115.

[12]See, for example, Florence Wolff, Nadine Marsnik, William Tacey, and Ralph Nichols, *Perceptive Listening,* Holt Rinehart and Winston, 1983, pp. 195–198.

[13]Osborn, Michael and Suzanne Osborn, *Public Speaking,* third Edition, Houghton Mifflin, 1997, p. 16.

[14]Hattersley, Michael and Linda McJannet, *Management Communication,* McGraw Hill, 1997, pp. 272–273.

[15]Sorenson, Ritch, Grace DeBord, and Ida Ramirez, *Business and Management Communication: A Guide Book,* Prentice Hall, 2001, p. 70.

[16]Brendan Francis has been described as an "American Writer" and several clever quotations have been attributed to him. He is regularly cited in quotation books and on the web. Interestingly, there is no known reference of any book or article that "American Writer" Brendan Francis has written. One reference librarian has opined that Francis might not be the actual name of the quote author. (Brendan Francis should not be confused with author Brendan Francis Behan). Interested readers might want to see http://www.cuis.edu/ftp/STUMPERS-L/STUMPERS-L.1997–11 for an assessment of the legitimacy of the name Brendan Francis. Nevertheless, Brendan Francis is the name used by collectors of quotations for attribution with this quote.

[17]Speakes, Larry (with Robert Pack), *Speaking Out,* Avon, 1988, p. 292.

[18]*The Saturday Evening Post* article was a reprint of a speech delivered by Max Isaacson, a Vice President of the Macmillan Oil Company. The article appeared on page 46 of the July/August 1980 edition. The Isaacson speech had been previously published in *Vital Speeches of the Day,* March 15, 1980, pp. 351–352. Isaacson is one of several persons who has made the claim about public speaking being more feared than death. His reference to that appears on page 352 of the *Vital Speeches* version of the speech text.

[19]Op. cit., Sorenson, DeBord, and Ramirez, *Business and Management Communication*, p. 224.

[20]McCroskey, James, "The Communication Apprehension Perspective," in J. A. Daly and J. C. McCroskey (editors), *Avoiding Communication: Shyness, Reticence and Communication Apprehension*, Sage, 1984, pp. 13–38. See also Michael Beatty, "Situational and Predispositional Correlates of Public Speaking Anxiety," *Communication Education*, vol. 37, January 1988, p. 28. McCroskey's full list of factors includes the items mentioned in the text: novelty, conspicuousness, prior history, and dissimilarity; as well as formality, subordinate status, unfamiliarity, degree of attention from others, and degree of evaluation.

[21]McCroskey, James, "Oral Communication Apprehension: A Summary of Recent Theory and Research," *Human Communication Research,* vol. 4, 1977, p. 78.

[22]Adler, Ronald and George Rodman, *Understanding Human Communication,* Harcourt College, 2000, p. 376.

[23]Op. cit., Ayres and Hopf discuss visualization benefits and approaches on pp. 31–47.

[24]Ibid., pp. 41–43.

10

Improving Interpersonal Communication: Working with Difficult (and Not So Difficult) People

I feel that instead of any inability to communicate there is a deliberate evasion of communication. Communication itself between people is so frightening that rather than do that there is a continual talking about other things, rather than what is at the root of the relationship.

—Harold Pinter, Playwright

It's odd that you can get so anesthetized by your own pain or your own problem that you don't quite fully share the hell of someone close to you.

—Lady Bird Johnson, Former First Lady

Humankind cannot bear very much reality.

—From T. S. Eliot's *Murder in the Cathedral*

© GETTY IMAGES/PHOTODISC

Case 10.1—*Communicating with Chuck*

Sam Ramirez supervises a group of 14 engineers. The company he works for is a very large communications provider. Each engineer is considered the company's subject matter expert (referred to as SME), for her or his particular assigned technology. These engineers procure test equipment, provide technical support, and purchase spare circuit packs in support of front-line employees. The minimal experience required for an engineer's position is five years in Operations and two years in Engineering. Engineers typically experience a learning curve of one to two years and it is very difficult to recruit good people for the job.

Due to the results of several early retirement incentive programs, there are few individuals in the company qualified to work in the engineering group Sam supervises. Members of Sam's team are frequently offered jobs by other departments within the organization and also are lured away by competitors. The last time one of Sam's engineers chose to move to another job, Sam lost the vacancy as a result of downsizing.

Chuck, one of Sam's engineers, has been rated "outstanding" for the past five years. Chuck's technical expertise and knowledge are extraordinary. In recognition of Chuck's value to the company, he has received a large bonus in each of the past five years. Unfortunately Chuck's interpersonal and communication skills are minimal at best. Chuck is often perceived as condescending, dominating, demeaning, unrelenting, and self-serving. Nearly all of Chuck's peers avoid interacting with him and even avoid attending meetings in which he's involved. Chuck is not only verbally demeaning but also will make inappropriate facial expressions when dealing with others. Often, he'll pretend to be trying to suppress laughter when someone asks a serious question that Chuck considers foolish.

An internal customer phoned Sam one day to "express his condolences" for Sam having to be Chuck's manager. There is an even split among customers who call to praise Chuck's excellent work and those who refer to him as a *prima donna* and refuse to ask him for assistance.

Last year, Sam Ramirez's annual performance feedback session with Chuck took three hours, even though Chuck was to receive a significant bonus. Chuck vehemently disagreed with the "Needs Development" rating Sam gave him in the "Working with Others" skill category. *Chuck even offered to trade his bonus in for an improved rating in this deficient skill category!* Chuck argued that Ramirez had only heard from the people who did not like or appreciate Chuck. Chuck asked Sam to cite specific examples of poorly executed interpersonal exchanges. Sam decided to accommodate Chuck and began to list event after event. Ramirez stopped suddenly when he realized that Chuck was recording the names of the individuals involved in each example that Sam cited. To make the case that he had been unfairly criticized by the others, Chuck began to attack the character of each person involved in the cited examples.

"Oh, you can't be serious believing Olga. She is an idiot."

"Pat is a loser, and you know that as well as I do, Sam."

"Harry? Please. Give me a break."

Chuck's basic response was, "I'm okay. It's the rest of the world that's crazy."

In order to improve his skill rating, Chuck worked diligently at improving his interpersonal interactions during the first half of last year. In response to the significant progress made, Sam rated Chuck's behavior as "Acceptable" during his mid-year review. Unfortunately, immediately after that rating, Chuck stopped working on improving his behavior with others and quickly slid back into his old habits. On the basis of this regression, Sam wants to again rate Chuck as, "Needs Development," during the current review period. Sam dreads the session and is considering giving Chuck an "Acceptable" rating just to avoid the tension.

☐   *Are people like Chuck uncommon?*

☐   *How should Sam Ramirez deal with Chuck during the current annual review?*

☐   *Is there anything anyone can do to change Chuck's behavior?*

☐   *Can an organization afford to fire an employee like Chuck who is so unusually capable?*

ABSTRACT

Organizational men and women engage in multiple interpersonal exchanges each day. These dyadic communications take place on both the formal and informal networks and include task, maintenance, and human messages. Since we communicate interpersonally so often, we may, incorrectly, assume that the process of dyadic interaction is simple. As we discussed in Chapter 3, communication is problematic due to a number of factors that are collectively called communication noise. In this chapter we discuss two models for conceptualizing the interpersonal communication process: Rules Theory and Transactional Analysis. Both have contemporary applications to organizations and organizational communication. Type *transactional + analysis + communication* into the Yahoo search engine, and you may be surprised to see how many contemporary consultants use Transactional Analysis as a method for improving organizational communication.[1] The *Transactional Analysis Journal*, in 1993 and then again in 1996, devoted special issues to the application of Transactional Analysis to organizational contexts. Rules theory is particularly relevant in the multicultural organizational environments of the twenty-first century. Both approaches are practical and can help readers become more adept at communicating with others in the organization.

When you have completed this chapter, you should be able to:

□ Explain what is meant by a *rules approach* to dyadic communication.
□ Describe the evolution and principles of *Transactional Analysis.*
□ Discuss how rules approaches and Transactional Analysis can help individuals become more effective interpersonal communicators.
□ Use rules approaches and/or Transactional Analysis to improve communication with difficult people in your organization.

PERVASIVE INTERPERSONAL COMMUNICATION

Interpersonal communication is our most common communication context. Individuals periodically communicate in groups and occasionally deliver and attend speeches. However, people engage in multiple dyadic exchanges daily.

It is no different in organizations. Occasionally there are presentations to attend or make, more frequently there are meetings, but employees are constantly involved in interpersonal interactions either on the formal networks or more commonly on the informal networks. These interpersonal interactions and the residuals from these exchanges affect productivity, managerial decisions, the nature of relationships within the organization, and the communication climate.

The examination of interpersonal communication is a relatively recent area of investigation for those who are involved in communication study. Until the 1970s the focus of most scholars' attention was on communication in public speaking or group communication contexts. Because interpersonal exchanges are so common in daily life, many students of communication began to turn their attention to the investigation of those factors that affect interpersonal interaction.

The analysis of interpersonal communication is complex. There are many variables that affect the process, and there have been multiple theories offered to explain its nuances. In this chapter we will take a pragmatic approach to the analysis of interpersonal communication in the organization. We will examine two ways to improve interpersonal communication that can be useful, and easily used. One approach—*rules theory*—assists in visualizing the dynamics of the process and the other—*Transactional Analysis*—is an unusually practical method for improving interpersonal communication that is employed regularly by communication and organizational consultants and trainers. Both approaches can be utilized to examine our individual communication tendencies and to assist us when dealing with difficult organizational others.

A RULES APPROACH

DeVito describes rules theory as "an approach . . . that attempts to identify the communication rules that operate in a communication act, rules that determine or influence the messages that are encoded or decoded."[2] Schall defines communication rules as "tacit understandings (generally unwritten and unspoken) about appropriate ways to interact (communicate) with others in given roles and situations."[3]

Essentially, a rules approach to interpersonal communication views communication as an act akin to a game that has a set of rules. Just like Checkers or Ping Pong has rules that govern playing, so does interpersonal communication. However, unlike board or table games, communication rules are implicit—and not explicitly articulated. Nevertheless these rules regulate interpersonal interactions. That is, the quality of the communication will depend upon the extent to which participants adhere to the "tacit understandings." The following example may help to illustrate the applications of rules theory:

Assume Person A and Person B are playing Checkers. Assume that A gets a piece to the back of B's row. Person A would then likely say, "King Me."

At that point Person B should take a piece and place it atop Person A's marker. Those are the rules of the game of Checkers. When one moves a piece to the back of an opponent's row, one is entitled to be Kinged. When Person A began the game with B, that was an assumption that A brought to the encounter. She'd be Kinged if she moved a token to the back of B's row.

Assume, however, that Person B decides not to "King" Person A and simply responds to A's "King Me" request by saying "No." The conversation that would ensue might proceed as indicated below.

A: "What do you mean, 'no'? King Me."

B: "I'm not going to. I don't want to."

A: "Why? What is wrong with you? You're supposed to 'King Me' when I get to your back row."

B: "I'm not into that today."

A: "Well forget it then. I'm not playing with you."

This scenario is unlikely to unfold when playing board games like Checkers. However, if it were to occur, if someone were to clearly violate the rules while you were playing, you would likely do just what Person A did above. You would quit.

Similarly, in interpersonal communication if someone were to violate a principle regarding *how* one should communicate, or *what* someone should say during an exchange, you might also quit. You might not physically remove yourself from the dialogue (though you might), but the nature of your subsequent interactions and your perceptions of the other communicator would change.

If a salesperson was describing a product in a formal business context, and the salesperson used what are typically referred to as profanities during the course of the presentation, you might well begin to dwell on why that person used the profanities, and not focus on the message. The use of profanities might affect your willingness to listen to that person again, your attitudes toward that individual, or even your perception of the quality of the product. If you brought into the meeting a rule stipulating that in "formal business situations one should not use profanity because it is unprofessional" then the use of vulgarities will break that rule and you may quit the interaction, at least in the cerebral sense.

If you expect a supervisor to express appreciation for the outstanding effort you put in while working on a project—and instead you are ignored—you may feel as if a rule of interpersonal communication has been broken. The rule that you bring to the table is that excellence, particularly excellence beyond what is expected, should be acknowledged. The absence of such acknowledgment appears to your conscious or subconscious self as a violation. The perceived breach may affect your perception of your supervisor and interfere with subsequent exchanges between you and the supervisor. Perhaps you have no right to expect congratulatory comments. However, as a practical matter as it pertains to rules theory, whether you have a right to your rule or don't have a right, when another breaks the rules as you see them, interpersonal communication is affected.

Chuck, the Subject Matter Expert in the case that begins this chapter, would pretend to suppress laughter when an internal customer asked questions that Chuck felt were foolish. The suppressed laughter was intended to ridicule the integrity of the question and questioner. This was perceived by internal customers as a violation of an interpersonal communication rule. The result was that some internal customers refused to interact with Chuck. They "quit" on him. Chuck's value to the firm, despite his expertise, was limited thereafter when internal clients refused to work with him.

We have all experienced situations when someone has communicated with us in a way that we felt was inappropriate. A supervisor may have been gruffly condescending; a roommate may have barked criticisms; a subordinate may have sounded sarcastically indifferent. We may not have always "quit" in these instances, but the violation likely had an effect on subsequent exchanges. Also, we probably all have been in situations when a person's communication was atypically considerate and went beyond the reasonable expectations of our rules. These considerate behaviors are, of course, the opposite of violations and can have a positive effect on the nature of current and subsequent interpersonal communications with that other individual. Consider the next three cases.

McDonald and Barrett

Gene McDonald, an associate manager, walked into the mailroom to check his box and noticed that a package was sitting on a table addressed to Sandra Barrett. Barrett was a new employee at the company and one of McDonald's peers. McDonald's office cubicle was not far from Barrett's, and he decided to be helpful and bring the package over to the new employee. McDonald took the package from the mailroom, walked onto the office floor, and approached Barrett's desk.

"Sandy," said McDonald, "This came for you. I spotted it in the mailroom."

Barrett took the package, clipped a staccato, "Thank you" and then made the following comment:

"Don't ever call me Sandy, again. My name is Sandra. I'm not a 'Sandy.' Please don't forget it."

McDonald's immediate response was to nod a stunned, "Okay," and return to his desk. As he told me subsequently, he decided after that encounter never to speak with Sandra Barrett again unless it was absolutely essential. He stated definitively that he wasn't going to call her Sandra, Sandy, or Mudd, unless he was compelled to. McDonald commented that Barrett's remark was unnecessary and he wanted nothing to do with her after her rebuke (his word), particularly considering that he'd been doing her a favor when she accosted (his word) him.

Joiner and the MBM

Angela Joiner is a product manager at a chemical company. The products that she manages are used in several markets, including aerospace, electronics, and pharmaceuticals. At 50 million in revenues the chemical company is a "small cap" public company which is run with a very serious focus on accounting and accountability. Every month, business meetings (MBMs for Monthly Business Meetings) are held with senior level management to review the financial health of the company. The product managers are not permitted to attend the meetings unless they are "called on the carpet" during the MBM to justify the numbers.

An MBM was scheduled for a Tuesday at 9 A.M. That day at 8 A.M. Joiner was walking through the door of her office—coat on and briefcase, purse, and bag lunch in tow—when she was anxiously greeted by her supervisor, one of the senior level officers involved in the MBMs. Even though he said, "Good morning," Joiner knew from his loud, rushed speech and nervous motions that the boss, Roger, wanted to get right to his questions rather than engage in friendly morning salutations. Joiner had only the opportunity to take off her coat and unload her things. Her attempt to motion Roger to the coffeemaker failed. She felt physically trapped as she braced for his questions.

There were, however, no questions. Instead, Roger curtly told Angela—while pointing a finger in her face—that not only were her aerospace film revenues down to date compared to forecast, they were also down compared to last year's actuals. Continuing, Roger told Angela that he would spare her the embarrassment of being called into the MBM, but that she'd better have a plan to rectify the situation.

Angela was shaken by Roger's approach. Nevertheless when he left her office she promptly reviewed the numbers in question and determined that while sales might be below forecast, they were, in reality, 50 percent *above* last year's actuals. Angela confronted Roger with the corrected information before the 9 A.M. MBM, but Roger barked a response, saying that it was not important to "rationalize or justify" the deficiencies, only to make things better. This infuriated Angela Joiner. She did not appreciate Roger's accusations and was distraught that the misrepresentation of her work might be brought to the MBM.

The Dean's Visit

On my first day as a university professor there was a grand, thunder crackling rainstorm. In consecutive periods on that rainy day I taught two classes. After dismissing the second group, I stayed in the room for a while reflecting on the moment. There was a knock on the classroom door. I looked to my left and saw the door open and my Dean enter the classroom. "Well, how did it go?" he asked.

I told him that it had gone well, but that was not what I was thinking. I was thinking, and still think, what a considerate gesture it was for the dean to walk close to a half mile from his office on a stormy day to ask how my first class had gone.

In the McDonald and Barrett example, Gene McDonald decided "not to play" with Sandra Barrett anymore. In the MBM example, Joiner's subsequent interactions with Roger were affected by what Joiner considered a gratuitious confrontation. In the instance with my Dean and the rainstorm, I thought that my boss had been very considerate, and my subsequent interactions with him and his staff reflected the positive way I thought he communicated.

Inherent Problems

The rules approach helps to visualize what takes place during interpersonal communication. Individuals who can assess the rules and "play" by the rules—while not altering the messages that they desire to communicate—increase the chances for message fidelity. The key to the successful application of rules theory is understanding and respecting your receivers so that you may honor their rules and communicate accordingly, while concurrently respecting and honoring your own rules.

There are, however, two obvious problems with the successful implementation of rules theory. The first is that it is nearly impossible to predict all the rules that another might bring to the table. We all have personal "landmines" that others could not identify. One would need a crystal ball to be able to predict all of your colleagues' communication rules. The longer you work with someone the easier it is to predict the rules, but initially, "since communication is such a personal process, [predicting rules] may be quite challenging."[4]

The second problem is that too many organizational persons are unwilling to accept "the challenge" even when predicting rules is not particularly demanding. Would a person like Chuck (the SME from Case 10.1) be concerned with predicting the rules of others?

Consider the following incident which took place at a large midwestern university.

A portly admissions counselor at this prestigious institution was meeting with a hopeful high school student and his parents. During the course of the interview, the mother of the applicant inquired about the food in the dormitories. The admissions' agent commented that he'd heard that the food was quite good. Incredibly, the father quipped, "Well, it looks like *you* haven't missed too many of the meals."

This was perceived by the counselor (and probably to you the reader) as inappropriately tactless. Can you imagine how tactful the father might have been if the son had *not* been a university applicant, hoping to gain admission? Imagine what it might be like to work with the father. Imagine what it might be like to work in a department where there are many such "fathers" all indifferent to the sensitivities of others.

Some readers might think, "Well, forget about the admissions' counselor if he can't 'take a joke.' " That may be a desirable notion. That is, we may wish that those with whom we interact can "take a joke" or be able to endure some comments that we consider innocuous. Nevertheless, not all people can "take a joke," and what one person deems harmless may be bruising to another. Most significantly—in organizations at least—it is short-sighted to assume that damage to a relationship will not have a consequent effect or effects on some aspect of the organization. One can't "forget about him if he can't take a joke." There are likely to be insidious reminders.

Using Rules Approaches

Rules theory is a very effective way to conceptualize the dyad. If one wants to improve interpersonal communication with difficult people, one should try to get into the head of those people, and imagine their rules.

Also, if you have been told, on occasion, that you are a difficult person, consider examining how adept you are at assessing the rules of others when you are engaged in interpersonal communication.

Sometimes we become so accustomed to counterproductive communication patterns that we cannot see them as counterproductive. If we have been weaned in an environment where certain communication behavior is accepted and encouraged, it may be difficult to understand that another might find that behavior unacceptable—or even that there is a need to examine communication behavior.

There's an old joke about the grade school teacher who is stunned when, after offering cookies to a student, the young boy says, "Nah, I don't want any of your rotten, miserable cookies." After reprimanding the child, the instructor returns the next day, and asks if the boy would like some cookies. The child responds as he had before, "Nah, I don't want any of your rotten, miserable cookies." Annoyed, the teacher hauls in the child's parents and asks them to observe the situation. She asks the boy on the third consecutive day if he would like some cookies. The youngster is nothing if not consistent. He responds as he has, "Nah, I don't want any of your rotten, miserable cookies." The teacher turns to the parents and says, "See? See the way your child talks?" The parents shrug, "So?" they say, "The kid doesn't want any of your rotten, miserable cookies."

Often we cannot see others' rules because of our experience. It's wise to consider that our experience is not the only experience, and to facilitate effective communication we need to predict the rules of others. Goldhaber framed it academically when he wrote, "When people define a situation differently, that is apply different rules, they will probably not co-orient to the event, and conflict may occur."[5]

Focus on Applications

What are your rules?

1. When you meet an instructor during office hours to discuss class progress, what rules do you think *your instructor* brings to the interaction in terms of

   a. Eye Contact?
   b. Word Choice
   c. Use of slang?
   d. Use of profanity?
   e. Use of technical terms?
   f. Use of appellations?
   g. Paralanguage (vocal qualities)
   h. Timeliness
   i. Content of discussion
   j. Accepting phone calls while you are in the room
   k. Eating during the meeting
   l. Drinking coffee or soft drinks during the meeting

2. What rules do *you* bring to the table regarding the same issues?

3. When you interact with people at work who are acquaintances (as opposed to close friends) are you offended if they

   a. Refer to women as "girls"?
   b. Touch you on the shoulder when telling you that you did a good job?
   c. Use profanities when upset?
   d. Use profanities as adjectives?
   e. Invade your personal space?
   f. Appear to be bored when you speak with them?
   g. Seem indifferent to your time concerns?
   h. Develop and use nicknames for you?
   i. Tell ethnic "jokes"?
   j. Disparage others behind their back?
   k. Use sophisticated words when simpler ones will do?

Figure 10-1 Transactional Analysis

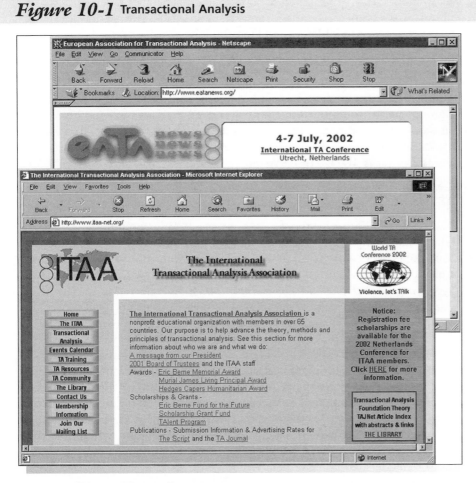

Throughout the World Transactional Analysis is currently used by consultants to improve interpersonal communication in organizations.

Courtesy of the ITAA, www.itaa-net.org
Courtesy of the EATA, www.eatanews.org

TRANSACTIONAL ANALYSIS

We are so accustomed to disguising ourselves to others that in the end we become disguised to ourselves.

—La Rochefoucauld

The meeting of two personalities is like the contact of two chemical substances: if there is any reaction, both are transformed.

—C. J. Jung

The Evolution of Transactional Analysis

In 1961, Eric Berne, a psychotherapist, published a book entitled, *Transactional Analysis in Psychotherapy.*[6] The book explained a self-help process for personal growth and psychological analysis. This process Berne called Transactional Analysis (TA). At its roots, TA is an analytic examination of interpersonal communication.[7]

Berne's book met with mixed reviews. The book, and the concept of Transactional Analysis, was not received positively by influential persons in the psychotherapeutic community.[8]Also, despite the fact that TA is a self-help process, Berne's book was academically written and difficult for many lay readers to understand.

In 1967 Thomas Harris published a book that explained Transactional Analysis more simply. Harris's book was entitled, *I'm O.K., You're O.K.* It was enormously successful. Four years later, Muriel James and Dorothy Jongeward published *Born to Win*, another book that presented the substance of Transactional Analysis in a manner that was accessible to almost any reader. Like the Harris publication, *Born to Win* sold millions of copies. Both books are still in print and are out in recent, post-1998, editions.[9]

In the early 1970s Transactional Analysis developed into a type of pop phenomenon. TA groups met throughout the country, and TA retreats took place with surprising, if not alarming, regularity. Harris's book and James and Jongeward's spawned additional volumes. *TA for Tots* appeared in print. *The O.K. Boss* was published, as was *Everybody Wins: Transactional Analysis Applied to Organizations*. Eric Berne himself wrote, *What Do You Say After You Say Hello?*[10]

Although Transactional Analysis was developed for use in psychotherapy, many Communication scholars use TA principles to examine interpersonal communication. Introductory Communication textbooks, sessions at scholarly communication conferences, and graduate seminars in communication all have discussed the applications of Transactional Analysis for improving dyadic communication. Also, many communication consultants use Transactional Analysis when working with their organizational clients. Type *transactional + analysis + communication* into the Yahoo search engine, and you may be surprised to see how many contemporary consultants use Transactional Analysis as a method for improving organizational communication.[11] (See Figure 10-1.) Three very recent academic articles in the *Transactional Analysis Journal* reflect this use and discuss how TA has been applied in organizational contexts to improve intrapersonal communication, interpersonal communication, and organizational creativity.[12] Wagner's *The Transactional Manager: How to Solve People Problems with Transactional Analysis* focuses entirely on the application of Transactional Analysis to organizational contexts.[13]

Transactional Analysis is presented here as a model for analyzing communication and not as a technique for psychotherapy. For people who want to improve their communications with others in the workplace or elsewhere, finding a more pragmatic method to facilitate such improvement would be difficult.

The discussion of Transactional Analysis will include sections on

- The transaction
- Ego states
- Types of transactions
- Communication modes
- Scripts
- Contracts

The Transaction

Berne uses the term *transaction* when speaking about dyadic exchanges. The word *Transaction* is used because it implies that there is an exchange between the source and receiver. The affix, *trans-*, means across, and according to Berne, something does go "across" from source to receiver when there is an interaction. When you speak to another you give something and get something back in return. Even in simple transactions when you say "hi" to colleagues whom you pass in the corridors, you are giving "acknowledgment" and getting "acknowledged" in return. If you were to pass another, say "hi" and be ignored, a message still would be coming across back to you.

For practical purposes, what Berne calls the transaction is synonymous with what is often called an interaction.

Ego States

Transactional Analysis is based on examinations (or "analyses") of interpersonal interactions (transactions).[14] In each analysis, there is an assessment made about the transaction based on the ego states of the involved sources and receivers.

Each person is said to have three ego states. These three are called the *Parent, Adult,* and *Child*—always written with a capital P, A, and C—to distinguish the ego states from parents, adults, and children.[15] That is, when writing about the *Parent* one capitalizes the P to make sure that readers do not confuse the ego state with a person who has children.

The Parent, Adult, and Child ego states are described as

- The **Parent ego state** is characterized by judgmental, nurturing, and/or admonishing communicative behavior. For example, were you to scold a colleague for being late to a meeting, you would be coming out of the Parent ego state.

- The **Adult ego state** is characterized by objective and rational communicative behavior. For example, were you to discuss plans for an upcoming project with your boss, you both would likely be speaking from your Adult ego state.

- The **Child ego state** is characterized by communicative behavior we would expect of children (i.e., needy, whiny, silly, and/or foolish communicative behavior). For example, if you were to ask a colleague to do you a favor and said, "Pretty please Sam, pretty please with polka dots, please fill in for me on Wednesday. I have tickets to see the 'Smoking Peppercorns', " you would be coming out of your Child ego state.

No matter how old or how young we might be, we all exhibit, at one time or another, all three ego states. Ego states are not theoretical concepts. They are "phenomenological realities."[16] In other words, they are real, and evident whenever we communicate with other people.

When conducting transactional analyses we assess what ego state the source is "coming out of" and what ego state the source attempts "to hook" or engage.

For example, if a passenger on a plane were to turn to you and say, "What time is it?" she or he would be coming out of the Adult ego state and would be attempting to engage or "hook" your Adult. The objective of the transaction would be to rationally inquire regarding the time. The source seeks a rational and objective response. Therefore, she or he would like to engage your Adult, expecting that you will respond rationally and objectively.

If your response to the query was, "It is 5:40," you would be coming out of your Adult and would be attempting to engage the source's Adult.

The determination of whether a message is coming from the Parent, Adult, or Child ego state is made on the basis of the content of the message, and the nonverbal factors that accompany the verbal content. Therefore, paralingual (vocal tone) and oculesic (eye contact), kinesic (body motion), and proxemic (spatial) factors are part of the determination. Were someone to thrust a finger in your face and growl, "What time is it?" the inquiry would be originating from the Parent ego state of the source.

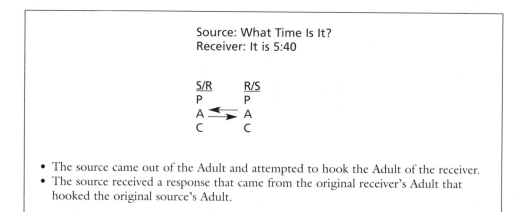

Figure 10-2 **Complementary Transactions**

> Source: What Time Is It?
> Receiver: It is 5:40
>
> S/R   R/S
> P   P
> A ⟷ A
> C   C

- The source came out of the Adult and attempted to hook the Adult of the receiver.
- The source received a response that came from the original receiver's Adult that hooked the original source's Adult.

The analyses of transactions are typically diagrammed. Figure 10-2 shows a Transactional Analysis diagram pertaining to the hypothetical conversation on the plane.

Types of Transactions

There are three types of transactions: (1) complementary, (2) crossed, and (3) ulterior transactions.

Complementary Transactions. The diagram in Figure 10-2 illustrates a complementary transaction. Any time the designated ego state is hooked, and the response returns to the source's emanating ego state, the transaction is complementary. If a colleague scolds you for coming to work late, coming out of his Parent and hooking your Child, and you respond coming out of your Child hooking the colleague's Parent, the result is a complementary transaction. The word *complement* means to complete. The response essentially completes the initial message. Complementary transactions may seem to be desirable. However, they are not necessarily desirable. A pattern of a colleague admonishing you and you humbly responding will consist of complementary transactions, but the pattern is likely to be unhealthy for both parties and unsatisfactory at least for one of the parties.

Crossed Transactions. Assume that when the stranger on the plane asks you for the time you say, "Fellow, why don't you get yourself a watch?" That transaction would be diagrammed as indicated in Figure 10-3 and would be an example of a crossed transaction. The stranger would have been rebuked, and would not have been successful at finding out the time. She or he would have come out of her Adult and attempted to engage your Adult. Instead you came out of your Parent and attempted to hook her Child.

Ulterior Transactions. Ulterior transactions are a bit more complicated and are the types of transactions that create insidious problems for the organization. Ulterior transactions are, by definition, deceptive transactions. In these exchanges, individuals

Figure 10-3 Crossed Transactions

> Source: What Time Is It?
> Receiver: Fellow, why don't you get yourself a watch?
>
> S/R   R/S
> P   P
> A   A
> C   C
>
> - The source came out of the Adult and attempted to hook the Adult of the receiver.
> - The source received a response that came from the original receiver's Parent that hooked the original source's Child.

Figure 10-4 Ulterior Transactions

> Source: What Time Is It?
> Receiver: I'd be delighted to provide the time to someone who doesn't wear a basic wrist watch. It is 5:40.

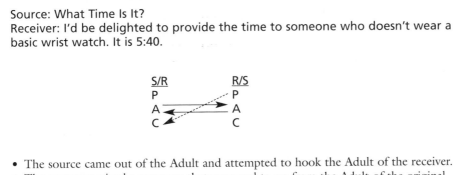

> - The source came out of the Adult and attempted to hook the Adult of the receiver.
> - The source received a response that appeared to go from the Adult of the original receiver and hook the Adult of the original source. However, the actual message came from the receiver's Parent and hooked the original Source's Child.

attempt to hook ego states indirectly. That is, deceptive individuals try to solicit desired responses by manipulating the other person. An ulterior transaction is diagrammed in Figure 10-4.

In organizations, far too often, individuals engage in ulterior transactions. Not all interpersonal exchanges, of course, are typically characterized by ulterior transactions. Enough are so characterized, however, to warrant attention to the possibility that our interpersonal exchanges are rooted in deception. Often, individuals do not even realize that they are being deceptive and manipulative when they're interacting.

Interpersonal communication characterized by ulterior transactions creates insidious problems for the organization.

© CORBIS

ETHICAL PROBE

IMPLICIT OR EXPLICIT CRITICISM?

Is it unethical to imply criticism as opposed to explicitly articulating your disapproval of another's actions?

Assume that you are annoyed at a colleague's perpetual tardiness. Instead of explicitly requesting that the person be more punctual, you could say, "I'm glad to see that you've arrived. It's good to have everyone here at last." Is it unethical to hide behind what may be perceived as an ambiguous message? Is there an ethical responsibility for communicators to own up to the position they appear to be making and not hide behind ambiguity? Do the positive benefits of being vague override whatever ethical responsibilities one might have to be explicit with communications?

Communication Modes

Transactional Analysis suggests that there are different degrees of substance in our dyadic exchanges. Berne categorizes these as rituals, pastimes, withdrawal, games, and intimacy.

Rituals. Rituals, sometimes called phatic communications, are characterized by small-talk exchanges. For example,

- Hi, how are you?
- Good and you?
- Fine, thanks.
- Good to see you.
- Thanks, so long.

Sometimes these exchanges take place so rapidly and are uttered by rote such that one party doesn't wait for the appropriate response before offering the next line. A co-worker may blurt, "Fine, thanks" after first saying "How are you?" regardless of whether the other individual utters a sound in response to the initial question.

Ritual transactions are intended more to acknowledge another's existence than anything else. A person who literally responded to ritualistic queries would be considered odd indeed. Assume that you were walking in a corridor in between classes and you were about to pass an acquaintance headed in the other direction. Imagine your reaction if, after you smiled and said, "What's happening?" you were pulled over to the side and heard the following in response:

> What's happening? I'll tell you what's happening, I have a bruise on my hip the size of Nebraska which I got from playing racquetball with Chris and it is killing me. It is absolutely killing me. It hurts every time I take a step. That's what's happening with me.

Your reaction to this outburst might well be, "Who asked ya?" You certainly had not. You were merely involved in a ritual transaction which was meant to acknowledge and not ignore an acquaintance. You don't want to hear about Chris and the racquetball bruise.

In fact, most people engage in rituals precisely because they don't want to become involved in an in-depth conversation. You may be in a hurry or you may just not want to speak about anything substantive. The following example illustrates how limited ritual communications can be.

Imagine that an employee at XYZ company walks into a supermarket, pushes her cart down the aisle, and spots an XYZ associate walking down the aisle toward her. Further, assume that the associate is not a friend, but only a peripheral acquaintance from work. The two are likely to engage in a ritual greeting.

> "Hi Brandon. How are you?"
> "Good, Nina. Thanks," says Brandon.

Nina passes the acquaintance, finishes up in aisle one, and turns down aisle two. There again she spots Brandon. This time as Brandon approaches, she might say, "Hi, again."

Brandon might contort his face in a "What do you know?" smile, then chuckle, then mimic, "Hi again," and walk on by.

Down aisle three she goes. Nina bumps into Brandon a third time and says with a dramatic smile, "We've got to stop meeting like this." Brandon concurs with a playful snort.

Nina turns down aisle five a few minutes later and there Brandon is again, and this time she doesn't want to see him. She has exhausted, "How are you," "Hi again," and "We've got to stop meeting like this." There is very little left in her ritual repertoire. She may well pick up a box of cereal, pretend to scrutinize the ingredients, wait for Brandon to pass by, put the box down, and proceed with shopping. Both Brandon and Nina are hopeful that they won't make eye contact in the store again.

Pastimes. Pastimes are exchanges that are a degree more substantive than rituals. Simply, they are nonsubstantive transactions, during which the participants attempt to pass the time. For example, while waiting for a meeting to be called to order, colleagues seated at the conference table may discuss the weather, other departments' idiosyncrasies, world news, or the local sport teams' successes. You might ask a co-worker about some personal matter but the discussions will probably be superficial.

"How are things going on the Mellen project, Zach?"

If Zach says, "Great just great," the superficial detail is likely to be fine with you.

When people engage in pastimes they are uninterested in discussing substantive matters. If you find yourself on a movie line waiting to buy tickets and notice your manager standing in front of you, you are likely to engage in pastimes as you await the line progression. You may not want to discuss anything meaningful related to your work and will probably be delighted if the line moves rapidly so that you will not have to search for comfortable topics to discuss.

Withdrawal. Withdrawal is a communication mode in which the person who withdraws attempts to avoid interpersonal transactions. The person, in the extreme case, may be agoraphobic, or, in a less serious situation, might simply want to be left alone for a particular time.

You may need time to work on a project alone so you decide to screen all incoming phone calls. You may feel besieged by a host of silly inquiries and therefore find a spot in the office where you sense that few can locate you. These examples are relatively innocuous, as they're likely not to be typical nor habitual avoidance behaviors.

However, if a person, as a matter of course, shuns external contacts, that person is likely to create communication problems for the organization that transcend the difficulties resulting from any one person not being able to locate the withdrawing other.

Games. Games refer to a communication mode that is typified by ulterior transactions. Employees and employers who engage in games generally want to manipulate others by communicating deceptively.

As an example, let us say that a manager is less concerned with productivity than maintaining power. By communicating deceptively, the manager may be able to manipulate the employee to continue to play an inappropriately servile role. Likewise, employees can be deceptive in order to ingratiate themselves with top management or avoid certain responsibilities.

Ingenuous Communication. Referred to as *intimacy* in Berne's nomenclature, ingenuous communication is defined as open, honest, and as it relates to TA, substantive communication.

An important note to make here is that ingenuous communication may or may not facilitate effective communication. While it is true that some people are impressed by ingenuous communicators, others are put off by such communication since it is so unusual. It is far more common for someone to initiate an interaction with a stranger that she or he would like to meet by discussing something peripheral than by stating simply that the approach is due to a physical attraction. In the hope of initiating a conversation, people will approach others in libraries and ask, "What time is it?" despite the fact that there might be six large clocks in the vicinity.

Scripts and Scripting

Nearly all human activity is programmed by an ongoing script dating from early childhood, so that the feeling of autonomy is nearly always an illusion—an illusion which is the greatest affliction of the human race because it makes awareness, honesty, creativity, and intimacy possible for only a few fortunate individuals.[17]

—Eric Berne

Scripting is the most controversial dimension of Transactional Analysis. It is, however, an important aspect to discuss in order to understand the nature of interpersonal communication problems in organizations.

According to Berne, much of what we say does not reflect our own personal beliefs and philosophies.[18] Not only what we say, but paralingual and other nonverbal communicative complements, may not be our own. He argues that many individuals as youngsters receive hundreds of messages that are sent from some others' Parent to the youngster's Child. The receivers do not evaluate the messages they receive in their Child, but simply "ship" these philosophies north to their Adult. Therefore, when people speak out of their Adult, according to Berne, they often are simply spewing a script that has been written by a host of aunts, teachers, neighborhood bullies, clergymen, cops, sports figures, parents, television personalities, etc. who have sent messages to this person that never were evaluated.

For example, if John is told and shown that it is acceptable for coaches to scream at youth soccer players, John may argue at a subsequent date that there is nothing wrong with coaches communicating gruffly. John will offer this opinion out of his Adult ego state. It may be, however, that the philosophy that John naturally puts forth was never internally questioned. That is, it is possible that John is under the illusion that he is speaking from his Adult, but he is actually only repeating a Script of messages he has previously heard.

Obviously the ramifications of this theory are enormous. It is very difficult to change how you communicate your thoughts, if your thoughts are, in fact, not yours but a composite of others'. Certainly, many take issue with Berne over this philosophy. To agree in entirety would be to acknowledge that the world is populated primarily by nonthinking robots. However, to improve interpersonal communication it is worth one's while to consider the possibility that one's transactions are a function of scripted input.

Focus on Applications

Assessing personal attitudes and scripts

Please respond to the following questions *and* in each instance explain why you feel the way you do.

1. Should employees use appellations when referring to superiors? That is, should an employee call the boss *Ms. Diego* or *Mr. Warren,* or are first names just as appropriate?
2. Should an employer shout at an employee who has done something incorrectly? Should a coach shout at a player who has done something incorrectly?
3. Is there anything wrong with taking a sick day and going out in the evening of the same day (assuming you feel just as healthy at night as you did in the daytime)?
4. Should you dress differently on a day when you will be interacting with senior management as opposed to days when you will be interacting with your regular colleagues?

Is it possible that your responses to these questions reflect scripted reactions?

Contracts

The "bottom line" in Transactional Analysis is related to the employment of *contracts*. A *contract*, in TA terminology, refers to a specific technique for improving interpersonal communication with individual others. The process involves a number of steps. An example is provided below. In this case, an employee has experienced difficulty communicating with a colleague named Williamson. Using contracts, the employee writes in the first person to explain how to proceed to improve communication with the colleague.

Step 1: Identify the communication problem in terms of TA terminology. Williamson frequently comes out of his Parent ego state during our interactions. Too often I find that he is successful hooking my Child. I don't want that to continue. I want to communicate out of my Adult with complementary transactions when dealing with Williamson.

Step 2: Specify a strategy to deal with the problem in terms of relevant communication factors. (*Typically, these factors are visual, verbal, and vocal dimensions of communication.*) The strategy is to cross Williamson's Parent-Child messages with Adult-Adult messages. The goal is to compel Williamson to come out of his Adult as opposed to his Parent when we are engaged in interpersonal communication. By continuing to cross the transaction, Williamson will either have to perpetuate the uncomfortable crossed transaction or come out of his Adult.

- *Visually:* Maintain steady eye contact at all times during the exchange.
- *Vocally:* Speak slowly and evenly using a steady tone.
- *Verbally:* Use no slang. Speak in clear sentences that refer specifically to the topic of discussion. When appropriate, comment that Williamson's remarks can sound condescending.

Step 3: Practice role playing with a friend. (In this stage, ask an acquaintance to assume Williamson's traits in order to practice and hone the approach identified in step 2).

Step 4: Interact with the person. (In this case Williamson.)

Step 5: Subsequent to the interaction, play your (cerebral) "tapes" of the conversations, and diagram a transactional analysis of the communications.

Step 6: If necessary, go back to step 2 and reevaluate the strategy.

Step 7: Continue with steps 3–6 until satisfied with changes when communicating with the other person.

Contracts work if persons are willing to work at them. They are a systematic method of changing communication patterns with individuals who may be abrasive.

PRACTITIONER'S PERSPECTIVE

Duane Vild, Complex Warden for the State of Arizona Department of Corrections; Bureau Administrator, Department of Corrections

In the Arizona State system, a Complex Warden is the chief administrative officer of a cluster of three to five prisons that are all located in the same region of the state. Mr. Vild served as Complex Warden in Douglas, Arizona and also in Tucson, Arizona. These were both five prison complexes. At each location, Mr. Vild supervised 100–200 Complex staff employees, 500 to 900

Unit employees (A Unit refers to one of the prisons in the Complex), and some 4,000 inmates. After his work as a Complex Warden, Mr. Vild became a Bureau Administrator for the Arizona Department of Corrections. In that role he was responsible for training persons who would work in Complex prisons.

Communication wasn't simply *central* to what I did. It was imperative. It could make me or break me as warden. You want to talk about communicating with difficult people? I had to communicate with difficult people and I'm not referring primarily to the inmates who, relatively speaking, were not a problem in terms of communication.

The key to success as a communicator in my situation is being sensitive to your audiences, paying attention to them, knowing your audiences—*and knowing yourself.* Don't forget that last part. You have to know yourself and develop—if you don't have it—some humility.

When I first became warden I thought that the best way to communicate was to write memos. I wrote 50 memos a day. I thought I could write well and this way I would get my message across. I thought because of who I was and how well I could express myself I could communicate. But I needed to listen more, understand my audiences, and become a little more humble. We live in a fast-food society. I call it a Jack in the Box society. People need information presented concisely and quickly that is germane to their needs. Sometimes managers get too impressed with themselves. Their egos get in the way and they think that the message they're relaying has clout and meaning because of how well they speak or write, and how much wisdom or power they have. Your writing skills and intelligence means little unless you know the people whom you're writing to and can get a concise understandable message to them. In a world as diverse as a prison in terms of race, gender, educational background, and power, administrators must learn and listen, and not let their egos get in the way.

Prisons foster poor communication. There is a great deal of pressure on wardens to communicate effectively to all of the constituents: the media, your supervisors, your staff, and the inmates. You have a great many people who are entrenched in their positions or who want to retain power and their fiefdoms. You have people who do things that are inappropriate—and I'm not talking about inmates here—yet your staffers may stonewall you when you try to address a situation. If you want to get a message through to those who are stonewalling you, you better not rely on your writing skills, but rely on your ability to discover what makes these people behave the way they do. And again, take a look at why you behave the way you do.

When I worked as the Bureau Administrator a supervisor came to me and said, "Vild, we have a problem with race and communication. I want you to run a half-day workshop and educate these people." Imagine that? Run a half-day workshop and deal with issues of race. Training regarding intercultural communication is doable, and we worked on a program for our staff, but it takes more than a half a day to conduct such training.

I think there's a 33-33-33 rule when it comes to coaching people about communicating interculturally. One third of the people are going to be unwilling to acknowledge that there is a problem because they're stuck on their cultural orientation as being superior. One third of the population doesn't need the training because they communicate cross-culturally without the differences creating rifts, and one third of the people have problems but can be transformed.

The nature of my work at the complexes really tested my ability to communicate. Communication training should be part of any manager's background. People should be coached when they come into a managerial position and then annually discuss issues related to communication. You can be brilliant, personable, knowledgeable, but if you can't communicate to your internal audiences you can't function.

SUMMARY

A Toolbox

1. Interpersonal communication is the most prevalent organizational communication context. We occasionally deliver and listen to presentations. More frequently we attend and participate in meetings. However, daily, we engage in multiple dyadic interactions.

2. One technique for improving interpersonal communication involves applying a rules approach. This approach requires:

   • Assessing your audience and identifying the rules that they bring to the communication setting.

   • A self-examination of the rules you yourself bring to dyadic communication settings.

3. A second technique is called Transactional Analysis. Transactional Analysis requires:

   • Identifying the ego states you use when communicating with others.

   • Identifying the type of transactions you desire when communicating with others.

   • Employing contracts to increase the chances that your actual communications with others will be consistent with your desired patterns of communication.

DISCUSSION QUESTIONS

1. In a typical month

   a. How many presentations are you required to deliver?

   b. How many meetings do you attend?

   c. How many interpersonal exchanges do you have within any one of the organizations to which you belong?

2. How can rules theory be applied to interpersonal contexts?

3. How can Transactional Analysis be applied to interpersonal contexts?

4. Think about an individual who is difficult in terms of interpersonal communication. What are the rules that she or he brings to a dyadic encounter?

5. When you meet colleagues or classmates for the first time, what rules do you bring to these interpersonal exchanges? Do you consider yourself difficult?

6. Think about the same individual whom you identified in response to question 4. When you interact with that person what ego state does she or he typically come out of? What ego state does she or he attempt to engage? What ego state do you come out of during these encounters?

7. Identify a current communication problem you have with another. How would you employ contracts to remedy that problem?

8. Please read the case that appears below and respond to the questions that follow it.

CASE FOR ANALYSIS

Case 10.2—Using Rules Theory and Transactional Analysis

Background. Two employees have been assigned by their respective supervisors to cross train one another in their areas of expertise for a period of approximately three weeks. Neither supervisor has provided specific instructions for the assignment, expecting that each employee will be able to handle the cross training responsibilities without direction.

Both employees work for a conservative bank in the reporting and analysis division of the Treasury Department. In addition, both employees are being groomed as potential managers. One employee is 28 and male, while the other employee is 46 and female. The tenure of the male employee is only five weeks, while the tenure for the female employee is three years. Each employee has considerable professional experience along with a documented history of achievement and advancement throughout his or her career. The workload for both employees is heavy—particularly in the morning hours, near every month's end, and at every quarter's end. In addition, the reports that each employee is responsible for are very time sensitive (most need to be submitted before noon to various groups). The afternoon is considerably less hectic than the morning. Nevertheless, in order to learn the dynamics of the positions, it is imperative to cross train in the morning.

Problem. During the cross training session of the male employee, tension developed between the two employees very quickly. The male employee perceived the training to be rapid and superficial, while the female employee perceived the male employee to be disrespectful, lazy, and intent on delaying the training schedule.

The tension culminated a few days later in a loud outburst by the female employee. As a result of this outburst, a communication gulf quickly developed between the two employees. Communication between the two was limited to a critical needs only realm. Neither one of the employees trusted the other one and both refused to address the issue with their supervisors. Colleagues and management were aware of the problem, but perplexed by it and took no specific action. The original goal of cross training was never accomplished. Furthermore, neither employee worked with the other one ever again. Both employees left the Treasury Department approximately six months later.

Each employee recognized the importance of learning from one another, but due to the communication breakdown neither was willing to continue with the cross training.

- How would a rules theorist analyze this communication problem?
- How would you analyze this problem using Transactional Analysis?
- How could either party have used rules theory or Transactional Analysis to avoid the tension that surfaced?

ENDNOTES

[1]On February 28, 2002 there were 31,500 hits for that combination. By adding the word *organization* to that combination the number was reduced to 9,210.

[2]DeVito, Joseph, *The Communication Handbook,* Harper and Row, 1986, p. 270.

[3]Schall, Maryann, "A Communication Rules Approach to Organizational Culture," *Administrative Science Quarterly,* 1983, vol. 28, p. 560.

[4]Goldhaber, Gerald, *Organizational Communication,* Sixth Edition, Brown/Benchmark, 1993, p. 132.

[5]Ibid., p. 131.

[6]Berne, Eric, *Transactional Analysis in Psychotherapy,* New York, Grove Press, 1961.

[7]Wagner, Abe, *The Transactional Manager,* Prentice Hall, 1981, 1992, p. 5 (page number is from 1981 edition).

[8]Ian Stewart in his book, *Eric Berne,* discusses two major critics of Berne: Joel Kovel and Irvin Yalom. Stewart defends Berne against these criticisms in the chapter entitled, "Criticisms and Rebuttals," pp. 105–128. Ian Stewart, *Eric Berne.* Sage Publications, 1992.

[9]James, Muriel and Dorothy Jongeward, *Born to Win, Transactional Analysis with Gestalt Experiments,* 25th Anniversary Edition, Perseus Books, January 2000. Thomas Harris, *I'm Ok. You're Ok. A Practical Guide to Transactional Analysis.* Galahad Books edition, March 1999.

[10]Freed, Alvyn, *TA for Tots,* Sacramento: Jalmar Press, 1973.
Berne, Eric, *Games People Play,* Grove Press, 1964.
James, Muriel, *The Okay Boss,* Addison Wesley, 1973.
Berne, Eric, *What Do You Say after You Say Hello,* Grove Press, 1972.
Jongeward, Dorothy and contributors, *Everybody Wins: Transactional Analysis Applied to Organizations,* Reading, Addison Wesley, 1973.

[11]As indicated in footnote number 1, there were thousands of web pages with this combination. Many of these discussed workshops for organizations that employed Transactional Analysis as the vehicle for improving communication. The web pages provided as illustrations on page 243 are examples.

[12]Nuttal, John, "Intrapersonal and Interpersonal Relations in Management Organizations," January 2000. Melanie Lewin, "I'm Not Talking to You: Shunning as a Form of Violence," April 2000. Eric William Sigmund, "Using Transactional Analysis for Creativity," July 1999.

[13]Op. cit., Wagner.

[14]Ibid., Abe Wagner, p. 5.

[15]Perhaps this sentence should read that ego states *should* always be written with the capital P, A, and C. There are publications that have printed articles relating to TA where the capital lettering did not appear. For example, "Parent-adult-child segments in Marketing," in *Journal of Advertising Research,* April–May 1987, vol. 27, no. 2, p. 38. There are several other similar examples.

[16]Op. cit., Eric Berne, *Transactional Analysis in Psychotherapy,* Grove Press, 1961, p. 24.

[17]Berne, Eric, "The Relationship Between Transactional Analysis and Other Forms of Treatment," in *Principles of Group Treatment* (Berne), Grove Press, 1966, p. 310.

[18]Ibid.

11

Improving Written Communication

I have received memos so swollen with managerial babble that they struck me as the literary equivalent of assault with a deadly weapon.[1]

—Peter Baida

Whether viewed with a futuristic foresight or in retrospect, they point to an enlargement of the functionary aspects of the business; hence a greater degree of risk to try management acumen.

—Excerpt from Ivy League MBA student memorandum

Incomprehensible jargon is the hallmark of a profession.[2]

—Kingman Brewster, Jr., Former Yale University President

© GETTY IMAGES/PHOTODISC

The Washington bureaucrat's guide to chocolate chip cookies

Total Lead Time: 35 minutes.

Inputs

1 cup packed brown sugar
1/2 cup granulated sugar
1/2 cup softened butter
1/2 cup shortening
2 eggs
1 1/2 teaspoons vanilla
1 teaspoon baking soda
1/2 teaspoon salt
12-ounce package semi-sweet chocolate pieces
1 cup chopped walnuts or pecans

Guidance

After procurement actions, decontainerize inputs. Perform measurement tasks on a case-by-case basis. In a mixing type bowl, impact heavily on brown sugar, granulated sugar, softened butter and shortening. Coordinate the interface of eggs and vanilla, avoiding an overrun scenario to the best of your skills and abilities.

At this point in time, leverage flour, baking soda, and salt into the mixing type bowl and aggregate. Equalize with prior mixture and develop intense and continuous liaison among inputs until well-coordinated. Associate your key chocolate and nut subsystems and execute stirring operations.

Within this time frame, take action to prepare the heating environment for throughput by manually setting the oven baking unit by hand to a temperature of 375 degrees Fahrenheit (190 degrees Celsius). Drop mixture in an ongoing fashion from a teaspoon implement onto an ungreased cookie sheet at intervals sufficient enough apart to permit total and permanent separation of throughputs to the maximum extent practicable under operating conditions.

Position cookie sheet in a bake situation and surveil for 8 to 10 minutes or until cooking action terminates. Initiate coordination of outputs within the cooking rack function. Containerize, wrap in red tape, and disseminate to authorized staff personnel on a timely and expeditious basis.

Outputs

Six dozen official government chocolate chip cookie units.

Source: Susan E. Russ.

ABSTRACT

Writing is central to organizational activity. Managers must write memos, letters, reports, electronic messages, meeting minutes, personnel evaluations, funding proposals, and assorted other materials. Nonmanagerial employees may not need to write as often as their supervisors, but most employees regularly have to write for various internal audiences.

Effective business writing can be difficult for even the most intelligent persons. People often become frustrated and stymied when they sit down to write. Individuals who claim to have no anxiety about business writing are either exceptional or—more likely—not being candid. This chapter discusses how organizational men and women can become more comfortable and effective when writing.

OBJECTIVES

When you have completed this chapter, you should be able to:

- ☐ **Explain why apprehension related to writing is common.**
- ☐ **Identify methods for reducing tension associated with business writing.**
- ☐ **Describe common problems that contribute to poor writing.**
- ☐ **Discuss how to avoid these problems.**
- ☐ **Explain the characteristics of persuasion and persuasive communication.**

THE IMPORTANCE OF BUSINESS WRITING

Some would argue that good writing and good speaking are out of date on the information highway. Nothing could be further from the truth. The same principles that applied to delivering a good speech in the Roman Senate apply to sending an effective e-mail message.[3]

—Michael Hattersley and Linda McJannet

Business leaders often complain about the written communication skills of their managers and employees.[4] It may well be, however, that these complaining leaders themselves have difficulty putting pen to paper or fingers to keyboard. In "Why Executives Can't Write: The Power of Poor Communication" freelance writer Dick Brown comments that most executives "can not write well enough to pass a Freshman English exam."[5] Brown characterizes executive writing as "ambiguous, weak, indirect, and pompous."[6]

Most of us, at one time or another, have grumbled about the quality of written communications that we have received. Faculty members admonish students for poor written submissions. Part-time graduate students, who themselves are full-time managers, are perplexed and put off by the turgid composition of many articles in academic journals.[7] Undergraduates shake their heads at the confusing language in course description catalogues. Organizational end users read "explanatory" manuals over and over in order to make sense out of dense paragraphs *intended to clarify* procedures. Employees use the grapevine to poke fun at managerial missives that contain illogical arguments or grammatical errors. Poor writing is not uncommon.

Matejka and Ramos argue that poor writing has deleterious effects on the reputations of employees. Poor writing is perceived as a reflection of:

- A lack of <u>d</u>edication
- Weak <u>e</u>ducational background
- In<u>a</u>ttention to detail
- Lack of industry and <u>d</u>iligence[8]

By cleverly playing with the underlined letters in each item, the authors form an acronym suggesting that employees who are incapable of writing are, in essence, "dead" in terms of career advancement. This seems to be a severe assessment, but it is worth your while to consider the ramifications of writing inadequately. Otherwise intelligent, industrious, and dedicated employees can earn a negative reputation.

WHY WRITING IS DIFFICULT

Writing Is Work

The act of writing can be uncomfortable for several reasons. First, it is work. You may have been in a situation where you were working on a letter or memo, became frustrated with the process, and then said to yourself, "Never mind. I'll call her up." It is easier to have a conversation with another (assuming that the content of the message is not sensitive) than it is to force yourself to find the right words, construct the sentences correctly, and provide for the adequate segues that help the writer make transitions from one thought to another. Working at composition is a chore. There are values to undertaking the task—and being able to write is an imperative for organizational communication excellence—but the task of writing is a chore nonetheless.

When bruised by some municipal or corporate offender you may have promised to complain and write a letter. How often do these missives get mailed? Occasionally, as you travel to work or school, you may write letters in your head to other people. These cerebral compositions are brilliant. You think of something that is wise, and somehow when you consider it during the morning drive, word choice and sentence structure is outstanding. However, when you sit down at the computer to write the message, the words do not seem to flow as easily. At the computer, the thorny obstacles of subject/verb agreement and appropriate word choice are staring at you front and center. The letter you "penned" on the 20-minute commute may absorb an hour and 20 minutes of a busy day. In short, one reason writing creates anxiety is because it can be a time-consuming and onerous process.

Not Being Clear About Your Own Message

A second explanation for writing tension is that often when people sit down to write, they discover that they are not exactly sure what it is that they want to express. In these situations it is less a matter of how to construct what you desire to communicate than a matter of being clear about the substance of your message.

If you have attempted to petition for a scholarship or academic program you may have experienced this uncomfortable sensation. The application probably required that you explain why you would be a strong candidate for the program. You may have been very certain that you wanted to be in the program and that you would be a strong applicant.

However, you may not have sorted out exactly what you want to say about *why* you would be a strong candidate. After repeated attempts to explain on paper what you had yet to explain to yourself, you may have become frustrated, which added to the accrued tension that surrounds the experience of writing.

Not Knowing Your Audience

A third explanation for writing anxiety is related to not knowing your audience. In some situations, you are very sure about what it is that you want to express, but your inability to focus on the nature of your readers makes it difficult for you to frame your message.

You may be writing to a large audience, and you may not know much about that population. Therefore, repeated attempts at getting your message right are exasperating. Whether you realize it or not, you are having problems because you don't know how to direct your comments. You know what bullets you want to shoot, but you can't focus on the targets.

You may even be writing to only one reader, but are not sure of her or his attitudes on the subject. You have difficulty expressing yourself because of uncertainty regarding how she or he will receive the message. In a face-to-face interaction, you can gauge reactions on the basis of nonverbal expressions and can adapt, modify, or restate your message on the basis of these reactions. In a face-to-face interaction you can even say, "Do you follow me?" or "Is this clear?" or "Do you have any questions?" In written situations, there is no opportunity for immediate feedback. Guiding nonverbal and verbal reactions are absent. Therefore, not knowing your audience can increase the tension for the writer, particularly in a business context where advancement, evaluation, and personal job satisfaction may be at stake.

Prior Negative Experiences

A fourth reason for writing anxiety can relate to having had negative experiences with persons who were highly critical of your composition. At some point, destructive evaluations of your written communications may have left a scar. You may be reluctant to write because somewhere in your memory you recall Mr. Gruff from high school who tore apart your compositions for what appeared to be sport.

A related explanation for anxiety can be due to some genuine gaps in your education in terms of grammar and spelling. For whatever reason, you may have reason not to be confident about how you write. You may have gotten Mr. Gruff's papers back and never understood why the red marks were placed where they were. You may have had training that emphasized the conceptualization of the writing process and not the nuts and bolts of subject/verb agreement and basic rules of grammar. Therefore, you may be anxious when you write because you have a fear of being exposed.

While it may take only a few training sessions to learn the basics, you may not want to identify yourself as someone in need of special training. You may decide to fake your ability to write. Of course, by continuing to fake it, you increase your anxiety level each time you need to sit and compose a memorandum.

Written Communication Creates a Record

Finally, a reason for writing anxiety is related to the reality that writing creates a record of what has been communicated. When you sit down to write a letter in an organization, you need to get the message right or face the consequences of being responsible for getting it wrong. Therefore, the occasion of writing an important memo may be anxiety provoking because there can be a great deal riding on how you express yourself.

ETHICAL
PROBE

GHOST WRITTEN DOCUMENTS: TESTING FOR WRITING COMPETENCE?

Let's assume that you are a manager in an organization and have high writing anxiety. You are intelligent, responsible, and industrious, but you have trouble writing and avoid doing so. Further, let's assume that your ideas are typically very good and very helpful for your department and the organization as a whole.

1. Is there anything wrong with:

☐ Outlining your ideas for a written document
☐ Handing the outline to your administrative assistant
☐ Having your administrative assistant write the documents and then
☐ Signing *your* name on the documents (and not your administrative assistant's) after you have approved what he or she has written?

2. Is there anything unethical about your organization:

☐ Compelling you to learn to write (assuming that they discover your avoidance tendencies)
☐ Removing you from managerial responsibility if you cannot pass a reasonable writing test?

In sum, writing may create anxiety because

• It requires hard work.
• There can be some uncertainty regarding what it is that you want to write.
• There can be some uncertainty regarding the profile of your audience.
• You may have had prior destructive criticism of your writing efforts.
• You may have a weak background in composition basics.
• Writing provides a record of your message.

Do any of these affect your desire and comfort level when you write? Which of these items are most difficult for you to overcome?

WRITING EFFECTIVELY

I write to understand as much as to be understood.

—Elie Wiesel, author

One reason for writing is that it helps individuals become clearer about what they want to say. By forcing yourself to put word to paper, you fine tune your own thinking regarding the subject.

Another reason for writing relates to the simple fact that our jobs often require us to write. Specifically, we need to write in order to:

• Persuade
• Advise, educate, and inform others

- Make inquiries
- Protect ourselves[9]

A third reason is important to emphasize here. While much of the discussion thus far has addressed the *problems* associated with composition, writing can be an empowering and even exciting activity. You have an opportunity when you write to match the precise word with your creative and intelligent ideas. In interpersonal communications you must find the words as you speak. This phenomenon explains the obnoxious speech fillers, "You know," "Okay," and "Um" which litter conversation and drive receivers to distraction. However, when you write, you can get it right. You can pluck the right words from your vocabulary reservoir and construct a message that makes you smile when you reread it. And perhaps your written communications will make readers nod and smile when they receive your messages.

Since writing can be beneficial to us, and also because we must write to be effective organizational communicators, we should consider methods for overcoming whatever anxieties we have about the writing process in order to become comfortable and capable writers.

Demystifying the Process

Davidson, in *Business Writing: What Works What Won't,* suggests that effective writing begins with a demystification of the process. She argues that three common misconceptions about writing need to be dispelled:

1. "Correct writing" guarantees effective business writing
2. The more words contained in a document the better the document
3. Creative writing and business writing are fundamentally the same.[10]

Let's consider each of Davidson's myths.

Myth 1: Correct writing guarantees effective business writing.
Typically, when people complain about poor writing they cite the following.

- **Poor Grammar.** For example, problems with subject and verb agreement, *John, Abigail, Juan, and Libby, **knows** how to use the videoconferencing equipment.*
- **Misspellings.** For example, *In order to create a team atmosphere we need to conduct some **roll** playing experiments.*
- **Confusing Sentence Structure.** For example, *Having been told that he was a fraud, the manager investigated the background of the employee.*
- **Existence of Malapropisms.** For example, *It's about time that our department stopped being the **escape goats** for the entire organization.*[11]

These problems can certainly affect written documents. However, the *absence* of these problems does not render a document well-written. One can make sure that subjects and verbs agree and can check to correct spelling errors. All confusing constructions from a letter can be purged. Nevertheless, the document may be dull, inappropriate for the given audience, pompous, and/or illogical. An operations manual may contain not one single grammatical error and yet be so poorly written that even the most responsible employees will bury it in a desk and never review the material.

Myth 2: The more words contained in a document, the better the document. Most people know intuitively that this statement makes little sense. Nevertheless, many documents are far too wordy. Effective business writing should be concise—not brief at the expense of essential content—but to the point. We are flooded with written material and our time is valuable. A lengthy memorandum wastes readers' time. For this reason, some companies require that memorandums must be shorter than one or two pages.

Myth 3: Creative writing and business writing are fundamentally the same. Many people believe that James Joyce is one of the greatest writers who has ever put pen to paper. Read the first few pages of *Finnegan's Wake* and you will see that if Joyce applied the same writing principles that guided his novel to the challenges of writing safety guidelines for machine operators, days lost to injury figures would soar astronomically. Business writing is different from creative writing, in large part, because business readers are different from those who read novels. When people sit down to read a novel, they are interested in discovering the plot, trying to understand the theme, and becoming familiar with the characters. When people read a business memorandum, they seek out the information that can help them do their jobs. This doesn't mean that business writings need to be lifelessly constructed, but business writers have objectives that differ from novelists'.

STEPS IN THE WRITING PROCESS

There are several notions, all somewhat similar, about the best step-by-step approach to writing. Munter identifies five stages in the process:

- Gathering
- Organizing
- Focusing
- Drafting
- Editing[12]

Ramirez et al. recommends a slight variation that involves breaking up the editing stage. They propose the following sequence:

- Planning
- Drafting
- Revising
- Proofreading[13]

Dumaine, in *Write to the Top: Writing for Corporate Success,* breaks down the planning stages in more detail. She recommends these stages:

- Analyzing your purpose and your audience
- Generating ideas
- Grouping ideas
- Sequencing ideas
- Writing a first draft
- Editing and revising[14]

Let's highlight the recurring elements of these recommendations. In the following section, I will discuss several writing steps and provide readers with a sequential procedure that may be helpful for business writing.

Step 1: Know Your Task

Before you begin to write, explore in detail the reason for your writing and what it is that you desire to express. You need to be clear about your writing goal. To facilitate this, try writing a mission statement for the communication. For example,

A. *"My goal for this writing is to explain why I am well suited for graduate study in terms of my work experience, academic performance, career objectives, related co-curricular activities, and personal needs."*

B. *"My objective for this report is to describe why our department needs additional staffing on the basis of past performance, present staffing level, comparative staffing level, potential for greater production with new members, and overall benefit to the organization."*

C. *"The purpose for this document is to explain why we cannot honor your request for extended personal leave, because of specific organizational policy, the extent of your present leave, the precedent for such activity, our desire to maintain a positive organizational climate, and our need to have your services in order to meet our organizational mission."*

In each instance, the mission statement describes the general objective and then specifies the particular components that will be part of the message. These mission statements may take some time to construct, but you might actually *save time* by working on them. Once you're clear about what it is that you want to express, it will take less time for you to communicate your message.

Step 2: Know Your Audience

Matejka and Ramos suggest a series of questions that you should ask about the persons who will be receiving your message:

- Who are they?
- What do they know?
- Where can they be reached?
- When would they be receptive?
- Why should they read what you have to write?
- How might they react to your message?[15]

It's difficult to overstate the importance of audience analysis. Throughout this book we have emphasized the importance of assuming a receiver orientation toward communication. What we communicate is irrelevant if our receivers do not get the messages. If we discover the answers to the above questions and then use that information to aid us in the construction of our message, we have a good chance of being effective communicators—all other factors being equal. If we do not analyze our audience, only good fortune will yield positive results.

After clarifying the writing objective and analyzing the audience, you are ready to consider the information that could be included in your document.

Step 3: Generation of Ideas

In step 1 you identified the focus and components of your message. In step 3 you want to generate the information that will be included in your message.

If, for example, the goal is to explain your qualifications for promotion in terms of past performance, you would have to gather information that would support the contention that your past performance has been meritorious.

In order to do that you might "brainstorm" and simply list all possible incidents that would be supportive. You might want to list these incidents by speaking into a tape recorder, or by jotting the items down on an index card.

You may need to go through old performance evaluations to remind yourself about the ways people commended you for your work. You may decide to conduct research that would reveal what performance criteria have been used in the past when promotion determinations were made.

In short, in step 3 you review your mission statement. Then you list any and all items that you might want to include in your document that would support your writing objectives. At this point there is no need, nor is it a good idea, to place these items into categories or even evaluate the legitimacy of each item. You simply want to identify all possible inclusions for your document.

Focus on Applications

Generating Ideas

Assume your writing goal is to:

1. Construct a report that evaluates your five subordinates and provides a rationale for annual salary increments.
2. Explain to end users how they can send Word attachments on electronic submissions.
3. Justify your request for temporary help from the accounting department for two weeks in order to prepare for an internal audit.

Brainstorm to decide what types of information you might include in each of these reports.

It's difficult to overstate the importance of audience analysis for effective communication.

GETTY IMAGES/PHOTODISC

Step 4: Place Similar Ideas into Topical Categories

In Step 4 you evaluate and categorize your ideas. For example, regarding the temporary accounting help in the Focus on Application feature on the previous page, you might categorize the ideas into:

- Benefits to department
- Benefits to organization
- Costs to organization
- Precedent of other departments hiring when under in need

Step 5: Decide on a Format for Sequencing

As a result of step 4 you have a series of categories. Now what you need to do is structure the various categories so that the entire document will make sense. That is, what should be the progression of the categories? Should you present information in terms of the strongest argument for your case to the weakest, or from the weakest to the strongest? Should you organize it in terms of benefits to the individual, benefits to the department, or benefits to the organization as a whole? Is this report such that a chronological organizational pattern makes sense?

Consider the goal of the communication and select a format that is consistent with your goal. If, for example, the report describes the evolution of some organizational phenomenon, then select a chronological format.

Step 6: Write a First Draft

The tensions associated with writing may have dissipated somewhat because of the steps you have already taken. Keep in mind the essential criteria for effective business writing. Hattersley and McJannet argue that effective writing is characterized by accuracy, clarity, brevity, and vigor.[16]

You want to ensure that information is factually accurate. You want to present information clearly, and you want your writing to be as succinct as it can be without omitting important information. Finally, an objective of business writing is this: You want what you write to be read. Therefore, your writing should be vigorous in the sense that it has life and is engaging to the reader.

Davidson suggests a number of ways to overcome anxiety that you may experience just prior to a drafting stage. She suggests:

- Adopting a "can-do" attitude
- Giving yourself permission to get it wrong before you get it right
- Giving yourself a deadline for the first draft[17]

All three of these ideas are sound ones. The first two in particular may help you overcome some tense moments. Think about all the poorly written documents you have read. Assume a "can-do" attitude, because it is likely that by preparing adequately you "can do" far better than many others who, apparently, did not prepare before constructing their reports or letters or memorandums. Also, remember that you are not expected to write something perfectly in the initial draft. Putting on paper the first difficult paragraphs may allow you to gather momentum and confidence so that the next few paragraphs are easier to construct. You can (and should) always go back and revise what you've written. Therefore, you need not become stymied out of fear that the first run through won't be perfect. By giving yourself a deadline (and adhering to it) you make sure that a first draft will get written.

Step 7: Proofread and Edit for Readability

Contemporary word processing software is a godsend in terms of proofreading. Most programs signal the writer when: words are spelled incorrectly, commas are in the wrong place, and even when subjects and verbs do not agree. Nevertheless, it is foolish to assume that the computer will catch it all or catch all well. You need to do your own proofreading.

In addition, writers will need to format the text so that it includes, when applicable:

- Headings
- Lists
- White space
- Graphs and charts
- Boldface type
- Italics
- Different fonts
- Different font sizes
- Pull quotes

Remember a goal of the writing is that the message be read. To the extent that any of these formatting aids will make a document easier to read, or more likely to be read, you want to use them.

How do you feel when you turn the page in a text and all you see is text—no pictures, no white space, and no bolded headings to divide sections? Business writing is not *Crime and Punishment*. Readers need help, and by creating an attractive look to your document you can provide some help. The idea is not to impress your reader with so many clever print dimensions that they begin to focus on the esthetics of your report as opposed to its essence. However, by being concerned with presentation, you increase the chances of the document being read by the readers.

Step 8: Polish, Rewrite, and Distribute

On the basis of your editing, you rewrite your document and then distribute it to receivers. Many authors advise writers to give the report or letter some time "to rest" before you construct the final version. The idea is that the author may be too familiar with the document to catch all those problems that need to be caught prior to distribution. A graduate professor suggested that students let papers "sleep" before they were reviewed for the "final coat of varnish." In business environments, often there is not time "to sleep" nor time for exquisite refinishing. But when possible, allow a period of time before revision. You might consider giving a report to some trusted other who will try to catch errors that you may have missed. Again, time may prohibit an external review. It is not uncommon in business environments, however, for colleagues to read reports, letters, and even important electronic mailings, to make sure that the piece is as strong as it can be before distribution.

Step 9: Follow-Up and Evaluation

Writers should attempt to follow-up and make sure that consumers received, understood, and had a chance to react to the material you created. The follow-up not only gives you an opportunity to clarify any information that requires clarification, but it may provide you with some suggestions that may help when you work on other documents.

Do I need to go through all nine steps every single time I write an e-mail or memo?

Obviously, writers need not (and often could not) follow each of these steps every time they sit down to write a note. However, the more regularly you go through this process, the less likely you are to experience tension associated with writing. Also, the more regularly you adhere to the procedure, the more natural the procedure becomes. You might, eventually, find yourself following these steps very rapidly—perhaps even subconsciously—because you have become accustomed to approaching writing in this manner. You may even develop your own writing steps that make you comfortable writing and confident in your writing.

IDENTIFYING COMMON PROBLEMS

As we conclude this section of the chapter, it seems wise to identify some very common problems with business writing. Leonard and Gilsdorf listed a number of the most distracting business writing lapses. They included:

- Run-on sentences
- Poor use of commas
- Unclear antecedents
- Incorrect word choice
- Spelling errors[18]

Previously it was mentioned that computer software can notify the writer who wishes to be so notified that there are grammatical or other related problems with the text. However, it is remarkable how intelligent people, despite these notifications, still churn out material that is pervaded with these errors. Below is a checklist of other common writing difficulties. For each item, I have included some examples and/or recommendations for avoiding the problem.

✓ Sentence Fragments: Subject/Verb Agreement

Identify the subject and verb in sentences to make sure that there are no sentence fragments in the material. Check to make sure that the subject and verb agree. For example, John and Wilma *are* managers, not *is* managers. Our team *needs* to be more dedicated to organizational goals.

✓ Use of Jargon

Ask yourself if people outside your area of expertise would be able to understand the words you are using in the document. You might want to ask others who are, in fact, outside of your area of expertise if they know the meaning of certain terms. Also, be careful about using so-called buzz words (like *buzz word*) that may be commonly used but are either trite or vague, or *both* trite and vague. For example, *reengineer, interface, rightsize, or paradigm-shift*.

✓ It's and Its

Check to make sure you have used the word *its* correctly. *Its* is only spelled with an apostrophe if it's a contraction for *it is*. If, when the sentence with *its* is reread, you are unable to substitute *it is* for *its,* then the word should not be spelled with an apostrophe.

✓ Use of i.e. and e.g.

Check to make sure that *i.e.* is not used synonymously with *e.g.* It is truly stunning how often this mistake is made. While preparing for this book I was reading a well-touted text in a related area and saw that, repeatedly, this error appeared. E.g. means *for example;* i.e. means *that is.* It has become so prevalent for these initials to be used interchangeably that at some juncture i.e. will come to be synonymous with e.g. However, we are not there yet. Below is an illustration of how the two can be used:

Appropriate word choice is the key to effective business writing, i.e., selecting the right words to match your thoughts is the essence of quality composition. If you select the incorrect words there can be unpleasant ramifications, e.g., loss of department reputation, loss of resources, and loss of job.

✓ Redundant Construction

Be careful to proofread in order to ensure that you haven't repeated yourself within the same sentence. My brother, Dr. Robert Zaremba, collects redundancies in written and spoken communication. Below are a few examples from his extensive collection.

- Our unit has met its projections for two consecutive quarters in a row.
- This was clearly an example of a group acting together in unison.

- He permanently maimed him for life.
- We think the trend is for it to fluctuate back and forth.

✓ Use of Nonapplicable Qualifiers

Check your text to make sure that words like *unique* or *discrete* are not modified by adverbs like *very* or *unusually*. *Unique* means one of a kind. *Discrete* means clearly separated. An item cannot become any more unique than unique. A discrete entity can't be particularly discrete or tremendously discrete. Your e-mail address has to be unique for you to receive electronic mail. It couldn't be any more unique than it is already.

✓ Misuse of Homonyms

Most, if not all, spell check software can*not* make usage distinctions between *stationary* and *stationery*, or *their* and *there*, or even *write* and *right*. Similarly, software checklists will not highlight incorrect words if the incorrect word in that context is, in fact, a real word. For this reason I read many papers that discuss the dilemma of *mangers*, not *managers*, and even have read about vice presidents who are the *air apparent* to the presidency. Business writers must proofread papers to ensure that words are spelled correctly—even after the spell checker has been used.

> The Spellchecker's Nightmare
>
> I have a spelling checker.
>
> It came with my PC.
>
> It plainly marks four my revue.
>
> Mistakes I cannot sea.
>
> I've run this poem threw it.
>
> I'm sure you're pleased too no.
>
> Its letter perfect in it's weigh.
>
> My checker tolled me sew.[19]

✓ Pronoun Reference

When using a pronoun, make sure that (1) the antecedent is clear and (2) the pronoun form agrees with the subject. Below are incorrect pronoun usage examples for both (1) and (2).

1. "When Harry meets Sam you know *he's* going to be in for a surprise." Who's *he*?
2. "The company decided to change *their* logo." The subject is singular, but the pronoun in the example is plural.

✓ Absence of Transitions

Brusaw, Alred, and Oliu define a transition as a "means of achieving a smooth flow of ideas from sentence to sentence, paragraph to paragraph, and subject to subject."[20] After you finish one section of a document you need to provide a transition to the next part of the text. The following paragraph is an example of a transition.

In the previous sections we have looked at general issues pertaining to business writing. In the next few pages we examine a specific dimension of business writing: persuasive messages.

Persuasive Messages

The pen may not always be mightier than the sword, but no country ever took up the sword without first having been convinced it should do so.[21]

—Melvin Grayson, former vice president of public relations for Nabisco

In organizations, as well as in national politics, it is important to understand how to persuade others. Many of our written communications involve some persuasive content. Organizational communicators may be appealing for additional funding, arguing for greater departmental autonomy, or requesting employee support for new corporate programs. Even factual reports are likely to contain implicit persuasive dimensions. A project status report distributed to superiors not only describes the status of the project, but also is intended to persuade readers that the department has diligently and responsibly addressed its organizational responsibilities. A manual that explains how to operate certain equipment is intended to describe a procedure *as well as* persuade readers that the equipment is valuable and that the recommended operation procedure is logical.

The following section discusses the subject of persuasion as it pertains to organizational communication.

What Is Persuasion?

When communicators try to persuade others they are attempting to do one of four basic things:

- Influence others to consider changing attitudes or behavior
- Change behavior or attitudes
- Reaffirm existing behavior or attitudes
- Actuate (i.e., persuade readers to do something or act)

Persuasion often involves combinations of these goals. One might want to influence someone to consider changing an attitude and then subsequently attempt to convince her or him to do something on the basis of his or her newly held belief.

Any communicative effort to facilitate meeting one or more of these goals is a persuasive attempt. The only such attempt that would not be considered persuasion would be one that did not allow the receiver a genuine perception of choice.

It is not persuasion to threaten subordinates with physical violence if they do not agree to work overtime. That is coercion, not persuasion. Therefore, blackmail is not technically considered persuasion. The act of blackmailing someone might be, in fact, persuasive, and in organizations there are, no doubt, instances when threats have been extraordinarily convincing. However, as we analyze persuasive organizational communication, we are discussing messages that allow the receiver a genuine choice. They can, upon reading the message, make a decision comfortably about whether to agree or disagree with the perspectives taken by the author.

The key question to ask is this: What facilitates persuasion? That is, what methods are most effective in helping those who persuade reach their goals?

Persuasive Approaches

The foundation for any persuasive communication is the persuader's knowledge of the audience. The more the writer can find out about the demographics and attitudes of the receivers, the better off she or he is in preparing to persuade them. Earlier in the chapter we discussed a series of questions that communicators should consider when analyzing an audience. In persuasive communications discovering the answers to these questions are crucial. A writer should consider which of the following persuasive techniques are most appropriate given the audience and his or her particular persuasive goal.

Use of Yourself as a Credible Source. These arguments are called arguments of ethos. As discussed in Chapter 8, ethos refers to the status that receivers attribute to those people who speak (or in this case write) to them. Nothing is more important to a persuasive communicator than ethos. Once credibility is forsaken, persuading audiences that poverty is pervasive becomes difficult.

Simply, who you are is often perceived as more important than the logical or emotional impact of any other arguments you might employ. Therefore, any organizational communicator who has earned a reputation for honesty and wisdom can often persuade others by relying heavily on that reputation.

For example, depending on the strength of the writer's ethos, the following communication will be viewed as either supportive and encouraging, or tactlessly insincere:

> As many of you are aware, I've been with the company for many years. I can assure you that while times are presently lean our next quarter forecast is appropriately optimistic. We will come out of these post-September 11th economic doldrums with the same kind of strength we possessed before any of us had ever heard the word Taliban.

Logical Arguments. Persuasion that attempts to convince the receivers that it makes sense to do what the writer is suggesting is often successful. The source should attempt to explain that there is a logical reason to change one's attitude or behavior.

The goal with this strategy is to have the receiver think that it is logical to behave in a certain way. If an employee suggests that a department package a product in a new, more cost-effective manner, the employee is trying to reach the rational spot in the receiver that is receptive to that type of logic. For example,

> This plan can save us money. If this recommended procedure is as sound in other ways as our prior policy, then we should use this new approach and apply the savings to other projects.

If a human resource representative suggests that signing up for a series of workshops will have specific long-range value, she or he is appealing to employees to think logically about the workshops and the merit of education.

Not all "logical arguments" are indeed logical. The history of advertising, for example, is full of persuasive campaigns that used "logical" argumentation that, under scrutiny, was found not to be logical at all. A soup company once tried to persuade consumers to buy their vegetable soup product by visually illustrating the huge amount of vegetables in the soup. Pictures of the soup made the broth look as if it was brimming with all types of tasty vegetables. An examination, however, revealed that the persuaders had placed shards of glass at the bottom of the soup bowl to force the relatively few vegetables to the surface of the bowl.

The implicit "logic" of this persuasion was:

- One can see that this soup contains plenty of vegetables.
- No one wants soup that requires a search party for the legumes.
- Therefore, buy our product, which is loaded with vegetables.

This is a clear example of a "logical argument" because it attempted to persuade receivers to think that the argument being made was logical. It is also a clear example of a logical argument that is not, in fact, logical.

Emotional Arguments. A very effective method of persuasion is one that attempts to engage the emotions of those being persuaded. Persuasive messages that involve sympathy, fear (still allowing the receiver a genuine perception of choice), guilt, humor, and intimations of physical pleasure are often extremely successful. The most cursory review of persuasive campaigns would indicate that this emotional strategy is used quite frequently, often complementing logical strategies.

Campaigns for charitable causes, insurance needs, cosmetic products, even toothpaste have included these emotional arguments. Writers who enumerate the potential repercussions of not adopting a policy are using emotional appeals. There may be no logical evidence to support the contention that a particular company will lose competitive advantage if it doesn't expand immediately to South America, but a communication that comments that several competitors have already set up satellite operations in Paraguay and Brazil may create some anxiety and therefore be persuasive.

Use of Reservations. Any persuasive effort has an opposing side. The arguments that are the arsenal for the opposing side are called reservations. Effective persuasion considers these reservations. One can effectively incorporate the reservations into his or her persuasive effort by doing one of three things with each reservation:

1. Refute the reservation outright if the counterargument is refutable.

2. If the reservation is not refutable, then one should downplay the significance of the reservation. For example, assume that two candidates, Mason and Ramirez, are applying for a position. You support Ramirez and are writing a report explaining your endorsement. Assume further that you know that Ramirez will require a higher salary than Mason. A reservation would be that the company will incur greater salary costs with Ramirez. You might deal with that reservation as indicated below:

   While it is true that it will cost you less to hire Mason, Mason does not have nearly the experience and expertise that Ramirez has. Therefore, I recommend that we go with Paola. She'll demand more money, but would be a better value.

3. The last resort in dealing with reservations is to ignore the reservation in your persuasion. It *is* a last resort. The only reason one should rely on this last resort is if the reservation is truly insignificant, and one's best guess is that very few, if any, receivers will have thought of it. If it is insignificant then the persuader is not avoiding his or her ethical obligations by omitting it. If no receiver will think of it, then bringing it up will make your report less concise than it needs to be.

One final comment needs to be made regarding content strategies in persuasion. It relates to ethical considerations. We discussed ethical factors in detail in Chapter 4. However, in any dedicated discussion of persuasion it is important to include a section on ethics.

Simply, there are two basic routes one can take when persuading. One route is to say, "Never mind ethics. Let the receivers/customer beware. It is fine to write anything in order to persuade another." The other route is to use valid arguments when persuading. For two simple reasons the valid route is strongly recommended. Dishonest persuasion makes subsequent persuasive efforts more difficult. A writer might be able to short cut persuasion by deceiving once or twice, but in the long run the persuader's "ethos" is damaged and persuasion becomes very difficult.

Moreover, at one point or another, we are all in the position of being receivers. Never have I met anyone who enjoyed being duped. If you bought an inefficient car, and subsequently discovered that the salesperson knew it was a lemon when you bought the auto, it is highly unlikely that you would return to the dealer and say to the salesperson,

You sly fox. That was very clever of you, convincing me to buy that old lemon. Very good. Very good indeed.

The contention that "unethical" persuasion is normal certainly cannot be refuted. In writing and teaching about persuasion, however, I emphasize that for pragmatic and ethical considerations, persuaders are wise to be honest.

PRACTITIONER'S PERSPECTIVE

Jeremiah Cole, Director of the Office of Strategic Initiatives

Jeremiah Cole has worked for the Commonwealth of Massachusetts in the Division of Medical Assistance for the past 10 years. The Division has an annual budget of five billion dollars. Mr. Cole's office makes recommendations on initiatives that affect how the five billion dollar budget is spent.

We have a saying in the agency, "If you want the document fast, it's going to be long. If you want it short, it's going to take time." Writing effectively in organizations requires distilling information and presenting it in a concise way so that readers can easily consume the information. Often we write these lengthy documents that we did not distill. The sheer number of words affects the chances of the document being read.

Time demands create the biggest problems for organizational communicators. People tend to prioritize what they have to do. Evaluating communication alternatives, thinking about how to organize your information, considering your audience, or even thinking about what should or should not go into a communication, is often placed on the back burner. Therefore, when information gets communicated, it's often done haphazardly. Poor choices are made.

There's a phenomenon I call the *tyranny of the immediate.* Sometimes we in the organization have legitimate time constraints that inhibit communication quality. However, there are also times when there *seems* to be a pressing problem that we feel we must (or are told we must) address immediately. This so-called immediate need displaces everything else—including matters related to how we express ourselves to our subordinates, superiors, and peers.

Employees don't all get information simultaneously, nor do they all get the same message that was initially sent. We have what I call "cascading information" in organizations. I may send a document to person 2, but before person 2 gets to relay it to person 3, person 3 has heard the message through the grapevine. Maybe they heard it the way I wanted them to hear it, but maybe they didn't. [This phenomenon was discussed in Chapter 6 under the heading "serial distortion."]

The issue of time is significant, but it also seems to me that writing skills in general are deteriorating. Some writers are incompetent because the same things that make them incompetent with their job tasks make them incompetent communicators. That is, they don't work diligently and responsibly to complete the job. As it relates to written communication, this means they don't work hard enough to express their messages clearly.

Another big problem is that people who are not physically at a central office feel as if they are not getting the same information as the people who are located at central. Sometimes this, in fact, is the case, but whether it is the case or is not, the perception persists that they're not getting information or timely information, and are therefore some type of second-class citizen. This perception, regardless of accuracy, creates additional communication problems for management.

E-mail is wonderful. E-mail has enabled matters to be discussed and decided in hours instead of days or weeks. It is extraordinarily difficult to quickly schedule a conventional meeting time for busy professionals. Without e-mail, it might take a week to find a time which is convenient for everyone to discuss a matter. Also, e-mail has democratized the organization by allowing people to have a voice who would previously not have been heard. However, this doesn't mean that e-mail is always the best way to interact. It's fast and we do have time pressures, but that doesn't always make e-mail the smartest choice.

SUMMARY

A Toolbox

1. Writing is a central component of organizational communication.
2. It is common to feel anxious and insecure about writing.
3. There are techniques for reducing writing anxiety which involve
   - Clarifying the writing goal
   - Analyzing the audience
   - Generating information
   - Organizing information
   - Getting an initial draft on paper
   - Editing and revising
4. Business writing often has persuasive dimensions.
5. Persuasive content can include several types of arguments
   - Logical
   - Emotional
   - Arguments of ethos
   - Arguments based on audience reservations
6. Persuasive communicators have ethical responsibilities

DISCUSSION QUESTIONS

1. What are four typical causes for writing anxiety?
2. What situations create the most anxiety for you as a writer?
3. Which three writing problems discussed in the chapter are problems you notice when you read through other students' materials or colleagues' documents at work?
4. Assume your writing goal was to describe what you have done in your Communication class to date. How would you compose your writing mission statement?
5. Of the four types of persuasive arguments identified in the chapter, which do you find the most persuasive when you read a document. That is, do you find logical arguments more persuasive than emotional? Arguments of ethos more persuasive than arguments employing receiver reservations?
6. Of the four types of arguments identified in the chapter, which do you believe is most effective when writing to mass audiences?
7. Do writers have a moral responsibility to be truthful when they compose their documents?
8. Please read the case that follows and respond to the questions at the end of the case.

CASE FOR ANALYSIS

Case 11.2—Tanya and the TASC

Tanya Nalbandian works for a telephone service provider and has commented that she cannot do her job because of her company's poor communication.

Nalbandian's company is composed of eight different strategic business units all located within a 250-mile radius of Scranton, Pennsylvania. Each business unit is a separate entity but relies upon one Technical Assistance Support Center (TASC) in Syracuse, New York. This center is staffed by technical matter experts in each of the organization's related technologies. The principal function of TASC is to provide technical assistance to persons like Tanya Nalbandian who staff the eight business units. TASC provides service-user guides and publishes technical journals that describe the specific services offered by the company.

The problem is that the service-user guides and technical journals are written at a high technical level. This presents a communication problem that has a dramatic effect on different aspects of the company from Operations to Marketing. Field personnel like Nalbandian simply can't interpret the information provided in these publications. The Operations employees have difficulty troubleshooting problems and Marketing employees have difficulty selling the services. The TASC may be providing technical assistance, but the employees at the company—who are all literate and intelligent persons—can't access the assistance. TASC personnel do not understand that their outstanding work is not totally utilized because of this problem.

To some extent the problem is compounded because too many people in the business units are embarrassed to indicate that they cannot access the technical materials. Nalbandian claims that some staffers may ask their friends and associates to explain some information, but others are reluctant to tell their superiors that they don't get it.

Documents continue to arrive in the field that are too sophisticated in terms of language and jargon. Also, the TASC folks don't seem to comprehend the fact that tiny fonts are not inviting. While small fonts may save paper, the field personnel are even less likely to read the documents if they have to read the tiny print.

- How should employees like Nalbandian articulate their concerns to TASC?
- What can the people at TASC do to make their publications more valuable to the end users?

ENDNOTES

[1] Baida, Peter, "Managerial Babble," *American Heritage,* April-May 1985.

[2] Brewster, Kingman, Jr., speech delivered December 15, 1977.

[3] Hattersley, Michael and Linda McJannet, *Management Communication,* McGraw Hill, 1997, p. xii.

[4] Matejka, Ken and Diane Ramos, *Hook 'Em: Speaking and Writing to Catch and Keep a Business Audience,* AMACOM, 1996, p. xii.

[5] Brown, Dick, "Why Executives Can't Write: The Power of Poor Communication," *World Press Review,* 1981, p. 52.

[6] Ibid.

[7] In graduate Managerial Communication courses I regularly ask students to review and rank some of the more prestigious articles in the general area of communication study. Repeatedly these very bright and extraordinarily responsible women and men comment that the writing in the journals is too dense. Since the assignment requires that they read through articles and digest them, they typically find merit in the pieces once they have completed the reading. However, they argue that the inherent values of the article would be lost on them if they were not compelled to read the material. Simply, they wouldn't bother to read what they consider poorly written prose in order to extract any possible nuggets that might be contained therein.

[8]Op. cit., Matejka and Ramos, p. xii.

[9]Ibid., p. 27.

[10]Davidson, Wilma, *Business Writing: What Works What Won't*, St. Martin's Press, 2001, p. 6.

[11]This malapropism may seem bizarre, but it was excerpted from a written document as were all of the items in the section.

[12]Munter, Mary, *A Guide to Managerial Communication*, Fourth Edition, Prentice Hall, 1997, p. 37.

[13]Sorenson, Ritch, Grace DeBord, and Ida Ramirez, *Business and Management Communication*, Prentice Hall, 2001: pp. 71–72.

[14]Dumaine, Deborah, *Write to the Top: Writing for Corporate Success*, Random House, 1989.

[15]Op. cit., Ken Matejka and Diane Ramos, p. 4.

[16]Op. cit., Hattersley and McJannet, p. 10–11.

[17]Op. cit., Davidson, p. 17.

[18]Leonard, Donald and Jeanette Gilsdorf, "Language in Change: Academics 'and Executives' Perceptions of Usage Issues," *Journal of Business Communication*, 1990, p. 146. This very interesting study compared academics' and executives' perceptions of distracting writing lapses.

[19]Adapted from H&L Enterprises, EL Cajon, CA, 92020.

[20]Brusaw, Charles, Gerald Alred, and Walter Oliu, *The Business Writer's Handbook*, St. Martin's Press, p. 679.

[21]Grayson, Melvin, "The Last Best Hope: Words," *Vital Speeches of the Day*, July 15, 1981, vol. 47, p. 585.

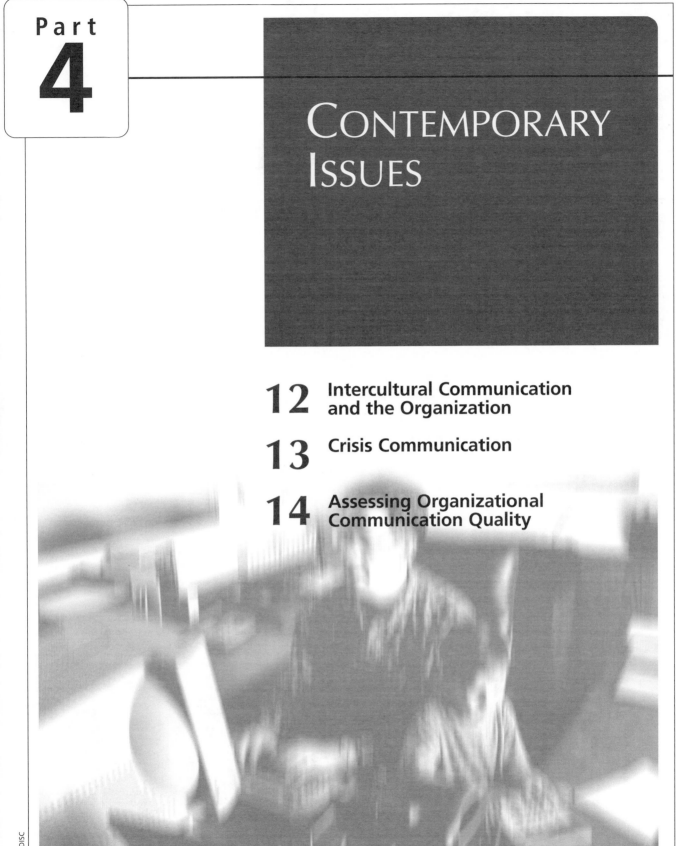

CONTEMPORARY ISSUES

© PHOTODISC

Intercultural Communication and the Organization

The world teems with people who are sensitive to prejudice only when it is against them, not when they are inflicting it on others.[1]

—David Maraniss, author

. . .too many American business people are not aware of the importance of understanding cultural differences. Business is business they think. And they are wrong.[2]

—John Reeder in *Business Horizons*

© CORBIS

Case 12.1—*Rando Systems Expands Internationally*

R ando Systems, Inc., based in an Atlanta suburb, is a developer and marketer of speech recognition software. The company was founded in 1984 and since 1990 has been actively developing and marketing products for foreign consumers—in particular, consumers in Western Europe, Australia, New Zealand, South Africa, and Asia. Until recently, all international operations were managed by a small team based in the Atlanta office that worked closely with a network of trusted distributors and resellers.

In the late 1990s the company decided to open commercial offices in France, Germany, and the United Kingdom, staffed with all local employees. These new employees were to take over the sales and marketing activities for Europe and Africa. The company also hired a sales manager based in San Francisco for the developing markets in Asia. Research and Development and Training/Technical Support services are still based in the United States at the Atlanta office.

Until the opening of the European and California offices, most organizational communications involved face-to-face discussions, meetings, telephone conversations, and informal sessions such as lunches, after-work drinks, and weekend parties. These types of interactions resulted in a very tightly knit group and a constant flow of information about the market and the peculiarities of the technology. When the United Kingdom, French, German, and San Francisco offices were set up and new personnel hired, communication methods became less informal. The company began to use electronic mail extensively. Some people in the Atlanta office said that e-mail was used exclusively. Occasionally, but rarely, overseas managers would come to Atlanta for very brief visits to headquarters. No lengthy training period was set up by the home office to get international personnel acquainted with the teams in the United States.

Many communication inefficiencies occurred in the beginning of the expansion due to a few obvious reasons: (1) new personnel had to learn a fairly sophisticated product and the peculiar market of speech recognition, (2) new personnel were unfamiliar with the organization, and (3) time differences. The first two problems would be overcome as time went by, and the time zone factors were easily adjusted to by adapting to different business hours.

However, communication breakdowns persisted. European offices were not on the same e-mail system as the rest of the organization, causing messages to get lost—especially company-wide broadcasts. As the European personnel got more involved in the markets, they felt that they had less time available for communication with the San Francisco and Atlanta offices. As a consequence, there was very little information exchange between parallel departments in the United States and Europe. Sales and Marketing missed many opportunities for joint sales and marketing efforts, especially with clients that had a global presence. That cost the company several accounts. Also, international service departments, such as Training and Technical Support, found the European personnel unresponsive to solicitations about training needs and scheduling service events for clients. The European office only seemed to be responsive if the need was expressed as urgent. Those in the Atlanta office found the Europeans aloof and inaccessible. It was almost as if the European office envisioned itself as an autonomous entity. The European managers considered their Atlanta counterparts to be dictatorial and oppressive.

To improve communication, Rando Systems built a secure website for employees-only use, and a parallel one for partners (distributors and resellers). Unfortunately, the site wasn't well maintained and the information was not updated regularly, so people stopped using it.

Expanding internationally has hurt the consistency of Rando's product and services. The problems related to communicating with the European offices have made it difficult for Rando to maintain what had been an excellent reputation.

☐ *What are the roots of Rando's communication problems?*

☐ *What could Rando Systems have done before the international expansion to reduce the communication problem?*

☐ *Given the present situation, what can Rando do to improve communication between the Atlanta and European offices?*

ABSTRACT

Our world is shrinking. Foreign countries are increasingly less foreign. It can be cheaper to fly roundtrip from Boston to Ireland than it is to fly back and forth from Boston to New York. Because of the ease of travel, the pervasiveness of communication technology, and economic reliance on other countries, the societies of the twenty-first century are, and will continue to be, multicultural in a way that is more obvious than ever before. The effects of cultural diversity on organizations are significant. In this chapter we will examine intercultural communication in terms of why it is important for organizational success and how persons who need to communicate interculturally can do so efficiently.

OBJECTIVES

When you have completed this chapter, you should be able to:

☐ **Explain why intercultural communication is essential for organizational success and organizational communication.**
☐ **Describe what we mean by *culture* and *intercultural communication.***
☐ **Identify barriers to effective intercultural communication.**
☐ **Identify steps that can be used to overcome these barriers.**
☐ **Discuss the Hofstede dimensions as they apply to organizational contexts.**

WHY STUDY INTERCULTURAL COMMUNICATION?

Nearly 40 years ago, media scholar Marshall McLuhan argued that we would soon be living in what he called a global village.[3] McLuhan felt that media innovation would make our planet akin to the small villages of earlier centuries.

We are there.

In the fall of 2001 we find out about events in Afghanistan more swiftly than our ancestors discovered what had taken place in the town square. We can e-mail colleagues in other countries as quickly as we can walk across the street and ask our neighbor to borrow a quart of milk. We can travel to other countries and meet members of other cultures as easily as we can take a five-hour bus ride. At the time of this writing, November 12, 2001, a Jet exploded in Rockaway, New York and within minutes the information was posted on Internet search engines like Yahoo. Depress a button on a remote control device and we can observe newscaster Bryant Gumbel interviewing a woman who lived blocks from the scene. Colleagues of mine outside of Paris can find out as much about this tragedy as members of my extended family who live within 10 miles of the crash site. The world is shrinking. We are a global village.

The ramifications of living in a global village extend to organizational contexts and organizational communication. Organizations are "going Global," that is, expanding beyond their domestic borders, because it is easier to "go Global" in the twenty-first century. However, expanding operations to other nations means that organizations have to concurrently expand their communication capabilities so that they can interact efficiently with their foreign offices and markets. Within domestic offices the shrinking world coupled with greater employment opportunities have created a work environment that is increasingly pluralistic. The demographics of the workforce in the twenty-first century reflect far more heterogeneity than those of your grandparents' and even your parents' generation.

The workforce diversity as well as the proliferation of multinational businesses compels organizations to expand their capabilities in terms of communication. As we discussed in Chapter 3 there is sufficient noise in most communicative interactions to create distortion. The problems of communication are exacerbated in intercultural contexts. There is, simply, more "noise." If we are interested in studying organizational communication, we must acknowledge the mosaic that is the contemporary workforce, identify the challenges of diversity for efficient organizational communication, and examine how these intercultural challenges within organizational contexts can be addressed.

Effective Intercultural Communication Has Become Essential

DeVito identified three reasons to explain why intercultural communication has become an imperative in contemporary society: *mobility, economic* and *political interdependence*, and *communication technology*.[4] Let's examine each of these three factors.

Mobility. Over the last 10 years my university has established an extensive study abroad program that allows qualified juniors to travel and study at any 1 of 34 colleges representing 24 separate countries. This program was set up by college administrators who were able to easily travel to other universities, establish relationships, and discuss the mutual benefits of "study abroad." Our students can journey to these other countries because air travel has become relatively inexpensive and, no longer, foreign. An advertisement suggests that it is just as cost-effective to fly from Boston to Lisbon as it is to take the Boston to New York airline shuttle.

Simply, time and distance no longer restrict intercultural encounters as they once did. Individuals have tremendous mobility and the direction and composition of organizations reflect that mobility.

Economic and Political Interdependence. To some extent the countries of the world have always been economically and politically interdependent. However, with the expansion of military capabilities, international safety is largely a function of economic and political cooperation.

Economic interdependence is apparent nearly any time you glance at the label of a garment and notice where the product was manufactured. On the morning news, North Americans are likely to hear how the Asian markets closed, and how the Asian markets closed is likely to affect what happens in the economies of the West. The Middle East countries, beset with historical tensions, are the focus of international concern in large part because of the political and economic significance of the region.[5] Another contemporary illustration of political interdependence is seen in the 2001 United States war on terrorism in Afghanistan. American military activity required the cooperation of several other bordering countries for its success.

Clearly, the countries and cultures of the world are economically and politically interdependent. Therefore, we must be concerned with how we communicate to those persons, countries, and cultures with whom we are so interdependent

Communication Technology. How many people do you know who do not have an e-mail address? The Maytag repairman used to be lonely. Soon, the loneliest folks are likely to be postal clerks. It is as simple to transmit a message overseas as it is to write your roommate a note reminding him to pay the phone bill. Electronic mail and teleconferencing have reduced barriers to communicating that had restricted the frequency of intercultural communication. Costs associated with international telephoning have been reduced so that it no longer is prohibitive to call persons in localities thousands of miles away from our homes. Satellite television transmissions make it as simple to witness demonstrators in Pakistan as it is to observe the pedestrian traffic outside of your window.

If we needed a catalyst to improve intercultural communication capabilities, we now have such a catalyst. Technology has put us in easy contact with people from other worlds. We need to know how to communicate with them.

WHAT DO WE MEAN BY *CULTURE?*

In order to examine intercultural communication we will need to clarify what we mean both by *culture* and *intercultural communication.*

Benedict defines *culture* as the "relatively organized set of beliefs and expectations about how people should talk, think, and organize their lives."[6] Haviland writes that culture refers to the "abstract values, beliefs, and perceptions of the world that lie behind people's behavior, and which are reflected in their behavior."[7] Triandis and Albert, writing in the *Handbook of Organizational Communication,* use Herkovitz' definition that culture is the "human made part of the environment" and go on to clarify that by *the human made part of the environment* they refer to the subjective culture of "norms, roles, belief systems, laws, and values" of a particular group.[8]

Essentially, *culture refers to the multiple perspectives a group has on the world and worldly phenomena.* The Triandis and Albert description is helpful as it breaks down cultural perspectives into categories of these "multiple perspectives."

- **Norms.** What does a group consider normal and abnormal? Is having a monogamous relationship normal in your culture? Is rearing children before the age of 30, normal? If your Uncle Wick is 45 and unmarried is he considered peculiar, or normal in your culture?

- **Roles.** What are the responsibilities of certain persons in society? What is the role, for example, of the husband, or eldest son, or educators in a community?

- **Belief Systems.** Does the group believe in monotheism? Life after death? That the land belongs to the creator and therefore no human can really "own" land?

- **Values.** Does the group consider education more valuable than wealth? Is a high school athlete more respected than someone who excels on academic examinations?

- **Laws.** What are the laws of the group which, if violated, are punishable either by governments or the governance systems of the culture?

Culture is learned. It is not biologically transmitted.[9] *Enculturation* refers to the process of how one learns the perspectives of the culture. *Acculturation* refers to the ways your culture is modified by exposure to other cultures.

Elashmawi and Harris identify several ways that cultural differences are manifested in people:

- Language
- Nonverbal messages
- Space and time orientation
- Patterns of thinking
- Self-images
- Aesthetics[10]

Focus on Applications

Do cultures really differ?

Is the above list by Elashmawi and Harris accurate? Do cultures differ in these ways?

- ☐ Can you identify language differences by cultural group?
- ☐ Are some nonverbal messages meaningful and/or appropriate in one culture and not another?
- ☐ Do different groups of people have different perceptions of space needs or the importance of time?
- ☐ Do members of cultures have variant perspectives on beauty?
- ☐ Can you identify cultural group members on the basis of how persons perceive themselves?

Do any of these factors create noises for intercultural interactions in organizations?

INTERCULTURAL COMMUNICATION IN ORGANIZATIONAL CONTEXTS

Defining Intercultural Communication

As we discussed in Chapter 3, message fidelity is affected by the abilities of sources and receivers to overcome impediments that collectively are called *communication noise*. What makes intercultural communication especially problematic is that in intercultural contexts there is the possibility of additional noise that is a function of the disparate cultures of source and receiver. Samovar and Porter in *Communication Between Cultures* define intercultural communication as "communication between people whose cultural perceptions and symbol systems are distinct enough to alter the communication event".[11] Essentially, intercultural communication is a more complex form of interpersonal communication. It's more complex because there are more variables that can serve as impediments.

One step that can be taken to reduce intercultural noise involves becoming aware of how frequently we participate in intercultural interactions. This can be valuable because it may highlight how many of our interactions are, in fact, intercultural and how many are, consequently, affected by additional culture-related impediments.

Types of Intercultural Exchanges and Problems

We engage in intercultural interactions regularly. We may be involved in communications with people from different countries, races, and religions. We may interact with those who are members of our own country but are representative of different regions of the country. We may communicate with those who share our own basic religious beliefs but are followers of different sects within the religion.

The list below identifies different types of intercultural interactions and suggests how pervasive intercultural communications are in our daily activities:

- An African-American conversing with a Caucasian.
- An African-American speaking with a Kenyan
- A Jew speaking with a Christian.
- A Chasidic Jew speaking with a Reform Jew.
- An American speaking with a Brazilian.
- A rural Arkansan speaking with a person from inner-city San Francisco.
- An Hispanic corporate executive communicating with an Anglo executive.
- A corporate executive communicating with members of the custodial staff.
- A Canadian from Toronto communicating with a Canadian from the Gaspé.
- A homosexual communicating with a heterosexual.
- A man communicating with a woman.
- An affluent man living in suburbia communicating with an indigent man living in a subsidized urban apartment.

All of these are examples of intercultural communication because, in each situation, cultural factors will likely create additional obstacles for the communicators. Because of the frequency of intercultural interactions in organizations (and elsewhere) organizational men and women are occasionally, if not regularly, faced with communication challenges related to cultural differences.

Take a moment to consider the three scenarios presented in the following box "How Would You Handle These Situations?" How would you respond?

How would you handle these situations?

1. Prior to Ramadan, Sophia, a practicing Moslem, approaches her manager with a request. During the holy month she wishes to be excused during portions of the day so that she may go to a local mosque to pray as, she claims, she is required to do during this period. Assume that Sophia is a vital member of the organizational team. If she is to leave the office, the manager will have to pay another person to assume Sophia's duties during her absence. Further assume that typically requests for personal time off during the day are not honored at this company except in cases of illness or family emergency.
   a. *How should the manager respond?*
   b. *How should the manager communicate the response?*

2. A bank manager is faced with a problem. She has hired several tellers whose primary language is Spanish. These persons are excellent employees. They are responsible, honest, and capable. When they speak to customers they demonstrate that their English is adequate. However, when they speak among themselves they always speak in Spanish. If a customer has a question that one teller cannot answer, the teller will use Spanish to ask another one of her Spanish-speaking colleagues about the customer's inquiry.

   A few customers have approached the manager and have expressed concern. These customers feel uncomfortable not knowing what the tellers are saying about their accounts.

   In addition, some of the non-Spanish-speaking tellers have approached the manager about a similar concern. They fear that the Spanish-speaking tellers are talking about them. Both the non-Spanish tellers and the customers have asked the manager to forbid the Hispanic employees from using Spanish at work.
   a. *Should the manager request that Spanish not be spoken at work?*
   b. *How should the manager communicate her decision?*

3. A professor in a course entitled Contemporary Drama passes out a syllabus that contains the reading list for the semester. An African-American student raises his hand and (politely) comments that all of the plays on the list have been written by authors of European descent. The student asks if there could be some representation of authors of African descent in the course. The professor (politely) comments that the semester is only so long and that all of the plays on the list are "must reads." After class, the student approaches the chairperson of the department and restates his request.
   a. *Should the chairperson honor the student's request?*
   b. *How should the chairperson communicate her reaction to the student?*
   c. *How should the chairperson communicate her reaction to the professor?*

Barriers to Effective Intercultural Communication

There are a number of communication noises that are specific to—or become more prominent within—intercultural contexts. Let's consider a few of these intercultural barriers.

- Perceptual disparity
- Ethnocentrism
- Language dissimilarity
- Nonverbal dissimilarity

Perception. Singer defines perception as the process by which an individual selects, evaluates, and organizes stimuli from the external world.[12] We know from Chapter 3 that in any interpersonal exchange the selectivity process inherent in perception can create or reduce communication noise. In intercultural contexts, selective perception and retention can be a function of disparate belief and value systems.

Let's assume that during your senior year in high school you met a young man from another country. Assume that you began to discuss your post high school plans with this new acquaintance. Further, let's assume that you said to him that you "could not wait" until high school was over because you wanted to "get out of the house" and "away from your mother and father."

In many parts of the United States such an expression would not be particularly unusual. However, in other countries where family and respect for parents is an inviolable component of the belief system, your comment might have made you seem to be irresponsible as opposed to simply independent. In an intercultural context, your message may have become distorted because of the perceptual lens of your culturally different receiver. While it may have been clear that you wanted to leave your home and go off to college, you may also have unwittingly communicated that you were a ne'er do well and would soon be a community pariah. Of course, you would not have likely become a pariah, because your expressed desires would have been normal within your own culture, but your acquaintance might not have seen things that way and his cultural vision may have affected (1) his notion of who you were and (2) the subsequent interactions you two may have had.

Consider some work-related examples.

1. Assume that during a work break you are having an informal conversation with a colleague. Further, assume that your colleague is new to this country.
   During the conversation you make a disparaging comment about your boss. If your colleague comes from a culture where employees consider it a duty to respect and honor one's employer, your colleague may attach more meaning than you intended to your casual remark.
2. Assume that you insist on being clear and certain about facts and deadlines relating to a task assignment. This may be perplexing to another who perceives your insistence as peculiar, given his orientation that considers ambiguity to be normal, and time relatively unimportant.

In short, cultural orientation can affect perception. According to Singer, "We experience everything in the world not as it is—but only as the world comes to us through our sensory receptors."[13] Our culture affects our sensory receptors.

Ethnocentricity. The bane of intercultural communication (and a barrier that is particularly problematic in businesses that expand globally) is called *ethnocentrism.*

As we discussed in Chapter 8, ethnocentrism refers to the perspective that your world view is superior to another's world view. Cushner and Brislin define ethnocentrism as "the tendency of people to judge others from their own culture's perspective, believing theirs to be the only 'right' or 'correct' way to perceive the world."[14]

It is one thing to have beliefs and value systems that are different from others, and quite another to assume that those who don't share your beliefs are misguided. If one consciously or subconsciously assumes that one's cultural group's world view is superior to the perspectives of another's, any interaction with members of other groups will be ineluctably fraught with communication noise. An ethnocentric communicator implicitly considers alternative perspectives to be substandard. No person warms to the notion that his or her cultural orientations are inferior. Inevitably, then, ethnocentric perspectives create cacophonous interference.

Consider the following exercise. It may help you assess the extent of your own ethnocentrism. Think about a religious, national, racial, or ethnic group with which you identify.

- How would members of that group and you react to the following statements?
- More significantly, how would members of that group and you react to other cultural groups that, generally, take different positions regarding the statements?

1. Getting a college education is essential for individual success.
2. Men can engage in intimate relationships promiscuously.
3. Women should not engage in intimate relationships promiscuously.
4. A man should be a breadwinner for the family.
5. Organized religion is the "opiate of the masses." That is, religion is a drug for fools.
6. Gambling on sporting events reflects irresponsible behavior.
7. Business people should wear formal attire at the workplace.
8. Love is more important than money.
9. Athletic achievements are as valuable as academic achievements.
10. A female child should not move out of the parents' home until she is married. However, a male child may move out of the parents' home before he is married.
11. Cheating in business is acceptable if one can get away with it.
12. Adult men should not cry in public.
13. Some colors are appropriate for little boys and other colors are appropriate for little girls.
14. Pornography is an abomination.
15. Heterosexual promiscuity is as good or bad as homosexual promiscuity.
16. A person who works hard, regardless of salary, should be respected.
17. Capitalism is a better economic system than any other.
18. Osama bin Laden is the Hitler of the twenty-first century.
19. Countries that win territory during wars should not have to return the land.
20. In the world of business, making a profit is the only real organizational consideration.

Let's assume that a few of the items in the above list generate some strong emotional reactions from members of a particular ethnic group. Further, let's assume that the same items generate either little reaction or the opposite reaction from members of a different group. Might it be difficult for the people in the former group to respect people in the latter group who held such disparate opinions? Might it be difficult to communicate with members of another group *on any matter* if one internalized the notion that people within this other group were generally misguided and, perhaps, intellectually or ethically inferior?

In any context, disparate attitudes between source and receiver can undermine attempts to communicate effectively. However, if from the start of any intercultural encounter you assume that the person with whom you are conversing is intellectually or ethically inferior because of disparate world views, then nearly any communicative attempt will be drowned out by deafening noise. Even an innocent comment like,

"How are you, Armindo?" is subject to distortion, if Armindo believes that you perceive his cultural background to be inferior to your own.

Effects of Language. An obvious barrier to intercultural communication relates to the use of common language. Simply, a Spaniard may have difficulty speaking to a Finn if the two do not share the same language. As we discussed in Chapter 3, language issues need not only pertain to common languages, but also to the use of slang, regional expressions, and terms that have high levels of abstraction.

As it relates to intercultural communication, a more subtle language factor is related to what has come to be called the Sapir-Whorf hypothesis (sometimes called the Whorfian hypothesis or Linguistic Relativity).

Edward Sapir and Benjamin Whorf posited that words affect our ability to conceptualize (i.e., the way we think is dependent upon the language that we have). In the language of academics, "The lexicon of a given language shapes our thought processes by providing a specific repertory of cognitive schemata."[15] Simply, a cultural group may actually think in a way that is distinctive because its language is distinctive. If conceptualization is dependent on language, then language differences do not only make understanding what we *say* difficult, but language differences make it difficult for people to conceptualize phenomena similarly.

This can be a complicated idea to grasp so let us consider a number of examples.

In a family of several siblings, a Chinese family member doesn't simply refer to a sister as a sister, but rather older sister, or small older sister—the former meaning the sister who is the eldest and the latter meaning a sister who is older than the person with the sibling, but not as old as the eldest sister. Because of the specificity of language in regard to siblings and children, there is, it is argued, a clearer sense of the importance of family, and individual roles of family members, in Chinese culture than in cultures that simply refer to sisters, regardless of relative age, as sisters.[16] Is it possible that a conversation about filial responsibility that takes place between a Chinese employee and an American employee could become complicated because of conceptual variation based on language?

Another regularly cited example has to do with the numbers of words for snow that Eskimos are said to have. It has been argued that Eskimos, who have several words for snow, think of snow differently than those persons from cultures with only one word for snow?[17] The Eskimo/snow example has been challenged,[18] but the point remains the same. If a group has multiple words for a concept, doesn't that group conceptualize differently than a group that has fewer words for the same concept? Do multiple words with shades of conceptual differences create the possibility of greater and more sophisticated conceptualization?

Let's assume that your home is near the equator. Would you distinguish between heavy snow and light snow, or would you have only one word for, and therefore one way to think about, snow? If all snow was one kind of snow, then would it affect how you could think about traveling, playing, shoveling, or working in cities where there often was snow?

Do the multiple words in the English language that are antonyms for authenticity (e.g., counterfeit, phony, bogus, artificial, specious, ersatz, spurious) make it easier to conceptualize nonauthentic behavior at the workplace? If you know what *specious* means, are you more likely to persuade using specious arguments?

Do you know what the word *usurp* means? If you do, are you more capable of usurping authority in a meeting, because you have a word for that concept? If a language had no equivalent word for usurp would usurpation be an alien notion to persons who used that language? If a culture had no word that was the equivalent of *alien* would the concept of intercultural communication be difficult to contemplate?

Is it true, as the Sapir-Whorf hypothesis suggests, that language affects our sense of the world, and therefore, groups of people who do not share the same language will inevitably have different perspectives?

© GETTY IMAGES/PHOTODISC

The meaning of non-verbal gestures and behavior can vary depending on one's cultural background and orientation.

These questions have no irrefutable answers, yet it can be valuable, or at least interesting, to consider the effects of language on thought and intercultural relationships.

Nonverbal Disparities. Nonverbal messages vary significantly on the basis of culture. Many research articles on intercultural communication are filled with examples of gestures that mean one thing in one culture, but something quite different in others. For example, the "ok sign" commonly used in the United States is an example of a gesture that has various meanings depending on the country. "In France it means zero. In Japan it is a symbol of money and in Brazil it carries a vulgar connotation."[19]

There are "dos and don'ts" papers published for business people who are traveling overseas reminding them to be cognizant of nonverbal differences. For example one is told that while in Indonesia one should not touch anyone on the head nor cross one's feet at a business meeting. "In India, an up and down nod can mean 'no' while a side to side toss of the head can mean 'yes.' "[20]

As we discussed in Chapter 3, an *emblem* is a nonverbal motion or gesture for which there is a discrete one-to-one relationship between that motion/gesture and a unit of meaning. A gesture that is emblematic in one culture may well be emblematic in another culture. However, the meanings of the emblems could be different. Also, what is not emblematic in one culture may well be emblematic in another. In short, one cannot assume a universal nonverbal language.

In the following sections we will look at some specific applications of intercultural communication to organizational contexts. We will discuss:

- Structural approaches to multinational expansion
- Disparate perspectives of workers in various countries
- Some suggestions for overcoming barriers to intercultural communication in organizational contexts.

Approaches to Multinational Expansion

Adler has identified five structural orientations of multinational organizations:

1. Cultural dominance
2. Cultural accommodation
3. Cultural compromise
4. Cultural avoidance
5. Cultural synergy[21]

The **cultural dominance** model assumes a monocultural style and, as one might predict, encounters resistance. When this orientation is in evidence, the parent organization superimposes its culture on the subsidiary offices in other nations. Despite the clear problems with it, the cultural dominance model is the most common of the approaches.[22]

The **cultural accommodation** model is in contrast to the cultural dominance approach. This model assumes that a company should accept and assume the cultural values of the host country. Those who follow this model "do what the Romans do" while they are in Rome.

The **cultural compromise** orientation requires an attempt to identify the divergent cultural orientations among managers who represent the organization. However, only the similarities among the disparate managers are used in the formation of policies. The compromise model is more sensitive than the dominance model in that it is, at the very least, conscious of and sensitive to cultural diversity.

The **cultural avoidance** orientation is, indeed, an avoidance approach. Those who follow this model pretend as if there is no distinction between the cultures.

ETHICAL PROBE

IS THERE ANYTHING WRONG WITH CULTURAL DOMINANCE?

Assume that you own a factory in Pennsylvania and you have decided to expand and set up another factory operation in Montreal. Assume that you know that the workers you hire in Montreal are bilingual, and that the persons you hire would prefer to speak French at work. Assume that your French is limited and several of the senior administrators at the Montreal facility (who have been moved to Montreal in order to run the plant) speak only English. Finally, assume that French could be the language used at the factory without affecting any relationship with external customers who speak English as a first language.

Is there anything unethical with compelling workers to use English in their written and oral communications while at the factory?

For the purposes of this exercise, do not consider the practical benefits of allowing the workers to speak French. Also eliminate from your thinking anything about any legal requirements of the Province of Quebec where Montreal is located. The hypothetical question is this: If you could so require that English be spoken and you knew that most workers would prefer to speak French, would there be anything unethical about compelling workers to speak English at work? Is there anything unethical about saying, "This is my factory and in my factory if you can speak English—and since all of you can—you'll speak English?"

Should you hire executives for the Montreal plant who can speak French? Should you learn to speak French or not open the factory in Montreal?

The **cultural synergy** model is, as the name implies, a synergistic approach to multinational operations. The policies and procedures of the organization are not superimposed by the parent organization, or only a reflection of similar perspectives, but an amalgam of the various inputs of the evolving multifaceted organization.

What problems can the cultural dominance model create? What problems can the cultural accommodation approach create? Do you think that the preference of the dominance model is a function of ignorance? indifference? ethnocentrism?

In the next section we will be discussing what has been referred to as the Hofstede Studies. As you read through this portion of the chapter, consider the possibility that the results of these studies suggest a contributing explanation for cultural dominance in organizations.

The Hofstede Studies

Geert Hofstede conducted a study that is cited in many books and articles about intercultural differences in organizations. His study (1) suggests that there are perceptual differences based on culture and, moreover, (2) implies that these perceptual differences can account for misunderstanding and intercultural tensions in organizational contexts.[23]

Hofstede distributed surveys to over 116,000 employees in 72 different countries.[24] All of the respondents worked for the same multinational organization. The goal of the research was to see whether attitudes toward similar phenomena related to organizations and organizational work would vary depending on country and culture.

Hofstede found that there were differences and he categorized the differences into four groupings: (1) uncertainty avoidance, (2) power distance, (3) individualism versus collectivism, and (4) masculinity versus femininity.

Uncertainty avoidance refers to the extent to which members of a cultural group require certainty, and disdain ambiguity and uncertainty. A culture high in uncertainty avoidance would seek formal regulations and tolerate less in the way of aberrant behaviors and personalities. Low uncertainty avoidance cultures are less concerned with specificity. In a meeting, members of high uncertain avoidance cultures might want to "nail down" all relevant information whereas members from low uncertainty avoidance cultures might be content with greater degrees of abstraction.

Power distance refers to the acceptance of supervisor/subordinate authority distinctions in organizations. A high power distance culture would respect their superiors and have disdain for those who challenge them. Low power distance societies would have little inherent respect for authority. If an organizational leader were to address a congregation from a high power distance society, that leader would be regarded more deferentially as a matter of course. However, if the same leader were to speak in a low power distance country, speaker authority would not be elevated solely on the basis of organizational role.

The category called **individualistic versus collective** relates to whether persons in the group value free-spirited independence, or community cooperation and compromise. Citizens of the United States who made popular the music of Sammy Davis Jr. singing "I Gotta Be Me" and Frank Sinatra crooning "My Way" are typically high on the individualistic side of the individualism collective continuum. A mission statement created for an individualistic society might emphasize the respect for individual self-expression and creativity, whereas a collective society is likely to consider a "mission" emphasizing teamwork and cooperation more consistent with their cultural orientation.

The **masculine versus feminine** scale pertains to whether the dominant values of the society emphasize assertiveness or nurturance. Adler and Rodman consider the labels of "Masculine/Feminine" inappropriate and counterproductive to a discussion of intercultural communication. They have changed the title of the masculine/feminine

TABLE 12.1   TOP FOUR COUNTRIES IN EACH CATEGORY

High Power Distance	Low Power Distance
Malaysia	Austria
Guatemala	Israel
Panama	Denmark
Philippines	New Zealand

High Masculinity (Task Orientation)	High Femininity (Social Orientation)
Japan	Sweden
Austria	Norway
Venezuela	Netherlands
Italy/Switzerland	Denmark

Individualism	Collectivism
United States	Guatemala
Australia	Ecuador
Great Britain	Panama
Canada/Netherlands	Venezuela

High Uncertainty Avoidance	Low Uncertainty Avoidance
Greece	Singapore
Portugal	Jamaica
Guatemala	Denmark
Uruguay	Sweden/Hong Kong

Adapted from tables in Hofstede, Geert, *Culture's Consequences: Second Edition, Comparing Values, Behaviors, Institutions and Organizations Across Nations,* Sage Publications, 2001, pp. 87, 151, 215, 286.

index label to task versus social orientation.[25] A high masculine or task-oriented society would admire a committee leader who takes control of the session and is clearly the committee chief, whereas a feminine or social orientation society would identify with a committee leader who sought to make sure all participants were comfortable in their role as members of the group.

Hofstede ranked the countries he explored in terms of those strongest in each of the categories. Table 12.1 is a list of the top four countries in each of the areas.

Triandis and Albert argue that the Hofstede dimensions have predictive value in that they can help multinational organizations expect how members of certain cultures "will respond to social situations."[26] This makes some sense and highlights the main value of Hofstede's study. At the very least, Hofstede has demonstrated that what some persons may assume are universal values and perspectives are not universal. For multinational organizations and for domestic organizations with a diverse workforce, it is important to consider that there are different perspectives related to the same phenomena. Samovar and Porter suggest that these culturally different perspectives affect interactions dealing with business protocol, the use of time, and business negotiation.[27] Others comment that recognizing these cultural disparities affect greetings, telephone communication, cross-cultural meetings, presentations, and written communications.[28]

Suggestions for Overcoming Barriers

We have identified a number of obstacles to effective intercultural communication. Let's review them here.

1. There are verbal and nonverbal differences among cultural groups. These language barriers range from the existence of separate language systems, to diverse meanings attributed to the same words, to varied interpretations of nonverbal behav-

iors. These language differences can make it difficult for managers to communicate with members of different cultural groups.

2. There are perceptual disparities. That is, people from different backgrounds tend to perceive the same phenomena in various ways. Cultural groups have different "world views" and these disparities can create confusion and/or disrespect. Disrespect or chauvinism can breed ethnocentrism—a perspective on ethnicity that assumes that your group and your way of perceiving phenomena is superior to another's. Ethnocentrism is toxic to intercultural communication as it immediately places the perceived other in a position of diminished credibility and legitimacy.

3. Finally, there is ignorance. That is, in addition to language, perception, and ethnocentrism, a barrier to effective intercultural communication is simply not knowing what you don't know. Asante, originally a communication scholar and now more closely associated with African-American studies, made a related claim. He argued that some persons had a "peculiar arrogance, the arrogance of not knowing that they do not know what it is that they do not know, yet they speak as if they know what all of us need to know."[29] This arrogance is the marriage of ignorance and ethnocentrism—a diabolical amalgam for intercultural communication in any context and certainly in organizational contexts. The question becomes, How can people overcome these obstacles?

Following Prescriptions. There is a distinction between having a prescription and following a prescription. It is easy to enumerate the steps for many tasks, yet sometimes difficult to follow the steps. Many people, and certainly any nutritionist, can explain how to lose weight. If you eat healthy foods and consume fewer calories than you expend, you will lose weight. Yet for many individuals the process of losing weight is extraordinarily difficult. If you've ever tried to lose weight you know that it can be painstaking and frustrating work. Weight loss businesses are lucrative *not* because the entrepreneurs who run them have a secret prescription, but because it is so very hard for so many people to follow the prescription. Indeed, if the formula was easy to follow, then these businesses would have a limited clientele.

Similarly, solving intercultural communication tension is difficult *not* because there is a secret regarding how to become effective in these contexts, but because the process of adhering to the how-to steps can be more difficult than it seems. Often people get off the track. One might know that it is important to adopt an egalitarian as opposed to an ethnocentric frame when engaging in intercultural interactions. Yet, it may be difficult to shed your ethnocentric perspectives. You may know that communication noise is a function of perceptual differences, but you may become fatigued straining to view the world from another's perceptual lens, when you feel as if the other is not making a similar effort.

Overcoming the barriers to intercultural communication is hard work. The formula is not difficult. The prescription, in fact, is remarkably basic as will become apparent in the next few pages. The challenge relates to being willing to follow the steps.

Learn About Other Cultures. In their book, *Multicultural Management,* Elashmawi and Harris identify several characteristics of "multicultural managers"—people who can overcome cultural noises in order to communicate effectively in organizations. The essence of their argument is that multicultural management requires learning about diversity.[30] Specifically they suggest that multicultural managers:

1. *Acquire multicultural competencies and skills including foreign languages.* The authors use a tree metaphor to explain their notion of cultural competence. A tree is a function of its roots. People, similarly, are a product of cultural roots. A culturally competent manager is someone who is aware of her or his own roots and is willing

to learn about the foundations of others with whom they interact. This includes learning and respecting customs, norms, values, and to some extent, language systems of the other cultural groups represented in the manager's organization.

DeWine comments that international business managers identify "showing respect" as a very important managerial skill for U.S. international business success.[31] Demonstrations of respect are reflected by learning about your employees' customs and respecting those customs. Ruben has indicated that respect can be demonstrated through nonverbal gestures suggesting interest and awareness of cultural rules.[32]

To show appropriate respect, endeavor to learn the nonverbal language of others with whom you will be in contact when working in countries that are foreign to you. Try to learn the language, or about the language, of the countries where you will be working. Just because "everyone there speaks English" doesn't eliminate the need to become familiar with the host language. Making no attempt to use the language of the host can, in and of itself, be a sign of disrespect.

2. *Become students of worldwide human relations and values.* This item is an extension of the previous one. A multicultural manager becomes a student, one who not only focuses on specific needs pertaining to managing a diverse workforce, but someone who continually attempts to broaden her or his knowledge base as it relates to diversity. The idea is that the more knowledgeable one becomes regarding global diversity, the more sensitive one will be when dealing with any one particular situation.

3. *Think beyond local perceptions and transform stereotypes into positive views of people.* This is certainly easy enough to write, and more difficult to accomplish. The idea is for managers to work toward adopting a perspective that embraces diversity.

4. *Become open and flexible in dealing with diversities in people.* This is another item that is easy to write and difficult to accomplish. Yet the authors' point is important here. It is one thing to become knowledgeable and another to apply your knowledge appropriately when "dealing with diversity."

Rancer et al. discuss two types of training that can be used to assist those who seek to become more aware of other cultures. *Cultural Specific Training* educates motivated learners on the mores, attitudes, and world view of a particular culture to which individuals will be visiting or working. *Cultural General Training* refers to training where persons become more aware of cultural issues by learning about one's own culture and intercultural variables.[33]

Novinger, in *Intercultural Communication*, writes about the advantages of learning about other cultures. She argues that education can preempt default tendencies that are counterproductive in the intercultural context:

> The raising of one's culture consciousness through education. . .gives the intercultural communicator the freedom to consciously choose behavior and attitude in personal interaction, rather than submitting to the control of subconscious cultural norms and just reacting, usually negatively, to any deviation from these norms.[34]

Earlier in this chapter you were asked to consider the roots of cultural dominance in organizations. Novinger's remarks are worth considering particularly in this context:

If education provides the "freedom to consciously choose behavior," then ignorance coupled with the diverse perceptual perspectives described by Hofstede, may deprive communicators of this "freedom." If people are inclined to "react, usually negatively, to any deviation" from their own cultural perspective, that may account for the tendency for persons to assume a culturally dominant posture when interacting with culturally different others.

"The raising of one's culture consciousness through education" is a key factor in the elimination of impediments in the intercultural communication context.

Please visit my great aunt

A senior-level American businessperson was working for a 3-week period in Italy where his company had a satellite office. During his stay he was invited to attend the wedding of the daughter of his Italian counterpart. The late afternoon celebration included a sumptuous feast at which the American ate far more than he wished he had. It seemed as if the meal consisted of a series of never-ending courses.

Buoyed by the events of the day and delighted to share his happiness with his new American friend, the Italian asked his guest if he would do him the honor of joining him as he visited his great aunt who lived nearby, but who had been unable to attend the celebration. To be polite, the American agreed despite the fact that he was feeling very uncomfortable from all that he had consumed at the wedding. The host quickly scribbled the directions to his relative's home and promised to meet the American there shortly after the celebration ended—as soon as he was able to say a private goodbye to his daughter.

The American arrived at the great aunt's home an hour after the wedding concluded. He was welcomed in and was told that the bride's father had yet to arrive. Almost as soon as he sat down in the great aunt's home, the American was asked if he wanted some pasta. The American declined, quickly commenting on how he was stuffed from the plentiful meals served at the wedding. The elderly woman smiled and then a moment later again offered some pasta. Again, the American politely declined, pointing to his burgeoning stomach. The woman asked a third time, and when this third offer was respectfully declined, the great aunt stood up and ordered the American out of her house, saying that anyone who would not eat pasta in her house did not deserve to visit. Hastily, the American apologized, and urged the woman to provide some pasta which he, painfully, consumed.

Recognize Diversity Within Cultural Groups. One problem with cultural-specific training, or any attempt to learn about the culture of another group, is that a learner can fall into the trap of assuming that each individual from that culture adheres to the same monolithic value system. While it is important to be sensitive to cultural differences, it is also important to recognize that individuals can vary from the norm.

How would you feel (or how do you feel) when someone approaches you and says, "Oh. You're Catholic. I understand Catholics go to mass regularly and are serious about religion. You, then, must be serious about religion."

It can be annoying to be categorized or generalized into one group. It can be exasperating to have people assume that everyone in that group, and therefore you, thinks and acts the same.

This makes cultural sensitivity a "slippery slope." On the one hand you are encouraged to become aware of cultural mores, and on the other you are discouraged from assuming that all members of a cultural group behave the same way. It is safe to wager that if you meet a Jewish employee who is wearing a skull cap, that he's unlikely to be receptive to attending a welcoming celebration held on a Saturday afternoon, the Jewish Sabbath. However, on the basis of the skull cap one could not determine the employee's nonreligious interests, capabilities, or what his precise position is on contemporary Israeli politics. To attribute prevailing cultural notions to all individuals is as insensitive as ignoring the possibility of cultural differences between you and another person. A component of successful intercultural organizational communication requires taking the time to acknowledge that within cultural groups there are individual differences.

Assume an Egalitarian Frame. Understanding the language, mores, attitudes, and customs of another culture is a limited asset in the absence of an egalitarian perspective. The fundamental plank for effective intercultural communication requires that individuals assume, from the start, that all people are inherently equal—and that culture in and of itself is not a factor that determines the quality of a person. One need not relinquish one's own cultural perspective in order to treat others as equals. Also, adopting an egalitarian frame does not mean that you must respect and honor a person whose behavior is reprehensible. It means that when you meet another person, either from your own culture or any other, you assume that neither you nor your culture is superior. It means that you do not attribute to a member of a group all characteristics associated with particular individuals of that group. The roots of cultural dominance may be ignorance and perceptual disparities, but the fuel that propels cultural dominance is a composite of ignorance and entrenched assumptions about the innate superiority of individual cultures.

Most people assume that they are, indeed, egalitarians. Are you? *Do you adopt an egalitarian frame when you meet people:*

- *From different regions of the country?*
- *From different countries?*
- *Of the opposite sex?*
- *Who have different sexual orientations?*
- *Who have a different religion?*
- *Whose race is not the same as yours?*
- *Who seem to come from a different economic bracket?*
- *Who have different careers or different career aspirations?*

An egalitarian predisposition coupled with a willingness to learn about the customs, language, and mores of another culture are the ingredients for successful intercultural communication in the twenty-first century.

We are a global village. It's easy to write "abandon ethnocentrism" on your managerial "to do" list. It's far more difficult to put in the time, effort, and introspection that will allow you to legitimately check the item off.

PRACTITIONER'S PERSPECTIVE

Steve MacLeod, Senior Vice President

Steve MacLeod has been with the Fluor Corporation for 28 years. During this period he has spent time serving as the company's president of its Middle East office, and also president of the South American office. Mr. MacLeod has lived and worked in Saudi Arabia, Chile, Puerto Rico, and Mexico City as well as several states in the United States. He has traveled extensively throughout the world as a businessperson. The Fluor Corporation, based in

California, is one of the world's largest publicly owned engineering and construction organizations. Fluor maintains a network of offices in more than 25 countries across six continents. It is consistently rated as one of the world's safest contractors.

Communicating is difficult enough for people who are from the same region, but when you are interacting with business partners who represent different cultures, the task of communicating effectively becomes particularly complicated. When you find yourself in a conference room and each person around the table has a different native tongue—even if all attendees can, and in fact do, speak the same language at the conference session—you are faced with a real challenge. In order to be a successful businessperson in an organization that has a global presence, it's important to be able to meet such challenges.

I think that the first step toward success in these contexts is to acknowledge that there are intercultural differences and to respect the diversity. Too many persons travel to another land and assume that any variation from their orientation renders the people from these lands somehow inferior. "How come these folks don't have a McDonald's in town?" "There are so few people here who speak English." "Gee, these people are not sophisticated." It seems to me that many American businesspeople are egotistical and view the world from their own cultural perspective. It's counterproductive to think and act this way. Also, you miss out on the chance to truly learn about other people.

My attitude when I went to a new country was to consider it a great opportunity. It was a wonderful chance for my family and I to learn about other cultures. You don't want to superimpose your attitudes on the people from another group. That kind of thing is disrespectful, and it creates impediments from the start that can make intercultural communication more difficult than it needs to be. It seems to me that the wisest tack to take was to learn about the group and attempt to meld in. It's a cliché, but "when in Rome. . . ."

Some intercultural issues are difficult to predict. Even the most sensitive and intelligent businessperson may not know the nuances of every cultural group. For example, in America it is quite common for business acquaintances to ask about the spouse and children of a business partner. In Saudi Arabia, such inquiries are considered inappropriate and it would be offensive to your colleague to pose such a question. While living in Saudi Arabia, I became personal friends with several Arab businessmen and if I were to meet privately with them I would always ask about their children. However, I would never insult them by asking such a question in the presence of others. Notions of time vary significantly from region to region.

Suppose you and I had an appointment to speak at 11 A.M. today. I could pretty much count on talking with you at 11. In Saudi Arabia, 11 A.M. could mean 10:45, 11:15, or tomorrow. Should one think that there's something inferior about the Saudis because their custom frowns on business partners asking about their family, or because their sense of time is different than it is here? I don't think one should and, as significantly, it would be counterproductive for businesspeople to make such assumptions.

I don't know how you can function in today's contemporary business arena without being sensitive to intercultural differences. Actually, I don't know how you can function without being bilingual or trilingual in this global environment. It's true that the new technology can allow for some greater ease in terms of international communication. For example, I have some software that allows me to translate documents relatively easily. E-mail and teleconferencing also eliminate some problems that distance creates. Yet it's difficult to have a heart-to-heart business negotiation with someone who is a relative stranger unless you can be with that person face to face and demonstrate that you respect that person and his or her culture.

SUMMARY

A Toolbox

1. The world is becoming smaller. Organizational men and women, sooner or later, will need to be adept at communicating interculturally.

2. Intercultural communication contexts have additional communication noises. Among these noises are:
   - Perceptual and world view disparities
   - Disparate language systems
   - Disparate nonverbal systems
   - Ethnocentrism

3. Overcoming these barriers requires:
   - A willingness to become knowledgeable about others
   - Respect for differences
   - Familiarity with other language systems, nonverbal behaviors, and customs
   - Awareness that cultures are not monolithic entities
   - Adopting an egalitarian frame and abandoning ethnocentric perspectives

DISCUSSION QUESTIONS

1. Why is effective intercultural communication essential for contemporary organizations?

2. How has ethnocentrism affected interactions you've observed between people at work?

3. Is intercultural communication noise inevitable, regardless of egalitarian perspectives of the communicators?

4. What types of intercultural encounters do you typically experience
   - At the university?
   - At work?

5. Do you think that the Sapir-Whorf hypothesis can affect the extent of communication noise in intercultural contexts? Explain.

6. As the world continues to become more and more of a global village, will results from Hofstede-type studies reflect fewer cultural distinctions?

7. Do events of September 11, 2001, create or reduce intercultural communication noise? Explain.

8. Please read the case that follows and respond to the questions at the end of the case.

CASE FOR ANALYSIS

Case 12.2—The Lady Bosses

[This case is presented in the first person for reasons that will become apparent].

The setting is a branch office in New Delhi, India, of a reputable financial company. The company has its central office in Bombay and is engaged in providing consultancy for project financing, mergers and acquisitions, and corporate restructuring to big industrial houses. The New Delhi branch office where I worked was a very small office where only six people used to work compared to a workforce of 50–60 employees in Bombay. I was the only one in the finance department in New Delhi. The rest of the employees were either in management or marketing.

I would directly report to the group company chairman, a Mr. Issar, who would visit New Delhi every Saturday to give out new assignments, and discuss the projects already assigned to me in the previous weeks. There were also two lady [sic] bosses in my office; one that was a cousin of Mr. Issar and the other who was his mistress. The cousin, Ms. Issar, was well educated, very dynamic, and the manager of the Delhi office. However, she had no knowledge of finance. The mistress was not well educated but enjoyed a special status in the organization due to her relationship with my boss. So I had to report to three different people in the organization—the chairman, Ms. Issar, and the chairman's mistress.

The lady bosses used to delegate tasks to me which I had to complete even if the tasks didn't have to do with the finance department or my interest. However, considering the fact that I was the most junior of the staff and the job was very well rewarded, I had to perform those functions delegated by them and report separately to each one of them.

The problem which I encountered was that I didn't like taking orders from the lady bosses at New Delhi who had nothing to do with the field of finance. No one took responsibility for the noncompletion of the core work in finance that I could not get to because I was taking orders from the lady bosses. As a result, I used to receive deadline warnings and efficiency warnings from the chairman. I tried to explain my problem to the chairman, but I could not do so effectively because he believed in the philosophy that the boss is always right and that I am well paid for this particular job.

Also, another problem was that the chairman did not communicate to me directly when he delivered the warnings. He would communicate mostly to the vice president in Bombay and I used to hear the bad messages from her, which sometimes would have lost their relevance due to late communication from her as she failed to understand the timely importance of the financial data and other bits of information. So this in turn made the problems of the delays worse.

I also noticed that the messages that the chairman used to communicate to me over the phone or in face-to-face meetings were different from the messages about the same projects he would communicate to the two lady bosses. This often led to conflicts in the organization, and also interpersonal tension between the chairman, the lady bosses, and the other staff in the office.

- What suggestions do you have for the narrator regarding how to communicate to the chairperson and his "lady bosses?"
- What suggestions do you have for the chairperson regarding how he should communicate to the narrator?
- Is your ability to analyze this case hampered because the ethnicity of the narrator is not identified? Why is that a factor?
- Is your ability to analyze this case dependent on your own cultural orientation?

ENDNOTES

[1]Maraniss, David, *When Pride Still Mattered*, Simon and Schuster, 1999, p. 242.

[2]Reeder, John, "When West Meets East: Cultural Aspects of Doing Business in Asia," *Business Horizons*, January/February, 1987, p. 69.

[3]McLuhan, Marshall, with Quentin Fiore and Jerome Agel, *The Medium Is the Message: An Inventory of Effects*, Bantam, 1967. Also referenced in Marshall McLuhan and Quentin Fiore, *War and Peace in the Global Village*, Bantam, 1968.

[4]DeVito, Joseph, *Human Communication: The Basic Course*, sixth edition, Harper Collins, 1994, pp. 417–419. Also the effects of new technology in particular on the creation of a shrinking world and the implicit need for intercultural communication is described in Francis Cairncross, *The Death of Distance: How the Communications Revolution Will Change Our Lives*, Harvard Business School Press, 1997, pp. 1–26.

[5]A study I conducted reflected this economic interdependence and demonstrated that mass communicated messages regarding perspectives on the conflict were a function of political and economic self-interest. Alan Zaremba, *Mass Communication and International Politics: A Case Study of Press Perceptions of the 1973 Arab-Israeli War*, Sheffield Press, 1988. This study examined newspaper reactions after the Yom Kippur War that began in October of 1973 and juxtaposed reactions prior to the oil embargoes and after the oil embargoes. Also the results of the study indicated clearly that political orientation had an effect on expressed attitudes regarding the conflict.

[6]Benedict, Ruth, *Patterns of Culture*, Mentor Books, 1948.

[7]Haviland, William, *Cultural Anthropology*, Holt, Rinehart, and Winston, 1993, p. 29.

[8]Triandis, Harry and Rosita Albert, "Cross Cultural Perspectives," in *Handbook of Organizational Communication*, 1987, p. 266. Herkovitz definition from *Cultural Anthropology*, Knopf, 1955. Triandis and Albert make a distinction between objective culture and subjective culture. The objective culture would be apparent by examining, for example, the "tools, roads, and gardens" of the group, and the subjective culture would be concerned with the "norms, roles, belief systems, laws, values." "Cross Cultural Perspectives," p. 266.

[9]DeVito discussing the same principle writes, "Culture is transmitted through learning, not through genes," p. 420.

[10]Elashmawi, Farid and Phillip Harris, *Multicultural Management: New Skills for Global Success*, Gulf Publishing, 1993, p. 50.

[11]Samovar, Larry and Richard Porter, *Communication Between Cultures*, Wadsworth, 1995, p. 58.

[12]Singer, Marshall, *Intercultural Communication: A Perceptual Approach*, Prentice Hall, p. 9.

[13]Ibid.

[14]Cushner, Kenneth and Richard Brislin, *Intercultural Interactions: A Practical Guide*, Second edition, Sage, 1996: p. 5. Similarly, see Richard Thompson, *Theories of Ethnicity: A Critical Appraisal*, Greenwood Press, 1989: p. 17.

[15]Maas, Anne and Luciano Arcuri, "Language and Stereotyping," in *Stereotypes and Stereotyping*, edited by C. Neil MacRae, Charles Stangor, and Miles Hewstone, The Guilford Press, 1996, p. 197.

[16]Infante, Dominic, Andrew Rancer, and Deanna Womack, *Building Communication Theory*, Waveland Press, 1997, p. 403.

[17]See discussion in *The Dictionary of Anthropology*, Thomas Barfield (editor), Blackwell Publishers, 1997, p. 492. Also, for example, Myron Lustig and Jolene Koester, *Intercultural Competence*, Addison Wesley, 1999, pp. 186–187.

[18]Pullum, Geoffrey K., "The Great Eskimo Vocabulary Hoax," in *The Great Eskimo Vocabulary Hoax and Other Irreverent Essays on the Study of Language,* University of Chicago Press, 1991, pp. 159–171.

[19]"Understand and Heed Cultural Differences," *Business America,* US Department of Commerce, January, 1991, page 26.

[20]Baraban, Regina, "Cultural Protocol Tips," in *Cultural To Do's and Taboos in the Marketplace. Cultural To Do's and Taboos in the Marketplace* is a reference and resource guide compiled by Karen Tucker and published by the Meeting Services Connection. Baraban's article was originally published in *Beyond Borders* in 1999.

[21]Adler, Nancy, *International Dimensions of Organizational Behavior,* Third edition, Southwestern, 1997, pp. 115–117.

[22]Triandis, Harry C. and Rosita Albert, "Cross Cultural Perspectives," in *The Handbook of Organizational Communication,* Frederic Jablin, Linda Putnam, Karlene Roberts, and Lyman Porter editors, Sage Publications, 1987.

[23]Hofstede, Geert, *Culture's Consequences: International Differences in Work Related Values,* Newbury Park, CA, Sage Publications, 1980. In 2001, Hofstede published a second edition of the book. The second edition was entitled somewhat differently: *Culture's Consequences: Second Edition, Comparing Values, Behaviors, Institutions and Organizations Across Nations.* A third Hofstede book, *Culture and Organizations: Software of the Mind,* McGraw-Hill, 1991, makes similar claims.

[24]Hofstede, 2001, p. 41. Several accounts of the Hofstede studies that came out after the first edition of *Culture's Consequences* reported that Hofstede's survey respondents were managers. Hofstede, in the preface to his 1991 book, *Culture and Organizations: Software of the Mind,* seems to be appalled by the misrepresentation. He affirms in that preface that the respondents in the studies were employees and not necessarily managers.

[25]Adler, Ronald and George Rodman, *Understanding Human Communication,* Seventh edition, Harcourt College Publishers, p. 260.

[26]Op. cit., Triandis and Albert, p. 277.

[27]Op. cit., Samovar and Porter, p. 224.

[28]Op. cit., Elashmawi and Harris, pp. 98–123.

[29]Asante, Molefi, *The Afrocentric Idea,* Temple University Press, 1987, p. 4.

[30]Op. cit., Elashmawi and Harris, p. 6.

[31]DeWine, Sue, *The Consultant's Craft,* Bedford St. Martin's, 2001, p. 374.

[32]Ruben, Brent, "Assessing Communication Competency for Intercultural Adaptation," *Group and Organization Studies: The International Journal for Group Facilitators,* September 1976, Volume 1, number 3, p. 339. Also see DeWine, 2001, p. 374.

[33]Op. cit., Infante, Rancer, and Womack, p. 410.

[34]Novinger, Tracy, *Intercultural Communication,* University of Texas Press, 2001, p. 158.

13

Crisis Communication

If fortune turns against you, even jelly breaks your tooth.

—Persian Proverb

When written in Chinese, the word crisis is composed of two characters. One represents danger and the other represents opportunity.

—John F. Kennedy

© CORBIS

Case 13.1—*The Nuance Group*

Background

A successful management consulting company, the Nuance Group, boasts that its consultants are all highly educated with significant consulting experience in the areas of marketing, economics, and finance. Nuance has created a glossy brochure that includes a description of its services, its contact information, and brief biographical statements about each consultant. Next to each biographical blurb is a photo of the consultant. Over 50,000 of these brochures have been mailed to people in organizations all over the world who have been identified as potential clients. In 2001 the brochure was reproduced for the Nuance Group website and has been continuously updated. The site can be accessed without any password simply by visiting nuanceconsulting.com

The Potential Client—Dorfman Associates

A potential client, Charlene Dorfman, the founder and director of Dorfman Associates, phoned the Nuance Group and requested some information about the services that the Nuance Group could offer. Dorfman had visited the website, but she had additional questions. She told the people at Nuance that she was considering several consulting firms and wanted literature that she could distribute to her senior associates. The associates would be meeting shortly to decide which consultant to hire. The Nuance Group sent Dorfman several dozen brochures and accompanying literature.

The senior associates at Dorfman met the following week to discuss which consulting group to hire. During the discussion, Randy, one of the associates, was scanning the Nuance Group brochure and was taken aback by a picture of one of the consultants. There was no doubt that the photo was a picture of one of Randy's college classmates, Jack Patten.

However, as Randy read Jack's corresponding bio he knew for certain that the biographical profile was a grand fabrication. The bio read that Patten had studied in New Haven attending Yale as an undergraduate. Patten had indeed studied in New Haven, having graduated from another college in the area. He may have attended Yale to use its library now and then, but he did not enroll nor graduate from the Ivy League school. Randy stopped the discussion and explained the misrepresentation. Charlene Dorfman immediately eliminated the Nuance Group from consideration.

Dorfman Contacts the Nuance Group— the Nuance Group Confronts Patten

After the meeting, Dorfman phoned the Nuance Group and described Randy's observation. When Jack Patten was confronted by his superior about the allegation, Jack did not deny the charge. He did, however, claim that all of the consultants had embellished their bios. Jack commented that he was told informally to "put his best foot forward."

"Apparently," his boss retorted, "You put someone else's foot forward."

However, as the boss continued to investigate the situation he discovered that several of the biographical blurbs were factually inaccurate and contained self-congratulatory embellishments.

☐   *Must the Nuance Group communicate to various audiences to address this problem?*

☐   *If the answer to the first question is "yes," who must be contacted? How should they be contacted? When should they be contacted?*

☐   *What must be communicated to each of these audiences?*

ABSTRACT

Crises happen. Organizations that are exceptionally profitable and well managed can encounter sudden problems that may rock their enterprise. When crises occur, organizations are compelled to communicate to various audiences. The quality of these communications is crucial for the success of the organization. Sloppy communication during crises can plague an organization right out of existence. Effective communication during these times can transform potential disasters into positive situations for a company. Tylenol, for example, will be remembered for years, as not only a pain remedy, but as a product associated with corporate responsibility. Tylenol will be so perceived because of how its company, Johnson and Johnson, communicated while in the throes of a crisis. This chapter discusses how to communicate during times of organizational crisis.

OBJECTIVES

When you have completed this chapter, you should be able to:

☐   **Describe what is meant by proactive crisis communication.**
☐   **Explain what is meant by internal and external stakeholders.**
☐   **List the steps of a crisis communication plan.**
☐   **Identify the responsibilities of crisis communication teams.**
☐   **Construct a plan that can be used for communicating during crises in an organization to which you belong.**

ORGANIZATIONS AND CRISIS COMMUNICATION

What Is a Crisis?

Laurence Barton, the author of *Crisis in Organizations: Managing and Communicating in the Heat of Chaos,* defines a crisis as "a major, unpredictable event that has potentially negative results. The event and its aftermath may significantly damage an organization and its employees, products, services, financial condition, and reputation."[1]

For example, a crisis for your university might involve:

- An epidemic illness spreading in the dormitories
- A fraternity hazing episode resulting in student injury
- A campus officer embezzling tuition dollars
- A professor's speech that's exposed as plagiary
- A student cheating scandal

A crisis for the airline industry might involve:

- A fatal crash
- The revelation that some pilots consume alcoholic beverages before flying
- Apparent conspiratorial fare-fixing among major carriers on common routes
- Skyjacking depicted as a reflection of poor security

What Is Crisis Communication?

Crisis communication involves identifying internal and external receivers who must receive information during times of crisis. Crisis communicators conceive, create, and disseminate messages to these internal and external receivers, and are ready to receive and respond to feedback from these audiences.

Sometimes the phrase *crisis communication* is used interchangeably with *crisis management*. The two are not synonymous. Crisis management involves communication, but is not only about communicating. Similarly, crisis communication is not synonymous with image management. Crises may require image restoration, and communicators may be able to repair damaged reputations. However, as we will see, crisis communication involves more than controlling or shaping how a company is, and will be, perceived by external others.

A result of effective crisis communication may be image restoration. A component of effective crisis management is crisis communication.

Why Study Crisis Communication?

Crisis communication is a very real problem for contemporary organizations. Not reacting well to a crisis can result in the generation of employee rumors, plummeting stock values, a lack of employee confidence, and a reduction in consumer trust.

The effect of not communicating well during a crisis can be an intensification of the crisis. To make this point more clear, consider two of the examples presented above. What would be the effects of poor communication during such crises?

If an epidemic of meningitis swept through your college or university, the school authorities would need to send messages out to various audiences, both within the organization and outside the organization.

- *What would be the (specific) repercussions of your university not communicating effectively if there were such an epidemic?*
- *Who, specifically, would have to be contacted?*

- *What information would these persons need to receive?*
- *What methods of communicating should the school utilize to get this information to these receivers?*

If an airline faced accusations that they had been derelict with their security checks, then employees and external customers would have to receive communications from the airline as quickly as possible.

- *What would be the repercussions of the airline not communicating to its internal and external audiences if faced with such a charge?*
- *Who, within the organization, would need to receive information immediately?*
- *Who, outside of the organization, would need to receive information immediately?*

There is nothing abstract nor artificial about the need for organizational men and women to communicate during these times. Consider a few very real examples of positive and negative communication during organizational crises.

- Deli meats produced by the Sara Lee Corporation were found to be tainted with a deadly microorganism. The contaminated meats were associated with 11 deaths, but the company remained silent for weeks. When the company finally addressed the issue their communications were considered "too little, too late."[2]
- Johnson and Johnson was faced with a colossal crisis when seven people died as a result of consuming cyanide-tainted Tylenol products. The company took immediate responsibility for protecting potential consumers. All Tylenol products were removed from retail shelves. Production and advertising were halted. Johnson and Johnson warned customers of the potential danger and their communications were characterized by candor, contrition, and compassion.[3]
- The EXXON *Valdez* was involved in an accident that resulted in thousands of barrels of oil being spilled in pristine Port Valdez, Alaska. The chairman of EXXON waited six days before making his first comments about the tragedy.[4]
- In Chicago, Melody Jones, a vice president and chief human resource officer for the international Aon Corporation, was in a meeting when she was informed that two planes had crashed into the World Trade Center. She watched a video replay of the explosion and was horrified. She realized that she must act immediately since 1,000 of her New York employees worked in the buildings that were now smoldering. Aon established a toll free number that employees and their families could use to get and share information regarding the status of employee safety. The company quickly began calling employees' homes in the hope of locating them. In addition, Aon used the web for communicating. By 1 p.m. on September 11, Aon had created a homepage with information for employees and families. By the morning of September 12 the Aon website had been completely redesigned and became "a portal for crisis communication."[5]
- President and head coach Dan Issel had been a revered member of the National Basketball Association's Denver Nuggets for 25 years. After a game on December 11, 2001, Issel became engaged in a verbal altercation with a

Focus on Applications

Crises in your organizations?

1. What was the last job you held?
2. What types of crises *could* have affected that organization?
3. What crises, if any, did affect that organization?
4. How did your company communicate during the crises?

fan who had been heckling him. One of Issel's retorts was recorded on audio tape. Issel told the heckler to "have another beer, you 'blankety' Mexican." Issel represents not only the Nuggets, but the entire NBA, an organization that consists of, and appeals to, a diverse racial constituency. On December 12 Issel participated in an emotional press conference during which he contritely apologized. The team suspended him for four days without pay. Members of the Hispanic community were not satisfied with the punishment nor the communications by Nugget management. Subsequently, Issel resigned from his positions with the Nuggets.

There is no doubt that organizations are faced with crises that require efficient communication. Firestone, Union Carbide, Coca-Cola, Ford Motor Company, Enron, the Catholic Church, Arthur Andersen, and Bendix comprise a list of major organizations that have had public crises in recent years to which they needed to respond.

However, it is not only the large companies that are at risk. All companies, regardless of size, and regardless of how fortunate they have been in the past, are susceptible to devastating crises.

CRISIS COMMUNICATION PLANNING

Proactive Versus Reactive Planning

Proactive planning refers to preparation before the fact. The word *proactive* is used in contrast to *reactive*. A reactive behavior occurs in reaction to a phenomenon. Proactive planning is something done in anticipation or in preparation for the phenomenon.

Reactive crisis communication planning, therefore, would take place subsequent to the crisis. As we will discuss in the pages that follow, an organization can put into place a communication plan well before any crises surface. Of course, there will have to be some components of the activity that will, inevitably, be reactions to unpredictable events. However, there is much that can be done in anticipation of a crisis so that in the event of calamity (or perceived calamity) the organization can begin to communicate as efficiently and rapidly as possible.

Steps to Crisis Communication Planning

Leaper identifies several stages of crisis communication planning. The list below is an edited version of these steps.[6]

1. Secure commitment from top management to be open and honest during crises
2. Establish a crisis communication team
3. Brainstorm regarding crises
4. Identify stakeholder & prepare appropriate message
5. Choose methods for communicating messages
6. Sequence messages
7. Identify spokespersons and establish a communication center
8. Record the Plan
9. Simulate and Coach
10. Update periodically

Let's consider each of these 10 stages.

1. Commitment from Top Management to Be Honest During Crises. In *Public Relations Quarterly*, James Lukaszewski lists what he calls categories of "trustbusting" behavior during crises.

- **Stonewalling** (e.g., issuing "No Comments;" stating "To the best of our knowledge, we have done nothing wrong in this matter")
- **Arrogance** (e.g., no expressions of apology or concern, telling media representatives or employees to keep out of "our" matters)
- **Defensive Threatening** (e.g., "Should you continue to insinuate. . . then we will have to. . .")
- **Delaying** (e.g., "We are hiring a consultant to investigate. . .")
- **Disdain** (e.g., "Only a fool would think that a company of our stature. . .")[7]

In order to plan meaningfully for crisis communication activities, an organization has to be committed to open, transparent communication and not trustbusting. We all have an ethical obligation to be honest in our communications. This moral responsibility complements the pragmatic value of open communication during crises.

Nearly all of the advice for crisis communication stresses the importance of honesty. Dishonesty and evasion might appear to be attractive when faced with the alternative of admitting to embarrassing activities. However, deceptive communication typically adds to the organization's crisis. Watson Wyatt consultant Linda Grosso comments that "the most critical challenge [in crisis communicating] is establishing a sense of trust. To that end, it's vital for management not to blow its credibility by putting out incorrect or confusing information."[8] Benoit writes that an "organization that falsely denies responsibility for offensive actions risks substantially damaged credibility if the truth emerges."[9]

If avoiding trustbusting and encouraging honesty is a crisis communication imperative, then an initial step in crisis planning requires obtaining a commitment from top management to be forthcoming when faced with crisis situations. Marra argues that the culture of an organization can dilute the effectiveness of crisis communication planning. "Many practitioners devote significant resources to produce a communication plan that is destined to fail because [it contradicts] the dominant and accepted communication plans used by their organizations."[10] If an organization typically is evasive, deceptive, or misleading in its communication, a plan based on forthcoming admissions is unlikely to succeed.

In short, the presence of a plan does not guarantee implementation. It requires a commitment from leaders to work the plan.[11] A first step is to get that commitment.

2. Establish a Crisis Communication Team. A crisis communication team is a committee composed of highly trusted members from various departments throughout the organization. Persons on this committee could be representatives from Corporate Communication departments and senior administration. It would be wise, however, to include persons on this team who represent various units of the organization and different organizational strata. By having a diverse membership in terms of experience, expertise, and culture, the crisis communication team can be better suited to deal with its mission as an anticipatory planning agent of the organization. Remsik recommends that the team have approximately six members and include persons who would fulfill identifiable roles. (The persons fulfilling the roles would not need to be members of the designated departments.)

- Team chairperson
- Representatives for
  - Government relations
  - Employee or internal relations
  - Operations/facilities
  - Community relations
  - Media relations[12]

3. Brainstorm Regarding Crises. Regardless of the nature of your organization, crises can occur both because of factors that have everything to do with your organization and because of factors that have nothing to do with your organization. A bank might lose its records because of a natural disaster like a hurricane or because of the actions of an outside thief or arsonist. The bank may also suffer a crisis because of the unethical behavior of an internal thief; for example, a manager who is embezzling client funds.

At this stage of the process, the crisis communication team must attempt to predict all possible crises that could surface in the organization. Subsequently, the team can place like types of crises into related groups. For example, the team could brainstorm and identify potential crises related to charges of racial, gender, sexual orientation, or age discrimination. While there are differences in the nature of each discriminatory type, the team could group all potential crises related to such charges into a single class.

Mitroff suggests that crises can be categorized as follows.

- **Economic:** e.g., in October 1987 the stock market unexpectedly drops four hundred points, affecting the fortunes of organizations and their customers.
- **Informational:** e.g., because of a computer glitch, a major university loses the names and related data of all students who have applied to the institution in a given year.

Focus on Applications

Brainstorming for crises

Assume you are on a crisis communication planning team for the organizations listed below. What potential crises might occur?

- ☐ The Islamic Student Association
- ☐ Your former high school
- ☐ A soft drink company
- ☐ *The Washington Post*
- ☐ The tobacco industry
- ☐ The National Guard
- ☐ A country club
- ☐ A theater company
- ☐ A furniture manufacturer
- ☐ A Wall Street investment firm
- ☐ The American Red Cross
- ☐ NATO
- ☐ A construction company
- ☐ The city council for St. Louis

- **Physical:** e.g., nuclear equipment at Three Mile Island appears to malfunction threatening the security of employees and all the citizens in the region.

- **Human Resources:** e.g., a highly successful mutual fund manager, in one of the largest investment firms in the world, suddenly leaves his position to begin his own investment company.

- **Reputational:** e.g., Procter and Gamble is faced with dismissing thousands of rumors suggesting that their logo indicates that the company is involved with the devil's work.

- **Psychopathic Acts:** e.g., a deranged employee enters Edgewater Technology in Wakefield, Massachusetts, and systematically shoots seven of his fellow employees.

- **Natural Disasters:** e.g., an earthquake in San Francisco hobbles the infrastructure of the city.[13]

4. Stakeholder Identification and Message Preparation. The word *stakeholders* is used in the language of crisis communication almost synonymously with what we have called *receivers* throughout the text. More specifically, a stakeholder is someone who has a stake in the information that an organization needs to communicate during a crisis *or* someone whom the organization wants to receive information, or have a stake, in the information during a crisis. An internal stakeholder is someone who is such a receiver *within* the organization. An external stakeholder is a receiver who is external to the organization.

For example, if there is a measles epidemic in your college dormitories, students who live in the same dorm as the infected persons would be considered one of several groups of internal stakeholders. The residence hall directors would be another group of internal stakeholders. The instructors who had been working with the infected students would be a third group of internal stakeholders. The editor of the campus newspaper would be an internal stakeholder. However, the editor of the town or city newspaper would be considered an *external* stakeholder. Parents of all students in the affected dormitory would be a group of external stakeholders. All parents of residential students (other than those in the affected dormitory) would be another group of external stakeholders. The news managers for the local radio stations would constitute a group of external stakeholders.

It's important for the committee to separate stakeholders into the smallest possible groupings to whom unique messages will need to be communicated. For example, in the case of a campus epidemic, it is not sufficient to identify students as internal stakeholders. The crisis communication team would have to break down the student population into discrete student populations that would receive unique messages from the university. For instance, students who live on the same floor as the infected persons would get a different message or messages than those students who lived in another dormitory, or off campus. Parents of the infected students would be sent messages that are different from the messages that would be sent to other dormitory student parents, or the parents of prospective university students.

Internal Stakeholders	External Stakeholders
Students who live in same dorm as those infected	Editor of city newspaper
Campus police	City police
Residence hall directors	Parents of prospective students
Instructors who've been teaching infected students	Area hospital physicians
All other dormitory students	Parents of all dormitory students

If there was a measles epidemic on your campus, crisis communicators would need to identify discrete groups of internal and external stakeholders that would need to receive unique messages from the university. Above are examples of such internal and external stakeholders.

It's essential that the identification of stakeholders be subdivided into these discrete units. If patrons of a restaurant suddenly complain of stomach cramps, then internal stakeholders do indeed include waitstaff, managers, and chefs. However, these populations should receive (or are likely to require) unique messages.

In the event of crisis, each discrete stakeholder population will receive a series of messages. The committee would list all types of messages that the identified discrete populations would need to receive.

For example, in the event of the campus epidemic, your committee might decide that all parents of prospective students receive:

- An updated account of the situation and how it has been addressed
- A history of the health records at the university
- A list of various medical services available for students
- A comparison of health records at your university as compared to national institutions

- A list of contact numbers for questions related to health services
- A message from the university president
- A message from the head of residential life
- Testimonials from the governor's office about health standards
- Clippings from media sources indicating the arrest of the illness

You will note that many of the items above can be prepared for in advance of any crisis. For example, the list of contact numbers, the various medical services for customers, the comparative health records of your university juxtaposed with others—these as well as other items on the list can be constructed and ready to disseminate well before any crisis develops. If you intend to release a report published by the FDA as part of your plan, then having this report ready for print or electronic dissemination is a component of your preparation. If an area is highly technical, prepare written "background" literature that will clarify the information for the lay receivers. Leaper suggests creating a glossary for terms that are likely to be unfamiliar to a stakeholder population.[14] In the best situation your organization will have paid for the production of materials that your team will never need to utilize.

5. Choose Methods for Sending Messages. As we discussed in Chapter 5, all communicators have options when they send information to receivers. In this phase of crisis communication planning, the team needs to consider the most effective ways to send the various messages to the particular group of stakeholders. For example, would

- The list of medical services *be mailed* to each prospective student's home?
- All parents receive a letter that identified a *website* that, when accessed, reveals all on-campus health service contacts?
- The "message from the president" be on *a videotape* that would be sent Priority Mail to each prospective student's home?
- A campus representative personally *phone* each prospective student updating the parents and student about the state of the epidemic?

The planning committee would decide what would be the best approach for each of the messages that needed to be communicated. Some decisions might be dependent on the specific nature of the actual, as opposed to anticipated, crisis. However, as you can see, some of the decisions could be made ahead of time and, therefore, reduce the chaos and increase the efficiency of communicating during crisis periods.

6. Sequence for Communicating Messages. The committee might decide to send out all messages to all stakeholders at once. It's unlikely, however, for that to be the wisest way to sequence the communications. For each crisis that has been anticipated, and each set of messages that needs to go to the stakeholders, the committee would want to consider who should get what messages when.

For example, if toxins were found in a cafeteria housed in an office building that served 20 independent businesses:

- Would you want external stakeholders to get messages before your internal stakeholders? For example, would you want media representatives to receive

© CORBIS

statements about corrective steps that will be taken, *before* you've explained these steps to your kitchen staff?

- Do you need to send messages to wholesalers who provide you with product, before you contact the local newspaper? Before you contact each of the businesses within your facility?

The sequencing, of course, will be dependent on the particular crisis identified. In terms of whom to contact first, Lukaszewski makes the following general recommendations:

First: Those most directly affected. For example, crisis victims
Second: Employee (i.e., internal) stakeholders
Third: Those indirectly affected. For example, neighbors of victims, friends, suppliers
Fourth: The news media[15]

It is also important to anticipate the need for follow-up messages. As indicated above, the committee might need to send out a series of messages to some stakeholders. The initial communications would be followed by a second group of messages that would depend on reactions to the initially communicated ones. These subsequent messages would be determined by the evolving nature of the crisis and/or reactions to the initial communications. It is impossible to predict every permutation in the evolution of a crisis, but the committee might want to anticipate what messages might need to be sent on the basis of potential developments.

For example, let's assume that a company's research and design facility has been inadvertently discharging noxious chemicals into nearby lakes. Your initial series of messages may precede any news of persons who became ill after swimming in these areas. In the initial messages you may comment that you are taking preemptive measures to ensure that people who did swim in the lakes can receive free medical attention so that the contact with the toxins will not result in illness. If persons, despite your company's efforts, do become ill, then your team would have to communicate the *reactive messages* you *proactively* determined to issue given such an eventuality.

In short, your committee should make an attempt to anticipate likely reactions and eventualities, and prepare for follow-up messages to meet the evolving communication needs of the crisis.

7. Identify Spokespersons and Establish a Communication Center. For each crisis, and perhaps for all crises, your committee should identify a spokesperson who will be the focal point for communications during the crisis period. An organization does not want to have several persons making comments to stakeholders. If that were to occur then it is possible that conflicting messages emanating from the same alleged source (your organization) could confuse the stakeholders and dilute the value of your overall communication plan. An organization doesn't want one person commenting that the procedure you are following is the official plan and another musing about whether in this instance your company will be following protocol.

The organization also needs to establish a place that will serve as the headquarters for communicating during crisis. This location needs to be equipped with phones, computers, fax machines, and any other equipment required for the "nervous system" of your operation. If print documents are part of any plan, then these materials should be located in or near this center. Monitoring media reaction is part of the crisis communication plan. The center therefore should be equipped with televisions, radios, and personnel to permit such monitoring. A place should be set aside for examining print and computer/electronic media content. An organization may decide to employ a "clipping service" like *Bacon's* to assess media reaction during crises. A clipping service is an organization that is hired to "clip" all relevant media messages related to a client's needs. "Clip," given contemporary media, is no longer a descriptive or inclusive word for what these clipping services, like Bacon's, do. However, the term clipping is still used. Should you wish to discover how the three local television stations have responded to a measles epidemic you could employ the clipping service to assess media reaction as opposed to doing the monitoring yourself. See Figure 13.1

8. Record the Plan. After creating the crisis communication plan for any anticipated event, the committee needs to prepare written versions of the plan. The committee should ensure that all persons who will be required to participate in the implementation of the plan have a copy and are familiar with their roles. As appropriate, the committee or committee representatives should meet with key organizational members and explain that a plan for crisis is in place. For example, all internal medical services staff at your university should be made aware that a crisis communication plan is in place in the case of a student epidemic—regardless of whether the informed persons will have an active role in the implementation of the communication plan.

9. Simulate and Coach. It is one thing to plan for a crisis and another to be able to implement the plan.

- If part of your approach to a particular crisis involves subjecting a spokesperson to a press conference, then it is wise to simulate the press conference for that spokesperson.
- If you intend for the head of campus public safety to meet with parents after an unfortunate incident on campus, you want to give the head of public safety an opportunity to practice, in a relatively safe environment, the presentation

Figure 13-1 **Clipping services**

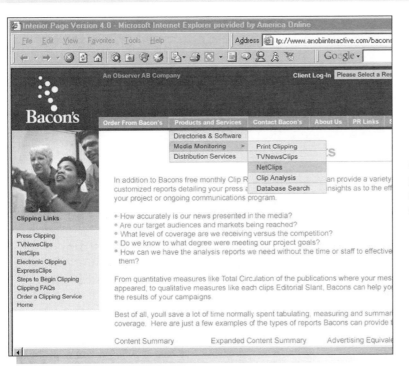

Clipping services can provide valuable services for crisis communications.

Courtesy of Bacon's Information, Inc. www.bacons.com.

she or he would give to the parents. Your group would be wise to simulate the tense and confrontational question and answer session that would likely follow that presentation.

- If in an attempt to reach your employees following an Anthrax-type scare, you intend to hold an immediate video teleconference to be "broadcast" internally, you would want to see how quickly you could set up that teleconference in terms of notifying audiences, setting up the studio, and "broadcasting" the message.

10. ***Update Periodically.*** The best scenario that can develop for the crisis communication team is that its plans are never implemented. However, the absence of crisis does not eliminate the necessity for the committee. Every 3 months the committee should reconvene to

- Review the crisis communication plans that are presently in place
- Ensure that all contact information for key persons remains the same
- Consider any other potential crises
- Plan for any other potential crises

ETHICAL PROBE

A CRISIS COMMUNICATOR'S CRISIS

Assume that you work in the corporate communication department for a struggling cooperative bank in a local municipality. Your job, in part, has involved creating crisis communication plans and, when necessary, implementing these plans.

Assume that you suspect that a manager—one of your colleagues—is sexually harassing one of the female employees. Further assume that you approach the employee and she reluctantly acknowledges that your suspicions are, in fact, the case. However, she requests that you not say anything about the harassment because she intends to leave the organization shortly and does not want to get involved with what she believes would be a drawn out battle of charges and countercharges.

You feel conflicted because you fear that while this woman might leave, your colleague may well begin to harass the employee who replaces the departed woman. In fact, for all you know, this manager may have been harassing others at the bank for years. Eventually, you decide to go to your superior and, without identifying the victim, you describe the charges. You are surprised to discover that no action is taken against the offending manager. Grapevine information suggests that senior management is aware of the intolerable behavior of your colleague, yet, apparently, is tolerating it.

The responsible position, you believe, would be to make public the harassment, and the fact that top management is ignoring it. To do this, however, would put your job in jeopardy. Even if you were to notify internal and external audiences anonymously, you would be jeopardizing the health of the struggling bank that pays your salary. In addition, because of your specific organizational responsibilities you would be placed in the awkward position of having to communicate to the internal and external stakeholders regarding the inevitable crisis that you, in actuality, precipitated.

Do you have an ethical responsibility to your firm to maintain silence in order to avoid a crisis to which you, yourself, would need to respond?

RECOMMENDATIONS FOR CRISIS COMMUNICATORS

When one reviews what has been written about crisis communication, a number of suggestions recur about how to act and respond in times of crisis. Below is a list of the recurring advice.

Respond quickly. All recommendations for crisis communicators emphasize the need for speedy reactions. Delayed comments by chief executives in the EXXON Valdez case, for example, proved disastrous for EXXON. The first 24 hours after a crisis is the most critical period.[16] Marra argues that excellent crisis communication "requires the ability to provide information to an organization's publics almost immediately."[17]

Use your plan. One of the problems with crisis communication is that in the throes of the crisis, organizations sometimes do not use the plan they have in place. This was the case with the Space Shuttle Challenger disaster in 1986. NASA had a

© 2002 THE NEW YORKER COLLECTION FROM CARTOONBANK.COM. ALL RIGHTS RESERVED.

"Look, Let's just say I haven't seen anything, Charlie hasn't heard anything, and Tom hasn't said anything."

In times of crisis, organizational communicators are urged not to stonewall, be silent, or be deceptive.

procedure for dealing with flight failure, but their plan was not implemented as designed. Your organization must be committed to using the plan that you have painstakingly established. The simulation step discussed earlier can be helpful in that your team will gain experience executing the plan prior to any incident.

Be accessible. Do not risk the wrath of internal or external stakeholders. Employees and media representatives will need information and will become frustrated if your plan doesn't include some way for these stakeholders to reach you.

Remember your internal stakeholders. The tendency is for crisis communicators to focus on the media and other external populations. Crisis communication is much more than external image management. Crisis communicators are compelled to consider internal stakeholders to be as central to the process as external stakeholders.

Avoid silence and "no comments." In Chapter 3, we discussed how messages are sometimes communicated regardless of speaker intent. We know that what has been communicated is not what we say, but how receivers perceive what we say. We also know that people can say nothing at all, and yet will still be communicating.

When spokespersons say "No comment," they are sending messages that are probably perceived negatively. A "no comment" is likely to imply that the company has something to hide. Kearns suggests that "silence in a crisis is never golden."[18] Olcott comments that one should never "hide behind a no comment. . . . If there's information you can't disclose, give a reason why."[19] Pirozzolo writes, "Never, never appear on camera with a lawyer, and remember saying 'No comment' is about as positive as taking 'the Fifth.' "[20]

Be truthful. Without question, the most oft-written recommendation pertaining to crisis communication relates to the requirement that communicators be open and "transparent" with their messages. Whether the suggestion is to be "credible"[21] "obviously open,"[22] "candid,"[23] or "scrupulously honest,"[24] the idea is the same: shoot straight. Clients are advised by one consultant to "be as forthcoming as they can be, and then be a little more forthcoming."[25]

Crisis communication is an important element of effective organizational communication. There is a cliché that suggests that the only things one can be sure of are "death and taxes." An organization might be wise to add, *crises,* to that list of inevitable eventualities.

Would you be able to create a crisis communication plan for an organization to which you belong? Could you develop a plan for your former high school? For your college?

Jason Vines, former Vice President for Communication, Ford Motor Company

Jason Vines is a principal in the Midwest Office of Strat@comm, a Washington D.C.-based firm dedicated to strategic communication counseling. Prior to joining his present company, Vines served as Vice President for Communication for the Ford Motor Company. In that role, Vines led the internal and external communications for Ford and was at the helm during the tempestuous crisis related to damaged Firestone tires that were on Ford vehicles. Prior to his stint at Ford, Jason Vines worked for Nissan North America. For his efforts in rebuilding Nissan's image worldwide, Automotive News named Vines the 1999 "All Star" in public relations. He began his career working for the Chrysler Corporation in 1983.

The key to crisis communication comes down very simply to this: openness, honesty, and credibility. Eventually the truth catches up. And it catches up a lot faster in the twenty-first century than it ever did before. Twenty years ago something that occurred in the Far East might take some time before people in the West would hear about it. Now the information is spread in 20 seconds.

You don't have to go much beyond the front pages of your newspaper to see why honesty is the key to effective crisis communication. Look at Enron and Arthur Andersen. They both were involved in deception. Citizens do not like companies and persons who are deceptive. Remember Nixon. When it became clear that he was covering up, the people went for the jugular. It's wise, in a very practical sense, to be sincere and apologize when you are wrong. If you remember, in the mid-1980s Chrysler was faced with a crisis. Some assembly plant officials were rolling back the odometers on so-called new cars and shipping these driven cars to dealers as new. What did Iacocca do? He came right out, apologized, acknowledged that some company people had engaged in that activity, said it was stupid, and promised that it would not happen again. People respect that kind of corporate behavior.

With all the communication tools we have, it all comes down to being frank. And a lie by omission is still a lie. Any notion that ambiguity is somehow strategic or justifiable, I categorically state is nonsense. Deception, whether explicit or implicit, is strategic—a strategic lie that will catch up to you sooner rather than later. When it does, your credibility is kaput.

The Ford-Firestone situation was a gut-wrenching time. Firestone was either constantly getting the facts wrong or not being forthright, and it was extraordinarily difficult to keep reacting to their bogus communications. We were getting "Scud Missile" attacks from them daily that we had to address. Eventually, the media caught on to them. When you lose your credibility in crisis communication, you are a "dead man walking."

You can plan for crises, but the best way to do this is get your team on board. You want to have a very solid communication system in place ahead of time. Some of the most powerful external communication is word of mouth. Your associates meet neighbors at soccer games, weddings, and various community activities. The neighbors may ask them about the situation at the company. If your organization has created a solid communication system, and has communicated credibly to its own employees, the messages the employees relay to their neighbors, friends, and relatives can very much enhance the quality of your overall crisis communication effort.

SUMMARY

A Toolbox

1. Crisis communication is an essential component of organizational communication.

2. Crisis communication is a component of crisis management; it is not the same as crisis management. Crisis communication is fundamentally different from image management, because not all messages that are communicated during crisis are related to building or restoring the company image. Also, crisis communication must involve communicating to internal as well as external receivers.

3. Effective crisis communication requires:
   - Support from top management
   - Comprehensive brainstorming regarding potential crises
   - Identification of internal and external stakeholders
   - Designated spokepersons
   - A commitment to implement the plan

4. Crisis communicators are advised to:
   - Quickly respond to crisis situations
   - Be scrupulously honest when communicating with your internal and external stakeholders.

DISCUSSION QUESTIONS

1. Why was crisis communication planning essential in the months preceding January 2000?

2. Why is the word *stakeholder* used in the language of crisis communication instead of *receiver*?

3. Why would a presidential aspirant be wise to have a crisis communication plan? What types of crises have presidential candidates faced? For those crises, who were the internal stakeholders?

4. At your university, who should comprise the crisis communication team?

5. How can poor communication during a crisis intensify a crisis?

6. Why do stakeholders have to be separated into discrete populations?

7. Is crisis communication planning an organizational communication imperative? Explain.

8. Please read the case below and respond to the questions at the end of the case.

CASE FOR ANALYSIS

Case 13.2—The Bayside Inn

A prestigious East Coast inn located in a resort community had enjoyed a fine reputation for decades. Sitting aloft a gorgeous bay, the inn had 70 rooms, a four star restaurant, an outdoor bar with magnificent views of the water, and several function rooms. The Bayside Inn was open year round and attracted affluent customers. Men and women were required to dress formally for dining and there was never a shortage of persons willing and eager—if one were to judge by the long waiting lists—to pay large sums and wear whatever was prescribed in order to dine (and be seen) at the Bayside Inn. In the worst of times—during the recession years of the mid-1970s and late-1980s—the Bayside was filled to capacity regardless of season.

In the summer of 2001 the Bayside Inn nearly went out of business. In July 1999 several persons who had eaten at the Bayside were hospitalized with food poisoning. Subsequently, articles in *The Gazette,* a local newspaper, suggested that the illnesses were likely the result of a problem with meat served at the Bayside.

When contacted by *The Gazette* the general manager of the Bayside indignantly refuted the charges. He characterized the rumors and newspaper articles as "absurd." His entire statement was printed in the newspaper:

> The Bayside Inn, as all who have dined here for years are well aware, has impeccable standards for quality and cleanliness. These rumors are absurd and slanderous. Anyone who assumes that these lies are truths is simply mistaken.

However, within a week of having made the remarks, several employees of the Bayside became ill and were bedridden. Matters became worse when a subsequent issue of *The Gazette* included a feature about seven persons who had become violently sick after attending a wedding that had been held at, and catered by, the Bayside.

Management attempted to thwart the negative publicity by quickly issuing statements reiteratively denying that any foodstuffs from the Bayside were responsible for the epidemic. The owner, the executive chef, and then again the general manager claimed that it was a matter of coincidence that these diners became ill after visiting the inn.

Nevertheless, the community grapevine continued to be active and *The Gazette* continued to pursue the story. At one point, a *Gazette* reporter interviewed a disgruntled former Bayside sous chef who commented that he had witnessed "iffy cleanliness" in the kitchen. The executive chef immediately denied the charge. However, a day after the "iffy cleanliness" comment appeared in *The Gazette,* a waiter was approached by a college student intern from a local radio station. The intern, prepared with a tape recorder and microphone, stopped the waiter and asked him what he thought of the conditions at the Bayside. The young man flippantly commented, "I've seen cleaner places." The waiter later said that he hadn't been thinking when he made the remark and had been "kind of in a hurry to get home." Nevertheless, the radio station played the "I've seen cleaner places" sound bite every hour on the hour during their local news segments.

The Bayside Inn management fired the waiter immediately. They then attempted to portray the sous chef's comments as the whinings of a bitter ex-employee.

"What do you expect Harold to say? We fired him because he was irresponsible. Of course, he would speak disparagingly about the inn."

The local radio station made the waiter's firing a cause celebre. *The Gazette* printed an interview with Harold, the former sous chef.

When the public outcry over the young waiter's treatment for being "honest" became too much for the inn, the general manager rehired the waiter and promised a "thorough investigation."

The thorough investigation never culminated with any conclusions. To date, there has never been any definitive evidence that customer or employee illness was related to food served at the Bayside. There has never been any acknowledgment by the inn that the community and staff illnesses were related to the Bayside.

Occupancy at the Bayside Inn dropped dramatically between 1999 and 2001. Despite offering several "specials," dropping the dress code requirements, and reducing room rates—even during season—the Bayside is struggling to stay in business.

- How could the Bayside have handled this situation differently?
- How should they have communicated to the public and to their staff?

Focus on Applications

Test your crisis vulnerability

1. Does your organization have a crisis communication plan in place?
2. If yes, is it up to date?
3. Has it been pre-tested?
4. Do you have a designated spokesperson?
5. Has the spokesperson had media training?
6. Do you have a crisis management team authorized and trained to be responsible and accountable in a crisis situation?
7. Has your organization evaluated what types of crisis situations are most likely to occur and which kind will have the most severe impact?[26]

ENDNOTES

[1]Barton, Laurence, *Crisis in Organizations: Managing and Communicating in the Heat of Chaos,* Southwestern, 1993, p. 2.

[2]Remsik, Jeffrey, "A Crisis Communication Plan—a Vital Element in Y2K Readiness," *Direct Marketing,* July 1999, p. 33.

[3]Ibid.

[4]Marra, Francis J., "Crisis Communication Plans: Poor Predictors of Excellent Crisis Public Relations," *Public Relations Review,* Winter 1998, p. 468.

[5]Kiger, Patrick, "Lessons from a Crisis: How Communication Kept a Company Together," *Workforce,* November 2001, pp. 28, 32. The entire article is found on pp. 28, 30, and 32–36. Aon's use of the web is explained in detail in the article.

[6]Leaper, Rae, ABC "Important Single Purpose Programs," in *Inside Organizational Communication,* edited by Carol Reuss and Donn Silvis, Longman, 1985, pp. 259–261. The list in the text is an edited version of her suggestions. The discussion that follows the list is not from the Leaper article.

[7]Lukaszweski, James, *Public Relations Quarterly,* Fall 1997, vol. 42, no. 3, pp. 13–14. The list that appears in the text comes from Lukaszewski; the examples do *not, but are similar* to examples that the author provides. There are several other items on the author's list of trustbusting behaviors including: aloofness, no commitment, and irritation.

[8]Cited in op. cit., Kiger, p. 34.

[9]Benoit, William, "Image Repair Discourse and Crisis Communication," *Public Relations Review,* Summer 1997, vol. 23, no. 2, p. 184.

[10]Op. cit., Francis J. Marra, p. 465.

[11]See Robin Cohn, *The PR Crisis Bible: How to Take Charge of the Media When All Hell Breaks Loose.,* Truman Talley Books, St. Martin's Press, 2000, p. xii.

[12]Op. cit., Jeffrey Remsik, p. 34.

[13]The categories come from Ian Mitroff, *Managing Crises Before They Happen*, Amacom, 2001, pp. 34–35. The examples are not from his book.

[14]Op. cit., Leaper, p. 161.

[15]Op. cit., Lukaszewski, p. 8.

[16]Op. cit., Remsik, p. 37. See also, op cit., Cohn, p. xi.

[17]Op. cit., Marra, p. 469.

[18]Kearns, I. M., "Protect Your Company's Image," *Communication World*, August/September 1998, vol. 15, no. 7, p. 42.

[19]Olcott, William, "Communicating in a Crisis," *Fund Raising Management*, October 1992, p. 6.

[20]Pirozzolo, Dick, "Crisis Communication Tips are Food for Thought:" *Nation's Restaurant News*, May 26, 1997, p. 22.

[21]Hoffman, Judith, "Stakeholder Focus, Effective Crisis Communication," *Chemical Market Reporter*, October 1, 2001, p. 28.

[22]Op. cit., Kearns P. M. p. 42.

[23]Op. cit., Lukaszweski p. 10–11.

[24]Op. cit., Olcott,

[25]Mitroff, Ian, *Managing Crises Before They Happen*, Amacom, 2001, p. 78.

[26]Op. cit., Remsik, p. 37.

14

Assessing Organizational Communication Quality

If you're not being critical about your business and yourself, you should be.
—Robert Heller, business author

We need very strong ears to hear ourselves judged frankly and because there are few who can endure frank criticism without being stung by it, those who venture to criticize us perform a remarkable act of friendship.
—Michel Eyquem de Montaigne, sixteenth-century French author

GETTY IMAGES/PHOTODISC

Case 14.1—*STIG: Perspectives of a Staffer*

Background

The Sales Technology and Information Group (STIG) of a large metropolitan HMO provides data analysis reports for the Sales and Services Department of the HMO. The STIG group is comprised of a manager, four analysts, one senior analyst, and two data coordinators. The nature of the work requires employees to have a strong technical background as well as business knowledge. Also critical to the position is the ability to communicate effectively with team members and other departments within the company.

Problem Description

The major communication problem in the department—according to one of the four analysts—is between the manager of STIG and her staff. The same staffer reports that a secondary problem relates to the communication between the manager and other departments, particularly the Sales and Services Department.

The analyst summarizes the nature of communication within STIG as follows:

☐ **One-on-one meetings:** *On a biweekly basis, the manager is scheduled to meet with each staff member to review projects and issues. The major problem with this forum is that the manager regularly cancels these meetings. Oftentimes, staff members will "save" information that they need to discuss with the manager only to find out that the manager is not available to meet as scheduled. This is particularly frustrating for staff members who spend time preparing for this meeting only to arrive at the manager's office and be told that the manager had to cancel. Because these sessions are regularly called off, information that the manager should be receiving is not communicated on time, and in other cases information the manager should receive is not communicated at all.*

☐ **Staff meetings:** *On a biweekly basis (alternative week of the one-on-one meetings), the manager holds staff meetings. The meetings are 2 hours in length and dreaded by most staff members. The manager sets the agenda for the meeting, but the staff does not receive the agenda until the time of the meeting. Therefore, staff often finds themselves unprepared to speak about specific topics on the agenda. In addition, the meetings often run over the allotted 2-hour timeframe. Furthermore, certain items on the agenda are not particularly relevant to the group (for example, information about sales presentations) and some team members feel that the manager "just likes to hear herself talk."*

- **Written communications:** *The majority of the written communication between team members and the manager is via e-mail. In fact, e-mail is often used instead of face-to-face interaction. The manager is very timely when responding to e-mail inquires and often forwards work requests and policy information via e-mail. In some cases, e-mail has been effective but in other cases, a face-to-face meeting may be more appropriate because of the nature of the topic being discussed or the need for immediate verbal and nonverbal feedback on the issue.*

As it relates to communication with other departments, the analyst contends that the Sales and Services Department repeatedly complains that information from STIG is not timely or clear. Occasionally, there are complaints about the accuracy of information. It is the STIG manager who is responsible for communicating information to Sales and Services.

- *Is there a communication problem in this department?*

- *Can you assume that the assessments of this one staff member are accurate?*

- *Assume that a number of staffers speak to the manager about problems with communication in the department. Further assume that the manager decides that it would be best to get an assessment of communication quality from a professional. Consequently, she hires you to examine the quality of organizational communication. How would you proceed?*

- *Assume that you conduct a test and find that the manager is indeed deficient in terms of organizational communication. How would you tactfully communicate these conclusions to her?*

ABSTRACT

In the preceding chapters we have made the case that communication is central to organizational activity and have discussed the various components of healthy organizational communication.

If communication quality is an essential component of organizational success, then an organization must be able to assess how well or how poorly it is communicating. Methods of measuring communication quality in organizations are called *communication audits*. These tests are designed to examine the communication skills, climate, networks, and information management within an organization. Successful audits require understanding audit objectives, selecting appropriate testing methods, and reporting results meaningfully. This chapter explains how you can examine the extent to which your organization is meeting its communication related responsibilities.

OBJECTIVES

When you have completed this chapter, you should be able to:

☐ Define the phrase *communication audit*.
☐ List what an audit must test in order for it to be valid.
☐ Describe the strengths and weaknesses of various audits.
☐ Describe the components of what is called the *ICA audit*.
☐ Identify responsibilities and challenges related to reporting audit results.

WHAT IS A COMMUNICATION AUDIT?

Most people are familiar with the word *audit* but associate the term with an accounting procedure or an action of the Internal Revenue Service. A financial audit is an assessment of the financial condition of a particular organization or person. The word *audit* has a similar meaning in organizational communication study. In the same way a financial audit tests the financial conditions of an organization, a communication audit is an examination of the quality of communication within an organization. In simplest terms, an audit is a test.

Sometimes the phrase *communication audit* is perceived to mean a particular type of audit called the *ICA communication audit*. We'll discuss the ICA audit technique later in this chapter. However, at this point keep in mind that a communication audit is *any* test that is designed to examine communication quality within an organization.

Gordon identifies several values of conducting communication audits. Communication audits can:

- Portray the overall nature of communication in a particular organization
- Describe the value and relevance of specific communication tools
- Assess whether employees have received key messages
- Help organizations develop a strategic plan for overall communication quality
- Develop an ongoing process for measuring effectiveness of communication in an organization.[1]

A key to effectively realizing these potential benefits is using an auditing technique that will provide meaningful results.

AUDIT QUALITIES AND COMPONENTS

Validity and Reliability

Two terms used in testing are **validity** and **reliability.** Regardless of what is being examined, your test needs to be both valid and reliable. A **valid** test is one that tests what it is designed to test. A **reliable** test is one that could be replicated; that is, if you were to employ a reliable test a second or third time, you would get similar results on the subsequent occasions as you did on the initial, or any other, occasion.

These qualities are very important to auditors or anyone who is conducting any research study. In order to clarify the terms, consider some examples related first to validity and then to reliability.

Validity. Assume you took a course called *The History of Direct Marketing.* If your 2-hour final exam for the course required that you analyze nine lengthy Direct Marketing campaigns, then that test would *not* be valid. It would not be considered valid for at least two reasons. The first reason is that your course covered the *history* of Direct Marketing. The final exam appears to be based on specific Direct Marketing campaigns. Therefore, the final exam did not test what it was designed to test. Also, since you needed to analyze nine lengthy cases, you would be tested on how quickly you could read, since you only had 2 hours for the exam. The test wouldn't be testing your knowledge of the history of Direct Marketing, it would be testing how quickly you could analyze Marketing cases. Therefore, it would be an invalid test.

Consider another example. Assume that you were being tested to see if you could *deliver* a business presentation. An exam that only asked you to provide definitions of extemporaneous and manuscript speaking would *not* be valid. The test would have to include some behavioral component that evaluated how well you could deliver a speech, not simply if you knew the names of different presentation styles. Otherwise it would be invalid since it would not assess if you could *deliver* a business presentation. Similarly, any comprehensive communication audit should test what it was designed to test in order for it to be valid.

Problems with Narrow Communication Skill Testing. If an auditor decided to assess the communication skills of all employees in terms of their written, oral, listening, and reading capabilities, then that auditor could—if the testing mechanism was a good one—derive some meaningful information about employees' communication skill sets. However, as we have seen in previous chapters, organizational communication consists of much more than just employee writing and speaking skills. Therefore, in order to conduct a valid audit, we need to assess much more than individual communication skill sets. Were we only to assess skill proficiency, and assume that what we discovered reflected the core communication problems in the organization, we would be making a serious testing error. Our results would be both invalid and illusory.

Consider the following paragraphs. Each paragraph reviews a principle that has been discussed in the book. Also, each example suggests why parochial skill set testing will provide incomplete, invalid, and illusory audit results.

- Contemporary organizational communication requires understanding the relative values of alternative approaches to communicating information. We know, for example, that indiscriminate and overabundant e-mail usage can swamp diligent employees and undermine the overall communication system.

  Excellent writers or speakers may be skilled and gifted, but if they do not make wise choices when selecting media for communicating, their writing and speaking skills will be a limited asset.

- Source credibility is a key factor in effective organizational communication.

  Communication skill sets are irrelevant if receivers do not perceive a source's communications, however eloquently articulated, to be credible.

- Since most organizations are made up of interdependent units or departments, it is important to establish channels for communication between these related units.

  Regardless of communication set skill levels, these networks must exist in order for employees to exercise their inherent skills.

In sum, we know that organizational communication is multidimensional. Therefore, if all a company did when conducting (what was intended to be) a comprehensive organizational communication audit was test how efficiently people could read, write, speak, and listen, it would obtain test results that were incomplete. The analysis of this incomplete data would be worse than meaningless. The organization would be under the illusion that it had assessed its internal communication when it had simply examined an aspect of it.

Consider this analogy: Assume that you sensed that you needed a complete physical check-up. You wanted to be very sure that you were in good health and that no insidious infections were pervading your body. Would you be content to visit a dermatologist, and then be relieved when an unattractive blemish was removed? It is not likely that you would feel relieved. You would want the physical examination to be comprehensive.

Similarly, an organization communication audit must be comprehensive. Otherwise the test would not be valid. It would not be testing what it was designed to test.

Problems with Reliability. If you are the type of person who gets on the scale in the morning, you are no doubt interested in finding out how much you weigh. If you stand on the scale once and check your weight, and then get on the scale a second time and see that you weigh 40 pounds more than you had only seconds earlier, you would assume that there was something wrong with your scale. The results you were getting from standing on the scale were, apparently, not reliable. If the device was providing reliable results, the test of standing on the scale would yield about the same result each time you got on it.

Similarly, when you conduct any test, you want to make sure that the testing mechanism is such that the results you obtain one time will be similar to the results you would obtain on a second or third or any other occasion.

Let's look at an organizational communication example. Assume that you were going to audit the communication at your university. In order to accomplish your goal you decide to interview four separate groups of six persons. Each group would include a randomly selected population composed of two students, a faculty member, a chairperson, an academic dean, and a student affairs dean. Let's assume that during the group interview you plan to ask a comprehensive set of questions pertaining to organizational communication and you intend to meticulously record the responses. Subsequently, you and your team of analysts would review the records from each of the four groups and then draw conclusions about the quality of communication in the organization. Would this test be reliable?

It could be, but only would be, if you could conduct this test again and reproduce the results.

There are a number of reasons why your test might not be reliable. Let's assume you, personally, were not conducting all of the focus groups, but that you had four associates who were helpers. It would be essential that each associate asked questions and perceived responses the same way. If Mary and John were researchers, but Mary and John draw different conclusions from the same observation, then your test does not have reliability. Depending on who is conducting the focus group, the results will vary.

Consider another example: Let's assume you *were* doing all of the interviewing. After you completed interviewing the first group, you went on to conduct the second, third, and fourth focus group. It is possible that your recording during the fourth session might not be as meticulous as it was during the first. By the time you interviewed the fourth group, you might have stopped asking follow-up questions or may have even altered the original questions you were to pose to the group. The test would not be reliable. Depending on fatigue and focus level, the test results will vary.

Relationship Between Reliability and Validity. Reliability is a precondition for validity, but does not determine validity. That is, a test would not be valid by virtue of it being reliable. However, if a test wasn't reliable then it could not be valid. *That is, if a test was not reliable it could not be actually testing what it was designed to test.*

If, of course, a test was not valid, the reliability of the test would be irrelevant. It would not matter if you could or could not replicate the results from a study that was not examining what it was designed to examine.

Audit Components

As we have discussed, a communication audit must be multidimensional in order to be valid. Two questions naturally surface: (1) What are those dimensions that need to be tested and (2) what does each dimension entail?

Dean suggests that an audit must examine information management, organizational networks, the communication climate, and individual communication skill sets.[2] Let's examine each of these areas.

Information Management. Organizations must intelligently communicate information to employees. A valid audit will test whether information is getting to employees and whether vehicles used for communicating information are effective. Specifically an audit will address the following questions:

- Are messages communicated to employees that describe job tasks, organizational policies, and performance evaluation?
- Are these messages communicated in a timely manner?
- Do employees consider these messages credible and pertinent?
- Are messages communicated clearly and accurately?
- Does the organization use appropriate methods for communicating information?

For example,

- Are e-mail, the intranet, and teleconferencing used appropriately?
- Are printed manuals, the company newsletter, and internal magazines effective?
- Are briefings efficiently conducted?
- Are messages disseminated at the annual meeting effective?
- Are bulletin boards used effectively?

- What "noises" typically create "message distortion?"

Communication Networks. In order for an audit to be valid it must test the quality of the various networks within the organizations. Specifically,

1. **Regarding Upward Networks**
    - Are the channels that link subordinates to superiors credible?
    - Can subordinates comfortably communicate
      - Problems?
      - Suggestions?
      - Feedback related to messages sent downward?
    - Is there a mechanism for providing feedback to upwardly sent messages?

2. **Regarding Downward Networks**

   - Are there channels that allow management to communicate to subordinates?
   - Do serial transmissions create
     - Serial distortions?
     - Untimely communications?

3. **Regarding Horizontal Networks**

   - Do networks exist that allow for interaction between interrelated departments?
   - Are there "redundancies" ensuring interdepartmental "penetration"? (See Chapter 6 for explanation of "penetration".)
   - Does interdepartmental communication reflect cooperation or does it reflect compeition?

4. **Regarding External Networks**

   - Are there navigable channels that permit prospective clients, or current clients, an opportunity to communicate with the organization?
   - Are there channels that allow organizational representatives easy access to clients and potential customers?

5. **Regarding Formal Network Systems**

   - To what extent does information travel on the informal network or grapevine, as opposed to the formal network?
   - Is the informal network overwhelming the formal network?
   - Who are the *isolates, bridges,* and *liaisons* within the organization?
   - How would employees describe the grapevine in the organization?

Communication Climate. As we saw in Chapter 7, Redding and others argue that the climate is a significant component for organizational success. Auditors, therefore, would need to test to see if the climate was conducive for quality communication. Specifically,

   - Is the organization's climate supportive or defensive?
   - Do employees consider the organization's communications credible?
   - Would employees characterize the organization as open or "transparent" in terms of willingness to share information?
   - Do communications reflect a credible desire to emphasize excellence?
   - Are employees encouraged to voice their opinions and participate in the decision making of the organization?
   - Do employees feel as if management communicates messages of support when supportiveness is warranted?

Communication Skill Sets. If, as we have seen, a large percentage of an employee's daily activities deal with some form of communication, then employees must possess basic communication competencies. Daly lists seven skill sets that need to be tested.[3]

1. **Predisposition to Communicate.** Specifically, are employees inclined to communicate or do they have a predisposition toward avoiding interaction? Shyness or communication apprehension is not an insignificant factor to examine. It is possible that when compelled to speak someone may reflect oral communication competencies. However, they may rarely exercise these skills if not compelled to do so.[4]

2. **Knowledge of Communication Principles.** Are individuals aware of basic tenets of communication, for example, the need for audience analysis, the concept of communication noise, message fidelity, and message distortion? The assumption is that understanding principles will affect communication competence.

3. **Public Speaking Capabilities.** Can individuals deliver messages clearly, use appropriate language, select appropriate speaking styles, use extemporaneous as well as manuscript formats, organize a message, handle questions, adapt to audiences, or use visual aids?

4. **Interviewing Skills.** Can individuals interview prospective employees? Can they interview for internal positions?

5. **Listening Skills.** Can employees comprehend information, evaluate what they hear, nonverbally display they are listening to messages, and successfully make use of what they have heard?[5]

6. **Conversational Performance.** Conversational performance includes abilities to express thoughts clearly; encourage and generate information from others; understand what others are saying; adapt to particular situations, persons, topics; and cope with deception, persuasion, and difficult people.[6]

7. **Communicate in Small Groups.** An assessment of one's ability to communicate in small groups would examine the ability to participate, focus on group goals, assess the process of group interaction while contributing (notion of participant-observation discussed in Chapter 8), and help make intelligent group decisions.[7]

METHODS FOR CONDUCTING AUDITS

Once you have clarified what it is you need to test, you are ready to begin to conduct the audit. Your primary consideration involves selecting an appropriate research method for collecting and analyzing the data.

Audit Techniques

There are several methods that can be used for conducting communication audits. Below you will find a brief description of a number of approaches. As will likely become apparent, each approach need not be used in isolation, but can be used in combination with some of the other methods. As will also become apparent, some of these techniques when *not* used in combination with other methods will present problems related to validity and reliability.

Focus Groups. Focus group is a phrase used to describe a group of individuals who convene to respond to questions about a particular issue. Marketing companies, for example, utilize focus groups to discover how customers react to certain types of products. Communication auditors can use focus groups as well. A group of organizational men and women are invited to meet, and they are asked questions pertain-

GETTY IMAGES/PHOTODISC

A communication log is difficult to keep. Employees may not always capture how they have reacted to the messages they receive, and this information can be relevant to the over-all assessment of communication in the organization.

ing to communication in the organization. The groups can be heterogeneous or homogeneous. Sometimes a facilitator will sit in a room and another researcher will be seated behind a one-way window. (The participants would be made aware that there is an external observer.) After concluding several focus groups, researchers compile information gleaned from the group interviews and draw conclusions based on that pooled information.

Communication Logs. A communication log is a diary completed by individuals who are asked to document their communication-related activities. Participants might record whom they phoned, when they responded to e-mail, reactions to briefing sessions, memoranda they received, and other communication-related information. Subsequently, researchers would collect the diaries, review them, and draw conclusions based on the information contained therein.

Observation. Sometimes this technique is called *shadowing*. Observers or shadowers simply follow a participant during a specific period of time. The observers record information regarding the persons' communication activities. It is, in part, an objective assessment of what is taking place and a subjective assessment of the quality of interaction. An observer may record that a manager met with four employees individually to discuss performance, and also that the manager spoke and listened effectively during the period. The subjective assessments could be based on objective criteria. That is, an observer might have a checklist of things to look for while observing, but still needs to make qualitative assessments of how well or how poorly the subject was meeting these communication objectives.

Executive One-on-One Interviews. Instead of a focus group composed of executives, this approach is dyadic. An auditor meets individually with several executives and asks questions pertaining to the executives' perspectives on organizational communication issues. The interview questions could be similar to those used for focus groups. For example, questions might include: What is your feeling about the value of your company's intranet? Do you prefer printed methods for communicating information? Are you comfortable using electronic media when you need to relay information to your subordinates? Do you feel as if you receive adequate information from related departments? Do you find that people communicate efficiently during your various meeting sessions?

Surveys. A survey used in this context is synonymous with what is typically called a questionnaire. Employees are asked to write responses to questions pertaining to organizational communication issues. Respondents will complete a questionnaire, leave the completed forms with an auditor, and subsequently these results will be recorded and analyzed. This approach offers the advantage of anonymity. Also, surveys provide quantitative data that can be attractive to people who respond positively to results presented statistically. Finally, this approach allows for easy demographic comparisons. Let's assume that an audit is being conducted at an organization that has multiple sites. Further assume that one demographic question asks respondents to indicate the particular site where they are located. Survey analysis will allow auditors to make distinctions between work sites in terms of communication quality.

Communication Experience or Critical Incident Interviews. Critical incidents refers to a particular type of interview where the respondent is asked, essentially, only two questions. He or she is asked to describe an excellent communication experience and to describe a poor communication experience. The incident must indeed be an experience. If a respondent were to say, "Our meetings are terrible," the auditor would ask for more specific information and ask the interviewee to describe a particular incident when a meeting was problematic because of some communication-related issue. Auditors would subsequently review these experiences and determine if certain types of problems and successes recur.

Publication Content Analysis. Content analysis is a very specific method of examining communication content. Some people use the phrase *content analysis* to mean any subjective assessment of communication content. However, originally the phrase was meant to describe a quantitative procedure that is used for examining such matters as sexist language in elementary school readers, national perspectives on international issues, language usage in novels, and so on.[8] For communication audits, content analysis would be used to examine publications, such as a company's rules and regulation manuals, newsletters, websites, or any other text-based communications. Content analysis has also been used to evaluate nontext material as well; for example, photographs in publications.

ECCO Analysis. ECCO analysis (Figure 14-1) was developed by Keith Davis who was mentioned in Chapter 6 when we discussed communication networks and the grapevine. ECCO is an acronym for Episodic Communication Channels in Organizations. The ECCO analysis procedure requires that participants complete a short survey referring to a particular unit of information they had received.

For example, a question might read: "Do you know that Joan Podkowsy has been appointed to be the head of Marketing?"

If respondents write "no," the survey is over. If the respondent writes "yes," she or he would be asked from whom they had first heard the information, and where they were when they heard it. If the respondent has the general idea that Joan Podkowsy has been hired but is not sure what she was hired to do, that information would be recorded on the form as well. With ECCO analysis, an auditor hopes to acquire a sense of message flow and use of organizational networks, both formal and informal.

Figure 14-1   Example of an ECCO analysis survey sheet

Gender: ☐ Female   ☐ Male
Age: ☐ Under 20 years   ☐ 21–30   ☐ 31–40   ☐ 41–50   ☐ Over 50 yrs
Post: ☐ Full-time   ☐ Part-time   ☐ Temporary full-time
            ☐ Temporary part-time
How long employed: ☐ Under 1 year   ☐ 1–5 yrs   ☐ 6–10 yrs
            ☐ 11–15 yrs   ☐ Over 15 yrs
Present position: ☐ I don't supervise anyone   ☐ Middle manager
            ☐ Senior manager
Other (please specify) _____
What is your job? _____

Please tick the box beside each of the statements below if you knew this information before you completed this questionnaire. If you did not know it, please leave the box blank. If you leave all boxes blank do not complete any more of the questionnaire.

☐ Sue Bloggs is leaving.
☐ Sue Bloggs is going to Head Office.
☐ Sue Bloggs was Head of Customer Services.
☐ The post of Head of Customer Services will not be re-advertised.
☐ The new Head of Communications is Davinder Patel.
☐ Davinder Patel will now be responsible for customer services.

From what *source* did you first hear or read about this information (please tick only one box)?

Written medium   Talking medium
☐ Company newsletter   ☐ Colleague
☐ Notice on staff board   ☐ Line manager
☐ Formal memo   ☐ Senior manager
☐ E-mail   ☐ Overheard someone
Other (please specify) _____

Through which *channel* did you learn about this information?

☐ Staff meeting   ☐ Informal conversation
☐ Company video   ☐ Telephone call
☐ Written communication
Other (please specify) _____

When did you first learn about this information (please circle only one)?

Days ago   Today   1   2   3   4   5   6
Weeks ago   1   2   3   4

Where were you when you first learned about this information?

☐ Cafeteria   ☐ At my normal working location
☐ While visiting another department   ☐ At a formal staff meeting
☐ Outside of the company
Other (please specify) _____

Sample ECCO survey adapted from Hargie, Owen, and Dennis Tourish, "Data Collection Log-Sheet Methods," in *Handbook of Communication Audits for Organizations*, Eds. Owen Hargie and Dennis Tourish, Routledge Press, 2000, pp. 109–110.

Skill Testing. Previously, we discussed the need for employees to have basic communication skill competencies. In the endnotes, there are references to tests and compendia of tests for skill assessment. (See notes 5, 6, and 7)

Some communication audits including the ICA audit described in the next section do not involve testing employee skill competence, but they do contain questions that ask employees if they perceive other employees to have such competence. That is, instead of testing to see if all those who give daily briefings can deliver these presentations well, the audit would assess whether those who listened to the briefings were satisfied with qualities of the presenter and the presentations.

ICA Audit

In the early 1970s, the International Communication Association (ICA) developed an audit tool in an attempt to address problems associated with the relatively weak communication audits that had been previously utilized.[9] The ICA audit is sufficiently well known (and auditing is sufficiently misunderstood) so that too many people are under the assumption that all communication audits are ICA audits. This is incorrect from two vantage points. First, as we have discussed, there are a number of types of communication audits. Second, the ICA audit has been in the public domain since 1979.[10] Therefore, any person can adapt what was the ICA audit, or use parts of it. Consequently, what passes for the ICA audit may be different from one user to another.

The International Communication Association is an organization of scholars and students (typically graduate students) who are interested in studying communication. It is the second largest such organization of communication scholars. (The largest is, ironically, the National Communication Association formerly called the Speech Communication Association. One might think intuitively that an international organization would be larger than a national organization, but the titles are misleading.) The ICA publishes several journals including the *Journal of Communication* and *Human Communication Research.*

When people join the ICA they become members of interest groups within the ICA. One might join the Interpersonal Communication interest group, Political Communication interest group, the Organizational Communication interest group, or any one of several others. In the late 1960s and early 1970s, scholars in the Organizational Communication interest group developed the ICA audit. In addition to creating a standard and valid auditing procedure, the ICA expected to collect sufficient data to create a data bank of information depicting how organizations communicated and the problems that might exist across organizations. There are five parts to what is referred to as the ICA audit.

1. Questionnaire. The questionnaire was a standard survey that was to be administered to all members of an organization.[11] There were 122 questions on the survey including demographic questions. An individual organization could add questions that were relevant to the particular organization. Persons responded to the audit anonymously and all respondents were told that they would receive a "short report" of the audit results. This short report was, essentially, a synopsis of the more detailed analysis provided to the client. Questions on the survey pertained to several communication areas including networks, information management, climate, and perception of skill sets. (See Table 14.1 for Sample Format)

2. Interview Procedure. Subsequent to the analysis of the survey data, auditors would ask a series of questions to a percentage of the population that had been either

TABLE 14.1   SAMPLE FORMAT OF ICA COMMUNICATION AUDIT SURVEY

Receiving Information from Others

Topic Area	This is the amount of information I receive now					This is the amount of information I need to receive				
	Very Little	*Little*	*Some*	*Great*	*Very Great*	*Very Little*	*Little*	*Some*	*Great*	*Very Great*
How well I am doing in my job	**1.** 1	2	3	4	5	**2.** 1	2	3	4	5
My job duties	**3.** 1	2	3	4	5	**4.** 1	2	3	4	5
Organizational policies	**5.** 1	2	3	4	5	**6.** 1	2	3	4	5
Pay and benefits	**7.** 1	2	3	4	5	**8.** 1	2	3	4	5
How technological changes affect my job	**9.** 1	2	3	4	5	**10.** 1	2	3	4	5
Mistakes and failures of my organization	**11.** 1	2	3	4	5	**12.** 1	2	3	4	5
How I am being judged	**13.** 1	2	3	4	5	**14.** 1	2	3	4	5
How my job-related problems are being handled	**15.** 1	2	3	4	5	**16.** 1	2	3	4	5
How organization decisions are made that affect my job	**17.** 1	2	3	4	5	**18.** 1	2	3	4	5
Promotion and advancement opportunities in my organization	**19.** 1	2	3	4	5	**20.** 1	2	3	4	5

Survey adapted from Gerald Goldhaber and Donald Rogers, *Auditing Organizational Communication*, Kendall Hunt Publishing Co. Dubuque, Iowa, 1979, p.6.

randomly or purposefully selected. There were two objectives for these interviews. The first was to obtain corroboration of the data gleaned from the survey. The second objective was to encourage respondents to elaborate.

Let's assume that data gleaned from the survey suggested that employees were very satisfied with information they had received regarding new products. During the interview respondents would be asked how they felt about information they received regarding new products. The hope would be that the respondents would comment that they indeed were satisfied with that information. If one respondent said they were unhappy, that would not be an issue. However, if several respondents indicated that they were not satisfied, then something would have had to have been wrong with the survey. Therefore an objective of the interview is to corroborate survey results.

After corroborating the information, an interviewer might pose the following question: What is there about the way the new product information was communicated that you liked? The respondent might comment that it was timely or that it was presented both orally and in writing. Whatever the response, the auditor would have additional explanatory information about the item in question.

3. Communication Experience. Originally, this was called a Critical Incident report. This technique used with the ICA audit is the same as the one described earlier in this chapter (see page 336).

TABLE 14.2   ICA COMMUNICATION AUDIT NETWORK ANALYSIS INSTRUMENT

During a typical workday, I usually communicate about work-related matters with the following people through the following channels:

	Identifi-cation	Formal Organizational Structure	Informal (Grapevine) Organizational Structure
Executive		**How important is the communication?**	
Stenographer-secretary	0001	_____ A B C D E	_____ A B C D E
Senior stenographer	0002	_____ A B C D E	_____ A B C D E
Executive secretary	0003	_____ A B C D E	_____ A B C D E
Assistant executive director	0004	_____ A B C D E	_____ A B C D E
Assistant manager	0005	_____ A B C D E	_____ A B C D E
Telephone operator	0006	_____ A B C D E	_____ A B C D E
Executive director	0007	_____ A B C D E	_____ A B C D E
Administration and Finance			
Assistant director for administration	0008	_____ A B C D E	_____ A B C D E
Typist	0009	_____ A B C D E	_____ A B C D E
Accounting clerk	0010	_____ A B C D E	_____ A B C D E
Accounting clerk-typist	0011	_____ A B C D E	_____ A B C D E
Assistant accountant	0012	_____ A B C D E	_____ A B C D E
Senior accountant	0013	_____ A B C D E	_____ A B C D E
Typist	0014	_____ A B C D E	_____ A B C D E
Stenographer	0015	_____ A B C D E	_____ A B C D E

Key: A = not at all important
   B = somewhat important
   C = fairly important
   D = very important
   E = extremely important

Gerald Goldhaber, *Organizational Communication*, Brown/Benchmark, sixth edition, 1993, p. 363.

4. Network Analysis. This component of the ICA audit involved employing a brief questionnaire as shown in Table 14.2. Members of a particular department were asked to complete the survey in order to gauge who in the group interacted with whom and to assess who was an isolate, a liaison, or bridge.[12] The goal of network analyses would be to juxtapose the formal network with the actual organizational network that involved both formal and informal channels.

5. Communication Diary. The communication diary component of the ICA audit was similar to the communication log explained previously in this chapter. Unlike the log, the ICA provided a form and a brief training session for participants. The ICA claimed that the diary would provide "indications of actual communication behavior among individuals, groups, and the entire organization."[13]

External or Internal Auditing

An audit can be conducted by external consultants or by internal agents. Some communication consulting companies will actually sell their products to clients. The clients can then administer the audit procedures themselves.[14] An organization would not have to buy any particular audit, however. An organization could—by studying

Measures of Organizational Communication

Comprehensive Measures of Organizational Communication

Communication Satisfaction Questionnaire (CSQ), Downs & Hazen
International Communication Audit Survey Questionnaire (ICA Audit)
Organizational Communication Development Audit Questionnaire (OCD Audit), O. Wiio
Organizational Communication Profile, R. W. Pace & B. D. Peterson
Organizational Communication Scale, K. H. Roberts and C. A. O'Reilley
Organizational Culture Survey, S. R. Glaser, S. Zamanou, & K. Hacker
Survey of Organizational Communication, S. DeWine & A. Taylor
Survey of Organizations, R. Likert.

Communication Competence

Communication Competence Scale
Communicator Competence Questionnaire
Interaction Involvement Scale
Relational Competence Scale, Cupach & B. Spitzberg

Conflict Communication

Conflict Management Message Style, R. Ross & S. DeWine
Conflict Management Survey, J. Hall
Conflict Management of Difference (MODE) Scale, K. Thomas & R. Kilman
Managerial Grid, R. R. Blake & J. S. Mouton
Organizational Communication Conflict Inventory (OCCI), L. Putnam & Wilson
Organizational Conflict Inventory (ROCI-II), Rahim

Leadership

Coaching Practices Survey, Mahler
Desirable Motivational Characteristics, D. C. McClelland
Grid Feedback from a Subordinate to a Boss, R. R. Blake & J. S. Mouton
Leader Effectiveness and Adaptability Description (LEAD) Questionnaire, P. Hersey & Blanchard
Leadership Opinion Questionnaire, Fleischman
Leadership Practices Inventory (LPI), J. M. Kouzes & B. Z. Posner
Management Practices Questionnaire, Miller & Zenger
Management Profiling: As Others See You, Daniels, Dyer, & Moffitt
Manager Feedback Program, Henrichs
Organizational Behavior Describer Questionnaire, Harrison & Oshrey

Communication Load

Three-Dimensional Communication Load Scale

Management Communication Style

Communicative Adaptability Scale
Communicator Style Measure
Focal Person's Communication Survey, R. Klauss & B. M. Bass
Management Communication Style, V. P. Richmond & J. C. McCroskey

(continued)

Figure 14-2 (continued)

Mentoring
Mentoring and Communication Support Scale,
Mentoring Questionnaire, Eubank

Group Communication
Inputs
Group Atmosphere Scale, F. E. Fiedler
Index of Work Cohesion, Price & Mueller
Interpersonal Trust Scale, Chun & Campbell
Measures of Morale, Scott
Process
Group Behavior Questionnaire, R. R. Blake & J. S. Mouton
Group Procedural Order Questionnaire, L. Putnam & Wilson
Interaction Behavior Measure, J. C. McCroskey & D. W. Wright
Input-Process
Decision Involvement Analysis, Thierback
Group Dimension Description Questionnaire, Hemphill
MultiStage
Group Atmosphere Scale, Hanson
Group Behavior Inventory
Job Reaction Questionnaire, Honeywell, Inc.

Team Building
Team Excellence Questionnaire, C. Larson & LaFasto
Team Interaction Profile, Wilson Learning Systems
Team Leadership Practices Inventory, J. M. Kouzes & B. Z. Posner
Team Review Questionnaire

Organizational Outcomes
Communication Satisfaction Questionnaire, C. Downs & Hazen
Job Description Index, Smith, Kendall, & Hulin
Organizational Commitment Instrument, Cook & Wall
Organizational Commitment Questionnaire, Mowday, Steers, & Porter
Organizational Identification Questionnaire, G. Cheney
Productivity Audit, Mali

Figure 14-2 is used with permission, Bob Sampson, University of Wisconsin-Eau Claire.

information that is available to the public—construct, administer, and then analyze its own communication audit. Figure 14-2 provides a list of several measuring instruments.

The value of hiring an external agent is that an organization runs less of a risk of the audit's credibility being questioned by employees who might speculate that the results have been laundered to portray the administration in a positive light. Another advantage of hiring external consultants is that they are allegedly experts in the area. Organizational women and men have other work to do. It may demand more time for internal agents to conduct the audit because of their lack of familiarity with the process.

Certainly it can't be ignored that an advantage of conducting the audit internally is financial. Audit expenses are not insignificant. An external communication audit can cost between $25,000 to several hundred thousand dollars.[15] The International

Communication Association is a not-for-profit organization and therefore, except for hotel and food expenses, no fees were charged for the ICA audit when the ICA owned it. Now, any audit can be expensive.

Another consideration that can affect cost is time frame and sequencing. How much time an organization can dedicate to conducting the audit can affect not only the expense but your decision to undergo the process altogether. It requires a relatively short amount of time to distribute questionnaires. Even the analysis of the survey data need not require a lengthy period. However, the interviews, network analyses, and communication experience evaluations can involve months of investigation. An external auditor needs to explain time issues to the client, and if a client undertakes the process as an internal project, time considerations must be a factor when deciding whether to proceed with the audit.

REPORTING RESULTS

When the audit is complete, whether conducted internally or externally, the data and recommendations must be presented to the client. This can be done by presenting a written report that is complemented by an oral presentation, or simply by submitting a written report and inviting questions subsequently. The written report should include

- Detailed explanations of the findings
- A set of specific recommendations that could be implemented by the client
- A schedule for implementation and follow-up assessment

SOFTENING THE BLOW

ETHICAL PROBE

Assume that you have conducted an extensive audit of an organization. Your findings indicate the following. Subordinates believe that

☐ Communication from upper management is not timely and not credible.
☐ Administrators actively discourage upward communication.
☐ They are not told whether they are performing well or poorly and, in general, feel that they are underappreciated.
☐ Administrators have very weak public speaking skills as demonstrated in large organizational meetings.

Further, assume that you had met with representatives of upper management before you began the audit. On the basis of what they told you then, you know that they will be stunned to hear the results of the audit. Management had essentially claimed that the company's communication problems were due to employees not paying attention to communications from management.

Finally, assume that you fear that the clients will reject your findings, even though you are certain that your test was both valid and reliable. You are concerned that the clients might be suspicious of your diagnostic abilities since your results vary from what the clients were certain would be the results. You wonder if perhaps they will not recommend you to other potential clients.

When you report your results to your clients, do you "soften" the nature of the information to make the results seem more palatable and less critical of management?

It's wise to consider an interesting and important conclusion from a 1983 study about audit reports. DeWine, James, and Walence conducted research to examine the value of the ICA audit instrument. While their work focused on the ICA audit, one conclusion they drew is likely applicable to any audit. They found that

> Managers maintain their own form of organizational reality. The administrators select and accept issue analysis and recommendations from an audit according to their own perceptions of organizational reality and what is most appropriate for their organizations *regardless of the nature of the recommendations*.[16] (Emphasis added)

This conclusion is both remarkable, yet not surprising. We discussed selective perception in Chapter 3 of this book. The value of any audit is a function of how willing administrators are to accept the conclusions of the auditors. It's easy for people to dismiss information that is inconsistent with what they want to hear. When I worked as an analyst for the ICA audit in its very early days, I confronted this phenomenon first hand. Administrators who very genuinely sought a communication analysis were nonplused when some conclusions were different from those that they had expected. It requires diplomacy and skill to inform administrators that a problem with communication may relate to their own habits that undermine efficiency. Such diplomacy may be as significant a factor for auditing as any measurement technique an auditor employs.

PRACTITIONER'S PERSPECTIVE

Angela Sinickas, Founder and President, Sinickas Communications

Angela Sinickas is a pioneer in the field of organizational communication measurement. Her company's recent clients include Merck, Nordstrom, 3M, Raytheon, ExxonMobil, and Lockheed Martin. Ms. Sinickas's work assessing communication quality has been cited in Harvard Business Review *and* Investor's Business Daily *as well as several other publications.*

The biggest challenge for auditors is to make sure that they're measuring the right things. All too often communicators measure only their outputs—the messages and channels they're producing—without connecting them to the outcomes of using these outputs.

For valid and reliable information, you need to use a quantitative auditing approach. In many cases, that means using a survey, but only if you're careful in selecting a large enough, and truly random, sample and being sure that the completed surveys are returned in the same proportions. There are also many other quantitative techniques that can be used in an audit. For example, a content analysis can quantify to what extent the communications you send out are aligned with the goals of your organization. You can also quantitatively track changes in your audience's behaviors due to your communications—either over time or using a pilot/control group study to isolate the impact of communication versus other possible change agents.

I have had situations where clients did not want to "hear" what our research had uncovered. Executives are all too often sheltered from the reality of their organizations by middle managers who don't want to be the bearers of bad news. Even when executives conduct meetings with employees, the employees won't always be candid if their supervisors are also in the meeting. Focus group findings are more often challenged than survey results, and with good reason. There are too many variables in how the focus group participants are selected and how the facilitators conduct the sessions. Plus, few organizations involve enough participants to constitute a valid sample for projecting findings to the entire group. I did have one executive who refused to believe some negative results from a survey administered to all employees, in spite of having a very large response rate. And I've known executives who give more credence to lots of direct quotes from focus groups than to survey results.

There's no reason an organization can't do an audit without outside help, as long as they have appropriate resources available inside. For example, if they're doing a survey, they should find someone in HR, Finance, or Marketing who can help them in determining sample sizes. They should use the experience of someone in Organizational Development or Market Research to ensure the questions they're asking and the response scales they're using will provide usable data. Most important, for any type of qualitative research, the facilitators must not be the individuals who are responsible for creating the communications that are being audited, for a number of reasons that affect the quality of the interaction in the sessions. However, if the communication department has recently hired someone who has no vested interest in the existing communication program, that person could conduct the qualitative research pretty well, assuming he or she had some training in the process. Otherwise, I'd recommend using someone from HR or Market Research to conduct interviews and focus groups more objectively.

The downside of doing it all yourself is that you will make mistakes and it will take longer because you're inventing everything yourself. The half-way solution is to do as much as you can in-house, but use outside resources judiciously, perhaps for peer review.

If you choose to hire someone from the outside, choose an auditor who has had lots of experience. Talk to his or her previous clients. Ask to look at samples of the types of reports she or he has presented to other clients. Determine if the reports would be useful to you or if they are organized and written in a way that only a researcher would find useful. Try to find an auditor who knows not only research but has also worked in communication. Preferably, find one who has spent some time working within organizations, not just in consulting firms. You'll find that the recommendations the auditor comes up with will be more practical and usable.

SUMMARY

A Toolbox

1. If communication is important, then testing communication becomes a priority.
2. Any method of auditing must examine organizational communication comprehensively.
3. There are several methods available. Consultants and techniques have proliferated over the last decade.
4. A manager can pick and choose from the available methods to suit the needs of the organization.
5. Audit findings should include a problem statement, a set of recommendations for solution, and a sequence for implementation.
6. Audit results may vary from client expectations.

DISCUSSION QUESTIONS

1. How would you describe the phrase *communication audit* to someone who was not familiar with the study of organizational communication?
2. What would make a test on this chapter material valid?
3. Why would a communication audit that only examined printed communications not be valid?
4. What must be tested in order for a communication audit to be valid?
5. What are the advantages of having a "communication experience" or "critical incident" component to an audit?
6. How does a method like ECCO analysis differ from what is referred to as the ICA audit?
7. How can reporting audit data to clients provide an ethical challenge?
8. Please read the case that follows and respond to the questions at the end of the case.

CASE FOR ANALYSIS

Case 14.2—James Whalen: Mired in Communication Problems

Background. James Whalen is an engineer who works with electronic medical imaging products, for example, MRI equipment. Whalen's company has a high ratio of technical employees who have the various skills required to carry out the development of sophisticated electronic products. However, according to Whalen, these persons do not have any intelligent notion regarding how to communicate within an organization. Whalen believes that his company is overwhelmed with communication-related issues that neither he nor anyone else in the company knows how to assess or remedy.

Details. The most prevalent formal communication tool used for interdepartmental communication within the company is memos—either electronic or print. There are few formal face-to-face interactions of any sort. When customers contact the organization they typically fax their communications. Many customers are foreign nationals with little or no background in the primary language used in Whalen's company, which is English.

There is an extremely high level of stress in the workplace, with a variety of causes including short development schedules, logistical problems caused by working with offshore customers, and an ever-increasing burden of paperwork required to satisfy regulatory requirements. It is not unusual for tasks to be assumed by multiple individuals unbeknownst to one another, causing a sort of "keystone cops" duplication of efforts. The fact of the matter is that the messages that inform Whalen and his colleagues of what they have to do are haphazardly distributed.

To further exacerbate the problem, many individuals in Whalen's department, as is the case throughout the company, are natives of foreign countries, who are struggling with the English language. Sometimes receivers simply do not understand precisely what they need to do, or who is to do what needs to be done, or deadlines for task completion. Informal interaction is restricted in part, because people who are comfortable speaking their native tongue tend to use their primary language with others with similar backgrounds. There are times when the company sounds like the Tower of Babel.

Another of Whalen's problems relates to subordinate-superior interaction. He reports that there is no formal path to superiors. Most often when subordinates communicate with superiors they tend to write short notes or use electronic mail. Frequently, these types of communications generate no response from the superior.

Finally, Whalen reports that one of the supervisors in a related department has extremely poor communication skills. This person listens only when he wants to—for example, he will ask questions, then turn and quickly walk away without waiting for a reply. This supervisor, whom Whalen characterizes as a Type AAA personality, is a direct report to the CEO. It is not unusual for the supervisor to take a call while conversing with another, leap from his chair, and head for the "front office" at a dead run—apparently oblivious to the effect this behavior has on the person with whom he had been talking.

- What recommendations would you have for Whalen?
- According to Whalen his company faces problems related to *Networks, Climate, Information Management,* and *Communication Skill Sets.* Now that you are nearing the final pages of this book, can you separate the specific problems and place them into the categories listed?
- How might you consider testing the company to ascertain the full range of communication-related issues that exist in the organization?

ENDNOTES

[1]Gordon, Greg, "A Buyer's Guide to Communication Audits," *Journal of Employee Communication Management,* March 2001.

[2]John Dean's list actually includes a fifth item, "communication systems controls." By this he means a person, persons, or mechanism for regulation or ensuring effective communication. This fifth feature is either implicit in the cases of networks, climate, and information management or a feature to be recommended as it relates to communication skill sets. Dean's article, "Internal Communication Management," appears in the edited volume by Howard Greenbaum entitled *Management Auditing as a Regulatory Tool.* The reference to the basic elements of internal communication appears on page 297. The description of the items continues from 297–303. The language Dean uses is somewhat different. He

does use Communication Climate, but instead of Individual Communication Skill Sets uses Interpersonal Communication Skills. He uses "Design of the Formal Communication Subsystem" and "Information Systems," for Communication Networks and Information Management, respectively.

[3]Daly, John, "Assessing Speaking and Listening: Preliminary Considerations for a National Assessment," *National Assessment of College Students Learning: Identification of Skills to be Taught, Learned, and Assessed: A Report on the Proceedings of the Second Study Design Workshop,* U.S. Department of Education, November 1992, NCES94–286.

[4]Daly comments further in the piece cited in the preceding note that Communication apprehension has been comprehensively examined over the last 20 years and that more than 2000 studies have been conducted related to communication apprehension. For more information see the book Daly and James McCroskey edited on the subject: *Avoiding Communication: Shyness, Reticence and Communication Apprehension,* Sage, 1984.

[5]Persons unfamiliar with communication study might wonder if these skills can, in fact, be measured. Such tests do exist. See Robert Bostrom, *Listening Behavior: Measurement and Application,* Guilford, 1990.

[6]See Brian Spitzberg's *Handbook of Interpersonal Competence Research,* Springer-Verlag, 1989, for testing techniques.

[7]There are several measurement devices for evaluating individuals' communication in small groups. Bales' SYMLOG is one. See Robert Bales, *Symlog: Case Study Kit,* Free Press, 1980.

[8]See Ole Holsti, *Content Analysis for the Social Sciences and Humanities,* Addison-Wesley, 1969, pp. 5–6. My first book, *Mass Communication and International Politics: A Case Study of Press Reactions to the 1973 Arab-Israeli War,* Sheffield, 1988, is an example of how the procedure can be used to examine communication content.

[9]Goldhaber, Gerald, *Organizational Communication,* Sixth Edition, Brown/Benchmark, 1993, p. 358.

[10]Ibid., p. 359.

[11]Optimally, all persons would in fact respond to the survey. Sometimes, however, the audit was conducted only with members of certain segments of the organizational population. In these cases generalizations about attitudes of all employees could not, of course, be made.

[12]As reported in *Organizational Communication* by Gerald Goldhaber (1993 edition), p. 362. There were occasions, however, when this component was not utilized as part of the ICA audit procedure. In at least one instance prior to 1979 when the audit ceased to be owned by the ICA, the audited organization was content with receiving data that excluded the network analysis and did not want to spend additional time participating with the network analysis.

[13]Goldhaber, Gerald, *Organizational Communication,* Fourth Edition, 1993, p. 366.

[14]Sinickas Communication is one such company. At the 2001 IABC annual meetings, I spoke with a Sinickas representative and was impressed with the comprehensive approach Sinickas had developed for audits. Sinickas will conduct audits for clients or sell the materials to the clients to allow clients to do the work themselves. Among Sinickas's materials are a Focus Group Discussion Guide, an Employee Communication Survey, and a Communication Vehicle Survey (which assesses whether clients are using the correct type of media when communicating internally).

[15]Op. cit., Gordon.

[16]The quote is from Sue DeWine, *The Consultant's Craft,* Bedford/St. Martins, 2001, p. 149. The referred to study was conducted by DeWine, S. James, and W. Walence, and presented in the paper, "Validation of Organizational Communication Audit Instruments" at the International Communication Association, May 1983 meetings in Hawaii.

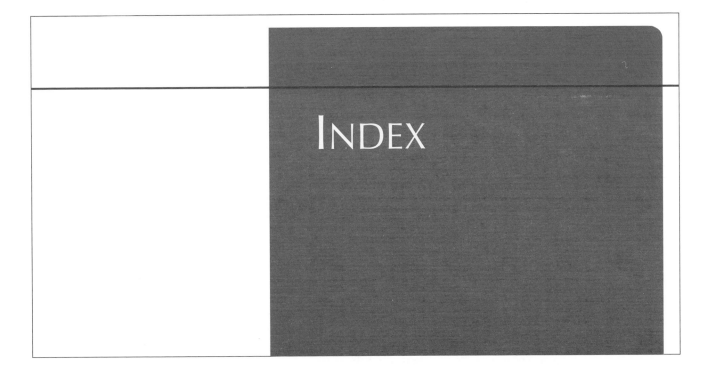

INDEX